T0213879

Lecture Notes in Computer Science 12101

More information about this series at http://www.springer.com/series/7407

Ting Hu · Nuno Lourenço ·
Eric Medvet · Federico Divina (Eds.)

Genetic Programming

23rd European Conference, EuroGP 2020
Held as Part of EvoStar 2020
Seville, Spain, April 15–17, 2020
Proceedings

 Springer

Editors
Ting Hu 🔾
Queen's University
Kingston, ON, Canada

Eric Medvet 🔾
University of Trieste
Trieste, Italy

Nuno Lourenço 🔾
University of Coimbra
Coimbra, Portugal

Federico Divina 🔾
Pablo de Olavide University
Seville, Spain

ISSN 0302-9743   ISSN 1611-3349   (electronic)
Lecture Notes in Computer Science
ISBN 978-3-030-44093-0   ISBN 978-3-030-44094-7   (eBook)
https://doi.org/10.1007/978-3-030-44094-7

LNCS Sublibrary: SL1 – Theoretical Computer Science and General Issues

This Springer imprint is published by the registered company Springer Nature Switzerland AG
The registered company address is: Gewerbestrasse 11, 6330 Cham, Switzerland

Preface

The 23rd European Conference on Genetic Programming (EuroGP 2020) took place at the Universidad Pablo de Olavide (UPO) in Sevilla, Spain, 15–17 April, 2020.

Genetic Programming (GP) is an evolutionary computation branch that has been developed to automatically solve design problems, in particular the computer program design, without requiring the user to know or specify the form or structure of the solution in advance. It uses the principles of Darwinian evolution to approach problems in the synthesis, improvement, and repair of computer programs. The universality of computer programs, and their importance in so many areas of our lives, means that the automation of these tasks is an exceptionally ambitious challenge with far-reaching implications. It has attracted a very large number of researchers and a vast amount of theoretical and practical contributions are available by consulting the GP bibliography.[1]

Since the first EuroGP event in Paris in 1998, EuroGP has been the only conference exclusively devoted to the evolutionary design of computer programs and other computational structures. In fact, EuroGP represents the single largest venue at which GP results are published. It plays an important role in the success of the field, by serving as a forum for expressing new ideas, meeting fellow researchers, and initiating collaborations. It attracts scholars from all over the world. In a friendly and welcoming atmosphere authors presented the latest advances in the field, also presenting GP-based solutions to complex real-world problems.

EuroGP 2020 received 36 submissions from around the world. The papers have undergone a rigorous double-blind peer review process, each being reviewed by multiple members of an international Program Committee.

Among the papers presented in this volume, 12 were accepted for full-length oral presentation (33% acceptance rate) and 6 as short talks. Authors of both categories of papers also had the opportunity to present their work in poster sessions to promote the exchange of ideas in a carefree manner.

The wide range of topics in this volume reflects the current state of research in the field. With a special focus on GP and artificial intelligence (AI) in 2020, the collection of papers cover interesting topics including designing GP algorithms for ensemble learning, comparing GP with popular machine learning algorithms, and customising GP algorithms for more explainable AI applications to real-world problems.

Together with three other co-located evolutionary computation conferences (EvoCOP 2020, EvoMusArt 2020, and EvoApplications 2020), EuroGP 2020 was part of the EvoStar 2020 event. This meeting could not have taken place without the help of many people. The EuroGP 2020 Organizing Committee is particularly grateful to the following:

---

[1] http://liinwww.ira.uka.de/bibliography/Ai/genetic.programming.html.

- SPECIES, the Society for the Promotion of Evolutionary Computation in Europe and its Surroundings, aiming to promote evolutionary algorithmic thinking within Europe and wider, and more generally to promote inspiration of parallel algorithms derived from natural processes.
- The high-quality and diverse EuroGP 2020 Program Committee. Each year the members freely devote their time and expertise, in order to maintain the high standards of EuroGP and provide constructive feedback to help the authors to improve their papers.
- Francisco Fernández de Vega from the University of Extremadura, Spain, and Federico Divina from UPO, Spain, as well as their local organizing teams.
- João Correia from the University of Coimbra, Portugal, for the EvoStar 2020 publicity and website.
- The School of Engineering at UPO in Sevilla, Spain, for supporting the local organization.
- Our invited speakers, José Antonio Lozano and Roberto Serra, who gave inspiring and enlightening keynote talks.
- The EvoStar 2020 coordinators: Anna I Esparcia-Alcázar, from Universitat Politècnica de València, Spain, and Jennifer Willies.

April 2020

Ting Hu
Nuno Lourenço
Eric Medvet
Federico Divina

Organization

Program Co-chairs

Ting Hu — Queen's University, Canada
Nuno Lourenço — University of Coimbra, Portugal

Publication Chair

Eric Medvet — University of Trieste, Italy

Local Chairs

Francisco Fernández
de Vega — Universidad de Extremadura, Spain
Federico Divina — Universidad Pablo de Olavide, Spain

Publicity Chair

João Correia — University of Coimbra, Portugal

Conference Administration

Anna I Esparcia-Alcazar — EvoStar Coordinator

Program Committee

Ignacio Arnaldo — Universidad Complutense de Madrid, Spain
R. Muhammad Atif Azad — Birmingham City University, UK
Wolfgang Banzhaf — Michigan State University, USA
Helio Barbosa — Federal University of Juiz de Fora, Brazil
Heder Bernardino — Federal University of Juiz de Fora, Brazil
Anthony Brabazon — University College Dublin, Ireland
Stefano Cagnoni — University of Parma, Italy
Mauro Castelli — Universidade Nova de Lisboa, Portugal
Ernesto Costa — University of Coimbra, Portugal
Marc Ebner — Universität Greifswald, Germany
Anna Esparcia-Alcazar — Universitat Politècnica de València, Spain
Francisco Fernández
de Vega — Universidad de Extremadura, Spain
Gianluigi Folino — ICAR-CNR, Italy
James Foster — University of Idaho, USA
Christian Gagné — Université Laval, Canada

Contents

Hessian Complexity Measure for Genetic Programming-Based Imputation Predictor Selection in Symbolic Regression with Incomplete Data

Baligh Al-Helali[✉], Qi Chen[✉], Bing Xue[✉], and Mengjie Zhang[✉]

School of Engineering and Computer Science, Victoria University of Wellington,
PO Box 600, Wellington 6400, New Zealand
{baligh.al-helali,Qi.Chen,Bing.Xue,Mengjie.Zhang}@ecs.vuw.ac.nz

Abstract. Missing values bring several challenges when learning from real-world data sets. Imputation is a widely adopted approach to estimating missing values. However, it has not been adequately investigated in symbolic regression. When imputing the missing values in an incomplete feature, the other features that are used in the prediction process are called imputation predictors. In this work, a method for imputation predictor selection using regularized genetic programming (GP) models is presented for symbolic regression tasks on incomplete data. A complexity measure based on the Hessian matrix of the phenotype of the evolving models is proposed. It is employed as a regularizer in the fitness function of GP for model selection and the imputation predictors are selected from the selected models. In addition to the baseline which uses all the available predictors, the proposed selection method is compared with two GP-based feature selection variations: the standard GP feature selector and GP with feature selection pressure. The trends in the results reveal that in most cases, using the predictors selected by regularized GP models could achieve a considerable reduction in the imputation error and improve the symbolic regression performance as well.

Keywords: Symbolic regression · Genetic programming · Incomplete data · Feature selection · Imputation · Model complexity

1 Introduction

Researchers in different fields often face the problem of having missing values when dealing with real-world data sets. One common way to work on incomplete data is called complete case analysis (CCA) [4], which restricts the analysis to complete instances causing a reduction in the sample size which in turn may result in biased estimates. Imputation is an alternative approach, which works by replacing the missing values with the estimated values using estimation models based on the available data. Statistically speaking, even very simple imputation

© Springer Nature Switzerland AG 2020
T. Hu et al. (Eds.): EuroGP 2020, LNCS 12101, pp. 1–17, 2020.
https://doi.org/10.1007/978-3-030-44094-7_1

approaches can provide less biased estimates than CCA [4]. In machine learning, imputation is utilized in many tasks, however, very few studies have been conducted on imputation for symbolic regression with incomplete data [1]. This is probably because most symbolic regression studies are conducted on data which are generated using artificial functions for benchmark problems rather than real-world data. Unlike real-world data sets, artificial data sets can be guaranteed not to contain missing values.

In 1605, Johannes Kepler launched a scientific revolution by discovering that Mars' orbit has an ellipse shape based on planetary orbits data tables [15]. This is an example of symbolic regression: discovering a symbolic expression that fits a given data set [30]. Such a problem is a core challenge for both statistics and artificial intelligence (AI). Although it is likely to be an NP-hard problem [30], symbolic regression plays an important role in many prediction analysis tools, especially because of its so called "WhiteBox" properties [14]. Another advantage of symbolic regression over traditional regression methods is the non-requirement of pre-assumptions on the structure of the regression model [16].

Although there are various methods to address symbolic regression problems [5], the most commonly used one is genetic programming (GP) which is outlined in [16] and also used successfully in commercial softwares such as Eureqa [10]. GP is a biological evolution inspired technique for evolving programs to solve a particular task by applying nature-inspired operations. When producing the prediction models, GP has the ability of selecting the features implicitly. GP has been successfully used for feature selection to enhance the performance of different learning tasks such as clustering, classification, and symbolic regression [35]. However, one of the most serious issues of GP is model complexity. GP tends to produce overcomplex models which could not generalise well on unseen data and have a low interpretablity. Therefore, model complexity measures and reducing the model complexity have received considerable interest from the research community [17].

Model selection refers to the task of choosing the best model among a set of candidate models. The term "best" has different interpretations based on the research perspective. When comparing models with similar empirical performance, the model with lower complexity is usually preferred hoping that it has good generalization properties. This is often described as Occam's razor in machine learning [26]. Its main idea is that given two models with similar performance, the simpler one should be preferred as simplicity is desirable in itself [17]. Therefore, it is essential in model selection to avoid choosing unnecessarily complex models rather than just relying on their goodness of fit.

Although the primary use of model complexity measures is in model selection, some of these methods can also be used for feature selection. For example, the Lasso technique can also be used for feature selection in addition to regularization. Another example is Akaike information criterion (AIC), which has been suggested as a useful technique for assessing the relative importance of features [3]. This can be done by summing the AIC weights across all models in which each feature appears and the relative importance is assessed via a rank ordering of the sums for all features. The larger the sums, the higher relative importance for the feature [22].

This work proposes a GP-based feature selection method based on a new complexity measure. The main goal is to construct regularized GP models for each incomplete feature using other features as predictors. The predictors selected by these GP programs are then utilized to impute the missing values using different imputation methods. The imputation methods are applied to symbolic regression on incomplete data. The specific objectives of this study are as follows:

- Proposing a new complexity measure for GP programs based on the analytical characteristics of the produced GP phenotypes.
- Utilizing the proposed measure to regularize GP models and using these models for feature selection.
- Investigating the impact of the proposed method on imputing predictor selection in symbolic regression with missing values.
- Comparing the proposed method with different GP-based feature selection variations.

2   Background

2.1   Missing Value Imputation

According to [19], there are three missingness mechanisms that cause incompleteness. If the probability of having a missing value does not depend on any other data, the missingness is called missing completely at random (MCAR). However, it is called missing at random (MAR) if this probability depends on the observed data, but not the missing data, whereas the missingness is missing not at random (MNAR) if the probability depends on both observed and missing data.

Missing value imputation (MVI) has been considered as a basic solution method for incomplete data set problems [18]. Unlike the complete case analysis strategy, where incomplete cases are deleted, missing value imputation does not have the risk of reducing the data size. In general, imputation is a process in which the missing data are replaced with the estimated values. Imputed data can be produced using two approaches: single imputation and multiple imputation [9]. Single imputation provides a specific value in place of the missing data directly. However, multiple imputation selects such an imputed value from several possible responses based on the variance/confidence interval analysis.

2.2   Model Complexity in GP

Model selection should not only be based on goodness-of-fit, but also model complexity must be considered [17]. Model complexity can be measured using different characteristics of the learned models such as non-linearity or/and number of parameters [17]. For example, in polynomial regression, the higher the degree of the polynomial, the more degrees of freedom, and the more capacity to overfit the training data. Therefore, the polynomial degree can be used as a complexity measure [33]. However, there are some more sophisticated complexity measures.

In addition to reducing the empirical error of the learned model, it is desired for the model complexity to be as small as possible (i.e. without suppressing the model performance). This goal can be achieved by minimising a fitness function augmented with a regularisation term as in Eq. (1).

$$fitness = empirical\_error + \lambda \times complexity\_penalty \qquad (1)$$

where $fitness$ is the regularised fitness function, $empirical\_error$ is the training error, and $complexity\_penalty$ works as a regulariser which is a measure of the model complexity. The influence of the model complexity on the fitness function is controlled by the regularisation parameter λ, that is, complexity has an impact on the selection process only if the models have comparable performance. This happens only if $\lambda \ll 1$.

Some of the regularisers that have been proposed for genetic programming are derivative-based complexity measures. A regulariser based on curvature (second order Tikhonov functional) of evolved polynomial models is applied in [25]. In [34], curvature is used as a regulariser. Regularisers based on the first derivatives of the evolved functions and their curve length are used in [36]. An approximation of the Vapnik–Chervonenkis (VC) dimension is used as a regularizer in [6,8], while in [28], Rademacher complexity is incorporated into the fitness function of GP individuals to control their functional complexity.

2.3   GP for Feature Selection

Feature selection is the process of choosing a subset of relevant features [35]. In feature selection, the two main components are the search strategy and the evaluation criteria. The search strategy tries to find the best feature subset(s). A feature selection method employs an evaluation criterion to measure the quality of the feature subsets. Feature selection methods can be classified as the wrapper, filter and embedded approaches based on the way of involving a learning algorithm in the evaluation procedure.

GP performs implicit feature selection as the features used in a GP program represent a set of selected features. For example, in tree-based GP, the target variable is represented as an expression tree in which the leaf nodes can be chosen from a terminal set that contains the independent features. Any feature appears in the constructed program is considered as a selected feature by this program. GP has been successfully used for feature selection to enhance the performance of different learning tasks such as clustering, classification, and symbolic regression [29].

For symbolic regression, a feature selection method to improve the generalisation ability of GP is proposed in [7]. This method works by obtaining the features that appear in the best-of-run GP individuals, and uses a permutation measure to get the features importance. Artificial bee colony programming is proposed for symbolic regression with feature selection in [2]. In [14], deep learning feature selection is utilized in symbolic regression-classification. In these feature selection for symbolic regression studies, the missing data are removed.

2.4   Symbolic Regression with Incomplete Data

The existing research on dealing with missing values mainly focus on the classification tasks. In symbolic regression, removing the incomplete cases is the most common strategy to deal with missing vales [1]. The symbolic regression research is mostly focusing on artificial functions that have no missing values.

In [32], missing values in certain ranges of the feature space are considered as an imbalanced data problem. To handle this problem, a framework for automatic weighting the data points is suggested, which considers the relative importance of the points using four importance weighting schemes according to the proximity, remoteness, surrounding, and nonlinear deviation from nearest neighbors. The methods are used to balance synthetic data sets drawn from mathematical functions. The limitation of these method is that the unability to estimate the missing values and their applicability is not validated on real-world incomplete data.

A hybrid imputation method called GP-KNN is presented in [1]. This method is employed for symbolic regression with missing values. The main idea of this method is to combine the regression-based imputation of GP and the instance-based selection of KNN. This method is evaluated using two measures; the imputation accuracy and the symbolic regression error. The experimental results show that GP-KNN outperforms state-of-the-art imputation methods on both imputation accuracy and the symbolic regression performance. However, the main limitation of the GP-KNN method is the time complexity of the imputation process. This drawback is due to the need for building new imputation models for each missing value in the test data using the training data.

3   The Proposed Method

In order to perform symbolic regression on incomplete data, the missing values can be imputed and the resulting complete data are then used. To impute an incomplete feature in a data set, other features are used in predicting its missing values. These features are called imputation *predictors* for the incomplete feature to be imputed. The main goal of the proposed method is to select imputation predictors for each incomplete feature using regularized GP models. A good selection of the predictors can improve the imputation performance and reduce its computation time as well.

3.1   The Overall System

There are three main components of the adopted framework in this work: the predictor selection process, the imputation process, and the symbolic regression process. These processes are carried out in two stages, one for training and the other for testing, as shown in Fig. 1.

In the process of predictor selection, the incomplete training data set is used by several GP runs to select a set of predictive features (predictors) for each incomplete feature. GP is used to evolve prediction models from independent runs and the predictors that appear in the best-of-run of models are selected. For the imputation process, the selected predictors are fed into an imputation method for estimating the missing values in the associated incomplete features. The imputed complete data sets are then used for the symbolic regression process.

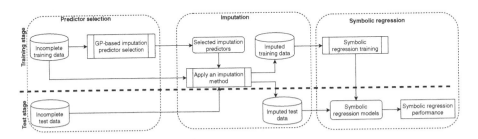

Fig. 1. The overall framework.

3.2   Standard GP-Based Predictor Selection

Given an incomplete data set, GP can be used to select the predictors for imputing the incomplete features. For an incomplete feature, f, the data set is reformed to consider this feature as the target variable for the GP modeling process. The other features (predictors) are used as input variables. Although all the other features including those containing missing values are considered, only the complete instances are used.

The fitness of the prediction model is measured based on the data type of the target incomplete feature. If it is numerical, the prediction process is a regression task and its goodness is measured by the regression error computed using relative squared error (RSE) shown in Eq. (2).

$$RSE = \frac{\sum_{i=1}^{n}(y_i - \hat{y}_i)^2}{\sum_{i=1}^{n}(y_i - \bar{y})^2} \tag{2}$$

where n is the number of instances, y_i $(\hat{y}_i)$ is the target value (predicted value) of the ith instance, and $\bar{y}$ is the average of the target values.

For categorical incomplete features, GP classifiers are constructed and the empirical error is the classification error rate shown in Eq. (3). The translation of the numerical outputs of GP individuals into class labels is done following [37] using Eq. (4).

$$Error\_rate = \frac{\#incorrectly\ classified\ instances}{\#instances} \tag{3}$$

$$class(output) = Class_j, \text{if } (j-1) * T < output \leq j * T, \tag{4}$$

where $Class_j$, $j = 1, 2, ..., C$ are class labels representing the available C distinct values in the feature of interest (classes), $output$ is the output of the evolved GP individual, and T is a random positive constant. In summary,

$$fitness_1 = empirical\_error = \begin{cases} \text{error rate (Eq. (3))}, & \text{for categorical,} \\ \text{regression error (Eq. (2))}, & \text{otherwise.} \end{cases} \tag{5}$$

3.3 GP-Based Predictor Selection with Feature Selection Pressure

To select the imputation predictors for an incomplete feature, f, the GP-process can be designed to emphasize reducing the number of involved predictors by using a selection pressure based on the generation number and the number of selected features as in Eq. (6). The first factor is the ratio of the number of the current generation, g, to the maximum number of generations, G. When the value of g increases, the importance weight of feature reduction increases monotonically. It is designed in this way to allow including more predictors in the early generations and then in the later generations, where individuals are supposed to be fitter, have more contribution to selecting the predictors.

The other factor is the ratio of the number of selected predictors, p_s (i.e. the features that are used in the individual), to the number of all available predictors in the data set, p. If two individuals in a generation have the same prediction error, a lower fitness value is given to the one with fewer predictors.

$$selection\_pressure = \frac{g}{G} * \frac{p_s}{p} \tag{6}$$

This pressure function is combined with the empirical error to form the fitness function for the evolving GP models to minimise the number of predictors in addition to minimising the prediction error. As shown in Eq. (7), the fitness function has two parts: the empirical error ($empirical\_error$) and the selection pressure ($selection\_pressure$). The empirical error measures how accurately the current GP individual fits the incomplete feature, whereas the selection pressure pushes towards using a smaller number of features.

$$fitness_2 = empirical\_error * (1 + \alpha * selection\_pressure) \tag{7}$$

where α is a positive real value less than 1 used to control the balance between the empirical error and the feature selection pressure, and it is set empirically to be 0.2 because the prediction performance is more important. In order to ensure that the selection pressure will not be the dominant part of the fitness function, especially when the empirical error is very small, it is multiplied by the empirical error to be a proportional ratio of the prediction performance.

3.4 The Proposed Method: GP-Based Predictor Selection with Model Complexity Pressure

The complexity of GP models can be indicated by different factors such as the involvement of complex functions or more complicated building blocks. Geometrically, the function $sin(x)$ is more complicated than x^3 which is in turn more complicated than x^2. Similarly, for more than one variable, the complexity can be indicated from the containing algebraic term and obviously a term like $x_1 * x_2$ is more complex than $x_1 + x_2$. Complexity is usually used to select the model, however, it can be also utilized for feature selection. For example, the GP model with the expression $y_1 = x_1^7 + x_2^5$ is more complex than the model $y_2 = x_1^2 + x_3$. If the empirical error difference between the two models is not significant, the less complex one is preferred. This implies that if it is planned to rely on the model for feature selection, the feature set $\{x_1, x_3\}$, which is selected by the model y_2, is more likely to be chosen over the one selected by y_1, $\{x_1, x_2\}$.

The key idea of the proposed complexity measure is that instead of checking the mathematical form for each term, partial derivatives are considered to measure whether the input predictors are involved in complex models. For each independent predictor, x_i, the partial derivative of the dependent variable y is derived w.r.t x_i, i.e. $\frac{\partial y}{\partial x_i}$. If the obtained derivative is 0, the predictor x_i has no impact on y at all (it does not appear in y). If $\frac{\partial y}{\partial x_i} = c$ for a non-zero constant, $c \neq 0$, x_i is linearly related to y. Otherwise, the relationship is functional which can be further examined by taking higher order derivatives and the above relational types still hold true. The predictor x_i is linearly related to y with order n if $\frac{\partial^n y}{\partial x_i^n} = c$. However, to take into account the interaction between different features, the mixed partial derivatives are also considered. For example, if $n = 2$, $\frac{\partial^2 y}{\partial x_i \partial x_j}$ are also considered in addition to $\frac{\partial^2 y}{\partial x_i^2}$.

Let y be the symbolic expression of a GP individual whose terminal set is $X = \{x_i\}_{i=1}^p$. The partial derivative of y w.r.t X can be denoted by the *Jacobian* matrix of y as in Eq. (8). If all second partial derivatives of y exist, then the *Hessian* matrix $\mathcal{H}$ of y is a square $n \times n$ matrix, usually represented as in Eq. (9).

$$\mathbf{J}(y) = \left[\frac{\partial \mathbf{y}}{\partial x_1} \cdots \frac{\partial \mathbf{y}}{\partial x_n} \right] \tag{8}$$

$$\mathcal{H}(y) = \begin{bmatrix} \dfrac{\partial^2 y}{\partial x_1^2} & \dfrac{\partial^2 y}{\partial x_1 \partial x_2} & \cdots & \dfrac{\partial^2 y}{\partial x_1 \partial x_n} \\ \dfrac{\partial^2 y}{\partial x_2 \partial x_1} & \dfrac{\partial^2 y}{\partial x_2^2} & \cdots & \dfrac{\partial^2 y}{\partial x_2 \partial x_n} \\ \vdots & \vdots & \ddots & \vdots \\ \dfrac{\partial^2 y}{\partial x_n \partial x_1} & \dfrac{\partial^2 y}{\partial x_n \partial x_2} & \cdots & \dfrac{\partial^2 y}{\partial x_n^2} \end{bmatrix} \tag{9}$$

By stating an equation for the coefficients using indices i and j, the entries of the Hessian matrix are denoted as $\mathcal{H}(y)_{i,j} = \frac{\partial^2 y}{\partial x_i \partial x_j}$. The mixed partial derivatives of y are the entries off the main diagonal in the Hessian. Assuming that they are continuous, the order of differentiation does not matter (Symmetry of second derivatives, Schwarz's theorem). Thus, $\frac{\partial}{\partial x_i}\left(\frac{\partial f}{\partial x_j}\right) = \frac{\partial}{\partial x_j}\left(\frac{\partial f}{\partial x_i}\right)$.

To measure the complexity of an evolved mathematical expression y, we count the number of predictors that are involved in highly non-linear terms. This is done by counting the number of predictors that survive after taking a specific number of derivatives. In the case of $n = 2$, the second order derivatives, the model complexity can be calculated as the ratio of the non-constant Hessian entries of the constructed GP model, $C^{(2)}(y)$ defined as in Eq. (10), then the model complexity can be calculated as in Eq. (11).

$$C^{(2)}(y) = \{\mathcal{H}(y)_{i,j}, \mathcal{H}(y)_{i,j} \neq c, \text{ for any real constant c}\} \tag{10}$$

$$model\_complexity = \frac{|C^{(2)}(y)|}{|\frac{\partial^2 y}{\partial X^2}|} \tag{11}$$

Model selection can be done by searching for a model that directly minimizes the weighted sum of empirical loss (goodness of fit) and the complexity of the model, as follows:

$$fitness_3 = empirical\_error * (1 + \lambda * model\_complexity) \tag{12}$$

where $\lambda \in [0, 1]$ is a constant value that assigns weight for the contribution of the model_complexity in the fitness value. If the model complexity is given a high weight then the model is pushed towards being too simple which has the risk of underfitting, hence, λ is set empirically to 0.2. Similar to $fitness_2$, the complexity is multiplied by the empirical error to guarantee that the focus will be always on minimizing the empirical error even when there is a big difference between the two factors.

4   Experiment Setup

For evaluation purposes, real-world regression data sets with various numbers of features and instances are used. The statistics of the data sets are shown in Table 1. A reference is made to the data repository OpenML [31] for more details. Each data set is split randomly into 70:30 as training and test sets. For each data set, 30 synthetic incomplete data sets are generated by imposing 30% missing at random (MAR) probability on 20% of the features. The synthetic incomplete data sets are generated using the R package SIMSEM [27].

Table 1. Statistics of the data sets

Data set	#Instances	#Features
fri_c0_100_25 (Fri)	100	25
CPMP-2015-runtime-regression (CPMP)	2108	24
Bank32nh (Bank)	8192	33
Selwood	31	54
MIP	1090	145
Mtp	4450	203

The effectiveness of the selected predictors is evaluated by the effect on enhancing the imputation performance of some widely used imputation methods including linear regression (LR), predictive mean matching (PMM), and K-nearest neighbour (KNN) [12]. These methods represent different imputation strategies and we use their implementations in the R package Simputation [20]. For GP-based methods, Table 2 shows the settings used for predictor selection and symbolic regression. The two processes have different settings (e.g. number of generation, population size, and tree depth) due to the difference in their objectives. The selection process is more tolerant regarding the prediction accuracy. It works by selecting the features that appear in a set of weaker prediction models. However, symbolic regression tries to deliver more accurate models. The implementation of these methods is carried out under the GP framework provided by distributed evolutionary algorithms in python (DEAP) [11]. The analytical derivatives are calculated using the python package SymPy (symbolic computing in Python) [21]. SymPy provides all the basic operations of calculus, such as calculating limits, derivatives, integrals, or summations. Derivatives are computed with the *diff* function, which recursively uses the various differentiation rules.

As the Hessian matrix requires calculating the partial derivatives of the evolved programs, all GP-generated individuals have be to analytic [24]. Conventional (un)protected division can produce discontinuities [13] and lead to individuals which are non-differentiable. So, it is replaced with an analytic quotient operator [23], defined in Eq. (13), which satisfies the differentiability condition. In addition to eliminating discontinuities, using analytic quotient systematically has been shown to improve the performance compared to conventional protected division [23].

$$AQ(x,y) = \frac{x}{\sqrt{1+y^2}} \tag{13}$$

Table 2. GP settings

Parameter	GP predictor selection	Symbolic regression
Generations	50	100
Population size	256	1024
Crossover rate	0.9	0.9
Mutation rate	0.1	0.1
Elitism	Top-1 individual	Top-5 individual
Selection method	Tournament	Tournament
Tournament size	3	7
Maximum depth	17	9
Initialization	Ramped-half and half	Ramped-half and half
Function set	$+, -, *$, AQ	$+, -, *$, protected %
Terminal set	Predictors and constants	Features and constants
Fitness function	Eq. (5)/Eq. (7)/Eq. (12)	Eq. (2)

5   Results and Discussions

To evaluate the different predictor selection methods, three measures are used: the imputation accuracy, the symbolic regression performance, and the ability of reducing the number of selected predictors.

5.1   Imputation Performance

The imputation error is the difference between the original complete data and the imputed data computed using RSE (Eq. (2)). The imputation results obtained using the imputation methods LR, KNN, and PMM are shown in Table 3. For each data set, the average imputation error of 30 copies of synthetically generated incomplete (test) data sets is shown. The table presents the imputation performance of each imputation method using different predictor selection methods. Column "Full" refers to the use of all the available predictors to impute the incomplete features, "GP" to the use of the predictors selected by standard GP ($fitness_1$ Eq. (5)), "GPFS" to the use of the predictors selected by GP with feature selection pressure ($fitness_2$ Eq. (7)), and "GPMC" to the use of the predictors selected by GP with model complexity measure ($fitness_3$ Eq. (12)).

Column "ST" refers to the significance of the difference between the results of different predictor selection methods based on pair-wise Wilcoxon test with a significance level of 0.05. The symbol "+" ("−") means that the corresponding method outperforms (is outperformed by) the compared method, whereas "=" refers to no significant difference. However, # means no comparison with the same method. These symbols are shown in an ordered 4-tuple form to show the test sign of the comparison with the methods in order. For example, (+, =, #, −) for the LR method using GPFS on the Fri data set (Table 3) means that the result of applying LR to impute Fri using the predictors selected by GPFS, is significantly better/equal/the same method/worse compared to applying LR using the predictors selected by Full/GP/GPFS/GPMC. To compute the number of the selected predictors, the average of number of predictors used to impute each incomplete feature is computed and then these averages are averaged.

From the shown results, it can be seen that the use of GPMC to select the predictors has more win cases than the use of other selection methods by any of the considered imputation methods. For example, when using LR imputation, it outperforms Full predictors on all data sets. Out of six imputation comparisons, GPMC outperforms GPFS and GP in five and four cases respectively. This reveals the superiority of the proposed method over the benchmark methods. Similar conclusions can be deducted from the results of using KNN and PMM.

Table 3. The imputation performance of using imputation methods with different predictor sets (Symbols "+", "−", "=", and # mean that the method in the column is significantly better, significantly worse, similar, and the same compared to the method in the corresponding row)

		Full		GP		GPFS		GPMC	
		Err	ST	Err	ST	Err	ST	Err	ST
LR	Fri	0.0564	(#, −, −, −)	0.0553	(+, #, =, −)	0.0561	(+, =, #, −)	0.0533	(+, +, +, #)
	CPMP	0.1976	(#, −, −, −)	0.1850	(+, #, +, +)	0.1901	(+, −, #, =)	0.1886	(+, −, =, #)
	Bank	0.1349	(#, =, −, −)	0.1351	(=, #, −, −)	0.1339	(+, +, #, −)	0.1194	(+, +, =, #)
	Selwood	0.2141	(#, −, −, −)	0.2106	(+, #, +, −)	0.2130	(+, −, #, −)	0.2025	(+, +, +, #)
	Pah	0.0733	(#, −, −, −)	0.0679	(+, #, =, −)	0.0660	(+, =, #, −)	0.0488	(+, +, +, #)
	Mtp	0.1712	(#, −, −, −)	0.1674	(+, #, =, −)	0.1667	(+, =, #, −)	0.1593	(+, +, +, #)
KNN	Fri	0.0536	(#, −, −, −)	0.0513	(+, #, =, −)	0.0512	(+, =, #, −)	0.0503	(+, +, +, #)
	CPMP	0.1764	(#, −, −, −)	0.1501	(+, #, +, +)	0.1560	(+, −, #, +)	0.1141	(+, +, +, #)
	Bank	0.1229	(#, −, −, −)	0.1205	(+, #, −, −)	0.1196	(+, +, #, −)	0.1141	(+, +, +, #)
	Selwood	0.1874	(#, −, −, −)	0.1756	(+, #, +, −)	0.1772	(+, −, #, −)	0.1744	(+, +, +, #)
	Pah	0.0545	(#, −, −, −)	0.0505	(+, #, =, −)	0.0513	(+, =, #, −)	0.0402	(+, +, +, #)
	Mtp	0.1312	(#, =, −, −)	0.1328	(=, #, −, −)	0.1318	(+, +, #, =)	0.1314	(+, +, =, #)
PMM	Fri	0.0511	(#, −, −, −)	0.0503	(+, #, −, −)	0.0490	(+, +, #, =)	0.0489	(+, +, =, #)
	CPMP	0.1489	(#, =, =, =)	0.1480	(=, #, =, =)	0.1487	(=, =, #, =)	0.1466	(=, =, =, #)
	Bank	0.1166	(#, −, −, −)	0.1157	(+, #, =, −)	0.1016	(+, =, #, −)	0.1051	(+, +, +, #)
	Selwood	0.1551	(#, =, +, =)	0.1554	(=, #, +, =)	0.1603	(−, −, #, −)	0.1556	(=, =, +, #)
	Pah	0.04953	(#, −, −, −)	0.0488	(+, #, =, −)	0.0498	(+, =, #, −)	0.0374	(+, +, +, #)
	Mtp	0.1122	(#, −, −, −)	0.1028	(+, #, =, =)	0.1075	(+, =, #, =)	0.1014	(+, =, =, #)

5.2   Symbolic Regression Performance

Regarding the symbolic regression performance, after applying each imputation method on each incomplete data set, 30 sets of experiments on GP for symbolic regression are performed. Table 4 shows the amount of the win cases when comparing the symbolic regression performance associated with different predictor selection method. Each value in the table refers to the number of times in which the *column* method is significantly better than the *row* method.

Table 4. Number of comparisons in which the method in the column has a significantly better symbolic regression performance than the method in the row

	Method	LR				PMM				KNN			
		Full	GP	GPFS	GPMC	Full	GP	GPFS	GPMC	Full	GP	GPFS	GPMC
Fri	Full	0	17	19	22	0	18	19	17	0	14	15	22
	GP	1	0	5	13	2	0	7	18	3	0	17	21
	GPFS	1	3	0	14	2	6	0	17	3	5	0	8
	GPMC	0	2	5	0	0	6	7	0	3	5	6	0
	Sum	2	22	29	49	4	30	33	52	9	24	38	51
CPMP	Full	0	18	14	12	0	14	18	19	0	5	6	5
	GP	5	0	6	12	6	0	4	6	4	0	7	8
	GPFS	5	16	0	6	3	16	0	8	1	6	0	5
	GPMC	2	13	7	0	2	15	17	0	1	7	6	0
	Sum	12	47	27	30	11	45	39	33	6	18	19	18
Bank32nh	Full	0	6	17	16	0	17	16	21	0	17	14	16
	GP	4	0	15	17	5	0	17	16	4	0	5	13
	GPFS	4	8	0	5	4	5	0	12	5	6	0	17
	GPMC	3	4	4	0	4	4	5	0	5	4	7	0
	Sum	11	18	36	38	13	26	38	49	14	27	26	46
Selwood	Full	0	13	21	19	0	16	17	17	0	5	5	7
	GP	5	0	5	15	2	0	14	15	8	0	8	6
	GPFS	4	16	0	17	4	7	0	16	12	17	0	17
	GPMC	2	5	6	0	3	3	5	0	4	5	7	0
	Sum	11	34	32	51	9	26	36	48	24	27	20	30
MIP	Full	0	14	12	19	0	17	19	21	0	12	16	19
	GP	6	0	8	15	6	0	5	18	3	0	5	18
	GPFS	7	7	0	17	6	4	0	13	5	6	0	17
	GPMC	1	3	2	0	4	6	5	0	1	2	7	0
	Sum	14	24	22	51	16	27	29	52	9	20	28	54
Mtp	Full	0	11	14	18	0	6	17	14	0	17	17	21
	GP	7	0	5	10	4	0	14	12	3	0	5	8
	GPFS	6	7	0	15	4	6	0	7	6	7	0	8
	GPMC	3	3	4	0	7	6	6	0	3	3	5	0
	Sum	16	21	23	43	15	18	37	33	12	27	27	37
All	Total	66	166	169	262	68	172	212	267	74	143	158	236

As shown in Table 4, GPMC leads to better symbolic regression performance in most of the considered cases compared to any other method. Comparing the symbolic regression results along with the corresponding imputation results, it has been noticed that the better imputation accuracy, the better symbolic regression performance. For instance, when using PMM imputation on the Fri data set, GPMC wins the majority of the symbolic regression comparisons against Full and GP but not GPFS. This is because GPMC significantly outperforms Full and GP in the imputation performance, whereas, there is no significant imputation difference between GPFS and GPMC. Such a pattern is clearer on the CPMP data set, where all methods are almost equivalent in the imputation performance. Similar patterns can be observed for the different methods.

Regarding the performance per data set, GPMC has better performance on four data sets. On CPMP, GPMC could not have better symbolic regression performance. This might be due to the poor imputation performance. For the imputation methods, the lowest errors are obtained when using PMM to impute the missing values on all data sets regardless of the used predictor selection methods.

5.3   The Number of Selected Predictors

For the number of selected predictors, the average number of selected predictors using different methods is shown in Table 5. GPFS reduces the number of predictors more than any other method. This is not surprising since the number of features is introduced into the fitness function in GPFS. However, it does not guarantee the improvement of the performance over the standard GP. Overall, the use of the full set of predictors results in the worst performance.

On the other hand, although GPMC can reduce the imputation predictors more than Full and GP in most cases, the GPMC method usually has a larger number of predictors compared to GP. An example of this situation is on the data set CPMP. This is because the GPMC method prefers models with a smaller number of predictors in complex terms rather than models with a small number of predictors in general. For example, if the models $y_1 = x_1^3 + x_3^3 * x_1$ and $y_2 = x_1^3 + x_2 + x_3 + x_4$ have comparable performance, the model y_2 is more preferred although it has more predictors. This is because y_1 contains more predictors with non-constant Hessian entries (i.e. 2-order derivatives).

Table 5. The average number of selected predictors using different methods

Data set	Full	GP	GPFS	GPMC
Fri	25	9	6	7
CPMP	24	7	4	9
Bank	33	16	9	15
Selwood	54	31	17	21
MIP	145	54	16	22
Mtp	203	73	31	44

6   Conclusions and Future Work

This work designed a feature selection method that incorporates the number of features in an analytical complexity measure. The results show that the proposed method mostly provides better performance in terms of both imputation accuracy and symbolic regression performance. The contribution of this study is three fold. First, proposing a new analytical complexity measure for GP models. Second, utilizing model selection for feature selection. Third, we conduct experiments to demonstrate that our approach is effective in symbolic regression with missing values.

The main drawback of the proposed method is the need for explicit derivative of the produced expressions. Such requirement may not be hold when using more complicated function set (some cause discontinuity). This limitation is a subject of more research. Another future work is testing the generalizability of the proposed complexity measure considering the regularized GP models. Moreover, new analytical complexity measures can be examined using some mathematical-based characteristics such as higher order derivatives and determinant of Hessian. Furthermore, the computation cost of the proposed method will be addressed and its complexity will be analysed. Meanwhile, the applicability of the developed method can also be extended to other machine learning tasks such as classification and clustering.

References

1. Al-Helali, B., Chen, Q., Xue, B., Zhang, M.: A hybrid GP-KNN imputation for symbolic regression with missing values. In: Mitrovic, T., Xue, B., Li, X. (eds.) AI 2018. LNCS (LNAI), vol. 11320, pp. 345–357. Springer, Cham (2018). https://doi.org/10.1007/978-3-030-03991-2_33
2. Arslan, S., Ozturk, C.: Multi hive artificial bee colony programming for high dimensional symbolic regression with feature selection. Appl. Soft Comput. **78**, 515–527 (2019)
3. Burnham, K.P., Anderson, D.R.: Model Selection and Multi-model Inference: A Practical Information-Theoretic Approach, 2nd edn. Springer, New York (2002). https://doi.org/10.1007/b97636
4. Camargos, V.P., César, C.C., Caiaffa, W.T., Xavier, C.C., Proietti, F.A.: Multiple imputation and complete case analysis in logistic regression models: a practical assessment of the impact of incomplete covariate data. Cadernos de saude publica **27**(12), 2299–2313 (2011)
5. Chen, Q.: Improving the generalisation of genetic programming for symbolic regression. Ph.D. thesis, Victoria University of Wellington (2018)
6. Chen, Q., Xue, B., Shang, L., Zhang, M.: Improving generalisation of genetic programming for symbolic regression with structural risk minimisation. In: Proceedings of the Genetic and Evolutionary Computation Conference 2016, pp. 709–716. ACM (2016)
7. Chen, Q., Zhang, M., Xue, B.: Feature selection to improve generalization of genetic programming for high-dimensional symbolic regression. IEEE Trans. Evol. Comput. **21**(5), 792–806 (2017)
8. Chen, Q., Zhang, M., Xue, B.: Structural risk minimisation-driven genetic programming for enhancing generalisation in symbolic regression. IEEE Trans. Evol. Comput. (2018)
9. Donders, A.R.T., Van Der Heijden, G.J., Stijnen, T., Moons, K.G.: A gentle introduction to imputation of missing values. J. Clin. Epidemiol. **59**(10), 1087–1091 (2006)

10. Dubčáková, R.: Eureqa: software review. Genet. Program. Evolvable Mach. **12**(2), 173–178 (2011). https://doi.org/10.1007/s10710-010-9124-z
11. Fortin, F.A., Rainville, F.M.D., Gardner, M.A., Parizeau, M., Gagné, C.: DEAP: evolutionary algorithms made easy. J. Mach. Learn. Res. **13**, 2171–2175 (2012)
12. Heidt, K.: Comparison of imputation methods for mixed data missing at random (2019)
13. Keijzer, M.: Improving symbolic regression with interval arithmetic and linear scaling. In: Ryan, C., Soule, T., Keijzer, M., Tsang, E., Poli, R., Costa, E. (eds.) EuroGP 2003. LNCS, vol. 2610, pp. 70–82. Springer, Heidelberg (2003). https://doi.org/10.1007/3-540-36599-0_7
14. Korns, M.F., May, T.: Strong typing, swarm enhancement, and deep learning feature selection in the pursuit of symbolic regression-classification. In: Banzhaf, W., Spector, L., Sheneman, L. (eds.) Genetic Programming Theory and Practice XVI. GEC, pp. 59–84. Springer, Cham (2019). https://doi.org/10.1007/978-3-030-04735-1_4
15. Koyré, A.: The Astronomical Revolution: Copernicus-Kepler-Borelli. Routledge, New York (2013)
16. Koza, J.R.: Genetic Programming II, Automatic Discovery of Reusable Subprograms. MIT Press, Cambridge (1992)
17. Le, N., Xuan, H.N., Brabazon, A., Thi, T.P.: Complexity measures in genetic programming learning: a brief review. In: IEEE Congress on Evolutionary Computation (CEC), pp. 2409–2416. IEEE (2016)
18. Lin, W.-C., Tsai, C.-F.: Missing value imputation: a review and analysis of the literature (2006–2017). Artif. Intell. Rev. **53**, 1487–1509 (2020)
19. Little, R.J., Rubin, D.B.: Statistical Analysis with Missing Data, vol. 793. Wiley, New York (2019)
20. van der Loo, M.: Simputation: Simple Imputation. R package version 0.2.2 (2017)
21. Meurer, A., et al.: SymPy: Symbolic computing in Python. PeerJ Comput. Sci. **3**, e103 (2017)
22. Murray, K., Conner, M.M.: Methods to quantify variable importance: implications for the analysis of noisy ecological data. Ecology **90**(2), 348–355 (2009)
23. Ni, J., Drieberg, R.H., Rockett, P.I.: The use of an analytic quotient operator in genetic programming. IEEE Trans. Evol. Comput. **17**(1), 146–152 (2012)
24. Ni, J., Rockett, P.: Tikhonov regularization as a complexity measure in multiobjective genetic programming. IEEE Trans. Evol. Comput. **19**(2), 157–166 (2014)
25. Nikolaev, N.Y., Iba, H.: Regularization approach to inductive genetic programming. IEEE Trans. Evol. Comput. **5**(4), 359–375 (2001)
26. Niyogi, P., Girosi, F.: On the relationship between generalization error, hypothesis complexity, and sample complexity for radial basis functions. Neural Comput. **8**(4), 819–842 (1996)
27. Pornprasertmanit, S., Miller, P., Schoemann, A., Quick, C., Jorgensen, T., Pornprasertmanit, M.S.: Package 'SIMSEM' (2016)
28. Raymond, C., Chen, Q., Xue, B., Zhang, M.: Genetic programming with Rademacher complexity for symbolic regression. In: IEEE Congress on Evolutionary Computation (CEC), pp. 2657–2664. IEEE (2019)
29. Tran, C.T., Zhang, M., Andreae, P.: A genetic programming-based imputation method for classification with missing data. In: Heywood, M.I., McDermott, J., Castelli, M., Costa, E., Sim, K. (eds.) EuroGP 2016. LNCS, vol. 9594, pp. 149–163. Springer, Cham (2016). https://doi.org/10.1007/978-3-319-30668-1_10
30. Udrescu, S.M., Tegmark, M.: Ai Feynman: a physics-inspired method for symbolic regression. arXiv preprint arXiv:1905.11481 (2019)

31. Vanschoren, J., Van Rijn, J.N., Bischl, B., Torgo, L.: OpenML: networked science in machine learning. ACM SIGKDD Explor. Newsl. **15**(2), 49–60 (2014)
32. Vladislavleva, E., Smits, G., Den Hertog, D.: On the importance of data balancing for symbolic regression. IEEE Trans. Evol. Comput. **14**(2), 252–277 (2010)
33. Vladislavleva, E.J., Smits, G.F., Den Hertog, D.: Order of nonlinearity as a complexity measure for models generated by symbolic regression via pareto genetic programming. IEEE Trans. Evol. Comput. **13**(2), 333–349 (2008)
34. Wu, Y., Lu, J., Sun, Y.: Genetic programming based on an adaptive regularization method. In: International Conference on Computational Intelligence and Security, vol. 1, pp. 324–327. IEEE (2006)
35. Xue, B., Zhang, M.: Evolutionary feature manipulation in data mining/big data. ACM SIGEVOlution **10**(1), 4–11 (2017)
36. Yeun, Y.S., Lee, K.H., Han, S.M., Yang, Y.S.: Smooth fitting with a method for determining the regularization parameter under the genetic programming algorithm. Inf. Sci. **133**(3–4), 175–194 (2001)
37. Zhang, M., Ciesielski, V.: Genetic programming for multiple class object detection. In: Foo, N. (ed.) AI 1999. LNCS (LNAI), vol. 1747, pp. 180–192. Springer, Heidelberg (1999). https://doi.org/10.1007/3-540-46695-9_16

Seeding Grammars in Grammatical Evolution to Improve Search Based Software Testing

Muhammad Sheraz Anjum[(✉)] [ID] and Conor Ryan[ID]

Biocomputing and Developmental Systems Group, Department of Computer Science and Information Systems, Lero - The Irish Software Research Centre, University of Limerick, Limerick, Ireland
{sheraz.anjum,conor.ryan}@ul.ie

Abstract. Software-based optimization techniques have been increasingly used to automate code coverage analysis since the nineties. Although several studies suggest that interdependencies can exist between condition constructs in branching conditions of real life programs e.g. *(i <= 100) or (i == j)*, etc., to date, only the *Ariadne* system, a Grammatical Evolution (GE)-based Search Based Software Testing (SBST) technique, exploits interdependencies between variables to efficiently automate code coverage analysis.

Ariadne employs a simple attribute grammar to exploit these dependencies, which enables it to very efficiently evolve highly complex test cases, and has been compared favourably to other well-known techniques in the literature. However, Ariadne does not benefit from the interdependencies involving constants e.g. *(i <= 100)*, which are equally important constructs of condition predicates. Furthermore, constant creation in GE can be difficult, particularly with high precision.

We propose to *seed* the grammar with constants extracted from the source code of the program under test in order to enhance and extend Ariadne's capability to exploit richer types of dependencies (involving all combinations of both variables and constant values). We compared our results with the original system of Ariadne against a large set of benchmark problems which include 10 numeric programs in addition to the ones originally used for Ariadne. Our results demonstrate that the seeding strategy not only dramatically improves the generality of the system, as it improves the code coverage (effectiveness) by impressive margins, but it also reduces the search budgets (efficiency) often up to an order of magnitude.

Keywords: Automatic test case generation · Code coverage · Evolutionary Testing · Grammatical Evolution

1 Introduction

An important aspect of software quality assurance is software testing and, in practice, manual testing of a software system is laborious. It has been reported in

© Springer Nature Switzerland AG 2020
T. Hu et al. (Eds.): EuroGP 2020, LNCS 12101, pp. 18–34, 2020.
https://doi.org/10.1007/978-3-030-44094-7_2

the various studies that manual testing can consume up to 50% of the total development budget [1,2]. In order to reduce the associated cost, many researchers [3–6] have been investigating the use of metaheuristic techniques to reduce the need of human intervention in the testing process; this field of study is referred to as *Search Based Software Testing* (SBST).

Genetic Algorithms (GAs) [7] are the most widely employed heuristic-based search techniques [5,8] in SBST and this subfield of SBST is referred to as *Evolutionary Testing* (ET). The most commonly targeted test adequacy criterion in SBST is *full branch coverage* [5], which ensures that all parts of the code are reachable. For the purpose of this paper, we have chosen *full condition-decision coverage* as the target which is an extended and thus more challenging to achieve as compared to branch coverage (detailed in Sect. 2).

Condition predicates of real life programs often contain interdependencies between variables and constant values, e.g. a condition to check if two variables are equal or if the value of a particular variable is between 100 and 500, as branching conditions often include the boundary values as constants. These facts are well established and have been reported in several research studies, for example, [9] studied 120 production PL/I programs and reported that 98% expressions included less than two operators while 62% of them were relational operators. In another study [10], 50 COBOL programs were analyzed and it was reported that 64% of the total predicates were equality checks and 77% of the predicates contained only a single variable; which means that majority of these predicates contained the comparison between variables and constant values.

To the best of our knowledge, *Ariadne* [11] is the only SBST technique proposed to date that exploits the interdependencies between input variables; however, it does not benefit from interdependencies involving constants which are equally important constructs of condition predicates as also apparent from the studies discussed above. Furthermore, Ariadne is a Grammatical Evolution (GE) [12,13] based system and constant creation in GE can be difficult [14,15], particularly with high precision. Therefore, it can be very difficult for Ariadne to find test data that can satisfy conditions containing any dependencies on constant values, particularly in cases where search spaces are large and complex.

GE is a grammar-based evolutionary algorithm that uses a grammar-based mapping process to separate search space from solution space. In recent years, GE has been successfully adopted to solve many software engineering problems from a wide variety of domains, including software effort estimation [16], vulnerability testing [17], integration and test order problem [18], game development [19], failure reproduction [20], software project scheduling [21] and software product line testing [22]. To the best of our knowledge, Ariadne is the only system proposed to date that targets the structural coverage testing of procedural C/C++ programs.

In this paper, we propose an improved attribute grammar for Ariadne that enhances and extends its capability to exploit interdependencies between condition constructs, by harvesting constants from the code under test and then *seeding* the grammar with them, thus making them directly available to individuals, obviating the need to evolve specific constants, and hence improving Ariadne's ability to achieve higher code coverage. The new design of grammar allows variables to take values dependent on both the previously generated variables and the extracted constant values (detailed in Sect. 4), which enables the system to exploit all kinds of interdependencies (involving both variables and constant values) during the whole of evolutionary process.

For the purpose of our experimentation, we employed a large set of benchmark programs which includes 10 numeric programs (that heavily rely on constant values) in addition to the ones adopted by [11]. We also created three new, extremely difficult to test programs, which contain deep levels of nesting, compound conditions and interdependencies involving both variables and constant values. We adopted condition-decision coverage as the test adequacy criterion to make a fair comparison with both original results of Ariadne and well-known results from the literature [23,24].

Our results suggest that the improved grammar dramatically improves the effectiveness of Ariadne by achieving a 100% coverage (also referred to as full coverage) on **all** benchmark programs, while the original system was not able to achieve full coverage for any of the programs that heavily used constant values. Our results also demonstrate that the improved grammar does not trade off the efficiency of the system to improve its generality as it further reduces the search budgets often up to an order of magnitude.

This paper begins with an overview of search based test data generation techniques (Sect. 2), followed by an introduction to Ariadne: A GE-based test data generator (Sect. 3). In Sect. 4, we present our improved grammar for Ariadne and also the philosophy behind the proposed changes in the original grammar. Finally, in Sect. 5, we empirically evaluate the performance of our improved system of Ariadne on a large selection of benchmark problems.

2   Background and Related Work

Structural testing inspects the code based on knowledge of its internal structure. There are multiple code *coverage criteria* which are essentially conditions with varying strictness. A coverage criterion, if met, ensures the absence of certain types of errors in the code. For example, to achieve 100% condition-decision coverage (also referred to as full condition-decision coverage), a piece of code must be executed with a test suite (set of input values) such that all of both the condition predicates and branching conditions take both possible outcomes of TRUE and FALSE at least once.

Manually achieving any type of code coverage is a laborious and difficult task as a human tester has to find a set of input values that can satisfy the respective condition(s). In order to reduce this testing cost, researchers have been trying to minimize the need for human intervention in the testing process since the 1960s [25]. It has been the subject of increasing research interest in recent years [26].

In any SBST technique, the goal is to heuristically search for a test suite that satisfies a chosen test adequacy criterion for the given program. One of the earliest SBST techniques [25] used random search for this purpose. *Random test data generation* can adequately deal with simpler problems but its scalability can be a challenge when dealing with problems having significantly complex and large search spaces.

Another SBST paradigm, known as *static test data generation*, employs some mathematical system to find the test suite. Symbolic Execution (SE) [27] is one such technique, in which a mathematical expression is formulated by placing some symbolic values at the place of program variables. The result of this expression is a set of input values that can satisfy the adequacy criterion. SE is generally supposed to resolve constraints and variable interdependencies in order to execute the required parts of the program but it has its own shortcomings which include handling procedure calls, loops, pointers and complexity of constraints. Other notable static test data generation techniques include domain reduction [28] and dynamic domain reduction [29]. These techniques address some of the inherent challenges of SE but handling of loops and pointers remains an open question.

A relatively more refined SBST approach found in the literature is *dynamic test data generation*, which essentially involves running the program under test. The execution behavior of the program is observed and this information is used to guide the search towards the required test data. This approach was first proposed by [30] and later extended/improved by various researchers [31,32]. All the above mentioned research works employed some Local Search Algorithm (LSA) and hence involve the inherent risk of getting stuck in some local minima.

To address some of the inherent challenges associated with LSAs, some global search based techniques including GA-based techniques [23,33–36] and simulated annealing-based techniques [37] have been proposed by researchers. Further, to get the benefits of both local and global search algorithms, some Memetic Algorithm (MA) based techniques [24,38] have also been investigated in the literature.

SBST techniques conventionally search for one sub-goal at a time e.g. in the case of condition coverage, the set of input values that can result into a particular outcome of a specific condition predicate is searched at one time. Some proposed techniques including *whole test suite generation* [39], [38] and *many-objective optimization* [40], search for multiple targets simultaneously.

2.1   Evolutionary Testing

In Evolutionary Testing (ET), a GA is employed to find the test suite from the domain of all possible input values for the program under test. Each individual in the population represents one possible set of input values and its fitness is calculated based on the execution of target program when run with the respective input values (test case). The code of the target program is usually instrumented to monitor its execution behavior; this instrumentation is done in conjunction with GA's fitness function as both are designed according to the chosen test adequacy criterion.

Many variations of fitness functions can be found in the literature, but most of them rely on one or both of two measures, namely, branch distance and control flow information. The interested reader can refer to [31] and [35] for the concepts of *branch distance* and *approximation level* (control flow information) respectively.

The earliest ET technique to use a branch distance based fitness function was proposed by [41] and the earliest works that used control flow information for measuring the fitness include [33] and [34]. The fitness function deployed in [33] was primarily based on branch distance but some control flow information was also incorporated for loop testing, whereas [34] used a purely control flow based fitness function. Later, [35] proposed a hybrid fitness measures in order to attain the benefits associated with both of the measures.

2.2 SBST Techniques Benefitting from Seeding

As one of the key observations underpinning this work is the exploitation of domain knowledge in the process of test data generation, here we present some other SBST techniques that also take advantage of some related knowledge. In general, use of any previous knowledge to help solve a problem can also be referred to as *seeding*.

There are several papers in the literature on SBST that have shown that different seeding strategies can strongly influence the search process. For example, [42] proposed seeding the evolutionary algorithm with structural test data to efficiently find worst-case execution times of real-time systems. Later, [43] proposed to extract knowledge from source code, documentation and programmers and seed it to reduce qualitative human oracle costs. In another study, [44] investigated the impact of exploiting common object usage for the problem of automatic test data generation. Soon after that, seeding strategies were also explored in the domain of software product lines [45]. More recently [46, 47] studied the impact of injecting knowledge, through different seeding strategies, for the problem of service composition.

Previous work has also shown that extracting and directly seeding the constant values from source code of program can significantly improve the structural coverage testing [48–51], particular for programs heavily relying on constant values. However, the impact of seeding is prominent only in earlier phases of search as the seeded values can be modified (through the genetic operators of crossover and mutation) during the evolutionary process. In this paper, we propose to inject the extracted constants values in the attribute grammar of Ariadne (described in Sect. 4). This will permit the system to evolve the required dependencies involving both constants and variables throughout the search process. In other words, seeding the grammar allows the system to exploit the provided knowledge (i.e. the constant values) at any stage of the evolutionary process.

3   Ariadne: GE-Based Test Data Generation

Ariadne is an SBST technique that uses GE as a search algorithm to find/evolve the required test data from the set of all possible input values for the program under test. It uses a simple attribute grammar (presented in Sect. 3.2) to exploit interdependencies present among input variables.

Ariadne targets full condition-decision coverage, which is an extended and thus more challenging form of branch coverage. The overall operation of Ariadne is shown in Fig. 1, where o_1 to o_n represent the list of separate search objectives consisting of TRUE and FALSE outcomes of all the branching nodes (b_1 to b_l) and condition predicates (c_1 to c_m).

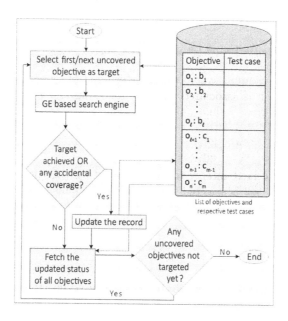

Fig. 1. System flow diagram of Ariadne: a GE-based test data generator.

Ariadne linearly selects its target from the list of search objectives and then performs a GE-based search to find the set of input values that can satisfy the current search objective. The GE-based search terminates as soon as the current target is achieved, otherwise, it keeps on running until the number of allowed generations are exhausted. This whole search process is repeated once for all the uncovered objectives, as some of the objectives are covered serendipitously (accidental coverage). The *efficiency* and *effectiveness* of any ET technique is measured in terms of total number of fitness evaluations and percentage of covered search objectives, respectively.

3.1   Grammatical Evolution

GE is essentially a GA that separates the search space (genotype) from solution space (phenotype) using a grammar-based mapping process. A problem-specific grammar is designed for this purpose which is comprised of four elements, i.e., terminals (T), non-terminals (N), productions rules (P) and a start symbol (S). Here, terminals are the only items that can appear in the final phenotype, while non-terminals are intermediate elements which are associated with the production rules. The mapping process always begins with the start symbol and, as it proceeds, production rules direct the mapping process.

In GE, the genotype is simply a list of integers which, in general, is represented using a binary string. GE consumes the genotype (integer-by-integer) in the process of making choices among available production rules using the following formula:

$Rule = (integer\ value)\ mod\ (\#\ of\ choices\ for\ the\ non\mbox{-}terminal\ at\ hand)$

Let us consider an example where the non-terminal of <operator> is about to be expanded, while it is associated with the following four production rules:

$$<operator> ::= *\quad [0]$$
$$|\ /\quad [1]$$
$$|\ +\quad [2]$$
$$|\ -\quad [3]$$

Assume that the next integer to be consumed by GE engine is 62, then *62 mod 4=2*, so option #2 is selected for the further expansion of <operator> i.e. (*<operator> ::= +*). A sample grammar with a complete genotype to phenotype mapping is presented in Fig. 2.

3.2   Grammar

In this section, we present the attribute grammar used in Ariadne [11] to exploit the commonly found characteristics of real life programs. The start symbol, in this case, is linked to the following production rule:

$$<start> ::= <var_1><var_2><var_3> \cdots <var_N> \tag{1}$$

where N represents the total number of input variables required by the target program. Each of the above non-terminals of the form $<var_M>$ is further linked with the following set of production rules:

$$<var_M> ::= 0|1| - 1|\ <rand>\ |\ <dep_{var_1}>\ |\ <dep_{var_2}>\ |\ \ldots| \tag{2}$$
$$<dep_{var_{M-2}}>\ |\ <dep_{var_{M-1}}>$$

The first three choices of the above rule enable Ariadne to quickly satisfy the commonly found zero, positive and negative value checks as the values of 0, 1 and -1 represent these domains, respectively. The next production rule of <rand> is responsible for the production of 32 bit signed random numbers.

The remaining non-terminals of the form $<dep_{var_X}>$ implement the dependency rules. These dependency rules essentially enable the system to exploit variable interdependencies as they allow the input variables to take values dependent on previously generated variables. These non-terminals of the form $<dep_{var_X}>$ are expanded using the following set of production options:

$$<dep_{var_X}> := var_X | (var_X + 1) | (var_X - 1) \tag{3}$$

where var_X refers to a previously generated variable. These newly generated values will be equal-to, greater-than or less-than the value of some previously generated variable; hence, the conditions involving comparisons/dependencies between the variables can be quickly satisfied.

4   Improved Grammar

A key distinguishing feature of Ariadne is its use of GE as a search algorithm (in place of conventional GAs). Design of a grammar is crucial and can have huge implications on the performance of any GE system; ideally the grammar used for test data generation should be both generic (so that it can be effectively applied to a wide range of programs) and efficient.

This section presents our newly proposed grammar design while its implications and the underpinning philosophy are detailed below in Sect. 4.1.

In our improved design, the non-terminal of $<var_M>$ is linked to the following set of production rules for their expansion:

$$<var_M> ::= 0|1|-1| <const> | <rand> | <dep_{var_1}> | <dep_{var_2}>$$
$$|\ldots| <dep_{var_{M-2}}> | <dep_{var_{M-1}}> \tag{4}$$

The newly introduced production rule of $<const>$ is further associated with the following choices of production rules:

$$<const> ::= 0|C_1|C_2|C_3|\ldots|C_N \tag{5}$$

where C_1 to C_N represent the list of seeded constant values which are simply extracted from the condition predicates in the source code. This innovation allows the variables to take values directly from the pool of seeded constants by right combinations of Rule 4 and 5. Once generated, these values become part of the grammar and remain available to be exploited by the dependency rules of the form $<dep_{var_X}>$, as described in Sect. 3.2. Consequently, the improved Ariadne can quickly evolve test data required to satisfy complex branching conditions that contain dependencies involving both variables and constant values.

The rest of the design is kept the same as that of the original grammar (presented in Sect. 3.2). An example with a complete grammar and grammar-based genotype to phenotype mapping for a program with three input variables and nine seeded constants is presented as Fig. 2. Note that this same generic grammar is used for all our experiments; only the number of input variables and the list of extracted constants (seeds) were modified as per each program.

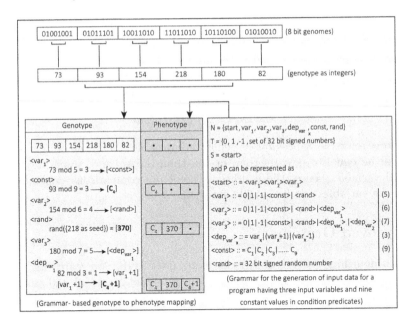

Fig. 2. An example with the genotype on the top, grammar on the right and the mapping sequence on the left.

4.1   Philosophy Behind the Proposed Changes

Ariadne, by design, does not solely rely on the evolutionary process to search for the required solution, but it also exploits variable interdependencies using its grammar, as described in Sect. 3. Results reported in [11] demonstrate that Ariadne clearly outperformed the well-known GA-based techniques by impressive margins. However, the original system of Ariadne is not capable of exploiting any dependencies involving constant values; furthermore, constant creation in GE with such an enormous range is a very difficult task.

Dependencies involving constant values are very common as discussed in Sect. 1. For example, a branching condition may contain a boundary value and look like this:

$$x > y \ \&\& \ z == 5000 \tag{6}$$

In general, it is very difficult for a conventional GA to fortuitously generate test data that can satisfy these kinds of branching condition, particularly when the search space is large. It becomes even more difficult for the original system of Ariadne as it additionally faces difficulties in the creation of constant values. To address this problem, we proposed an improved grammar for Ariadne that is capable of exploiting all kinds of interdependencies/comparisons involving both variables and constant values.

It is worth noting that the seeded constants stay available (as a part of grammar rules) throughout the search process; hence, they can also play their role in the evolution of the values required for satisfying some deeper level nested conditions, which are only reached after some initial generations of the evolutionary process. To conclude, our novel design greatly improves Ariadne's capability to exploit interdependencies present among all kinds of condition constructs by enabling it to exploit dependencies involving constant values.

5   Experimental Results and Discussion

An empirical study was performed using three different sets of benchmark functions. The first set, **Set 1**, contains ten numeric functions[1] that heavily rely on constant values. The second, **Set 2**, includes the same well-known numeric and validity-check functions[2] that were originally adopted by [11] to compare with the earlier GA based techniques proposed in [23,36] and [24].

Set 1 contains seven real life programs and three synthetic programs of varying complexity. The real life programs include Tax Calculator, Admission Merit, Vitamin D Levels, Birth-Time Weights, HBA1c Levels (blood glucose levels), Grade Point Average (GPA) Calculator and Volume Discount. These programs are well-known and self-explanatory and their branching conditions often contain the boundary values (which are essentially constant values). The synthetic programs $S1$, $S2$ and $S3$, are artificially created to be difficult coverage targets of varying complexity as they contain deep nesting (up to four levels), compound conditions and interdependencies among the condition constructs (involving both variables and constant values).

We employed Set 2 to make a fair comparison with the original system of Ariadne and also with earlier well-known results from the literature [23,24]. For the purpose of this paper, we adopted only those numeric functions that had average search costs of at least 10 fitness evaluations in the previously reported results [11] as the rest of the benchmark functions proved trivial for grammar-based approach. The adopted numeric function include Days, Quadratic Formula (QCF) and *Triangle Classification* which is one of the most commonly adopted functions in SBST [23,32,34,36] etc. While two validity-check functions named check ISBN and check ISSN are a part of an open source program, **bibclean-2.08** [52]. These all are among popular benchmark functions in SBST and their short descriptions as well as justifications for their selection can be found in [11].

5.1   Experimental Setup

We first conducted some initial experiments to identify reasonable settings for GE run. We noticed that the maximum of 200 generations with a population size of 50 were found appropriate for all but some synthetic functions. So the synthetic functions, being more complex, were run with a population size of 200 and maximum number of generations was kept at 500. For a fair comparison

---

[1] In order to facilitate future comparisons we have made available the source code at http://bds.ul.ie/?page_id=390/.

[2] The source code of these benchmark functions was made available by [11] at http://bds.ul.ie/?page_id=390/.

with [11], the crossover and mutation operators (i.e. One Point Crossover & Bit Mutation) and their probabilities (crossover: 0.9, mutation: 0.05) were kept the same as that of original system of Ariadne.

The input values generated by our improved grammar lie in the same range as that of the original system (i.e. from the range of $-2, 147, 483, 648$ to $2, 147, 483, 647$) as both systems generate 32-bit signed integers. These integer values directly serve as input values for most of the benchmark functions; for the functions of Days, check_ISBN and check_ISSN, an extra mod based step was deployed by [11] to convert these integer values into valid input formats as per the respective functions. For the sake of our experiments, we also used a similar mapping step for both input and seeding in order to have a fair comparison with the original system.

5.2   Detailed Analysis of Experiments

We performed **200 independent runs** for all the benchmarks and present their **mean** performance. We also repeated the same set of experiments using the original grammar in order to have a better statistical comparison with [11]; our results were very similar to the originally reported results.

We report our results in terms of three metrics, i.e., Maximum Coverage (MC), Success Rate (SR) and average number of fitness evaluations (AE). MC is the best performance (maximum achieved coverage) of all 200 runs. SR for each coverage target is the percentage of 200 runs/times that the target was successfully covered. AE is the average number of benchmark function executions that were performed in each run.

It can be clearly seen in Table 1 that the original system was not able to achieve a full coverage for any of the benchmark programs from Set 1 (which requires the generation of specific constant values). Despite being given a decent search budget, the maximum coverages achieved by the original system remain in the range of 25% to 75%. On the other hand, our improved system exhibited a full coverage (i.e a 100% coverage) in all of its runs; hence achieving a 100% SR for all the benchmark functions from Set 1.

The original system was never able to attain a full coverage as all these benchmark functions contain boundary values in their branching conditions. In other words, they contain interdependencies involving constant values. The original system is neither able to exploit these interdependencies nor able to successfully evolve constant values, therefore, it could never generate the test data required to satisfy these branching conditions. On the other hand, our improved system was able to exploit the presence of these boundary values as they were directly seeded in the grammar, and hence it was able to quickly evolve the test data containing all the dependencies (involving both variables and constant values) needed to satisfy these branching conditions.

For all the benchmark functions from Set 2, both the original system and our improved system were able to exhibit a 100% SR as presented in Table 2. As it was also reported in [11] that the original system was already able to achieve a full coverage for these programs, the purpose of adopting these benchmarks here

Table 1. A comparison of our improved Ariadne with the original system of Ariadne [11] on ten benchmark functions in Set 1. MC, SR and AE are maximum coverage, success rate and average number of fitness evaluations, respectively.

Branch ID	Original Ariadne [11]			Improved Ariadne		
	MC	SR	AE	MC	SR	AE
Tax Calculator	67%	0%	20108	100%	100%	27
Admission Merit	25%	0%	150759	100%	100%	827
Vitamin D Levels	63%	0%	30157	100%	100%	34
Birth-time Weights	67%	0%	20108	100%	100%	20
HBA1c Levels	75%	0%	10058	100%	100%	11
GPA Calculator	56%	0%	70359	100%	100%	96
Volume Discount	58%	0%	50259	100%	100%	57
S1	38%	0%	501003	100%	100%	134
S2	70%	0%	601223	100%	100%	2608
S3	56%	0%	801606	100%	100%	11202

was to study if our improved system was also able to retain similar good results (both in terms of effectiveness and efficiency) for these well-known benchmarks in SBST. In order to have a fair comparison with [11,24], the experiments for the validity check functions were performed on the same lines and the results were separately reported for all the non-trivial branches.

Table 2 shows that our improved system retained a 100% SR while consuming significantly smaller search budgets, particularly for the validity-check functions where the AE was reduced to anything just from 9% to 14% of that of the original system. The reason behind this dramatic improvement in efficiency is the presence of interdependencies involving constant values, which were successfully exploited by our improved system via seeding strategy. For example, the validity-check functions contained many constants in the condition predicates, which were made a part of the grammar using Rule 5. The conditions containing comparisons/dependencies involving these (seeded) constant were quickly satisfied by the function of dependency rules as described in Sect. 3.2. In can also be clearly seen that these improvements are even more impressive when compared to other GA-based techniques.

To conclude, the results presented in this section demonstrate that the grammar is made more generic without compromising on its efficiency as our improved system clearly outperforms the original system of Ariadne as well as the other GA based SBST techniques (both in terms of effectiveness and efficiency) by wide margins.

Table 2. A comparison of our improved Ariadne with the original system of Ariadne [11] and with earlier GA-based techniques [23,24]. MC, SR and AE are maximum coverage, success rate and average number of fitness evaluations, respectively.

Branch ID	Conventional GAs			Original ariadne [11]			Improved ariadne		
	MC	SR	AE	MC	SR	AE	MC	SR	AE
GADGET [23]									
Tri	94%	N/A	8000	100%	100%	958	100%	100%	355
Days	100%	N/A	N/A	100%	100%	288	100%	100%	218
QCF	75%	N/A	N/A	100%	100%	16	100%	100%	13
Harman and McMinn [24]									
B3-ISBN	100%	95%	7986	100%	100%	591	100%	100%	69
B4-ISBN	100%	95%	7986	100%	100%	581	100%	100%	69
B6-ISBN	100%	95%	8001	100%	100%	718	100%	100%	70
B7-ISBN	100%	95%	9103	100%	100%	4215	100%	100%	594
B3-ISSN	100%	98%	5273	100%	100%	525	100%	100%	47
B4-ISSN	100%	98%	5273	100%	100%	522	100%	100%	50
B6-ISSN	100%	98%	5324	100%	100%	584	100%	100%	53
B7-ISSN	100%	98%	6380	100%	100%	3755	100%	100%	344

6   Conclusion and Future Work

We have proposed to seed the grammar with constants extracted from source code in order to improve its effectiveness/generality; this improved grammar is capable of exploiting a richer class of dependencies (involving both variables and constant values). We compared our results with the original system of Ariadne against the same sets of benchmark functions that were originally used as well as against an additional set of 10 numeric programs. The results of our experiments show that the seeding strategy improves the effectiveness/generality of the system by impressive margins without compromising on its efficiency as it further reduces the search budgets often up to an order of magnitude. In other words, the improved system clearly outperforms both the original system of Ariadne as well as the other GA based SBST techniques both in terms of effectiveness and efficiency.

We believe that there is much potential to further improve this GE based SBST technique. For example, the seeding strategy can be further improved by adding support for numeric values observed at run time (dynamic seeding) and/or by exploring the possibility of accommodating other data types such as strings, as currently only numeric values are seeded in the grammar. The grammar can also be improved by systematically adding additional domain knowledge. Further, we are also conducting a rigorous study to investigate the scalability of GE-based test data generation.

This paper is the first to propose, investigate and discuss the implications of seeding the grammars in GE. Although we have used the seeding strategy in the area of SBST, we believe that there is huge potential to benefit from this strategy in other GE-based systems from different domains in which constants and other low level structures are present in the problem description.

Acknowledgments. The authors would like to thank Aidan Murphy, Muhammad Hamad Khan and Sehrish Saeed for their help with conceptualization of the idea, graphic designs and benchmark functions, respectively. This work is supported by the Science Foundation of Ireland (SFI) Grant Number 16/IA/4605.

References

1. Beizer, B.: Software Testing Techniques, 2nd edn. Van Nostrand Reinhold Inc., New York (1990). ISBN 0-442-20672-0
2. Myers, G.J., Badgett, T., Thomas, T.M., Sandler, C.: The Art of Software Testing, vol. 2. Wiley Online Library (2004)
3. McMinn, P.: Search-based software test data generation: a survey. Softw. Test. Verif. Reliab. **14**(2), 105–156 (2004)
4. Afzal, W., Torkar, R., Feldt, R.: A systematic review of search-based testing for non-functional system properties. Inf. Softw. Technol. **51**(6), 957–976 (2009)
5. Ali, S., Briand, L.C., Hemmati, H., Panesar-Walawege, R.K.: A systematic review of the application and empirical investigation of search-based test case generation. IEEE Trans. Software Eng. **36**(6), 742–762 (2010)
6. Anand, S., et al.: An orchestrated survey of methodologies for automated software test case generation. J. Syst. Softw. **86**(8), 1978–2001 (2013)
7. Holland, J.H.: Genetic algorithms. Sci. Am. **267**(1), 66–73 (1992)
8. Aleti, A., Buhnova, B., Grunske, L., Koziolek, A., Meedeniya, I.: Software architecture optimization methods: a systematic literature review. IEEE Trans. Software Eng. **39**(5), 658–683 (2013)
9. Elshoff, J.L.: An analysis of some commercial PL/I programs. IEEE Trans. Software Eng. **2**, 113–120 (1976)
10. Cohen, E.I.: A finite domain-testing strategy for computer program testing. Ph.D. thesis, The Ohio State University (1978)
11. Anjum, M.S., Ryan, C.: *Ariadne*: evolving test data using grammatical evolution. In: Sekanina, L., Hu, T., Lourenço, N., Richter, H., García-Sánchez, P. (eds.) EuroGP 2019. LNCS, vol. 11451, pp. 3–18. Springer, Cham (2019). https://doi.org/10.1007/978-3-030-16670-0_1
12. Ryan, C., Collins, J.J., Neill, M.O.: Grammatical evolution: evolving programs for an arbitrary language. In: Banzhaf, W., Poli, R., Schoenauer, M., Fogarty, T.C. (eds.) EuroGP 1998. LNCS, vol. 1391, pp. 83–96. Springer, Heidelberg (1998). https://doi.org/10.1007/BFb0055930
13. O'Neill, M., Ryan, C.: Grammatical evolution. IEEE Trans. Evol. Comput. **5**(4), 349–358 (2001)
14. Dempsey, I., O'Neill, M., Brabazon, A.: Constant creation in grammatical evolution. Int. J. Innovative Comput. Appl. **1**(1), 23–38 (2007)
15. Azad, R.M.A., Ryan, C.: The best things don't always come in small packages: constant creation in grammatical evolution. In: Nicolau, M., et al. (eds.) EuroGP 2014. LNCS, vol. 8599, pp. 186–197. Springer, Heidelberg (2014). https://doi.org/10.1007/978-3-662-44303-3_16

16. Barros, R.C., Basgalupp, M.P., Cerri, R., da Silva, T.S., de Carvalho, A.C.: A grammatical evolution approach for software effort estimation. In: Proceedings of the 15th Annual Conference on Genetic and Evolutionary Computation, pp. 1413–1420. ACM (2013)

17. Sparks, S., Embleton, S., Cunningham, R., Zou, C.: Automated vulnerability analysis: leveraging control flow for evolutionary input crafting. In: Twenty-Third Annual Computer Security Applications Conference (ACSAC 2007), pp. 477–486. IEEE (2007)

18. Mariani, T., Guizzo, G., Vergilio, S.R., Pozo, A.T.: Grammatical evolution for the multi-objective integration and test order problem. In: Proceedings of the Genetic and Evolutionary Computation Conference 2016, pp. 1069–1076. ACM (2016)

19. Patten, J.V., Ryan, C.: Procedural content generation for games using grammatical evolution and attribute grammars (2014)

20. Kifetew, F.M., Jin, W., Tiella, R., Orso, A., Tonella, P.: Reproducing field failures for programs with complex grammar-based input. In: 2014 IEEE Seventh International Conference on Software Testing, Verification and Validation, pp. 163–172. IEEE (2014)

21. de Andrade, J., Silva, L., Britto, A., Amaral, R.: Solving the software project scheduling problem with hyper-heuristics. In: Rutkowski, L., Scherer, R., Korytkowski, M., Pedrycz, W., Tadeusiewicz, R., Zurada, J.M. (eds.) ICAISC 2019. LNCS (LNAI), vol. 11508, pp. 399–411. Springer, Cham (2019). https://doi.org/10.1007/978-3-030-20912-4_37

22. Lima, J.A.P., Vergilio, S.R., et al.: Automatic generation of search-based algorithms applied to the feature testing of software product lines. In: Proceedings of the 31st Brazilian Symposium on Software Engineering, pp. 114–123. ACM (2017)

23. Michael, C.C., McGraw, G., Schatz, M.A.: Generating software test data by evolution. IEEE Trans. Software Eng. **12**, 1085–1110 (2001)

24. Harman, M., McMinn, P.: A theoretical and empirical study of search-based testing: local, global, and hybrid search. IEEE Trans. Software Eng. **36**(2), 226–247 (2010)

25. Sauder, R.L.: A general test data generator for COBOL. In: Proceedings of the May 1–3, 1962, Spring Joint Computer Conference, pp. 317–323. ACM (1962)

26. Harman, M., Jia, Y., Zhang, Y.: Achievements, open problems and challenges for search based software testing. In: 2015 IEEE 8th International Conference on Software Testing, Verification and Validation (ICST), pp. 1–12. IEEE (2015)

27. Clarke, L.A.: A system to generate test data and symbolically execute programs. IEEE Trans. Software Eng. **3**, 215–222 (1976)

28. DeMilli, R., Offutt, A.J.: Constraint-based automatic test data generation. IEEE Trans. Software Eng. **17**(9), 900–910 (1991)

29. Offutt, A.J., Jin, Z., Pan, J.: The dynamic domain reduction procedure for test data generation. Softw.: Pract. Exp. **29**(2), 167–193 (1999)

30. Miller, W., Spooner, D.L.: Automatic generation of floating-point test data. IEEE Trans. Software Eng. **3**, 223–226 (1976)

31. Korel, B.: Automated software test data generation. IEEE Trans. Software Eng. **16**(8), 870–879 (1990)

32. Ferguson, R., Korel, B.: The chaining approach for software test data generation. ACM Trans. Softw. Eng. Methodol. (TOSEM) **5**(1), 63–86 (1996)

33. Jones, B.F., Sthamer, H.H., Eyres, D.E.: Automatic structural testing using genetic algorithms. Softw. Eng. J. **11**(5), 299–306 (1996)

34. Pargas, R.P., Harrold, M.J., Peck, R.R.: Test-data generation using genetic algorithms. Softw. Test. Verif. Reliab. **9**(4), 263–282 (1999)

35. Wegener, J., Baresel, A., Sthamer, H.: Evolutionary test environment for automatic structural testing. Inf. Softw. Technol. **43**(14), 841–854 (2001)
36. Miller, J., Reformat, M., Zhang, H.: Automatic test data generation using genetic algorithm and program dependence graphs. Inf. Softw. Technol. **48**(7), 586–605 (2006)
37. Tracey, N., Clark, J., Mander, K., McDermid, J.: An automated framework for structural test-data generation. In: ASE, p. 285. IEEE (1998)
38. Fraser, G., Arcuri, A., McMinn, P.: A memetic algorithm for whole test suite generation. J. Syst. Softw. **103**, 311–327 (2015)
39. Fraser, G., Arcuri, A.: Whole test suite generation. IEEE Trans. Software Eng. **39**(2), 276–291 (2013)
40. Panichella, A., Kifetew, F.M., Tonella, P.: Reformulating branch coverage as a many-objective optimization problem. In: 2015 IEEE 8th International Conference on Software Testing, Verification and Validation (ICST), pp. 1–10. IEEE (2015)
41. Xanthakis, S., Ellis, C., Skourlas, C., Le Gall, A., Katsikas, S., Karapoulios, K.: Application of genetic algorithms to software testing. In: Proceedings of the 5th International Conference on Software Engineering and Applications, pp. 625–636 (1992)
42. Tlili, M., Wappler, S., Sthamer, H.: Improving evolutionary real-time testing. In: Proceedings of the 8th Annual Conference on Genetic and Evolutionary Computation, pp. 1917–1924. ACM (2006)
43. McMinn, P., Stevenson, M., Harman, M.: Reducing qualitative human oracle costs associated with automatically generated test data. In: Proceedings of the First International Workshop on Software Test Output Validation, pp. 1–4. ACM (2010)
44. Fraser, G., Zeller, A.: Exploiting common object usage in test case generation. In: 2011 Fourth IEEE International Conference on Software Testing, Verification and Validation, pp. 80–89. IEEE (2011)
45. Lopez-Herrejon, R.E., Ferrer, J., Chicano, F., Egyed, A., Alba, E.: Comparative analysis of classical multi-objective evolutionary algorithms and seeding strategies for pairwise testing of software product lines. In: 2014 IEEE Congress on Evolutionary Computation (CEC), pp. 387–396. IEEE (2014)
46. Chen, T., Li, M., Yao, X.: On the effects of seeding strategies: a case for search-based multi-objective service composition. In: Proceedings of the Genetic and Evolutionary Computation Conference, pp. 1419–1426. ACM (2018)
47. Chen, T., Li, M., Yao, X.: Standing on the shoulders of giants: seeding search-based multi-objective optimization with prior knowledge for software service composition. Inf. Softw. Technol. **114**, 155–175 (2019)
48. Alshahwan, N., Harman, M.: Automated web application testing using search based software engineering. In: Proceedings of the 2011 26th IEEE/ACM International Conference on Automated Software Engineering, pp. 3–12. IEEE Computer Society (2011)
49. Fraser, G., Arcuri, A.: The seed is strong: seeding strategies in search-based software testing. In: 2012 IEEE Fifth International Conference on Software Testing, Verification and Validation, pp. 121–130. IEEE (2012)
50. Rojas, J.M., Fraser, G., Arcuri, A.: Seeding strategies in search-based unit test generation. Softw. Test. Verif. Reliab. **26**(5), 366–401 (2016)

51. Bidgoli, A.M., Haghighi, H.: A new approach for search space reduction and seeding by analysis of the clauses. In: Colanzi, T.E., McMinn, P. (eds.) SSBSE 2018. LNCS, vol. 11036, pp. 343–348. Springer, Cham (2018). https://doi.org/10.1007/978-3-319-99241-9_19
52. bibclean.c   (1995).   http://www.cs.bham.ac.uk/~wbl/biblio/tools/bibclean.c. Accessed 15 Sept 2019

Incremental Evolution and Development of Deep Artificial Neural Networks

Filipe Assunção[1,2](✉) , Nuno Lourenço[1] , Bernardete Ribeiro[1] ,
and Penousal Machado[1]

[1] CISUC, Department of Informatics Engineering,
University of Coimbra, Coimbra, Portugal
{fga,naml,bribeiro,machado}@dei.uc.pt
[2] LASIGE, Department of Informatics, Faculdade de Ciencias,
Universidade de Lisboa, Lisbon, Portugal

Abstract. NeuroEvolution (NE) methods are known for applying Evolutionary Computation to the optimisation of Artificial Neural Networks (ANNs). Despite aiding non-expert users to design and train ANNs, the vast majority of NE approaches disregard the knowledge that is gathered when solving other tasks, i.e., evolution starts from scratch for each problem, ultimately delaying the evolutionary process. To overcome this drawback, we extend Fast Deep Evolutionary Network Structured Representation (Fast-DENSER) to incremental development. We hypothesise that by transferring the knowledge gained from previous tasks we can attain superior results and speedup evolution. The results show that the average performance of the models generated by incremental development is statistically superior to the non-incremental average performance. In case the number of evaluations performed by incremental development is smaller than the performed by non-incremental development the attained results are similar in performance, which indicates that incremental development speeds up evolution. Lastly, the models generated using incremental development generalise better, and thus, without further evolution, report a superior performance on unseen problems.

Keywords: Incremental development · NeuroEvolution · Convolutional Neural Networks

1 Introduction

Automated Machine Learning (AutoML) is a sub-field of Artificial Intelligence (AI) that automates with little or no human-intervention the application of Machine Learning (ML) approaches to the user's problem, avoiding the need for the manual tuning of the data pre-processing, the design and extraction of features, and/or the selection and parameterisation of the most suitable ML model. The current work focuses on a branch of AutoML: NeuroEvolution (NE) [1]. NE applies Evolutionary Computation (EC) to search for Artificial Neural Networks

T. Hu et al. (Eds.): EuroGP 2020, LNCS 12101, pp. 35–51, 2020.
https://doi.org/10.1007/978-3-030-44094-7_3

(ANNs), enabling the optimisation of their structure (e.g., number of neurons, layers, connectivity), and/or learning (i.e., weights, or learning algorithm and its parameters). In other words, the ultimate goal of NE is to empower non-expert ML users with the ability to design effective ANNs.

One of the main limitations of NE lies in the fact that the majority of the methods only address a specific problem, i.e., the ANNs are evolved for one task, and when there is the need to solve a new problem the entire search procedure is re-started from scratch. Therefore, the methods do not take advantage of any of the information available from addressing previous similar tasks. In addition, NE approaches tend to evolve large populations of individuals that are continuously optimised throughout a usually large number of generations. The evaluation of a single ANN is time-consuming, because it often requires the training of the networks with a defined (or evolved) learning strategy. Consequently, the search for effective ANNs resorting to NE tends to be slow. This problem is even more striking when optimising Deep Artificial Neural Networks (DANNs).

In this work we extend Fast Deep Evolutionary Network Structured Representation (Fast-DENSER) [2] to incremental development, i.e., we transfer and re-use the knowledge acquired when optimising DANNs (architectures and learning strategies) to previous problems, and cumulatively apply it to learn new classification tasks. The main contributions of this work are the following:

– The extension of the Fast-DENSER framework to incremental development;
– The demonstration that DANNs evolved by incremental development statistically outperform the canonical approach;
– The indication that incremental development speeds up evolution. When given the same number of generations, incremental development surpasses the performance of the evolution from scratch. For the same level of performance fewer generations are necessary;
– The evidence that the method works as expected in terms of evolution, i.e., knowledge from previously solved problems is introduced in any stage;
– The conclusion that the DANNs that are evolved by incremental development generalise better than those obtained by the non-incremental version. The performance of the incrementally generated DANNs is superior to their independent evolution counterparts in previously addressed, and in yet unaddressed problems.

The remainder of the document is organised as follows. Section 2 surveys related works in the field of NE applied to DANNs, and incremental development; Sect. 3 details Fast-DENSER; Sect. 4 introduces the extension of Fast-DENSER to incremental development; Sect. 5 presents the experimental setup and results; and Sect. 6 draws conclusions and addresses future work.

2   Related Work

NeuroEvolution (NE) approaches are usually grouped according to the target of evolution, i.e., topology [3,4], learning (i.e., weights, parameters, or learning policies) [5–7], or the simultaneous evolution of the topology and learning [8,9]. Nonetheless, more recent efforts have been put towards the proposal of methods that deal with the optimisation DANNs, and thus we feel that it is more intuitive to divide them into small-scale [5,8] and large-scale [7,10–13] NE. The current paper focuses on the latter; a complete survey can be found in [14].

The problem of most of the methods that target the evolution of DANNs is that, even aided by Graphics Processing Units (GPUs) they tend to take a lot of time to find effective models. For example, CoDeepNEAT [10] trains on 100 GPUs, and Real et al. use 450 GPUs for 7 days to perform each run [15]. Fast-DENSER takes approximately 4.7 days with a single GPU to perform each run, and that is the reason why we have selected Fast-DENSER for the current paper. There are methods that are computationally cheaper, e.g., Lorenzo and Nalepa [16] take about 120 min to obtain results; however, the speedup is obtained at the cost of the performance of the model.

To speedup evolution some authors have investigated the use of transfer learning in NE. The main goal of transfer learning is to make use of the knowledge acquired when solving previous tasks to facilitate the resolution of others, enhancing lifelong learning [17]. One of the most recurrent ideas is that of using past knowledge to provide a better start than random seeding (e.g., [18,19]).

A key problem on transfer (and even multi-task) learning is the representation. Verbancsics and Stanley [20] demonstrate that transfer learning is most effective when the representation is the same for the multiple problems that are to be addressed. That is one of the advantages of using a grammar-based NE approach such as Fast-DENSER: the grammar nature of the method makes passing from one task to the next one transparent, and requires no changes to the individuals' representation.

Whilst some transfer learning works seek to learn high-level features that are generalisable across multiple domains (e.g., [21]), our objective is to port individuals to warm start evolution to another problem, and in theory help to reach high performing solutions in less time. An example of a similar work, but where a hand designed network is used is introduced by Ciresan et al. [22], where there is the transfer of knowledge from Latin digits recognition to uppercase letters, and from Chinese characters to uppercase Latin letters.

3   Fast-DENSER

Fast-DENSER [2] is an extension of Deep Evolutionary Network Structured Representation (DENSER) [13]: a general-purpose grammar-based NE approach for optimising DANNs. DENSER can search for any type of DANN, and the target of evolution is specified in a Context-Free Grammar (CFG). An example of a CFG for encoding Convolutional Neural Networks (CNNs) is provided in Fig. 1. The typical structure of CNNs divides the topology into two parts: (i) layers for feature extraction (convolutional and pooling, lines 1–3), and layers for classification (fully-connected, line 11). The grammar of Fig. 1 explores these layer types, and also regularisation layers (dropout and batch normalisation, lines

$$
\begin{aligned}
&\text{<features> ::= <convolution> | <convolution>} && (1)\\
&\qquad\qquad\quad\ \ \text{| <pooling> | <pooling>} && (2)\\
&\qquad\qquad\quad\ \ \text{| <dropout> | <batch-norm>} && (3)\\
&\text{<convolution> ::= layer:conv [num-filters,int,1,32,256] [filter-shape,int,1,2,5]} && (4)\\
&\qquad\qquad\qquad\quad\ \text{[stride,int,1,1,3] <padding> <activation> <bias>} && (5)\\
&\text{<batch-norm> ::=layer:batch-norm} && (6)\\
&\qquad\text{<pooling> ::= <pool-type> [kernel-size,int,1,2,5]} && (7)\\
&\qquad\qquad\qquad\ \ \text{[stride,int,1,1,3] <padding>} && (8)\\
&\qquad\text{<pool-type> ::= layer:pool-avg | layer:pool-max} && (9)\\
&\qquad\text{<padding> ::= padding:same | padding:valid} && (10)\\
&\text{<classification> ::= <fully-connected> | <dropout>} && (11)\\
&\text{<fully-connected> ::= layer:fc <activation>} && (12)\\
&\qquad\qquad\qquad\qquad\ \text{[num-units,int,1,128,2048 <bias>} && (13)\\
&\qquad\text{<dropout> ::=layer:dropput [rate,float,1,0,0.7]} && (14)\\
&\qquad\text{<activation> ::= act:linear | act:relu | act:sigmoid} && (15)\\
&\qquad\qquad\text{<bias> ::= bias:True | bias:False} && (16)\\
&\qquad\text{<softmax> ::= layer:fc act:softmax num-units:10 bias:True} && (17)\\
&\qquad\text{<learning> ::= <bp> <early-stop> [batch\_size,int,1,50,500]} && (18)\\
&\qquad\qquad\qquad\ \ \text{| <rmsprop> <early-stop> [batch\_size,int,1,50,500]} && (19)\\
&\qquad\qquad\qquad\ \ \text{| <adam> <early-stop> [batch\_size,int,1,50,500]} && (20)\\
&\qquad\qquad\text{<bp> ::= learning:gradient-descent [lr,float,1,0.0001,0.1]} && (21)\\
&\qquad\qquad\qquad\ \text{[momentum,float,1,0.68,0.99]} && (22)\\
&\qquad\qquad\qquad\ \text{[decay,float,1,0.000001,0.001] <nesterov>} && (23)\\
&\qquad\text{<nesterov> ::= nesterov:True | nesterov:False} && (24)\\
&\qquad\qquad\text{<adam> ::= learning:adam [lr,float,1,0.0001,0.1] [beta1,float,1,0.5,1]} && (25)\\
&\qquad\qquad\qquad\ \text{[beta2,float,1,0.5,1] [decay,float,1,0.000001,0.001]} && (26)\\
&\qquad\text{<rmsprop> ::= learning:rmsprop [lr,float,1,0.0001,0.1]} && (27)\\
&\qquad\qquad\qquad\ \text{[rho,float,1,0.5,1] [decay,float,1,0.000001,0.001]} && (28)\\
&\qquad\text{<early-stop> ::= [early\_stop,int,1,5,20]} && (29)
\end{aligned}
$$

Fig. 1. CFG for the optimisation of the topology and learning strategy of CNNs.

1–3, and 11). Furthermore, the grammar enables the optimisation of the learning strategy (learning, lines 18–20). The parameters of each evolutionary unit (in the current work layers or learning algorithms) are kept in the grammar, and can be integer (e.g., the filter shape in line 4), float (e.g., the momentum in line 22) or closed choice (e.g., the bias in line 16). The integer and float parameters are represented by a block with the format: [variable-name, variable-type, num-values, min-value, max-value].

In addition to the CFG we need to define the macro-structure, that establishes the search space, and points directly to the grammar production rules. The macro-structure sets the sequence of evolutionary units that the individuals are allowed to use, and is encoded as a list of tuples, where each position indicates the non-terminal symbol (that establishes a one-to-one mapping to the grammar, and is used as starting symbol), and the minimum and maximum number of expansions for that non-terminal symbol. For example, for CNNs, an example of a macro-structure is [(features, 1, 10), (classification, 1, 2), (softmax, 1, 1), (learning, 1, 1)]. This macro-structure allows for CNNs with between 3 and 13 layers, and where the learning strategy is optimised.

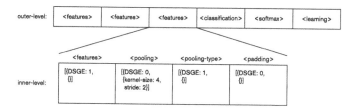

Fig. 2. Example of the genotype of a candidate solution that encodes a CNN.

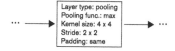

Fig. 3. Phenotype of the layer specified by the inner-level of Fig. 2

The genotype of the candidate solutions is organised into two levels: (i) the outer-level encodes the sequence of evolutionary units (with respect to the macro-structure), and sets the non-terminal symbol that is used as initial symbol for the grammatical derivation; and (ii) the inner-level corresponds to each outer-level position and encodes the parameters of a specific evolutionary unit. The inner-level genotype is similar to the genotype of Dynamic Structured Grammatical Evolution (DSGE); for more details on DSGE refer to [23]. An example of the genotype and corresponding phenotype of a candidate solution are represented in Figs. 2 and 3, respectively.

The representation of the candidate solutions in DENSER and Fast-DENSER is the same. The differences between the two approaches lie in the evolution of the population and in the evaluation of the candidate solutions. In DENSER evolution is conducted as in a standard Genetic Algorithm, where in each generation a large population of individuals is evaluated and offspring is generated. Contrary, Fast-DENSER follows a $(1+\lambda)$ Evolutionary Strategy (ES), and therefore in each generation fewer individuals are evaluated. The results have demonstrated that Fast-DENSER, with the same individual evaluation scheme, can generate individuals that have the same quality as those generated by DENSER, in a fraction of the time. More precisely, there is a speedup of 20x from DENSER to Fast-DENSER. In addition, Fast-DENSER is extended to enable the generation of fully-trained DANNs, i.e., networks that need no further training by the end of the evolutionary process. To this end, Fast-DENSER evaluates the individuals for a maximum GPU training time. However, the maximum training

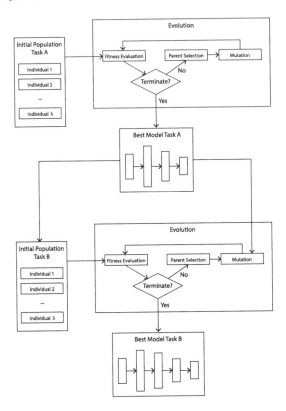

Fig. 4. Incremental development Fast-DENSER flow-chart.

time granted to each individual can grow continuously as required. The networks that are likely to benefit from longer training cycles are given access to a greater evaluation time as evolution proceeds.

4   Incremental Development of Deep Neural Networks

Experiments on previous work have shown that Fast-DENSER, given the same computational time budget, can obtain results that are superior to those reported by DENSER. The results are achieved without taking advantage of any of the knowledge acquired when solving other problems. In this paper we investigate the impact of building the networks incrementally, i.e., we take into account the DANNs that are generated for solving previous related problems, speeding up evolution, and possibly finding more effective solutions.

The flow-chart that illustrates the extension of Fast-DENSER to incremental development is depicted in Fig. 4. It shows how the method proceeds to address two different tasks A and B. For the first problem, task A, the method works similarly to Fast-DENSER: an initial population is randomly created and evolves until the stop criterion is met. The difference occurs when we solve a new problem, given that we have information on a prior one. For task B, the creation of the initial population takes into account the best model found for a previous problem (in this case task A). During evolution the past knowledge can also be incorporated. This rationale is generalised for more than two problems, i.e., in case we later address a task C, we use the knowledge obtained when addressing tasks A and B. Next, we will discuss how the prior knowledge is introduced in the initial population, and during evolution.

The initial population is formed by individuals that can be either entirely generated at random or that can use sets of evolutionary units from past models. The evolutionary units are transferred taking into account the macro-structure. For example, considering the macro-structure introduced above for CNNs, [(features, 1, 10), (classification, 1, 2), (softmax, 1, 1), (learning, 1, 1)], the initial population can contain individuals that (i) have all the layers comprising the feature extraction, and generate the classification layers at random; (ii) generate at random the feature extraction layers, and copy the layers that perform classification from previous models; (iii) copy only the learning evolutionary unit, and generate all the remaining ones at random; (iv) generate all evolutionary units at random, not using any previous knowledge; or (v) any other possible combination. It is important to mention that this incremental development approach only focuses on the evolutionary units, and consequently the weights are not transferred from previous models. At most we allow the learning strategy (which is an evolutionary unit) to be ported.

The models generated for solving each of the previously addressed problems are also important during evolution. The mutations in Fast-DENSER are tailored for manipulating DANNs: they enable the addition, removal, and/or duplication of any evolutionary unit, and the perturbation of the integer and/or float values. The duplication mutation, as the name suggests, replicates a given evolutionary unit by reference, and thus, any mutation that later affects this evolutionary unit changes all of its copies. In the incremental development version of Fast-DENSER the duplication can copy evolutionary units either from the individual or from any of the best models that were generated for solving previous tasks.

The individuals are evaluated only on the new problem. Therefore, up to the moment, this method is incremental in the sense that the DANNs for solving new and unseen problems do not kick off evolution from scratch. The incremental development does not mean that by the end of evolution the generated models can solve multiple tasks. However, it is expected that the models that are built considering previous knowledge generalise better than those that are always evolved from a random population. That is, we expect the models generated by incremental development to perform well in other tasks when re-trained.

5   Experimentation

To compare the incremental and non-incremental versions of Fast-DENSER we consider four computer vision datasets: MNIST, SVHN, Fashion-MNIST, and

Table 1. Description of the datasets.

Dataset	Train set size	Test set size	Number of classes	Shape
MNIST	60000	10000	10	$28 \times 28 \times 1$
SVHN	73257	26032	10	$32 \times 32 \times 3$
Fashion-MNIST	60000	10000	10	$28 \times 28 \times 1$
CIFAR-10	50000	10000	10	$32 \times 32 \times 3$

CIFAR-10 (summarised in Sect. 5.1). In particular, we conduct experiments for the following setups: (i) MNIST; (ii) SVHN; (iii) Fashion-MNIST; (iv) CIFAR-10; (v) MNIST $\rightarrow$ SVHN; (vi) MNIST $\rightarrow$ SVHN $\rightarrow$ Fashion-MNIST; (vii) MNIST $\rightarrow$ SVHN $\rightarrow$ CIFAR-10. The symbol $\rightarrow$ denotes the incremental build of the model from one task to the next. The setups are chosen according to the relatedness and expected difficulty of the tasks: the MNIST and SVHN datasets are composed by digits, and then transferred to two different domains, Fashion-MNIST, and CIFAR-10. The parameters required for the conducted experiments are detailed in Sect. 5.2. The experimental results are divided into three sections. First, in Sect. 5.3 we analyse the evolutionary performance when evolving DANNs for MNIST, SVHN, Fashion-MNIST, and CIFAR-10 with and without incremental development. Second, in Sect. 5.4 we investigate the incremental development of the topologies. Third, in Sect. 5.5, we analyse the generalisation ability of the different models. The experimental results are discussed in Sect. 5.6.

5.1 Datasets

The experiments are conducted in 4 datasets: MNIST, SVHN, Fashion-MNIST, and CIFAR-10. The characteristics of the datasets are summarised in Table 1. The shape of the instances is formatted as width $\times$ height $\times$ number of channels; grayscale images have one channel, and RGB images have three channels. A brief overview of the dataset instances is provided next.

MNIST [24] – handwritten digits from 0 to 9. The instances are pre-processed: size-normalized, and centered;

SVHN [25] – digits gathered from real-world images from house numbers in Google Street View images;

Fashion-MNIST [26] – similar to MNIST, where the images of handwritten digits are replaced by fashion clothing items: top, trouser, pullover, dress, coat, sandal, shirt, sneaker, bag, and ankle boot;

CIFAR-10 [27] – real-world pictures of objects that are of one of the following classes: airplane, automobile, bird, cat, deer, dog, frog, horse, ship, and truck.

5.2   Experimental Setup

The experimental parameters are detailed in Table 2. The table is organised into 4 sections: (i) evolutionary engine – parameters related to Fast-DENSER $(1+\lambda)$-ES; (ii) dataset – parameters concerned with the dataset partitioning; (iii) training – parameters associated with the training of the DANNs; and (iv) data augmentation – parameters required for the dataset augmentation strategy.

The number of generations is different for each of the datasets. In particular, we perform 20, 30, 50, and 100 generations for the MNIST, Fashion-MNIST, SVHN, and CIFAR-10 datasets, respectively. The number of generations for each dataset was set empirically based on previous experiments, and according to how challenging each problem is expected to be. The grammatical mutation rate is a DSGE parameter that stands for the probability of changing any of the grammar expansion possibilities or integer/float parameter values.

The dataset section of Table 2 defines how we partition the train set of each dataset, i.e., for each run the train set is divided (in a stratified way) into three independent folds: (i) evolutionary train – used for training the DANNs; (ii) evolutionary validation – used to perform early stop; and (iii) evolutionary test – used to measure the fitness of the individual, which is measured using the accuracy. The test set (that is different from the evolutionary test set) is kept

Table 2. Experimental parameters.

Evolutionary engine parameter	Value
Number of runs	10
Number of generations	20/30/50/100
λ	5
Add layer rate	25%
Duplicate layer rate	15%
Remove layer rate	25%
Grammatical mutation rate	15%
Dataset parameter	Value
Evolutionary Validation set	3500 instances
Evolutionary Test set	3500 instances
Evolutionary Train set	Remaining instances
Test set	Check Table 1
Training parameter	Value
Training Time	10 min
Loss	Categorical Cross-entropy
Data augmentation parameter	Value
Padding	4
Random crop	4
Horizontal flipping	50%

out of evolution and is used only after the end of the evolutionary search. It measures how well the models behave beyond the data used during evolution, and enables the unbiased evaluation of the performance.

The datasets, as discussed in Sect. 5.1, have different shapes: MNIST and Fashion-MNIST are $28 \times 28 \times 1$, and SVHN and CIFAR-10 are $32 \times 32 \times 3$. To facilitate the application of the optimised DANNs to all datasets we reshape the MNIST and Fashion-MNIST to $32 \times 32 \times 3$. The image width and height are resized using the nearest neighbour method, and to pass from one to three channels we replicate the single channel three times. All the datasets are applied the same data augmentation strategy: padding, random cropping, horizontal flipping, and re-scaling to $[0, 1]$. We do not subtract the mean image nor normalize.

Table 3. Average performance of the optimised DANNs. The results are averages of 10 independent runs. Bold marks the highest average performance values.

Dataset	Evolutionary accuracy	Test accuracy
MNIST	98.86 ± 0.465	98.80 ± 0.298
SVHN	93.28 ± 0.863	93.31 ± 0.955
MNIST → SVHN	$\mathbf{94.01 \pm 0.891}$	$\mathbf{94.04 \pm 0.887}$
Fashion	92.42 ± 1.224	91.41 ± 1.049
MNIST → SVHN → Fashion	$\mathbf{93.92 \pm 0.930}$	$\mathbf{92.96 \pm 0.742}$
CIFAR-10	87.18 ± 1.242	86.19 ± 1.672
MNIST → SVHN → CIFAR-10	$\mathbf{89.06 \pm 1.488}$	$\mathbf{88.19 \pm 1.669}$

The networks are trained for an initial maximum GPU time of 10 min, and thus it is important to mention that we are performing each evolutionary run in a GeForce GTX 1080 Ti GPU. For the experiments conducted on this paper we use the grammar of Fig. 1, and the macro-structure: [(features, 1, 30), (classification, 1, 10), (softmax, 1, 1), (learning, 1, 1)]. The code for Fast-DENSER can be found in the GitHub repository https://github.com/fillassuncao/fast-denser3.

5.3   Experimental Results: Incremental Development

We start by comparing the DANNs generated by Fast-DENSER with and without incremental development in terms of performance. The results are summarised in Table 3. We report the evolutionary accuracy (i.e., fitness), and the test accuracy (i.e., the accuracy of the models on an unseen partition of the datasets). The results are averages of 10 independent runs. The first conclusion is that given the same computational time (number of generations), the results reported by the incremental development are always superior to those of when evolution starts from scratch. In particular, the performance of MNIST → SVHN is superior to the performance of SVHN, the performance of MNIST → SVHN → Fashion is superior to the performance of Fashion, and the performance of MNIST → SVHN → CIFAR-10 is superior to the performance of CIFAR-10.

To better acknowledge the differences between the fittest DANNs generated with and without incremental development we use statistical tests. To check if the samples follow a Normal Distribution we use the Kolmogorov-Smirnov and Shapiro-Wilk tests, with $\alpha = 0.05$. The tests reveal that the data does not follow any distribution and thus the non-parametric Mann-Whitney U test ($\alpha = 0.05$) is used to perform the comparisons between the setups. The statistical tests show that the results of MNIST → SVHN → Fashion, and MNIST → SVHN → CIFAR-10 are statistically superior (in evolution and test) to Fashion (evolutionary p-value = 00736, test p-value = 0.00278), and CIFAR-10 (evolutionary p-value = 0.00804, test p-value = 0.01552), respectively. The effect size is large for all the statistically significant comparisons ($r > 0.5$). The difference between MNIST → SVHN and SVHN is not statistically significant (evolutionary p-value = 0.05876, test p-value = 0.0536). With only 20 generations the MNIST setup is the one that attains the highest average accuracy results. This indicates that it is an easy to solve problem and consequently no much knowledge is acquired from addressing it. This is a well-known fact: a simple fully-connected network is able to attain good performances in the MNIST dataset.

The above results prove that incremental development, given the same number of generations, designs DANNs that outperform those generated without incremental development. On the other hand, what happens when, for each setup, we only let evolution to be conducted for a smaller amount of generations, so that the cumulative number of generations is not superior to that of when evolution is conducted from scratch? The cumulative number of generations is the sum of the number of generations of each incremental step. For example, for the MNIST → SVHN, the cumulative number of generations is 70 (20 + 50). In this scenario we consider 30, 0, and 30 generations for the MNIST → SVHN, MNIST → SVHN → Fashion, and MNIST → SVHN → CIFAR-10 setups, respectively. The average evolutionary performance of the 10 fittest networks slightly decreases to 93.69 ± 0.912, 92.91 ± 1.15, and 87.13 ± 2.225, respectively for the MNIST → SVHN, MNIST → SVHN → Fashion, and MNIST → SVHN → CIFAR-10 setups. With these results there is no statistical difference for any of the setups, i.e., with incremental development, given a cumulative search time that equals the search time from scratch, we are able to generate DANNs that report the same performance as those optimised without incremental development for more generations. In other words, the use of previous knowledge speeds up evolution.

In addition to analysing the average performance over the 10 evolutionary runs we also focus on the overall best found DANN, i.e., the fittest DANN among the conducted runs. This analysis is important considering that in a real-world scenario by the end of evolution what really interests the user is the best found model, which is the one to potentially be deployed live. To avoid an unbiased choice of the best model for each dataset, the decision is taken only with regard to the evolutionary performance. The results are reported in Table 4, and once again show that the best results are obtained by incremental development. The most striking result is the one of CIFAR-10, where the difference introduced by incremental development is the highest.

Table 4. Accuracy of the best performing DANN for each of the setups. Bold marks the highest performance value.

Dataset	Evolutionary accuracy	Test accuracy
MNIST	99.46	99.12
SVHN	94.20	93.88
MNIST → SVHN	**94.80**	**94.14**
Fashion	93.91	92.92
MNIST → SVHN → Fashion	**94.80**	**93.92**
CIFAR-10	88.74	88.14
MNIST → SVHN → CIFAR-10	**91.06**	**89.79**

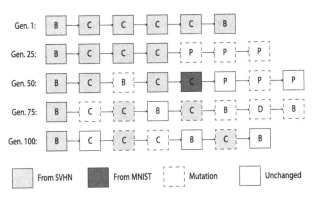

Fig. 5. Overview of the evolution on the incremental development setup MNIST → SVHN → CIFAR-10. We provide a snapshot of the feature-layers of the best individual on the 1st, 25th, 50th, 75th, and 100th generations. For space constraints we focus on the feature extraction layers: Convolutional (C), Pooling (P), Batch-Normalization (B), and Dropout (D).

5.4   Experimental Results: Topology Analysis

To analyse the behaviour of incremental development from a structural point of view we inspect the topology of the best networks as evolution proceeds. Figure 5 shows the evolution of the structure of the networks on the setup MNIST → SVHN → CIFAR-10. Because of space constraints we select the setup where more generations were performed, and present the snapshots of the run that generates the DANN with the median fitness value, i.e., we order the runs according to the fitness of the best generated DANN and select the 6th run. We choose the median run to avoid a biased selection over the worst or best results. We focus only on the feature extraction layers. The figure's goal is to illustrate the exploration of knowledge incorporation, and thus the parameters of the layers are omitted.

The figure makes it evident that the amount of layers that come from previously addressed tasks without any change diminishes as evolution proceeds. That is the expected behaviour: in the initial generation the fittest DANN reuses all layers from the best network generated to address the SVHN, and across generations these layers are adapted to tackle the CIFAR-10 (e.g., convolutional in generation 75). During evolution new layers are also randomly created (e.g., batch-normalization in generation 50), and others removed (e.g., dropout in generation 100). Similarly to the the non-incremental approach, new random layers can be added, but in addition, in the incremental development strategy we can also add layers that come from the previously solved tasks (e.g., convolutional layer that is transferred from the MNIST in generation 50).

The snapshots prove that incremental development is able to generate better results based on the re-use of evolutionary units that aid solving previous problems. The evolutionary units are not only incorporated in the generation of the initial population, but also during evolution. We also inspect the evolutionary results of other setups and the conclusions are inline with the reported.

5.5   Experimental Results: Generalisation of the Models

With the objective of studying the generalisation ability of the generated models we measure their performance on all the considered datasets. For example, we take the best generated solutions for the MNIST dataset and apply them to the SVHN, Fashion and CIFAR-10 datasets without further evolutionary optimisation. The networks are re-trained on the target datasets with the same topology and learning strategy that is optimised for the source task. Table 5 summarises the test results for all the setups. The values in bold mark the best generalisation performance, i.e., the best performance of the setup (row) that has not yet seen the dataset (column), e.g., for the CIFAR-10 dataset (last column), except for the setups that specifically target this dataset (CIFAR-10, and MNIST→SVHN→CIFAR-10), the setup that attains the highest performance is MNIST→SVHN→Fashion, and thus this is the setup that is marked in bold.

The analysis of the results shows that incremental development always generates better results, even for tasks that have not been addressed previously. To better understand the differences we perform a statistical analysis, and compare the performances reported by the non-incremental and incremental approaches. Therefore we compare the SVHN and MNIST→SVHN setups on the MNIST, Fashion, and CIFAR-10 datasets, and we do similarly with the remaining pairs: Fashion vs. MNIST→SVHN→Fashion, and CIFAR-10 vs. MNIST→SVHN→CIFAR-10. The same conditions of the above statistical comparison are applied. The statistical tests reveal that there are only significant differences between the Fashion, and MNIST→SVHN→Fashion setups, with p-values of 0.02574, and 0.01732, respectively for the SVHN and CIFAR-10 datasets (the effect size is large). The direct comparison for the dataset used for evolution (in this case Fashion) was performed above and revealed a statistical significance in favour of incremental development for the setups that include two incremental development steps.

Table 5. Performance of the evolved DANNs when applied to other datasets. The results are averages of 10 independent runs, where each DANN is trained 5 times. The setups are the table rows, and the datasets the columns.

	MNIST	SVHN	Fashion	CIFAR-10
MNIST	98.80 ± 0.298	71.31 ± 29.60	90.17 ± 1.842	63.63 ± 23.29
SVHN	96.87 ± 5.426	93.31 ± 0.955	91.60 ± 1.289	78.49 ± 7.899
MNIST→SVHN	98.93 ± 0.266	94.04 ± 0.887	91.83 ± 1.312	82.58 ± 2.414
Fashion	92.73 ± 16.75	89.16 ± 3.551	91.41 ± 1.049	77.32 ± 4.893
MNIST→SVHN→Fashion	98.89 ± 0.273	**92.48 ± 2.167**	92.96 ± 0.742	**83.47 ± 2.294**
CIFAR-10	99.06 ± 0.039	90.18 ± 9.282	92.91 ± 0.479	86.19 ± 1.672
MNIST→SVHN→CIFAR-10	**99.11 ± 0.071**	90.08 ± 5.924	**93.16 ± 0.3328**	88.19 ± 1.669

In case we order the datasets by difficulty, given by the non-incremental test performance on each dataset, we have MNIST, SVHN, Fashion, and CIFAR-10, where the leftmost is the easiest one, and the rightmost is the most challenging. From these results we hypothesise that superior generalisation performances are obtained by incremental development, when passing from more simple to more challenging datasets. That is the reason why there is no statistical difference in the CIFAR-10 vs. MNIST→SVHN→CIFAR-10 setups: the CIFAR-10 is per-se more challenging to solve than the remaining ones, and therefore, as already noticed in a previous article [13], the DANNs generated for addressing CIFAR-10 tend to be able to solve other easier problems. The remarkable aspect of incremental development is when a DANN optimised for Fashion is able to get better results on the CIFAR-10, compared to when the DANNs for Fashion are not evolved in an incremental fashion.

5.6 Discussion

The results presented in the previous sections compare in terms of performance, topology, and generalisation ability the search conducted by non-incremental and incremental development. The evolutionary results show that given the same search time the DANNs obtained by incremental development statistically outperform the non-incremental counterparts. On the other hand, the incremental strategy speeds up evolution, and given the same cumulative search time reports results that match the non-incremental performances.

The speedup in evolution is facilitated by the warm-start of incremental development, and possibility to still incorporate knowledge from previous tasks by mutation as generations proceed. We show an example of this by representing several snapshots of a network across generations. In particular for the selected run of the MNIST→SVHN→CIFAR-10 setup, on the first generation the best individual replicates all the layers from the MNIST→SVHN setup, which are continuously modified and adapted to the CIFAR-10. During evolution the parameters of the layers that are copied from the previous setup are changed, new layers (random, and from previous setups) are added, and others removed. That is, the behaviour of the incremental development evolution is the expected.

Finally, we analyse the generalisation ability of the generated DANNs. Without further evolution, i.e., with the same topology and learning strategy obtained when optimising a DANN for a specific task, we re-train the DANNs on the remaining datasets. The results show that, on average, the incremental development results are superior to the non-incremental results. Moreover, the results are statistically significant when the generated DANNs are applied to a more difficult task than that where they were generated. This indicates that incremental development helps in learning increasingly more challenging tasks, and that there are not major differences when performing the opposite.

6 Conclusions and Future Work

Motivated by the difficulty and burden in the design of DANNs we investigate how to incorporate past knowledge to aid evolution. In particular, we extend Fast-DENSER – a general-purpose grammar-based NE framework – to take advantage of the evolutionary units acquired when optimising DANNs for previous tasks. This novel incremental developmental approach enables the incorporation of knowledge from any of the previously addressed tasks in any stage of evolution: both during the generation of the initial population, and by the application of mutations, as the generations proceed.

The results prove that incremental development improves the search performed by Fast-DENSER enabling it to obtain statistically superior results. Additionally, incremental development speeds up evolution, being able to obtain the same results as non-incremental evolution given the same cumulative search time, i.e., less generations are used for the target dataset. In addition, the DANNs obtained by the end of evolution generalise better when we use incremental development in the search: the networks designed for easy problems perform better in more challenging and yet unseen tasks.

The future work will target three different directions: (i) apply the incremental development methodology to a wider set of tasks and domains; (ii) extend the approach to modular evolution; and (iii) seek ways to transfer not only the evolutionary unit but also the weights (in case the evolutionary units are layers).

Acknowledgments. This work is partially funded by: Fundação para a Ciência e Tecnologia (FCT), Portugal, under the PhD grant agreement SFRH/BD/114865/2016, the project grant DSAIPA/DS/0022/2018 (GADgET), and is based upon work from COST Action CA15140: ImAppNIO, supported by COST (European Cooperation in Science and Technology): www.cost.eu.

References

1. Floreano, D., Dürr, P., Mattiussi, C.: Neuroevolution: from architectures to learning. Evol. Intell. **1**(1), 47–62 (2008)
2. Assunção, F., Lourenço, N., Machado, P., Ribeiro, B.: Fast DENSER: efficient deep neuroevolution. In: Sekanina, L., Hu, T., Lourenço, N., Richter, H., García-Sánchez, P. (eds.) EuroGP 2019. LNCS, vol. 11451, pp. 197–212. Springer, Cham (2019). https://doi.org/10.1007/978-3-030-16670-0_13

3. Gruau, F., Whitley, D., Pyeatt, L.: A comparison between cellular encoding and direct encoding for genetic neural networks. In: Proceedings of the 1st Annual Conference on Genetic Programming, pp. 81–89. MIT Press, Cambridge (1996)

4. Miller, G.F., Todd, P.M., Hegde, S.U.: Designing neural networks using genetic algorithms. In: ICGA, pp. 379–384. Morgan Kaufmann (1989)

5. Whitley, D.: Applying genetic algorithms to neural network learning. In: Proceedings of the Seventh Conference (AISB89) on Artificial Intelligence and Simulation of Behaviour, pp. 137–144. Morgan Kaufmann Publishers Inc. (1989)

6. Gomez, F.J., Schmidhuber, J., Miikkulainen, R.: Accelerated neural evolution through cooperatively coevolved synapses. J. Mach. Learn. Res. **9**, 937–965 (2008)

7. Stanley, K.O., D'Ambrosio, D.B., Gauci, J.: A hypercube-based encoding for evolving large-scale neural networks. Artif. Life **15**(2), 185–212 (2009)

8. Stanley, K.O., Miikkulainen, R.: Evolving neural networks through augmenting topologies. Evol. Comput. **10**(2), 99–127 (2002)

9. Turner, A.J., Miller, J.F.: Cartesian genetic programming encoded artificial neural networks: a comparison using three benchmarks. In: GECCO, pp. 1005–1012. ACM (2013)

10. Miikkulainen, R., et al.: Evolving deep neural networks. CoRR abs/1703.00548 (2017)

11. Suganuma, M., Shirakawa, S., Nagao, T.: A genetic programming approach to designing convolutional neural network architectures. In: Proceedings of the Genetic and Evolutionary Computation Conference, pp. 497–504. ACM (2017)

12. Real, E., et al.: Large-scale evolution of image classifiers. In: ICML. Proceedings of Machine Learning Research, vol. 70, pp. 2902–2911. PMLR (2017)

13. Assunção, F., Lourenço, N., Machado, P., Ribeiro, B.: Denser: deep evolutionary network structured representation. Genet. Program. Evolvable Mach. **20**, 5–35 (2018). https://doi.org/10.1007/s10710-018-9339-y

14. Baldominos, A., Saez, Y., Isasi, P.: On the automated, evolutionary design of neural networks: past, present, and future. Neural Comput. Appl. **32**(2), 519–545 (2019). https://doi.org/10.1007/s00521-019-04160-6

15. Real, E., Aggarwal, A., Huang, Y., Le, Q.V.: Regularized evolution for image classifier architecture search. arXiv preprint arXiv:1802.01548 (2018)

16. Lorenzo, P.R., Nalepa, J.: Memetic evolution of deep neural networks. In: GECCO, pp. 505–512. ACM (2018)

17. Thrun, S.: Is learning the n-th thing any easier than learning the first? In: NIPS, pp. 640–646. MIT Press (1995)

18. Tirumala, S.S., Ali, S., Ramesh, C.P.: Evolving deep neural networks: a new prospect. In: ICNC-FSKD, pp. 69–74. IEEE (2016)

19. Wong, C., Houlsby, N., Lu, Y., Gesmundo, A.: Transfer learning with neural AutoML. In: Bengio, S., Wallach, H., Larochelle, H., Grauman, K., Cesa-Bianchi, N., Garnett, R. (eds.) Advances in Neural Information Processing Systems 31, pp. 8356–8365. Curran Associates, Inc. (2018)

20. Verbancsics, P., Stanley, K.O.: Evolving static representations for task transfer. J. Mach. Learn. Res. **11**, 1737–1769 (2010)

21. Long, M., Cao, Y., Wang, J., Jordan, M.I.: Learning transferable features with deep adaptation networks. arXiv preprint arXiv:1502.02791 (2015)

22. Ciresan, D.C., Meier, U., Schmidhuber, J.: Transfer learning for Latin and Chinese characters with deep neural networks. In: IJCNN, pp. 1–6. IEEE (2012)

23. Lourenço, N., Assunção, F., Pereira, F.B., Costa, E., Machado, P.: Structured grammatical evolution: a dynamic approach. In: Ryan, C., O'Neill, M., Collins, J.J. (eds.) Handbook of Grammatical Evolution, pp. 137–161. Springer, Cham (2018). https://doi.org/10.1007/978-3-319-78717-6_6

24. Lecun, Y., Bottou, L., Bengio, Y., Haffner, P.: Gradient-based learning applied to document recognition. Proc. IEEE **86**(11), 2278–2324 (1998)

25. Netzer, Y., Wang, T., Coates, A., Bissacco, A., Wu, B., Ng, A.Y.: Reading digits in natural images with unsupervised feature learning. In: NIPS Workshop on Deep Learning and Unsupervised Feature Learning 2011 (2011)

26. Xiao, H., Rasul, K., Vollgraf, R.: Fashion-MNIST: a novel image dataset for benchmarking machine learning algorithms (2017)

27. Krizhevsky, A., Hinton, G., et al.: Learning multiple layers of features from tiny images. Technical report, Citeseer (2009)

Investigating the Use of Geometric Semantic Operators in Vectorial Genetic Programming

Irene Azzali[1]([envelope]) [ORCID], Leonardo Vanneschi[2,3] [ORCID], and Mario Giacobini[1] [ORCID]

[1] DAMU - Data Analysis and Modeling Unit, Department of Veterinary Sciences, University of Torino, Turin, Italy
{irene.azzali,mario.giacobini}@unito.it
[2] NOVA Information Management School (NOVA IMS), Universidade Nova de Lisboa, Campus de Campolide, 1070-312 Lisbon, Portugal
lvanneschi@novaims.unl.pt
[3] LASIGE, Departamento de Informática, Faculdade de Ciências, Universidade de Lisboa, 1749-016 Lisbon, Portugal

Abstract. Vectorial Genetic Programming (VE_GP) is a new GP approach for panel data forecasting. Besides permitting the use of vectors as terminal symbols to represent time series and including aggregation functions to extract time series features, it introduces the possibility of evolving the window of aggregation. The local aggregation of data allows the identification of meaningful patterns overcoming the drawback of considering always the previous history of a series of data. In this work, we investigate the use of geometric semantic operators (GSOs) in VE_GP, comparing its performance with traditional GP with GSOs. Experiments are conducted on two real panel data forecasting problems, one allowing the aggregation on moving windows, one not. Results show that classical VE_GP is the best approach in both cases in terms of predictive accuracy, suggesting that GSOs are not able to evolve efficiently individuals when time series are involved. We discuss the possible reasons of this behaviour, to understand how we could design valuable GSOs for time series in the future.

Keywords: Vector-based genetic programming · Time series · Sliding windows · Geometric semantic operators

1 Introduction

A *panel dataset* is a dataset consisting of observations collected during time from multiple subjects [11]. As such, these datasets combine static features with time series data. An important issue involving panel datasets arises when we face the problem of predicting one of the time series variables. Table 1 shows a simple example of a panel dataset for three stores in U.S. regions over the course of several weeks, in which the data include the fuel price in the region (Fuel_pr),

T. Hu et al. (Eds.): EuroGP 2020, LNCS 12101, pp. 52–67, 2020.
https://doi.org/10.1007/978-3-030-44094-7_4

the unemployment rate of the region (Unempl_r), and the distance of the store from the nearest metro station (Dist_M). The goal is to predict the total sales (*Sales*) of each week, based on the explanatory variables introduced before.

Table 1. Example of a standard panel dataset.

Store ID	Fuel_pr	Unempl_r	Dist_M	Week	*Sales*
1	2.7	5.4	1800	12	3000
1	2.6	5.4	1800	13	1750
2	2.3	6.2	1400	11	440
2	2.3	6.2	1400	12	4100
2	2.6	6.5	1400	13	1800
3	2.1	2.2	8000	10	650

Classical machine learning (ML) techniques such as neural networks, random forests and genetic programming (GP) can be applied to forecast panel datasets, but their performance might suffer from considering independently each observation, therefore losing information on their temporal order. This would result in difficulties caused by the lack of meaningful predictive characteristics of time series such as peaks and regularities. In this perspective, besides known advanced ML techniques such as recurrent neural networks, a new approach of GP called vectorial genetic programming (VE_GP) was recently proposed in [4]. VE_GP extends the terminal set to vectors, providing a suitable representation for time series. In this way, the time series variables collected from each subject can be kept intact, making it possible to fully exploit the knowledge about the behaviour of the series. To clarify, Table 2 shows how the panel dataset of Table 1 changes representation in order to feed a VE_GP algorithm.

Table 2. The same data as in Table 1, but with the representation used for VE_GP.

Store ID	Fuel_pr	Unempl_r	Dist_M	Week	*Sales*
1	[2.7, 2.6]	[5.4, 5.4]	1800	[12, 13]	[3000, 1750]
2	[2.3, 2.3, 2.6]	[6.2, 6.2, 6.5]	1400	[11, 12, 13]	[440, 1100, 1800]
3	[2.1]	[2.2]	8000	[10]	[650]

To efficiently use the information contained in time series, VE_GP includes aggregation functions as primitives, as well as new strategies in the different steps of the classical GP search process.

VE_GP has already revealed advantages in benchmark problems [4], but noteworthy are the results on a real prediction of panel data [3]. In this last work, the predictive accuracy and the generalization ability of VE_GP were ascribed to the key feature of keeping together ordered sequences in vectors. This representation, in fact, lets the evolution discover the most informative aggregation functions to be used in the predictive model, which are responsible of inferring information on the time series behaviour.

Nonetheless, one of the major advantages of VE_GP was claimed to be its ability to evolve the window of time where the new aggregation functions are applied. VE_GP, in fact, adds to all the aggregation functions their parametric version, so that they can be applied only on a portion of the whole vector. The search for the best parameters, the ones that determine the most informative portion of the vector, is part of the evolutionary process, thanks to the introduction of a parameter mutation operator.

In recent years, the use of geometric semantic operators (GSOs) in GP [18] became popular and showed some interesting advantages with respect to GP with classical genetic operators [7,8,10,17]. GSOs, thus, deserve to be explored even in VE_GP approach to see if they still bring advantages in panel data forecasting, although they can not include a semantic parameter mutation. In this article, we investigate the use of GSOs in VE_GP by presenting a comparative study of GP techniques on two panel data forecasting problems. The first one consists in predicting mosquito abundance from climatic and environmental factors, a problem recently approached with standard GP in [12]. This dataset allows the inclusion of parametric aggregation functions as primitives, offering the possibility to explore the role of the windows evolution for the accuracy of predictions. The second dataset deals with the prediction of ventilation flow of running people, based on physiological parameters including the heart rate flow. In this case, the fact that the time series among different subjects have different lengths suggests the use of aggregation functions without parameters. Further explanations on the different use of aggregation functions will be provided in Sect. 5. The methods we compare are VE_GP and classical GP (ST_GP), both using classical and semantic genetic operators.

The paper is organized as follows: Sect. 2 presents an overview on previous attempts to apply GP to panel datasets. Section 3 introduces the problems used in the experimental investigation. Section 4 describes the use of GSOs in VE_GP. Section 5 presents the experimental setting and proposes an analysis of the obtained results. Finally, Sect. 6 draws the conclusions of the investigation.

2   Panel Datasets in GP: Literature Review

When dealing with panel datasets, researchers have employed a common strategy to avoid the use of the standard representation of panel data, the aggregation of vectorial information into a summarizing scalar value. However, such approach usually results in a loss of information. In [13], ECG signals recorded from different patients are substituted by important signal characteristics, such as the mean, the energy etc. This is the typical "collapse approach" where instead of letting the data reveal the most important series characteristics, these are *a priori* fixed before the evolutionary process. Again, in [20], the signals measured to be the predictors or the target are pre-processed before feeding the

GP algorithm. In [14], instead, GP is used to predict glucose values of diabetic people based on insulin values and food intakes without a pre-processing of time series variables. However, the panel data regression problem is transformed into 4 simple regression problems by fixing 4 time values of glucose as the target. As stated by the authors, the main drawback of this approach is the impossibility of predicting a continuous time series of glucose.

Some works have already explored the idea of using vectors to represent time series as terminals. In [15] the authors designed a vector-based GP to discover signal processing algorithm by means of evolution. As well as in VE_GP, they introduced functions to combine scalars and vectors, and advance signal processing functions specific for vectors. In [5] again vectors and vectorial functions are included in the primitive set. Even if VE_GP is strongly influenced by these contributions, the evolution of time windows to capture the most informative signal behaviours is totally new in the field.

3   Problem Description and the Datasets

3.1   Mosquito Abundance (P_Mosq)

The surveillance plan established in Italy in 2008 aimed at quantifying mosquito abundance in order to predict the emergence and the spread of West Nile virus. Predictive models of mosquitoes dynamics were therefore a valuable tool to fulfil the goal. For this reason, modelling techniques with the objective of forecasting mosquito abundance based on environmental factors were explored [6,12]. In this article, we use the dataset produced by the Casale Monferrato Agreement for mosquitoes control from 2002 to 2006 in the context of the Piedmont surveillance program, already used in [6,12]. Mosquitoes were weekly collected from 36 CO_2-baited traps from May to September with a total of 20 collections per year for each trap.

We consider the same scalar predictive variables selected by [6] and reported in Table 3.

Table 3. Scalar mosquitoes predictors.

Variable	Description
ELEV	Elevation of the sampling location
DISTU	Distance of the sampling location from the nearest urban area
DISTR	Distance of the sampling location from the nearest rice field
DISTW	Distance of the sampling location from the nearest woodland
RICEA	Area of the nearest rice field

Regarding the time series predictors considered by [6], we introduce some novelties according to the results of [12]. First, we discard the variable *SIN*.

In fact, according to [12], *SIN*, which is a sinusoidal curve with a phase of 1 year included as a suggester of mosquitoes seasonality, is too frequently used in all the evolved models. This fact prevents the discovery of how environmental variables interact to determine the peaks in abundance of mosquitoes. However, the function *SIN* plays a key role in exploiting the knowledge on the time order of the observations, since it gives a "score" to each collection according to the day in which it took place. As suggested in [12], the use of VE_GP makes it possible to avoid *SIN* without losing the time order information. Thus, our results will also contribute to confirm the advantages of the vector representation proposed by VE_GP. Second, to highlight the benefit of evolving temporal windows, we remove for VE_GP the prior aggregations of the time series predictors considered by [6]. Therefore, VE_GP handles daily values of land surface temperatures, normalized difference vegetation index and rainfalls which are the environmental time series predictor selected by [6]. On the contrary, ST_GP keeps the same variables aggregated as in [6]. Table 4 describes the time series variables for the two approaches of GP.

Table 4. Time series mosquitoes predictors.

Variable	ST_GP description	VE_GP description
TWEEK [2]	The average land surface temperature 8–15 days prior to trapping	Daily value of land surface temperature
NDVI [2]	16-days average of normalized difference vegetation index	Daily value of normalized difference vegetation index
RAIN [1]	Cumulative rainfall 10–17 days prior to trapping registered by the nearest weather station	Daily rainfall registered by the nearest weather station

The variables involved as predictors are therefore the time series *NDVI*, *TWEEK* and *RAIN* (with different definitions depending on the GP approach) plus the scalar variables *ELEV*, *DISTU*, *DISTR*, *DISTW* and *RICEA*. The target is the number of mosquitoes collected *Mosq*. We have two different dataset representation:

– ST_GP with classical and geometric semantic operators: the dataset is a matrix of 3600 rows and 9 columns. Columns one to eight indicate a predictor while the rightmost is the target; each row corresponds to a day of collection.
– VE_GP with classical and geometric semantic operators: the dataset is a matrix of 180 rows and 9 columns. Columns one to eight indicate a predictor while the rightmost is the target; time series variables (*NDVI*, *TWEEK* and *RAIN*) are represented as vectors of length 173 since they contain daily values from April 1st (37 days before the first collection of the year) to September

20th (the last collection day of the year). The target *Mosq* is instead a vector of length 20 representing the 20 collections per year from each trap. Each row corresponds to the collections from a trap during a year.

3.2 Ventilation Flow (P_Physio)

This task was proposed by the Centre of Preventive Medicine and Sport - SUISM - University Structure of Hygiene and Sport Sciences of Turin. The goal is to predict ventilation flow during outdoor activities based on physiological variables in order to monitor the intake of air pollution. We use the dataset employed in [3], which consists of static physiological data and time series variables such as heart rate and ventilation, recorded every 10 s from people running on a treadmill. We must point out that each person ran as long as he/she could, thus the heart rate and ventilation series have different lengths among people. The predictors are therefore the gender (*SEX*), the age (*AGE*), the body mass index (*BMI*) and the heart rate (*HR*). We use the acronym *VE* to indicate the target which is the ventilation. The dataset representation changes again according to the GP approach:

- ST_GP with classical and geometric semantic operators: the dataset is a matrix of 3600 rows and 5 columns. Columns one to four indicate a predictor while the rightmost is the target; each row corresponds to a recording instant of the heart rate from a person.
- VE_GP with classical and geometric semantic operators: the dataset is a matrix of 262 rows and 5 columns. Columns one to four indicate a predictor while the rightmost is the target; *HR* and *VE* are represented as vectors of variable length depending on the running time of the person. Each row corresponds to a person.

4 Methodology

4.1 Vectorial Genetic Programming

Vectorial genetic programming (VE-GP) is a recently developed approach of GP to properly deal with time series as predictors or targets. VE-GP allows vectors as terminals, providing a suitable representation for all time series. Besides the simple adjustments needed to cope with this new terminal structure, VE-GP includes other innovations to fully exploit vector representation. Here we describe the main novelties of this approach that we are going to use to carry out the experiments. Further details can be found in [4].

Primitive Set. In GP the primitive set consists of functions and terminals combined to build the individuals. In VE-GP, vectors join the classical scalar terminals and new functions are included as possible primitives. To avoid inconsistencies, vectors of length 1 and scalars are considered the same terminal form.

Functions of Arity 1. Aggregate functions are included in the primitive set in order to capture the behaviour of a vector. These functions group together multiple values to return a single summary value. Two main versions of aggregation functions are available in VE-GP: standard and cumulative. While standard aggregation functions collapse the whole vector into a single value, cumulative aggregation functions collapse only a portion of the vector. To clarify, let $v = [v_1, \ldots, v_n]$ be a vector terminal and Cf be the cumulative version of the aggregation function f; then $Cf(v) = [w_1, \ldots, w_n]$ where $w_j = f([v_1, \ldots, v_{j-1}, v_j])$ for each $j = 1, \ldots, n$. Standard aggregation functions are meant for problems where the recording time of predictors and target time series is different, cumulative aggregation functions are meant instead for problems where the predictors and the target time series are simultaneous. Both these versions have their parametric form that apply the aggregation function only to a window of the vector. In case of standard aggregation functions the window defined by the parameters can slide all the vector, while for cumulative aggregation functions the window slides only backwards. To explain, let p and q be two integer numbers where $p < q$; then $f_{p,q}(v) = f([v_p, \ldots, v_q])$. Let p and q, instead, be two integer numbers where $p > q$; then $Cf_{p,q}(v) = f([z_1, \ldots, z_n])$ where $z_j = f([v_{j-p}, \ldots, v_{j-p+q}])$ for each $j = 1, \ldots, n$. In both cases, if the window extends to not existing elements of the vector they are simply not included in the calculation. For a detailed explanation of these functions joined with numerical examples see Section 3, Table 3 of [4].

Functions of Arity 2. Regarding functions of arity 2, they are simply extended in order to manage the new vector inputs. In particular, when the inputs of a function are two vectors of length greater than 1, the shortest is completed with the null element of the function up to the length of the longest before applying the function itself. Differently, when a scalar and a vector of length greater than 1 are the inputs, the scalar is initially replicated up to the length of the other vector input. This different input preparation highlights the static nature of scalars: since scalars are constant over time we can not "complete" a scalar with the value representing missing values (the null element); we know that its value for every time instant is always the same, thus we have to "complete" the scalar with its value. To clarify, see Section 3 of [4] where Table 4 reports all the aggregation functions of arity 2 available in VE_GP, with an example of application.

Initialization. VE-GP proposes a new initialization strategy in order not to misuse the aggregation functions added to the primitive set.

- n_1 individuals, during the generation with one of the classical techniques [19], are forced to apply aggregation functions only to vectorial variables;
- n_2 individuals are generated with one of the classical techniques [19] and checked in their output. If individual t returns scalars for each observation, a vectorial terminal X and an arity 2 function F are randomly selected and the

individual t is replaced with the following individual, using post-fix notation, $(F\ t\ X)$;

- the remaining n_3 individuals are generated with one of the classical techniques [19].

Parameter Mutation. The genetic operator of parameter mutation (PM) is developed in VE_GP in order to let the evolution find the most informative windows of time. PM simply looks in an individual for parametric functions, randomly selects one of them and randomly changes one of its parameters. Depending on the kind of function, standard or cumulative, the parameter is mutated without violating the rule of superiority, i.e. $p < q$ for standard functions and $p > q$ for cumulative functions.

Fitness Evaluation. Some individuals may output a scalar for each observation, when the target instead is supposed to be a vector. In order to evaluate their fitness, each scalar is preliminary replicated up to the length of the corresponding target vector. Moreover, these individuals are penalized by multiplying their fitness for a huge constant (panel data prediction problems belong to the area of minimization problem). The wrong size of their output suggests, in fact, that they unlikely to be good predictive models.

4.2   Geometric Semantic Operators

Geometric semantic operators (GSOs) are genetic operators recently introduced for GP [18] to replace the traditional syntax-based crossover and mutation. The term *semantic* in GP community indicates the vector of outputs an individual produce on the training instances. Thus, any GP individual can be identified as a point (its semantic) in a multidimensional space (dimension equal to the number of observations) called *semantic space*. While traditional crossover and mutation manipulate individuals only considering their syntax, GSOs define transformation on the syntax of individuals that correspond to the genetic algorithms operators of geometric crossover and ball mutation in the semantic space. Geometric crossover generates an offspring that stand on the segment joining the parents; ball mutation is a weak perturbation of the coordinates of an individual. We report the definition of the GSOs as given in [18] for individuals with real domain and considering Euclidean distance as the fitness function, since these are the operators we are going to use in the experimental phase.

Geometric semantic crossover (GSXO) returns, as the offspring of the parents $T_1, T_2 : \mathbb{R}^n \to \mathbb{R}$, the individual:

$$T_{X0} = (T_1 \cdot T_R) + ((1 - T_R) \cdot T_2)$$

where T_R is a random number in $[0, 1]$. *Geometric semantic mutation* (GSM) transforms the individual $T : \mathbb{R}^n \to \mathbb{R}$ according to the expression:

$$T_M = T + m_s \cdot (T_{R1} - T_{R2})$$

where T_{R1} and T_{R2} are random real individuals with codomain in $[0, 1]$ and m_s is the mutation step. We refer to [18] for a proof of the fact that GSXO corresponds to geometric crossover in the semantic space, while GSM corresponds to ball mutation in the semantic space. The main advantage of these semantic operators is that they induce a unimodal fitness landscape, thus an error surface characterized by the absence of locally suboptimal solution, on every supervised learning problems. This property should enhance GP evolvability on all these problems. The main drawback that afflicts GSOs is that the size of the offsprings is larger than the one of their parent(s). To overcome this problem we use the implementation of GSOs proposed by [22] and the strategy of elitist replacement suggested in [9].

Unfortunately it is not possible to define the semantic equivalent of parameter mutation as described in Sect. 4.1. To clarify, let us assume that this operator exists, we call it geometric semantic parameter mutation (GSPM). GSPM has to change one of the parameter of a parametric aggregation function determining, as a result, a weak perturbation of the semantic of T, the individual containing the parametric aggregation function. However, modifying the window in which the aggregation function is applied means considering different values of the time series observed, thus the perturbation of the semantic of T depends on the semantic of T itself. Surely this fact is in contrast with the hypothesis of weak perturbation.

5   Experiments

5.1   Experimental Settings

We have adopted the Matlab implementations of ST_GP and VE_GP based on GPLab toolbox [21]. We have extended both implementations in order to include GSOs. The methods involved in the experiments are therefore ST_GP, VE_GP, ST_GP with GSOs (GSGP) and VE_GP with GSOs (GSVEGP). With each technique we have performed a total of 50 runs on both P_Mosq and P_Physio. Here we lay out the design of the experiments conducted on both problems. For the remainder of this paper, the training set is the portion of the dataset used to feed the algorithm in order to make it learn, while the test set is the remaining portion of the dataset which consists of unseen data used to validate the trained model performance.

P_Mosq. In each experimental run we have considered the same partition of training and test sets that follows the natural order of years: collections from 2002 to 2005 were used as the training set, while collections of 2006 formed the test set.

Fitness was calculated as the Root Mean Square Error (RMSE) between the output and the target. In case of vector based GP (VE_GP and GSVEGP) the output are the predictions of mosquito abundance over 173 days (April 1st– September 20th), thus for the evaluation of fitness we have considered as the actual output the predictions corresponding to the collection days. Since the output of trees built by VE_GP and GSVEGP is supposed to be a vector, for these latter algorithms we have calculated the RMSE vertically disbanding both output and target; in this way the measures of fitness were ensured to be comparable among all the techniques.

All the runs used population of 100 individuals and the evolution stopped after 50 generations. ST_GP and GSGP initialized populations using the Ramped Half-and-Half (RHH) method [16] with a maximum initial depth equal to 6, while VE_GP and GSVEGP initialized populations using the process proposed in [4] based on RHH with maximum initial depth again equal to 6. The functions set for ST_GP and GSGP contained the four binary arithmetic operators $+, -, \times$ and $/$ protected as in [16]. The days of mosquitoes collection are the same across years and traps, thus it is reasonable to look for common informative windows of time among all the observations. For this reason, the functions set for VE_GP contained the binary operators VSUMW, V_W, VprW, VdivW plus the parametric cumulative aggregation functions $C\_max_{p,q}$, $C\_min_{p,q}$, $C\_mean_{p,q}$, $C\_sum_{p,q}$. GSVEGP can not handle parametric functions, thus its functions set consisted of the binary operators VSUMW, V_W, VprW, VdivW plus the cumulative aggregation functions C_max, C_min, C_mean, C_sum. All the functions of the vectorial approaches are defined in [4]. The terminal sets contained the 8 variables as described in Sect. 3.1 plus random constants r between 0 and 1 generated in run time when building individuals. To select parents we used a tournament selection involving 4 individuals. To create new individuals, ST_GP used standard crossover and subtree mutation [16] with probabilities equal to 0.9 and 0.1 respectively. Besides crossover and mutation, VE_GP used parameter mutation with probabilities respectively 0.5, 0.1 and 0.4. The semantic algorithms of GSGP and GSVEGP, instead, used GSXO and GSM with probabilities respectively 0.1, 0.9 and 0.7, 0.3; the mutation steps were respectively 1 and 0.01. The different probabilities and mutation rates depends on a preliminary experimental study performed to find the best parameter setting. Survival of individuals was elitist for ST_GP and VE_GP, while we used the elitist replacement [9] for GSGP and GSVEGP. Maximum tree depth was fixed at 17 for ST_GP and VE_GP while no depth limit have been imposed in GSGP and GSVEGP.

P_Physio. Differently from the previous problem, a distinct partition of the training and test sets has been considered in each run. In particular, 70% of the data instances were randomly selected at the beginning of each run as training set, while the remaining 30% were used as the test set.

Fitness was calculated as the RMSE between the output and the target. In case of vector based GPs we followed the procedure described above to guarantee comparable measures.

All the runs used population of 100 individuals and the evolution stopped after 50 generations. ST_GP and GSGP initialized populations using the RHH with a maximum initial depth equal to 6, while VE_GP and GSVEGP initialize populations using the process proposed in [4] based on RHH with maximum initial depth again equal to 6. The functions set for ST_GP and GSGP contained the four binary arithmetic operators $+, -, \times$ and $/$ protected as in [16]. The subjects of the trial ran on the trade mill as long as they could, thus the HR and VE series have different lengths among the people. Looking for a common informative window of time across all the people may weaken the learning phase. In fact, some time windows may be more adequate for long time series compared to shorter ones, causing a loss of generalization ability. For this reason, the functions set for both VE_GP and GSVEGP contained the binary operators VSUMW, V_W, VprW, VdivW plus the cumulative aggregation functions $C\_min_{p,q}$ and $C\_mean_{p,q}$ as in [3]. All the terminal sets contained the 4 variables as described in Sect. 3.2 plus random constants r between 0 and 1 generated in runtime when building individuals. To select parents we used a tournament selection involving 4 individuals. To create new individuals, ST_GP used standard crossover and subtree mutation [16] with probabilities equal to 0.9 and 0.1 respectively. Besides crossover and mutation, VE_GP used parameter mutation with probabilities respectively 0.5, 0.1 and 0.4. The semantic algorithms of GSGP and GSVEGP, instead, used GSXO and GSM with probabilities respectively 0.3, 0.7 and 0.5, 0.5; the mutation steps were respectively 1 and 0.1. Also in this case, the different probabilities and mutation rates depends on a preliminary experimental study performed to find the best parameter setting. Survival of individuals was elitist for ST_GP and VE_GP, while we used the elitist replacement [9] for GSGP and GSVEGP. Maximum tree depth was fixed at 17 for ST_GP and VE_GP while no depth limit have been imposed in GSGP and GSVEGP.

5.2   Experimental Results

In this section, we report the results that we have obtained in terms of training and test RMSE. In particular, at each generation we stored the value of RMSE on the training and on the test set of the best individual in the population, i.e. the one with the smallest RMSE on the training data. The curves report the median over the 50 runs of all these values collected at each generation. The median was preferred over the mean due to its robustness to outliers which are common in stochastic methods. Figure 1 reports the training and test errors for P_Mosq and P_Physio.

These plots clearly show that VE_GP in both problems is the fastest in learning, with perspective of further improvement going on with generations, at least for the P_Mosq problem. Moreover, the fast decreasing of the test error confirms that VE_GP is learning with generalization ability. On the contrary, both GSGP and GSVEGP exhibit a slow and almost static (GSVEGP in particular) learning phase. We claim that the main reason behind this fact is the huge size of the semantic space. Considering in fact GSVEGP, in P_Physio problem the semantic space has dimension $(\text{length}(p_1) \times \cdots \times \text{length}(p_{183}))$ where 183 is the number of people in the training set (70% of data instances) and $\text{length}(p_i)$ is the length of the time series recorded for person p_i; in P_Mosq the size is still huge, being $(20)^{144}$ where 20 is the number of mosquitoes collections over a year and 144 is the number of collections in the training set (36 traps $\times$ 4 year).

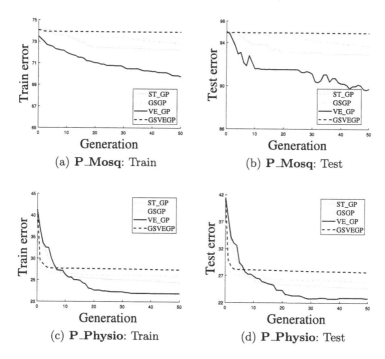

(a) **P_Mosq**: Train

(b) **P_Mosq**: Test

(c) **P_Physio**: Train

(d) **P_Physio**: Test

Fig. 1. ST_GP, GSGP, VE_GP and GSVEGP fitness evolution plots.

Since the goal of the paper is to understand how parametric functions influence the performance, we compared the RMSE on the test set of the models found out in the 50 runs by all the techniques. We consider as a model the best individual on the training set at the end of the evolution. Statistical significance of the null hypothesis of no difference among the methods was determined with pairwise Kruskal-Wallis non-parametric ANOVAs at $p = 0.05$. In both problems the resulting $p - value$ stated that there was a significant difference in performance among techniques, thus we performed multiple two-sample Wilcoxon signed rank tests to understand which method differs from the other. The significance level for each test depends on the Bonferroni correction. We report the values of the statistical tests in Table 5, as well as the boxplots of models test

Table 5. Results of comparison between techniques on P_Mosq and P_Physio. Significance level of Wilcoxon test after Bonferroni correction $p = 0.05/3 = 0.02$.

P_Mosq: Kruskal-Wallis ANOVA $p < 10^{-16}$		
VE_GP vs GSVEGP	VE_GP vs GSGP	VE_GP vs GP
$p < 10^{-16}$	$p = 5.7 \cdot 10^{-16}$	$p = 2.2 \cdot 10^{-14}$
P_Phisio: Kruskal-Wallis ANOVA $p < 10^{-16}$		
VE_GP vs GSVEGP	VE_GP vs GSGP	VE_GP vs GP
$p = 2.6 \cdot 10^{-10}$	$p = 2.1 \cdot 10^{-7}$	$p = 1.1 \cdot 10^{-5}$

fitness in Fig. 2. According to the statistical tests, VE_GP performance differs from all the other methods for both problems. Moreover, boxplots in Fig. 2 show that VE_GP is outperforming all the other techniques. This outcome confirms that VE_GP is the better GP approach when dealing with panel data, rather than classical GP approach.

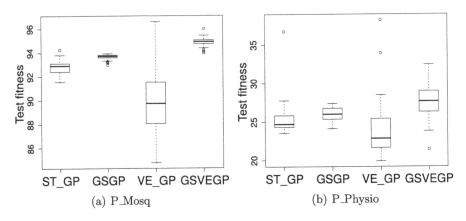

(a) P_Mosq   (b) P_Physio

Fig. 2. Test fitness boxplots of models found out by each technique. Figure (a) refers to P_Mosq, while figure (b) refers to P_Physio.

Regarding P_Mosq, the results confirm our intuition on the benefit of evolving time windows to discover the most informative ones without prior fixing them just by means of experts knowledge. Surely GSVEGP's slow learning is due to the semantic space dimension, but we claim that considering always all the data points of previous collections (classical cumulative functions) rather than an evolving windows over previous times may cause a loss in population diversity and thus be another reason of slow learning. In fact, in VE_GP we find individuals containing different aggregations that span different time series portion, while in GSVEGP we find surely individuals containing different aggregations, but they all span the same time series portion. To confirm this observation we report the median (over the 50 runs) diversity curves along generations for GSVEGP and VE_GP. We use as a subjective measure of diversity the standard deviation of the fitness values in the population at each generation. Figure 3 clearly shows that GSVEGP is unable to keep good diversity levels which is a key feature of a successful search process. We tried to give an explanation of other reasonable reasons responsible of this GSVEGP diversity drop. GSOs seems to quickly direct the diversified initial population towards the target; however, after the individuals have converged, the improvements are thinner and thinner and the weak perturbation of one of the components of one of the output time series results in a weak perturbation of the individual fitness. At a certain point, thus, GSOs seems to be less efficient due to the high dimension of the semantic space. In addition, the elitist replacement used to control individual growth [9], at that

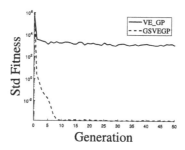

Fig. 3. Diversity evolution for VE_GP and GSVEGP on P_Mosq. Curves are plotted in logarithmic scale.

certain point, causes more frequently the replication of individuals instead of the offspring replacements. In fact, if the weak perturbations are not efficient (produce offsprings with bigger fitness) parents are preferred rather then their offsprings. All these behaviours are feasible reasons of GSVEGP loss of diversity.

Concerning P_Physio results, we expected GSVEGP to be the outperforming method, since parametric functions are not involved in any primitive set. However, statistical tests and the boxplots reveal that VE_GP is the method with the best performance. These results confirm that GSOs are not suitable to deal with time series variables, probably because of the high dimension of the semantic space induced.

6   Conclusions

This paper contains an investigation on the usefulness of evolving parametric aggregation functions for panel data forecasting. Aggregations of values may return informative features of predictors time series for the target, however aggregations on all historical times of predictors may not be needed to forecast the target series. The behaviour of the predictors over a window of time may in fact be more meaningful for the target. To clarify, let us consider the P_Mosq problem of predicting the abundance of mosquitoes during a year: mosquitoes collected at day t are more likely to be affected by the rainfalls over the week before t rather than on all the rainfalls of the days before t; mosquitoes growth in fact, lasts more or less one week, thus rainfalls over a week may cause the loss of eggs and thus adult mosquitoes at day t.

The recently developed vectorial genetic programming (VE_GP) includes in the functions set aggregation function depending on parameters to define time window in which to apply the function. The genetic operator of parameter mutation, moreover, gives the possibility to parameters to evolve in order to catch the most informative windows. The objective of the paper was therefore to highlight the benefits of tackling panel dataset forecasting using VE_GP. In particular, we compared VE_GP performance against VE_GP with geometric semantic operators (GSVEGP) on two problems. While the first one, P_Mosq, demanded for parametric aggregation functions in the functions set, the second problem, P_Physio, did not require evolving time windows. We chose GSVEGP as a benchmark because although geometric semantic operators should improve the performance, the geometric semantic awareness does not allow parameter mutation as a genetic operator.

The main contribution of this work consisted in showing that parametric aggregation functions can further improve the performance when the dataset hypothesis allow for their inclusion (P_Mosq). Moreover we found out that considering all the history of time series may influence the maintenance of diversity in the evolving population. Surprisingly, however, results achieved on P_Physio revealed a weakness of GP algorithms with geometric semantic operators. We impute this result to the high dimension of the semantic space caused by time series variables that slow the learning process.

The outcomes paved the way for future works on the design of more efficient geometric semantic operators for problems involving time series. A wider result is, however, the highlight of VE_GP as a successful approach in panel data forecasting, making the GP community aware of its value.

Acknowledgments. This work was partially supported by FCT, Portugal through funding of LASIGE Research Unit (UID/CEC/00408/2019), and projects PREDICT (PTDC/CCI-CIF/29877/2017), BINDER (PTDC/CCI-INF/29168/2017), GADgET (DSAIPA/DS/0022/2018) and AICE (DSAIPA/DS/0113/2019).

References

1. Arpa Piemonte. http://www.arpa.piemonte.it
2. NASA MODIS Web. https://modis.gsfc.nasa.gov/
3. Azzali, I., Vanneschi, L., Bakurov, I., Silva, S., Ivaldi, M., Giacobini, M.: Towards the use of vector based GP to predict physiological time series. App. Soft Comput. (forthcoming)
4. Azzali, I., Vanneschi, L., Silva, S., Bakurov, I., Giacobini, M.: A vectorial approach to genetic programming. In: Sekanina, L., Hu, T., Lourenço, N., Richter, H., García-Sánchez, P. (eds.) EuroGP 2019. LNCS, vol. 11451, pp. 213–227. Springer, Cham (2019). https://doi.org/10.1007/978-3-030-16670-0_14
5. Bartashevich, P., Bakurov, I., Mostaghim, S., Vanneschi, L.: Evolving PSO algorithm design in vector fields using geometric semantic GP. In: GECCO 2018: Proceedings of the Genetic and Evolutionary Computation Conference, pp. 262–263 (2018). https://doi.org/10.1145/3205651.3205760
6. Bisanzio, D., et al.: Spatio-temporal patterns of distribution of West Nile virus vectors in eastern Piedmont Region, Italy. Parasites Vectors **4** (2011). https://doi.org/10.1186/1756-3305-4-230
7. Castelli, M., et al.: An efficient implementation of geometric semantic genetic programming for anticoagulation level prediction in pharmacogenetics. In: Correia, L., Reis, L.P., Cascalho, J. (eds.) EPIA 2013. LNCS (LNAI), vol. 8154, pp. 78–89. Springer, Heidelberg (2013). https://doi.org/10.1007/978-3-642-40669-0_8
8. Castelli, M., Vanneschi, L., Felice, M.D.: Forecasting short-term electricty consumption using a semnatics-based genetic programming framework: the South Italy case. Energy Econ. **47**, 37–41 (2015). https://doi.org/10.1016/j.eneco.2014.10.009

9. Castelli, M., Vanneschi, L., Popovic, A.: Controlling individuals growth in semantic genetic programming through elitist replacement. Comput. Intell. Neurosci. (2016). https://doi.org/10.1155/2016/8326760

10. Castelli, M., Vanneschi, L., Silva, S.: Prediction of the unified Parkinson's disease rating scale assessment using a genetic programming system with geometric semantic genetic operators. Expert Syst. Appl. **41**(10), 4608–4616 (2014). https://doi.org/10.1016/j.eswa.2014.01.018

11. Dermofal, D.: Time-series cross-sectional and panel data models. Spat. Anal. Soc. Sci. **32**, 141–157 (2015). https://doi.org/10.1017/CBO9781139051293.009

12. Gervasi, R., Azzali, I., Bisanzio, D., Mosca, A., Bertolotti, L., Giacobini, M.: A genetic programming approach to predict mosquitoes abundance. In: Sekanina, L., Hu, T., Lourenço, N., Richter, H., García-Sánchez, P. (eds.) EuroGP 2019. LNCS, vol. 11451, pp. 35–48. Springer, Cham (2019). https://doi.org/10.1007/978-3-030-16670-0_3

13. Guo, H., Jack, L.B., Nandi, A.K.: Automated feature extraction using genetic programming for bearing condition monitoring. In: Proceedings of the 14th IEEE Signal Processing Society Workshop Machine Learning for Signal Processing, pp. 519–528 (2004). https://doi.org/10.1109/MLSP.2004.1423015

14. Hidalgo, J.I., Colmenar, J.M., Kronberger, G., Winkler, S.M., Garnica, O., Lanchares, J.: Data based prediction of blood glucose concentrations using evolutionary methods. J. Med. Syst. **41**(9), 1–20 (2017). https://doi.org/10.1007/s10916-017-0788-2

15. Holladay, K., Robbins, K.A.: Evolution of signal processing algorithm using vector based genetic programming. In: 15th International Conference on Digital Signal Processing, pp. 503–506 (2007). https://doi.org/10.1109/ICDSP.2007.4288629

16. Koza, J.: Genetic Programming: On the Programming of Computers by Means of Natural Selection. MIT Press, Cambridge (1992)

17. Vanneschi, L., Silva, S., Castelli, M., Manzoni, L.: Geometric semantic genetic programming for real life applications. In: Riolo, R., Moore, J.H., Kotanchek, M. (eds.) Genetic Programming Theory and Practice XI. GEC, pp. 191–209. Springer, New York (2014). https://doi.org/10.1007/978-1-4939-0375-7_11

18. Moraglio, A., Krawiec, K., Johnson, C.G.: Geometric semantic genetic programming. In: Coello, C.A.C., Cutello, V., Deb, K., Forrest, S., Nicosia, G., Pavone, M. (eds.) PPSN 2012. LNCS, vol. 7491, pp. 21–31. Springer, Heidelberg (2012). https://doi.org/10.1007/978-3-642-32937-1_3

19. Poli, R., Langdon, W.B., McPhee, N.F.: A Field Guide to Genetic Programming. Lulu Enterprises, UK Ltd. (2008)

20. Sannino, G., Falco, I.D., Pietro, G.D.: Non-invasive estimation of blood pressure through genetic programming - preliminary results. In: SmartMedDev 2015, pp. 241–249 (2015). https://doi.org/10.5220/0005318002410249

21. Silva, S., Almeida, J.: GPLAB a genetic programming toolbox for MATLAB (2007). http://gplab.sourceforge.net/index.html

22. Vanneschi, L., Castelli, M., Manzoni, L., Silva, S.: A new implementation of geometric semantic GP and its application to problems in pharmacokinetics. In: Krawiec, K., Moraglio, A., Hu, T., Etaner-Uyar, A.Ş., Hu, B. (eds.) EuroGP 2013. LNCS, vol. 7831, pp. 205–216. Springer, Heidelberg (2013). https://doi.org/10.1007/978-3-642-37207-0_18

Comparing Genetic Programming Approaches for Non-functional Genetic Improvement
Case Study: Improvement of MiniSAT's Running Time

Aymeric Blot[✉][iD] and Justyna Petke[iD]

CREST, University College London, London WC1E 6BT, UK
a.blot@cs.ucl.ac.uk, j.petke@ucl.ac.uk

Abstract. Genetic improvement (GI) uses automated search to find improved versions of existing software. While most GI work use genetic programming (GP) as the underlying search process, focus is usually given to the target software only. As a result, specifics of GP algorithms for GI are not well understood and rarely compared to one another. In this work, we propose a robust experimental protocol to compare different GI search processes and investigate several variants of GP- and random-based approaches. Through repeated experiments, we report a comparative analysis of these approaches, using one of the previously used GI scenarios: improvement of runtime of the MiniSAT satisfiability solver. We conclude that the test suites used have the most significant impact on the GI results. Both random and GP-based approaches are able to find improved software, even though the percentage of viable software variants is significantly smaller in the random case (14.5% vs. 80.1%). We also report that GI produces MiniSAT variants up to twice as fast as the original on sets of previously unseen instances from the same application domain.

Keywords: Genetic improvement (GI) · Genetic programming (GP) · Search-based software engineering (SBSE) · Boolean satisfiability (SAT)

1 Introduction

Genetic improvement (GI) [11,19] uses automated search to find improved versions of existing software. GI literature focuses on both improvement of functional properties, such as automated bug repair or introduction of new functionality, as well as improvement of non-functional properties such as running time, or memory or energy consumption.

Genetic programming (GP) has been used most often so far as the GI search process [11]. Even though previous work use GP as a theoretic common framework, most of it implements or uses very specific variants and parameter values for the GP algorithms that led to evolution of improved software. In order to

© Springer Nature Switzerland AG 2020
T. Hu et al. (Eds.): EuroGP 2020, LNCS 12101, pp. 68–83, 2020.
https://doi.org/10.1007/978-3-030-44094-7_5

shift the focus from the target software to the GI process itself, so it can be better understood, it becomes increasingly necessary to be able to compare and analyse all these proposed search processes.

In this paper, we aim to provide insights on how to compare GI approaches and improve the protocol for applying GI techniques. We consider an existing non-functional improvement GI scenario used in previous work [3,12,13], the improvement of the running time of MiniSAT [4] on combinatorial interaction testing instances, and a diverse range of various GP-based and random-based search processes. We consider the following research questions:

RQ1 (Effectiveness): *How often are noticeable improvements found?*
RQ2 (Efficiency): *How significant are the improvements found?*
RQ3 (Robustness): *How critical are the GP parameter values for GI?*
RQ4 (Consistency): *What is the impact of test cases on the results of GI?*

This paper is structured as follows. First, Sect. 2 provides the necessary GI background. Next, Sect. 3 presents the GP structure that will be used in the experiments. Section 4 then describes the experimental protocol and which specific GI search processes are compared. Experimental results are presented and discussed in Sect. 5. Finally, Sect. 6 concludes this paper.

2 Genetic Improvement (GI)

Genetic improvement (GI) uses automated search to find improved versions of existing software. In this section, we detail on how the software to be improved will be represented, how it will be modified, and how mutant fitness is assessed. In addition to the related work mentioned in this section see [11] for a more comprehensive survey of GI work.

2.1 Software Representations

This work focuses, as a lot of previous work [11], on processing software source code based on its underlying abstract syntax tree (AST). The main advantage of producing mutated source code, in contrast to, for example, producing mutated binary code [15], is that source code mutations and, in particular, patches can be expected to be much more easily understood and thus accepted by software developers [17].

Source Code Representation. Implementation-wise, this paper uses the latest version of the PyGGI[1] framework, and in particular its XML tree representation introduced in [1]. SrcML[2] is used to obtain an XML tree for the AST of the original source code file, which is then stripped down to only consider statements inside functions. No specific instrumentation is performed; the only source code

---

[1] https://github.com/coinse/pyggi.
[2] https://www.srcml.org/.

modification applied is the addition of explicit brackets around pseudo blocks (e.g., *if* statements containing a single line statement with no surrounding bracket) so that modifications of the AST are correctly translated back when generating the modified source code. A successful alternative to AST-based representations is BNF grammar-based representation (e.g., GISMOE [3,6,7,12–14]).

Mutants Representation. In contrast to the earliest GI work [2], in which populations of entire programs were evolved, most GI work nowadays consider intermediary representations for mutants, focusing on the changes that are applied to the original software. In this paper, the possible changes (or *edits*) considered are deletions, replacements, and insertions, relatively to any sub-tree of the original software AST. Mutants are then simply represented as a sequence of edits, only translated into source code and compiled for fitness assessment.

2.2 Fitness Assessment

The non-functional software property to be optimised is computational speed of software, in particular, its average running time. For all purposes, the original software will be considered already functionally correct and the correctness of mutants will be assessed in comparison with the original software execution (e.g., by providing the same output). Non-functional mutant will be discarded immediately. Previous work have shown that considering a multi-objective approach and using degree of functionality as another objective is a viable alternative that can sometimes even lead to a semantic gain [7].

Running time can be an extremely unreliable property to measure precisely, strongly impacted by the environment, with good measurements only achievable after a sufficient number of repetitions. As a proxy measure, previous work used, for example, the number of lines of code executed by the software (e.g., [11]). Major drawbacks include heavy source code instrumentation, same weight given to every statement, omission of impact of standard or external libraries, and an arguably strong impact of the compiler optimisation procedure. Instead, we propose to use the total number of executed CPU instructions as reported through the `perf` UNIX kernel monitoring tool[3]. While the number of CPU instructions still does not provide a deterministic measure [16], preliminary results have shown it to be well correlated with running time and several orders of magnitude more stable even when executing experiments in parallel on a single machine.

3 Genetic Programming (GP)

Since the inception of genetic improvement (GI), many variants of genetic programming (GP) have been successfully applied to the task of improving existing software. In this work, we focus on and extend a GP structure that has been used in recent non-functional GI work [7,12,13], and particularly has already been used on the specific software improvement scenario that we will consider.

---

[3] https://perf.wiki.kernel.org/index.php/Main_Page.

This structure is detailed in Fig. 1. It considers a fixed size population of n individuals that it will evolve until the training budget is exhausted. Individuals of the first generation are generated by considering a single random mutation of the original source code. Then, for all subsequent generations, offspring are generated in five successive steps.

Selection. The fittest individuals of the previous population are selected as parents. In this paper, selection simply amounts to discarding invalid mutants and sorting the remaining individuals according to their fitness.

Elitism. The best p_e parents are simply added back untouched to better ensure gene transmission.

Crossover. The best p_c parents are considered successively and crossed with another parent picked uniformly at random to produce a single offspring. GP crossovers in the GI literature include concatenation (e.g., in [7,12,13]), 1-point crossover (e.g., in [5,10,18]), or uniform crossover (e.g., in [9]).

Mutation. The first p_m best parents are considered successively again and mutated once. The most common mutations include either removing an edit from the edit sequence, selected uniformly at random, or appending a new edit at the end of the edit sequence.

Regrow. Finally, if not enough offspring have been generated (e.g., if the previous generation could not yield enough valid parents) then new individuals are generated at random with a single mutation.

This structure differs from the previous one by two major points: it includes an elitism step and enables explicit parameterisation. In the previous work up to $n/2$ parents were selected, and each of them had two offspring, one through crossover and one through mutation, with the risk of completely discarding the genetic material of a parent when both offspring are unsuccessful. In the worst case, the entire population can be decimated in a single population only to restart evolution from scratch [7]. The elitism step tries to alleviate this issue by providing a way to safely carry the best mutations over to the next generation.

4   Experimental Setup

In this section, we present the GI scenario—i.e., the target software to be improved, MiniSAT [4], together with the application scenario, combinatorial interaction testing instances—, clarify implementation specifics such as how the source code of MiniSAT is represented, how it will be modified, and how performance is assessed, before finally detailing the experimental protocol.

4.1   MiniSAT

This paper targets the automatic improvement of MiniSAT [4], a well-known Boolean satisfiability (SAT) solver. MiniSAT is open-source and can be downloaded online[4]. It has been used several times in previous GI work, such as in [1,3,12–14].

---

[4] http://minisat.se/MiniSat.html.

$\triangleright$ n: population size
$\triangleright$ p_e, p_c, p_m: number of parents selected for *elitism*, *crossover*, *mutation*
procedure $\mathrm{GP}(n, p_e, p_c, p_m)$
    $\triangleright$ Initial generation, generated at random
    $pop \leftarrow []$
    while $|pop| < n$ **do**
        $mutant \leftarrow$ new mutant
        append $mutant$ to pop
    end while
    $\triangleright$ Subsequent generations
    repeat
        $offspring \leftarrow []$
        $\triangleright$ (1) Selection (here: filter and sort)
        $parents \leftarrow selection(pop)$
        $\triangleright$ (2) Offspring by elitism
        for all $parent \in parents[0 \ldots k_e]$ **do**
            append $parent$ to $offspring$
        end for
        $\triangleright$ (3) Offspring by crossover
        for all $parent1 \in parents[0 \ldots k_c]$ **do**
            $parent2 \leftarrow$ individual from $parents$ (uniformly at random)
            $mutant \leftarrow crossover(parent1, parent2)$ or $crossover(parent2, parent1)$
            append $mutant$ to $offspring$
        end for
        $\triangleright$ (4) Offspring by mutation
        for all $parent \in parents[0 \ldots k_m]$ **do**
            $mutant \leftarrow mutation(parent1)$
            append $mutant$ to $offspring$
        end for
        $\triangleright$ (5) If not enough parents: fill with random mutants
        while $|offspring| < n$ **do**
            $mutant \leftarrow$ new mutant
            append $mutant$ to $offspring$
        end while
        $pop \leftarrow offspring$
    until training budget exhausted
    return overall best mutant ever evaluated
end procedure

Fig. 1. Genetic programming search

Two versions of MiniSAT were previously considered, `minisat2-070721` and `minisat-2.2.0`, based on the winning entries of SAT-Race 2006 and 2009, respectively. We used the latest version and focus on a single file, `core/Solver.cc`, which contains the code pertaining to the search process.

As input, we use combinatorial interaction testing (CIT) instances, a GI scenario proposed in [12] and reused in later work. In particular, we use the 130 instances described in [13], split following the 5 "bins" according to their satisfiability (SAT or UNSAT) and the time taken by MiniSAT to solve them[5].

4.2 Experimental Protocol

The purpose of GI is to obtain, from a given software, a *better* software, in terms of either functional or non-functional property. In previous work, especially in the case of automated bug fixing, only one test suite was often used, leading frequently to overfitting, as pointed out in [8]. For that reason, it is necessary to split data into at least two disjoint sets of inputs in order to properly control for generalisation, which has been done in the non-functional work to-date. Additionally, previous GI work [7,11] has shown that, especially using GP and edit list as representation for the mutated software, an intermediary filtering step was extremely useful to reduce bloat, focus on fewer edits, and improve generalisation. Our experimental protocol thus consists of the following steps:

Pre-processing. The set of inputs is disjointly split between training, validation, and test inputs. When considering multiple bins of input, all of them are split independently and then interwoven so that each of the training, validation, and test input sets also contains the same number of sub-bins, thus ensuring that they all follow the same distribution of bins as the entire set of inputs.

Training. Training is the main, most important, and most computationally expensive part of the experimental protocol. Starting from an initially empty mutant, the search process (e.g., GP) produces incrementally *better* individuals, before returning a single mutated software when the training budget is exhausted. The final training mutant can, for example, be the best individual of the last GP generation, or the best overall mutant for random search. No new software modification is to be investigated beyond this point.

Validation. The final training mutant very often overfits to the training data. The validation steps tries, by considering previously unseen input, to filter out mutations that do not seem to generalise. This step also allows for a simpler and more understandable software to be returned.

Test. Again, new unseen data is used to reassess the performance of the final validated mutant. It is extremely important that the final software is not modified: any decision or analysis process, including singling out individual mutations, should have been performed during the validation process.
Additionally, we also reassess the performance of the final training mutant to control the impact of the filtering performed during the validation step.

Additionally, to select the training, validation, and test sets, we propose to use a repeated procedure based on nested k-fold cross-validation. This procedure,

---

[5] Fastest SAT instances, fastest UNSAT instances, SAT instances, UNSAT instances, and slowest (both SAT or UNSAT) instances. Respective bin sizes: 50, 37, 17, 18, 8.

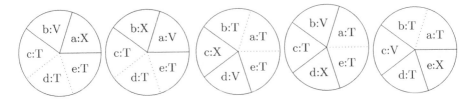

Fig. 2. Example of nested 5-fold cross validation using a single fold for test (X) and $k - 1$ folds for both validation (V: single random fold from the remaining $k - 1$ folds) and training (T: all remaining $k - 2$ folds). Each of the five folds is successively used once for the test step (X).

illustrated in Fig. 2, ensures a fair usage of every instance across the multiple steps and control the consistency of the GI process. Firstly, inputs (independently for each bin) are shuffled and split into k disjoint subsets (or *folds*). For k successive sets of experiments, each of the k folds is successively used during the test step, leaving $k - 1$ folds for both training and validation. Within these $k - 1$ folds, one is picked uniformly at random for the validation subset, leaving the last $k - 2$ for the training subset. In the experiments, we use $k = 5$, thus five sets of experiments will be conducted, each using 60% of each bin of inputs in the training step, 20% in the validation step, and 20% in the test step.

Note that while the validation and test steps will use every single of their respective instances, search processes will not necessarily use all the training instances during the training step. For example, previous GI work using GP advocated sampling a single instance from each bin before every generation [7], while for random search we will simply use a fixed subset of instances. The reason is the computational cost of evaluating software on all instances: impractical and inefficient for each and every mutant generated during training, but necessary to reliably assess performance in the two other much shorter steps. Finally, so that multiple approaches can be fairly compared, it is critical that every search process, disregarding their specific instance usage strategy, is given equal opportunity to all training instances: in no circumstance should the training set be tailored to a specific search process.

4.3   Search Processes

A total of eight GP search processes are compared, together with a baseline constituted of four random searches. The GP search processes follow the structure introduced in Fig. 1, with four different population sizes $n \in \{10, 20, 50, 100\}$ for a total budget of 2000 mutant evaluations. Half of them will use the elitism mechanism with $p_e = 0.1 \cdot n$ and $p_c = p_m = 0.45 \cdot n$, carrying the best 10% individuals to the next population[6], while the other half will follow previous work with $p_e = 0$ and $p_c = p_m = 0.5 \cdot n$. These very small populations sizes are

---

[6] After rounding, we use $\{p_e, p_c, p_m\} = \{1, 5, 4\}, \{2, 9, 9\}, \{5, 23, 22\}$, and $\{10, 45, 45\}$.

justified by the large amount of computational time used for fitness computation; the successful use of a population of $n = 10$ is corroborated in [7] while $n = 100$ is used, for example, in [13]. Furthermore, we deviate from previous work using a similar GP structure with a concatenation crossover in favour of a 1-point crossover, preliminary experiments having shown that the former generates unreasonable and unsustainable amount of bloat, especially with very small populations (thus at equal training budget, more generations).

In addition to these eight GP search processes, four random searches are included as a baseline, in which new individuals are simply generated independently and uniformly at random and the final mutant is the one with overall best fitness. These random searches are parameterised with the maximum number m of edits that are generated for each new mutant. We consider $m = 1$ (i.e., each mutant contains a single random edit), and $m = 2, 5, 10$ to enable generating more complex mutants.

The only difference between the two types of search processes is the number of training instances used and therefore the subsequent training budget. On the one hand, to compute fitness GP will use as in previous work five instances that are resampled at the start of every generation (a single instance from each bin). It arguably implies an initial very unreliable fitness in terms of both functional and non-functional properties, but the evolutionary process ensures that the longer a mutation lives in the population, the more instances it has been trained on and thus increasing reliability. On the other hand, fitness in random search cannot rely on subsequent evaluations so instead more instances are used: twenty in total, four instances from each bin. As a direct consequence, to keep the overall same number of software execution and ensure fair comparison, the training budget is reduced to 500 mutant evaluations, one forth of the GP training budget.

In the experiments the four approaches using GP without elitism will be referred to as $GP(n)$, with $GP_e(n)$ used for the four approaches using GP with elitism and $Rand(m)$ for the four random-based approaches.

4.4   Filtering

Two successive filtering procedures are applied during the validation step. The first filtering is based on the assumption that GP-based search may produce a large amount of bloat. Every edit is successively removed from the edit sequence and discarded if its omission has no impact on the mutated source code. More precisely, this filtering targets patterns in which, for example, a single statement is deleted multiple times, modified, then deleted. It is usually very cheap as it does not require any fitness computation, but has, however, no impact on the mutant performance.

The second filtering (from [13]) aims to improve generalisation by discarding edits that fail to generalise on previously unseen instances. The fitness of every edit is first computed independently, then edits are sorted by fitness, and the final mutant is constructed by adding edits one at a time if their addition has a positive impact. This process consumes at most twice as many fitness evaluations as the size of the edit sequence. This specific filtering works best when edits are independent.

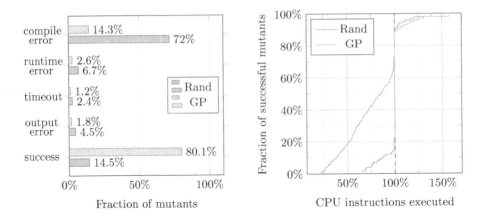

Fig. 3. Distribution of evaluation outcomes for random- and GP-based approaches

5   Results and Discussion

Training and validation step were conducted in parallel on four cores of a dedicated (8 × 3.4 GHz, 16 GB RAM) Intel i7-2600 machine, running CentOS-7 with Linux kernel 3.10.0 and GCC 4.8.5. The testing step was conducted sequentially on a single core.

5.1   Overall Training Results

The 40 GP training runs required between 7 to 13 h to complete, with an average of 10 h. The four random-based approaches required between 30 min to 5 h, with an average of about 2 h. Variance in training time can be explained by instances with different processing time being sampled.

Figure 3 shows the distribution of outcome of every mutant during the training step, separated between random search and GP, together with the empirical cumulative distribution function (ECDF), i.e., the fraction of the successful mutants better than a given fitness. Because fitness values are computed using different instances they are normalised and indicated as a ratio with the fitness of the original software on the same instances. Random-based approaches generated 10000 mutants, with only 14.5% of them viable and very few with a noticeable impact. 72% failed to compile, and the remaining 13.5% either crashed, stalled, or produced an incorrect satisfiability output. GP-based approaches generated 80000 mutants, within which only 14.3% failed to compile while 80.1% were successful, with a very large fraction of them reporting large improvements over the original software. This indicates that a very high efficiency for the 1-point crossover for combining existing mutations and generating valuable mutants.

Table 1. Experimental results for all variants (first split).

	Training		Validation				Test			
Search	Size	CPU	Size'	CPU	Size*	CPU*	CPU	Time	CPU*	Time*
$GP(10)$	16·	99.9%	11	99.9%	7	99.9%	99.9%	99.2%	99.9%	100.4%
$GP(20)$	32	92.7%	12	123.4%	5	93.5%	40.5%	52.7%	67.4%	76.1%
$GP(50)$	23	69.6%	11	102.6%	3	99.4%	77.7%	91.3%	99.6%	98.8%
$GP(100)$	16	63.8%	13	111.3%	4	99.9%	87.7%	100.3%	99.9%	100.6%
$GP_e(10)$	1304	33.5%	26	114.4%	13	90.8%	44.1%	50.5%	62.8%	70.6%
$GP_e(20)$	268	57.7%	21	105.5%	4	91.0%	43.7%	57.1%	63.0%	71.1%
$GP_e(50)$	15	78.2%	7	123.6%	5	96.7%	80.0%	87.9%	98.5%	99.6%
$GP_e(100)$	6	64.8%	6	107.1%	2	100.0%	36.2%	45.7%	100.0%	99.3%
$Rand(1)$	1	66.5%	1	114.0%	0	–	89.2%	101.4%	–	–
$Rand(2)$	2	67.0%	2	114.5%	0	–	89.7%	102.5%	–	–
$Rand(5)$	1	75.0%	1	109.0%	0	–	60.5%	66.9%	–	–
$Rand(10)$	2	74.9%	2	107.2%	1	100.0%	63.3%	66.3%	100.0%	99.3%

Size, Size', Size*: patch size (number of edits) of the final training mutant, of the cleaned-up mutant, and of the final validation mutant.
CPU, CPU* (**Time, Time***): percentage of CPU instructions (running time) of the final training and validation mutant, compared to the unmodified software.

5.2   Comparison of Approaches

Tables 1, 2, 3, 4 and 5 respectively report on the performance of the twelve approaches over the five repetitions and splits of instances. For each approach we first report, for the training step, the size and fitness estimate of the final training mutant. Then, for the validation step we report the cleaned-up size of the final training mutant and its fitness, and the size and fitness after filtering. Finally, for the test step, we report, for both the final training mutant and the final validation mutant, the fitness in terms of both the number of CPU instructions and the actual running time. Again, fitness values are indicated as a ratio of the fitness with the original software on the same instances. An illustration of the relationships between these results is presented in Fig. 4.

Firstly, while the results are mostly consistent within a single instance split, they greatly differ from one split to another. Furthermore, the instance sets of the validation and the test steps induce extremely different results, albeit being from identical size and sampled from the same distribution. This difference in results points towards a high heterogeneity in the data set, easily explained by the small number of SAT instances used (only 130 CIT instances).

The results do not show any noticeable impact on neither the size of the population nor the use of elitism on the performance of the GI process. While a statistical analysis using a considerably larger amount of GI runs for each approach might yield better insight on the impact of GP parameters, significant difference in performance within the selected parameter values is unlikely. The four random-based approaches also show no significant difference in performance.

Focusing on the very first set of experiments (Table 1), most of GP-based and random-based approaches report final mutants using around 70% of the num-

Table 2. Experimental results for all variants (second split).

	Training		Validation				Test			
Search	Size	CPU	Size	CPU	Size*	CPU*	CPU	Time	CPU*	Time*
$GP(10)$	71	38.6%	27	155.3%	3	93.6%	127.1%	135.8%	88.0%	88.2%
$GP(20)$	40	20.0%	13	117.7%	6	99.7%	98.5%	113.4%	99.6%	99.7%
$GP(50)$	16	54.9%	13	165.7%	5	99.9%	151.9%	205.6%	100.0%	100.1%
$GP(100)$	5	55.6%	5	136.6%	1	100.0%	126.4%	154.0%	100.0%	99.8%
$GP_e(10)$	45	38.6%	29	100.7%	2	100.0%	90.9%	91.5%	100.0%	99.8%
$GP_e(20)$	62	15.7%	19	117.7%	7	100.0%	102.9%	119.8%	100.0%	99.7%
$GP_e(50)$	31	44.2%	12	118.8%	5	99.7%	97.8%	112.7%	99.7%	99.6%
$GP_e(100)$	19	49.9%	12	123.8%	3	93.4%	90.7%	105.5%	81.2%	84.6%
$Rand(1)$	1	48.3%	1	151.1%	0	–	114.9%	123.0%	–	–
$Rand(2)$	2	44.4%	2	107.9%	1	100.0%	105.1%	106.8%	100.0%	99.7%
$Rand(5)$	2	70.2%	2	108.0%	1	100.0%	89.9%	86.8%	100.0%	100.5%
$Rand(10)$	1	51.8%	1	107.4%	0	–	91.9%	96.1%	–	–

Table 3. Experimental results for all variants (third split).

	Training		Validation				Test			
Search	Size	CPU	Size	CPU	Size*	CPU*	CPU	Time	CPU*	Time*
$GP(10)$	28	69.4%	9	102.5%	6	99.8%	76.5%	76.0%	99.7%	100.8%
$GP(20)$	63	86.7%	10	107.7%	6	100.0%	130.2%	138.0%	100.0%	99.8%
$GP(50)$	7	26.2%	7	151.1%	1	100.0%	74.9%	71.6%	100.0%	100.3%
$GP(100)$	8	60.8%	6	109.3%	1	100.0%	62.9%	64.1%	100.0%	98.4%
$GP_e(10)$	19	69.3%	5	93.2%	3	100.0%	98.5%	98.2%	100.0%	99.5%
$GP_e(20)$	1	100.0%	1	100.0%	1	100.0%	100.0%	100.4%	100.0%	99.4%
$GP_e(50)$	21	25.7%	9	111.2%	3	100.0%	102.2%	113.2%	100.0%	100.8%
$GP_e(100)$	5	48.2%	5	109.2%	2	93.6%	76.3%	74.6%	76.3%	74.7%
$Rand(1)$	1	64.9%	1	107.7%	0	–	50.1%	49.0%	–	–
$Rand(2)$	1	65.7%	1	118.1%	0	–	100.3%	108.4%	–	–
$Rand(5)$	2	52.2%	2	107.9%	1	100.0%	86.9%	89.0%	100.0%	100.3%
$Rand(10)$	3	69.0%	3	98.8%	2	98.8%	104.3%	105.3%	104.3%	106.9%

ber of CPU instructions executed compared to the original software, with the best mutant reporting using only as much as 33.5%. Mutants generated by GP approaches used between 6 and 26 edits, with the best mutants of random-based approaches containing only a single or two edits. The training performance of all mutants failed to generalise to the set of validation instances, with only three mutants surviving the filtering process with more that 5% fitness improvement. All three mutants did then further generalise on the final test set of instances, with a final improvement of 25% to 30% in running time. However, many unfiltered mutants, albeit slower on the validation set, showed on the test set much larger improvements in both number of CPU instructions and running time.

For this first split of instances, it appears that mutants generalised to the test instances but not the validation instances. The same situation occurs in Table 3, while Tables 4 and 5 show the inverse to be true. Finally, on the three

Table 4. Experimental results for all variants (fourth split).

| Search | Training | | Validation | | | | Test | | | |
	Size	CPU	Size	CPU	Size*	CPU*	CPU	Time	CPU*	Time*
$GP(10)$	26	93.8%	9	91.6%	6	91.6%	126.9%	121.4%	126.9%	121.1%
$GP(20)$	54	22.2%	13	55.0%	6	50.2%	126.3%	129.7%	124.7%	128.2%
$GP(50)$	9	82.8%	7	91.0%	6	54.0%	126.0%	120.7%	115.8%	111.8%
$GP(100)$	7	57.8%	5	75.4%	3	75.4%	92.0%	91.8%	92.0%	91.7%
$GP_e(10)$	2	99.8%	2	99.9%	2	99.9%	99.8%	101.0%	99.8%	101.1%
$GP_e(20)$	49	22.2%	9	54.9%	8	49.8%	126.2%	127.7%	123.8%	124.9%
$GP_e(50)$	6	82.8%	6	99.7%	4	99.7%	130.6%	135.6%	130.6%	134.6%
$GP_e(100)$	10	48.9%	9	119.6%	5	50.1%	111.2%	118.1%	124.7%	127.8%
$Rand(1)$	1	57.4%	1	77.2%	1	77.2%	122.8%	115.6%	122.8%	114.8%
$Rand(2)$	1	77.1%	1	75.4%	1	75.4%	92.0%	90.9%	92.0%	92.1%
$Rand(5)$	3	57.7%	3	99.9%	1	99.8%	96.4%	98.3%	96.1%	99.2%
$Rand(10)$	1	77.1%	1	75.4%	1	75.4%	92.0%	91.2%	92.0%	91.1%

Table 5. Experimental results for all variants (fifth split).

| Search | Training | | Validation | | | | Test | | | |
	Size	CPU	Size	CPU	Size*	CPU*	CPU	Time	CPU*	Time*
$GP(10)$	0	100.0%	–	–	–	–	–	–	–	–
$GP(20)$	36	21.6%	16	105.6%	4	75.1%	timeout	timeout	97.1%	96.9%
$GP(50)$	6	83.9%	5	91.5%	3	53.5%	89.0%	81.7%	119.8%	115.0%
$GP(100)$	4	54.7%	4	130.1%	1	100.0%	109.1%	108.8%	100.0%	99.4%
$GP_e(10)$	0	100.0%	–	–	–	–	–	–	–	–
$GP_e(20)$	88	29.6%	15	53.2%	11	53.2%	119.2%	116.6%	119.2%	116.5%
$GP_e(50)$	14	79.1%	9	54.1%	4	49.2%	73.5%	74.3%	98.6%	103.3%
$GP_e(100)$	20	55.1%	12	57.6%	5	53.4%	103.4%	99.9%	119.8%	116.8%
$Rand(1)$	1	65.4%	1	74.9%	1	74.9%	98.4%	96.4%	98.4%	98.9%
$Rand(2)$	1	65.4%	1	74.9%	1	74.9%	98.4%	96.7%	98.4%	96.8%
$Rand(5)$	1	65.6%	1	75.0%	1	75.0%	98.6%	95.7%	98.6%	95.5%
$Rand(10)$	1	69.8%	1	75.3%	1	75.3%	97.3%	94.6%	97.3%	95.6%

cases (first three folds) in which the validation step is able to catch overfitting on the training step, it efficiently is able to fix it on the test step.

5.3 Comparative Analysis

Figure 4 illustrates various relationships between mutant performance at different points of the experiments. Dashed lines highlight 100% thresholds and the identity function ($x = y$). Data points are simply denoted by the index of the fold they used in the test step.

Figure 4(a) shows the overfitting of the final training mutants on the validation set of instances. As expected, almost every single mutant overfits on the training set, with roughly half of the mutants using more CPU instructions than the original software on the previously unseen validation instances.

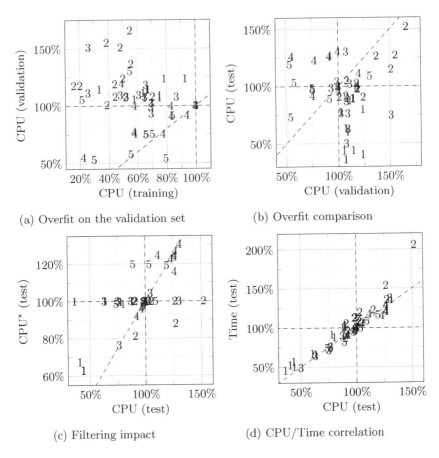

Fig. 4. Results correlations after the training, validation, and test steps

Figure 4(b) should ideally show very correlated results, as performance should be similar on both validation and test sets of instances, both unseen and following the same distribution. Instead, it highlights a previous conclusion: the set of CIT instances is too small to be randomly divided in five fair subsets.

Figure 4(c) shows the impact of the filtering step, comparing the performance on the test step of the final training mutant and the filtered one. Unfortunately, filtering had in most cases either no impact or a negative impact. This is due to validation and test sets of instances being inconsistent.

Figure 4(d), finally, shows the clear correlation between performance in terms of the number of CPU instructions executed and the running time. This, together with the very high stability of CPU instructions readings even in parallel contexts, confirms it as an excellent measure of computational speed.

5.4 Research Questions

RQ1 (Effectiveness): *How often are noticeable improvements found?*
In all but five GI runs improvements from 5% to 79% in the number of CPU instructions were found on training instances. In slightly more than half of the runs some of the mutations had a noticeable (>5%) impact during either the validation or the test step. However, considering only the performance on the filtered mutants, only nine GI runs had a noticeable positive impact during the test step. Seven of these GI runs used a GP search process, while the two other used random search.

RQ2 (Efficiency): *How significant are the improvements found?*
The improvements of the nine most successful GI runs vary between 8% and 37% in terms of the number of CPU instructions, and between 8% and 30% in terms of running time. Furthermore, among the many results with significant (>5%) improvements on unseen instances (validation and test) about two-thirds show improvements of at least 25%.

RQ3 (Robustness): *How critical are the GP parameter values?*
No particular impact of parameter values is noticed for neither GP-based approaches nor random-based approaches. While more GI runs based on GP ultimately produced significant improvements, performance of GP-based approaches was similar to the performance of random-based approaches. This could be partly attributed to the data set heterogeneity.

RQ4 (Consistency): *What is the impact of test cases on the results of GI?*
As clearly demonstrated in the experiments, results are strongly impacted by the way instances are split. The same final mutant trained on 60% of the instances can be reported as 50% faster on 20% of previously unseen instances while being at the same time 25% slower of the remaining 20% of equally unseen instances. As a consequence, it is highly recommended for future GI work to report repeated performance using multiple data splits, following, for example, the experimental protocol described in this paper. Failure to do so might result in overlooking major weaknesses in the dataset and highly overestimated final software performance.

6 Conclusions

This paper presented and compared several GP approaches for a GI scenario in which a Boolean satisfiability solver, MiniSAT, was evolved to optimise running time on combinatorial interaction testing instances. Number of CPU instructions was proposed as an alternative to source code instrumentation and was shown to be a reliable indicator of computational speed. Following a protocol based on repeated experiments, it showed that performance of GI processes was highly impacted by heterogeneity in the data set. While the training steps resulted in a very high number of mutants with excellent performance on *either* of the validation or test steps, very few of them had a significant impact after the complete GI process. Overall, GP approaches are mostly indistinguishable from one another and yet more efficient and effective than random search, suggesting that more consistent and reliable approaches are yet to be proposed.

The proposed protocol, with repeated experiments and disjoint validation and test sets, shows the potential for obtaining even better results than in previous work. Moreover, it shows that the largest impact on the performance lies in the set of test suites used, which requires further investigation in future work. Regardless, even in the simplest random search case, improvements can be found. However, the question of which is the most efficient and effective search process in GI remains open with this work being the first step towards answering that question.

Acknowledgement. This work is supported by UK EPSRC Fellowship EP/P023 991/1.

References

1. An, G., Blot, A., Petke, J., Yoo, S.: PyGGI 2.0: language independent genetic improvement framework. In: Proceedings of the 27th ACM Joint Meeting on European Software Engineering Conference and Symposium on the Foundations of Software Engineering (ESEC/FSE 2019), pp. 1100–1104. ACM (2019). https://doi.org/10.1145/3338906.3341184
2. Arcuri, A., Yao, X.: A novel co-evolutionary approach to automatic software bug fixing. In: Proceedings of the Congress on Evolutionary Computation (CEC 2008), pp. 162–168 (2008). https://doi.org/10.1109/CEC.2008.4630793
3. Bruce, B.R., Petke, J., Harman, M.: Reducing energy consumption using genetic improvement. In: Proceedings of the 10th Genetic and Evolutionary Computation Conference (GECCO 2015), pp. 1327–1334. ACM (2015). https://doi.org/10.1145/2739480.2754752
4. Eén, N., Sörensson, N.: An extensible SAT-solver. In: Giunchiglia, E., Tacchella, A. (eds.) SAT 2003. LNCS, vol. 2919, pp. 502–518. Springer, Heidelberg (2004). https://doi.org/10.1007/978-3-540-24605-3_37
5. Forrest, S., Nguyen, T., Weimer, W., Le Goues, C.: A genetic programming approach to automated software repair. In: Proceedings of the 4th Genetic and Evolutionary Computation Conference (GECCO 2009), pp. 947–954. ACM (2009). https://doi.org/10.1145/1569901.1570031
6. Langdon, W.B., Harman, M.: Evolving a CUDA kernel from an nVidia template. In: Proceedings of the Congress on Evolutionary Computation (CEC 2010), pp. 1–8 (2010). https://doi.org/10.1109/CEC.2010.5585922
7. Langdon, W.B., Harman, M.: Optimizing existing software with genetic programming. IEEE Trans. Evol. Comput. **19**(1), 118–135 (2015). https://doi.org/10.1109/TEVC.2013.2281544
8. Le, X.D., Chu, D., Lo, D., Le Goues, C., Visser, W.: S3: syntax- and semantic-guided repair synthesis via programming by examples. In: Proceedings of the ACM Joint Meeting on European Software Engineering Conference and Symposium on the Foundations of Software Engineering (ESEC/FSE 2017), pp. 593–604. ACM (2017). https://doi.org/10.1145/3106237.3106309

9. Le Goues, C., Dewey-Vogt, M., Forrest, S., Weimer, W.: A systematic study of automated program repair: fixing 55 out of 105 bugs for $8 each. In: Proceedings of the 34th International Conference on Software Engineering (ICSE 2012), pp. 3–13. IEEE Computer Society (2012). https://doi.org/10.1109/ICSE.2012.6227211
10. Le Goues, C., Nguyen, T., Forrest, S., Weimer, W.: GenProg: a generic method for automatic software repair. IEEE Trans. Softw. Eng. **38**(1), 54–72 (2012). https://doi.org/10.1109/TSE.2011.104
11. Petke, J., Haraldsson, S.O., Harman, M., Langdon, W.B., White, D.R., Woodward, J.R.: Genetic improvement of software: a comprehensive survey. IEEE Trans. Evol. Comput. **22**(3), 415–432 (2018). https://doi.org/10.1109/TEVC.2017.2693219
12. Petke, J., Harman, M., Langdon, W.B., Weimer, W.: Using genetic improvement and code transplants to specialise a C++ program to a problem class. In: Nicolau, M., et al. (eds.) EuroGP 2014. LNCS, vol. 8599, pp. 137–149. Springer, Heidelberg (2014). https://doi.org/10.1007/978-3-662-44303-3_12
13. Petke, J., Harman, M., Langdon, W.B., Weimer, W.: Specialising software for different downstream applications using genetic improvement and code transplantation. IEEE Trans. Softw. Eng. **44**(6), 574–594 (2018). https://doi.org/10.1109/TSE.2017.2702606
14. Petke, J., Langdon, W.B., Harman, M.: Applying genetic improvement to MiniSAT. In: Ruhe, G., Zhang, Y. (eds.) SSBSE 2013. LNCS, vol. 8084, pp. 257–262. Springer, Heidelberg (2013). https://doi.org/10.1007/978-3-642-39742-4_21
15. Schulte, E.M., DiLorenzo, J., Weimer, W., Forrest, S.: Automated repair of binary and assembly programs for cooperating embedded devices. In: Proceedings of the 18th International Conference on Architectural Support for Programming Languages and Operating Systems (ASPLOS 2013), pp. 317–328 (2013). https://doi.org/10.1145/2451116.2451151
16. Weaver, V.M., Terpstra, D., Moore, S.: Non-determinism and overcount on modern hardware performance counter implementations. In: Proceedings of the 2013 International Symposium on Performance Analysis of Systems & Software (ISSTA 2013), pp. 215–224. IEEE (2013). https://doi.org/10.1109/ISPASS.2013.6557172
17. Weimer, W.: Patches as better bug reports. In: Proceedings of the 5th International Conference on Generative Programming and Component Engineering (GPCE 2006), pp. 181–190 (2006). https://doi.org/10.1145/1173706.1173734
18. Weimer, W., Nguyen, T., Le Goues, C., Forrest, S.: Automatically finding patches using genetic programming. In: Proceedings of the 31st International Conference on Software Engineering (ICSE 2009), pp. 364–374. IEEE Computer Society (2009). https://doi.org/10.1109/ICSE.2009.5070536
19. White, D.R., Arcuri, A., Clark, J.A.: Evolutionary improvement of programs. IEEE Trans. Evol. Comput. **15**(4), 515–538 (2011). https://doi.org/10.1109/TEVC.2010.2083669

Automatically Evolving Lookup Tables for Function Approximation

Oliver Krauss[1,2(✉)] and William B. Langdon[3]

[1] Johannes Kepler University Linz, Linz, Austria
[2] AIST, University of Applied Sciences Upper Austria, Wels, Austria
`oliver.krauss@fh-hagenberg.at`
[3] CREST, Computer Science, UCL, London, UK
`W.Langdon@cs.ucl.ac.uk`

Abstract. Many functions, such as square root, are approximated and sped up with lookup tables containing pre-calculated values.

We introduce an approach using genetic algorithms to evolve such lookup tables for any smooth function. It provides double precision and calculates most values to the closest bit, and outperforms reference implementations in most cases with competitive run-time performance.

Keywords: Genetic Improvement · Objective function · Covariance matrix adaptation

1 Introduction

Newton-Raphson [11] is a widely applied method to approximate smooth mathematical functions. We present an approach that allows the fully automated generation of a lookup table for any given mathematical function, across a defined range. Newton-Raphson requires a known approximation and its derivative. Our approach is more accurate than comparable approximation methods and, except where hardware acceleration is provided, e.g. square root, it is also faster.

To validate the method we compare our approach to several reference implementations, including square root and cube root, in C, C++, Java. We give a detailed overview of the design of the fitness function and influencing factors, such as algorithm design and the occurrence of inflection points in the functions to be approximated.

The approach improves the performance of Newton-Raphson by reducing the amount of iterations required, and provides:

- High precision function approximation - all functions are calculated with double precision accuracy, and are more accurate than reference implementations in most cases.
- Auto generated lookup tables - Lookup tables are automatically generated without the need for configuration.

© Springer Nature Switzerland AG 2020
T. Hu et al. (Eds.): EuroGP 2020, LNCS 12101, pp. 84–100, 2020.
https://doi.org/10.1007/978-3-030-44094-7_6

– Fast run-time performance compared to algorithms that are not hardware accelerated.

The approach can be directly applied to various domains. Gauss-Newton, a modification of the original Newton-Raphson algorithm, is used in Genetic Programming [6] to guide the search through the search space [14]. Lookup tables are also used in Genetic Programming as function lookups [2,9]. Newton-Raphson is used in distributed optimization to drive the consensus between the different agents on a shared optimization problem, both synchronously [12] and asynchronously [1]. It is also used in Data Science to solve equations to categorize, group or predict data. In the case of Yap et al. [13], it is used for parameter estimation to fit the Lee-Carter numerical forecasting algorithm. When hardware architectures do not offer hardware acceleration, the square root and division operations as defined in the IEEE Standard for Floating-Point Arithmetic [5,10] are often implemented using Newton-Raphson in reference implementations. To further speed up these implementations reference implementations provide lookup tables to reduce the amount of Newton-Raphson iterations needed.

Previously Langdon and Petke [8] introduced a way to automatically generate the cube root function $\sqrt[3]{x}$ (cbrt) into the C Math library and automatically generate the lookup table required for it by using CMA-ES. We expand on their work, and show a way to generate a lookup table for any given mathematical function, within a predefined range. The goal is to provide a speedup for functions that need to be solved often during algorithmic evaluations and do not have hardware acceleration.

2   Background

2.1   Covariance Matrix Adaption - Evolution Strategy (CMA-ES)

The CMA-ES algorithm can be used to solve n-dimensional continuous numerical problems. It has been proven to work for local [4] and global [3] optimization. At the core of the algorithm is the covariance matrix of which a centroid is calculated that guides the search over several iterations of new population-generations by evolving a probability distribution. The essential operators in CMA-ES are mutation and crossover. Mutation happens around a standard deviation that is continuously updated during the run. Crossover is done by combining several individuals in the population to new points. Crossover and mutator are CMA-ES internal functions that are closely tied to the core covariance matrix, and were not adapted for our approach [4].

CMA-ES also does not require parameter tuning, as all values are calculated, and updated in regular intervals, internally around the core centroid [4]. Several parameters can be set, such as the initial standard deviation, an initial search position (centroid), but they only serve to speed up the algorithm by moving closer to an already known, or at least assumed, good global optimum, and an appropriate mutation size around it. Parameters relevant to the approach of this article will be discussed in the next section.

2.2 Evolving Better Software Parameters

The publication of Langdon and Petke [8] discusses the need to automatically evolve software parameters, and emphasizes on applications in the domains of automated bug-fixing, maintenance of legacy code as applications in the field of Genetic Improvement [7]. As a proof of concept that software parameters can be improved automatically their publication shows how to generate the cube root (cbrt) function for the GNU C library (glibc) which does not implement it. The cbrt algorithm itself was not generated, but rather copied and modified from the IEEE square root implementation as is provided in glibc. CMA-ES was used to generate the lookup table that cbrt used with only three iterations of Newton-Raphson. The goal was to achieve IEEE 754 double precision accuracy (1 sign bit, 11 bit exponent, 52 bit fractional [5]).

Algorithmic Implementation of Cube Root - Langdon and Petke [8] adapted the existing cube root function of glibc, which does not perform a pure Newton-Raphson approximation, but does several refinements to extend the limited range of the lookup table (between 0.5 and 2) to the entire range of values double can take. This includes splitting the double value into two 32 bit components and performing bitwise operations on them. Three Newton-Raphson iterations are taken, and finally the values last bit is modified to ensure the closest possible rounding [10].

CMA-ES parameters - All parameters were left as default except the following. The problem size in [8] was of $N = 2$ as they selected values for both 32 bit components in cbrt. All stopping conditions in [8] were set to 0 to ensure the algorithm would only stop when it found the exact values required for the lookup table. The seed for the random number generation was set externally for reproducibility.

Restarting Strategies - CMA-ES can have several reasons why it fails to produce an exact result. The primary reason when generating lookup tables is that the fitness landscape becomes too flat in the area it is searching for, as all individuals in the population come close to perfect accuracy, but will not reach it, due to bitwise imprecision, or due to not randomly mutating to the final correct bit. [8] opted for a restart in this case with a different seed. In all cases of their function it was enough to run CMA-ES no more than 3 times to reach the closest possible answer.

Fitness function - When generating a lookup table for cube root every value in the lookup table represents a sub-range of the range the table was generated for. The fitness function in [8] used three test points, the lower end, the higher end and the middle of the range, for each table entry. The fitness function was evaluated by calling the cube-root with the spot in the lookup table initialized with the values in the evaluated individual of the CMA-ES population.

The fitness function did a logarithm conversion. All values except 0 had the absolute logarithm of *DBL_EPSILON* added to it. *DBL_EPSILON* in C is the minimal difference when added to 1 changes results in a different double value. All values below 1 had the logarithm taken as well. This essentially 'zooms' into the fitness when values extremely close to zero are dealt with.

Table 1. Analysis of Langdon and Petkes fitness function [8]. Modifying the fitness function with a *logarithm* has no effect. Their method is more accurate than the Java and C++ reference implementations. Total Error is the difference between x and $cbrt(x)^3$ over 512 test values.

Implementation	Distribution	Total error $\times 10^{-10}$
C - with log	Even	3.1451
	Random	3.3231
C - without log	Even	3.1451
	Random	3.3231
Java	Even	3.3322
	Random	3.6071
C++	Even	6.2851
	random	7.2275

Listing 1.1. Conversion of qualities close to 0.

```
if(quality==0.0) return quality;
if(quality< 1.0) return (-log(DBL_EPSILON))+log(quality);
return (-log(DBL_EPSILON))+quality;
```

2.3 Investigating Evolving Better Software Parameters

As the CMA-ES stopping condition is targeted towards 0 already, and the standard deviation does reduce its size to a DBL_EPSILON during runs, this adaption to the fitness function should not impact the algorithm. To check this assumption we compared two different versions of Langdon and Petkes code. One of them was modified to not apply the logarithm in their fitness function. A batch file then applied this compilation process:

1. Compilation of the entire project, to ensure the CMA-ES algorithm runs no old versions.
2. Running the original Genetic Improvement script with a *seed* that the compilation script takes as input.
3. A script then created the new lookup table from the compilation results.
4. Recompilation of the project with the new lookup table.

A test harness generated values ranged between 0.5 and 10000. The amount of positions in the lookup table, 512 values, were evenly spaced inside the range (e.g. 0.5, 20, 30.5, ..., 9980.5, 10000). An additional 512 values were randomly selected inside the range. The test harness then randomly created 1000 seeds between 1 and 1000000. The compilation batch file was run with every seed, and all 1024 values were tested on that seed. The measurement was done by taking the result values given by the implementation and cubing them again. The difference between the original value and the re-cubed cube root values was calculated as the error. The total error is the sum of these over all test-values as shown in Table 1. On all executed tests the results were equivalent, with every single seed, and in both versions of the code. This means that neither applying a log, nor selecting a seed has an impact in their approach.

Accuracy of the results - One noteworthy finding that is not mentioned in [8] is that their generated cube root function outperforms implementations of other programming languages as shown in Table 1 with Java and C++. We compared their algorithm not only to our adaption, but to the Java and C++ implementations of cbrt as well, and [8] outperforms all implementations.

3 Methods

We extended the original approach of [8], to be used for any function that can be approximated with the Newton-Raphson method. The method generates only the lookup table for a function defined by a developer. Our method can generate a lookup table with the parameters:

- Range - from a *lower end* to a *higher end*. The range restricts the space in the double values the lookup table is being generated for. This is necessary as not all functions can benefit from refinements such as the cube root.
- Table Size - The number of entries in the table essentially splits the range into sub-ranges. By increasing the size of the table precision in a smaller range can be improved. Alternatively a larger range can be covered with no loss of precision.
- User Function - the user function allows the user to define an entry point to handle operations in addition to the Newton-Raphson approach.
- Approximation function and its derivative - are required by the approach. They are used both in the fitness function of CMA-ES to generate the lookup table, and in the Newton-Raphson approach that uses the lookup table.
- Iterations - the number of iterations in the Newton-Rapson approach. Increasing the number of iterations can improve the range the lookup table can be used for, and improve upon the precision.

3.1 CMA-ES Settings

Listing 1.2. Cube Root implementation.

```
// Function for Newton-Raphson
double fn(const double approx) {
    return approx * approx * approx;
}

// Derivative of fn
double derivativeFn(const double approx) {
    return 3 * approx * approx;
}
```

```
// Function that allows user to modify input and result
double userFunction(const double x) {
    // accept negative numbers in cube root
    if (x < 0) return approximate(0.0 - x);
    if (x > 0) return approximate(x);
    return x;
}
```

Table 2. Analysis of the strategy to restart the algorithm if no exact value is found. Not restarting has a higher (better) mean. Restarting is not relevant.

	Mean	Std. deviation	Median	Min. exact values	Max. exact values
No restarts	**496.33**	1.9646	496	491	**502**
3 restarts	495.87	1.7271	496	**492**	499

Algorithmic Implementation - The algorithmic implementation was done with only Newton-Raphson. An example of the approximation function for cube root can be seen in Listing 1.2.

CMA-ES parameters - Similar to [8] we did not change any of the default parameters of CMA-ES except the stopping conditions, which were set to 0 for the fitness as well. The seed is provided externally as well. Our method takes a problem size of 1 instead of 2, as the values will be selected for the entire double value instead of its 32 bit components.

Restarting Strategies - Langdon and Petke [8] opted to apply a restart in case the CMA-ES run did not find an exact value according to their fitness function. Their results showed that no more than 3 restarts were necessary and in most cases the first seed was acceptable. To check if this option impacts the results we compared 100 different runs without restarting, and 100 runs with restarting.

As Table 2 shows, the runs without any restarting have a higher mean and a higher maximum in the amount of exact numbers found. An analysis of the medians over 100 runs (same values used for no restarts/3 restarts) showed that the differences are not statistically significant (expecting 5 out of 100 - p of 0.05). Shapiro Wilk shows (p 0.0023) which means the data is not normally distributed, Mann-Whitney-U for two independent samples shows a normalized (p 0.0566). Repeating the test multiple times with different sets of 100 runs showed similar behavior, sometimes even with statistical significance, with both no-restarts and 3 restarts having the better mean. This lets us assume that the restarts have less impact on the run than the random seed values. While restarts can positively impact the results due to choosing a new seed, omitting them greatly improves the runtime of the approach.

3.2   Test Setup and Measurements

To enable a better comparability over all tested root functions, as well as the different applied fitness functions, the range of the lookup table was set from 0.5 to 2. For all tests the table size was set to 512. All functions depend only upon the approximation and its derivative, with no additional steps taken to improve or change the results. To enable comparability with reference approaches the iterations of Newton-Raphson were fixed at 3. The tests in Subsect. 3.3 are conducted with 3 restarts, while the tests in Sect. 4 were done with no restarts as the runs with inflection points proved to be too time-consuming.

The tests were always conducted over two separate sets of 512 values. One set was evenly spaced in the given range of 0.5 to 2, the second set was generated randomly using a uniform distribution. These two sets were always generated for one group of tests. The only thing changing when repeating the tests was the random seed value which was randomly selected between 1 and 1000000.

The tests show two different quality measurements:

– *Total Error* - which is calculated from applying the approximation function fn to the approximated value of a given input, and then subtracting that input from it. The *err*or value is always summed over all test-values to produce the total error.

$$\text{err} = \text{abs}(\text{fn}(\text{approximation}) - \text{input})$$

– *Exact Values* - Which are the amount of values that were met exactly by Newton-Raphson using the fitness function. In the double range not all continuous numbers can be represented, so this measure takes into account if the approximation is the closest that could be represented with double. This is done by comparing the *err*or of the approximation, as well as one bit lower and one bit higher. The bit addition and substraction are conducted by copying the value into a long with memcpy adding or removing 1, and conducting another memcpy back to double.

$$\text{exact} = \text{err}(\text{appr.}) \leq \text{err}(\text{appr.} - 1\text{bit})\&\&\text{err}(\text{appr.}) \leq \text{err}(\text{appr.} + 1\text{bit})$$

3.3   Fitness Function Design

In Subsect. 2.2 we showed that applying a log to the fitness function had no impact. To check if this depends on the implementation of the algorithm we redid the test with our implementation of cube root as shown in Listing 1.2.

The results (see Table 3) show that applying the logarithm not only has an effect, but that effect is statistically significant, with the logarithm application achieving better results. The fact that there is a deviation from the mean as well, means that the seed also seems to have an impact. We assume that this is due to the additional steps that the algorithm implements, which allows finding exact values with different initial seed values, making the algorithm more robust.

As applying a logarithm to CMA-ES does significantly impact the results we chose to compare several other methods of modifying the fitness function:

- *No mod.* - the fitness function without any modification.
- *Log.* - as was done in [8] adding log(quality) + log(DBL_EPSILON).
- *Inc. Log.* - it stands to reason that if the fitness function does benefit from applying a log that increasing the log value (== getting the value closer to zero) should provide more benefit. Thus, we applied log(quality) + log(DBL_EPSILON × DBL_EPSILON ×DBL_EPSILON) instead of just log(DBL_EPSILON).
- *Mul.* - Adding a logarithm has the benefit of representing smaller changes in the fitness function. A multiplication log(quality) *1000 should have the same effect.
- *Bitwise* - The actual double fitness value is copied into a long with memcpy, and then cast back to double. This sets the value equal to all bits that were off from zero. This modification brings the largest transformation, and ensures that all values that are just one bit off will result in a fitness of 1, while all exact values will have a fitness of 0.

In their original work Langdon and Petke decided on a fitness function that takes three values for every value in the lookup table. Those three values were the lower end, the upper end and the center of the range an entry in the lookup table represented (see a in Fig. 1) [8]. The lookup table for Newton-Raphson does require a good staring point for all values covered in the range. Selecting both ends and the center of the sub-range, that one individual position represents, ensure a good starting position for the entire range.

There are other ways to represent the fitness function, and arguments to be made for each of them. We selected several options for comparison:

(a) *Outer* - The outer points - upper and lower end - and center of the range, which is the original from [8] (see a in Fig. 1)

Table 3. Analysis of the influence of applying *log* in our approach. *Log* improves the accuracy and makes a significant difference in most cases (bold).

Distribution	Value	Fitness	Mean	Min	Max	Significance (p)
Even	Total error $\times 10^{-14}$	No log	9.02	8.93	9.13	1.5×10^{-133} (yes)
		Log	**8.62**	**8.49**	**8.73**	
	Exact values	No log	472.64	467	478	3.7×10^{-124} (yes)
		Log	**493.06**	**487**	**501**	
Random	Total error $\times 10^{-14}$	No log	9.03	**8.78**	9.16	5.58×10^{-7} (yes)
		Log	**8.97**	8.8	**9.15**	
	Exact values	No log	480.79	473	492	0.8929 (no)
		Log	480.86	471	489	

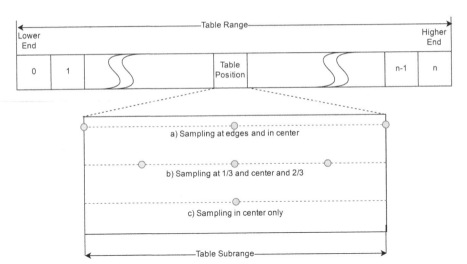

Fig. 1. Sampling point options (a–c) used in the fitness functions when generating a cell in the lookup table.

(b) *Inner* - ⅓, the center and ⅔ of the range (see b in Fig. 1). The argument for this option is that the points are more evenly distributed over the entire range, than (a).

(c) *Center* - Only the center of the range (see c in Fig. 1). To verify that there is cause in the assumptions of (a) and (b) that multiple points per lookup table entry make a difference.

In these fitness functions there are several approaches as to what can be used to calculate the target for the lookup table positions. In all of them the goal is to set the currently searched lookup table position with the individual in the population to be evaluated and check that value for accuracy by applying it to the test-positions:

1. *Approx* - By comparing the result of the Newton-Raphson approximation, exactly as how the error in the tables is calculated
2. *Rem.Err* - By taking the last error after applying Newton-Raphson, essentially returning the difference instead of the desired result
3. *Direct* - By simply taking the individual of the population and applying the error function without applying Newton-Raphson at all. This is the most run-time efficient way to calculate a lookup table position as it requires only one call to fn(x) instead of three iterations, it is only viable when applying it to the center of the range.

When creating all valid combinations of the options above from the fitness function adaptions, test points and evaluation options a total of 35 functions have to be considered.

4   Results

To evaluate and validate our approach we selected these functions for testing:

- Square Root - as this has a reference implementation available in all languages (C, C++, Java)
- Cube Root - to offer a comparison with the work in [8]
- Super Root ($\sqrt[4]{x}$) - to provide new functionality in a similar area
- A polynomial with inflection point - to test how the lookup table behaves with an inflection point, which have difficulties for Newton-Raphson
- A function with many inflection points - to test what happens with multiple inflection points

Figure 2 shows the mathematical definitions of the above function and provides plots for them. For the polynomial with only one inflection point the lookup table range is outside of where the inflection occurs (around 0).

The results show that the approach is best suited for smooth functions, as the single inflection point influences the outcome. While most results can provide acceptable results (Error $\leq 1.5E-8$) some runs fail to produce a valid lookup table. This happens even though the inflection is outside of the generated range for the lookup table. With multiple inflections inside the range not a single attempt generated an acceptable solution.

With the smooth square- cube- and super- root functions the fitness functions only taking the center point, and applying fn(x) instead of Newton-Raphson continuously provided good results in the random range. Using the outer test points and Newton-Raphson tended to produce better results in the even range. The fitness function continuously providing the worst results was using the center point and applying Newton-Raphson with the logarithm.

We attempted to test all algorithms with all fitness functions. This was achievable for square-, cube-, and super root. All results except the multiple inflection were calculated from 100 repeats. For the single inflection function we were only able to test 23 of the 35 defined fitness functions, as several took multiple hours per run to finish. For the multiple inflection function we were only able to test 15 repeats for all fitness functions.

The results for square root (see Table 4) cannot compete with the existing square root functions of all reference languages (C, C++ and Java). They do however show a trend that in the even distribution fitness functions that use the outer test values and approximate produce perfect results in the evenly distributed test set. This is similar over all functions without an inflection (see Tables 5 and 6).

The results of Cube root (see Table 5) show the same trend as square root concerning the even distribution. Similar to the super root the fitness functions which only use the center point and apply the value of the approximation function directly instead of Newton-Raphson produce much better results in the randomly distributed set. Unlike the square root our approach is more accurate than C++ and Java in both test distributions.

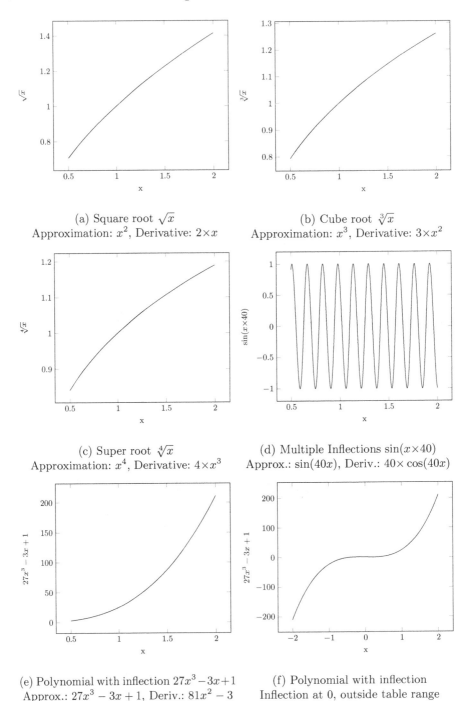

(a) Square root $\sqrt{x}$
Approximation: x^2, Derivative: $2 \times x$

(b) Cube root $\sqrt[3]{x}$
Approximation: x^3, Derivative: $3 \times x^2$

(c) Super root $\sqrt[4]{x}$
Approximation: x^4, Derivative: $4 \times x^3$

(d) Multiple Inflections $\sin(x \times 40)$
Approx.: $\sin(40x)$, Deriv.: $40 \times \cos(40x)$

(e) Polynomial with inflection $27x^3 - 3x + 1$
Approx.: $27x^3 - 3x + 1$, Deriv.: $81x^2 - 3$

(f) Polynomial with inflection
Inflection at 0, outside table range

Fig. 2. Plots of functions under test in the 0.5 to 2 range the lookup tables were generated for. (f) shows an extended range of (e) which includes the inflection point around 0.

Table 4. Square root - comparison of lookup tables generated with different fitness functions. Our approach is less accurate than C, C++ and Java.

Distribution	Value	Fitness	Median	Min	Max
Even	Total error $\times 10^{-14}$	C comparison	5.31	–	–
		C++ comparison	5.31	–	–
		Java comparison	5.31	–	–
		(Bitwise- Inc. Log.- Mul.- NoLog.-) Outer approx	5.31	5.31	5.31
		Log center approx	6.58	5.55	12.5
	Exact value	**(Bitwise- Inc. Log.- Mul.- NoLog.-) Outer approx**	512	512	512
		Log center approx	465	284	500
Random	Total error $\times 10^{-14}$	C comparison	5.27	–	–
		C++ comparison	5.27	–	–
		Java comparison	5.27	–	–
		(Bitwise- Inc. Log- Log- Mul.- No Mod.-) Center direct	5.37	5.37	5.37
		Log inner approx	6.55	5.50	9.63
	Exact value	**Log Center Rem. Err.**	506.5	499	511
		Log center approx	466.5	352	501

The super root function behaves nearly exactly the same as the cube root concerning which fitness function works. The functions that used only the center test point and directly applied the approximation instead of Newton-Raphson had nearly the same results. This indicates that the smoother the function, the more consistent the approach becomes. The accuracy of the reference implementation is not a valid comparison as we simulated the super root by applying the square root twice which results in a consequential error.

Table 7 shows that the approach can still work with a single inflection point. While the margin of error becomes considerable, several runs still managed to provide accurate results. Considering the amount of exactly calculated values it seems that points influenced by the inflection point can be problematic. A results table for the multi-inflection function is not provided as not a single run produced any value below a total error of 100 over 512 test values. Between 150–250 values still are calculated exactly, so this supports the assumption that points influenced by the inflection(s) are the source of the problem.

4.1   Run-Time Performance

The Run-Time performance of our approach is faster than Java, and slightly slower than the approach of Langdon and Petke. It is slower than approaches that are hardware accelerated. To enable a comparison we tested the cube root approximation of the approach against the C cube root of [8], and the native C++ and Java implementations. To have a baseline comparison for hardware accelerated functions in C we tested against the C square root as well.

Table 5. Cube root - comparison of lookup tables generated with different fitness functions. Our approach is more accurate than C++ and Java.

Distribution	Value	Fitness	Median	Min	Max
Even	Total error $\times 10^{-14}$	Langdon and Petkes cbrt	8.33	–	–
		C++ comparison	14.5	–	–
		Java comparison	8.72	–	–
		(Bitwise- Inc. Log.- Mul.- NoLog.-) Outer approx	8.33	8.33	8.33
		Log center approx	10	9.07	14
	Exact value	**(Bitwise- Inc. Log.- Mul.- NoLog.-) Outer approx**	512	512	512
		Log center approx	449	361	480
Random	Total error $\times 10^{-14}$	Langdon and Petkes cbrt	8.78	–	–
		C++ comparison	17.0	–	–
		Java comparison	9.34	–	–
		(Bitwise- Inc. Log- Log- No Mod.-) Center direct	9.13	9.1	9.17
		Log center approx	10.6	9.69	14
	Exact value	**(Bitwise- Inc. Log- Log- No Mod.-) Center direct**	492	491	493
		Log center approx	448	369	474

Table 6. Super root - comparison of lookup tables generated with different fitness functions. Our approach is more accurate than C, C++ and Java, possibly due to the consequential error introduced by applying square root twice. This had to be done as the languages do not implement super root.

Distribution	Value	Fitness	Median	Min	Max
Even	Total error $\times 10^{-13}$	C comparison	1.32	–	–
		C++ comparison	1.32	–	–
		Java comparison	1.32	–	–
		(Bitwise- Inc. Log.- Mul.- NoLog.-) Outer approx	1.18	1.18	1.18
		Log Center Approx	1.37	1.23	1.79
	Exact value	**(Bitwise- Inc. Log.- Mul.- NoLog.-) Outer approx**	512	512	512
		Log center approx	459	371	490
Random	Total error $\times 10^{-13}$	C comparison	1.30	–	–
		C++ comparison	1.30	–	–
		Java comparison	1.30	–	–
		Log Outer Rem. Error	1.19	1.17	1.21
		Log center approx	1.42	1.28	1.68
	Exact value	**Log Outer Rem. Error**	490	482	496
		Log center approx	451.5	400	480

Table 7. Single Inflection function - comparison of lookup tables generated with different fitness functions. Our approach can still produce satisfying results though the inflection, which is outside of the lookup table range, has a negative impact on the achieved accuracy as shown by the large medians (10^{27}).

Distr.	Value	Fitness	Median	Min	Max
Even	Total error	**Mul. Outer Rem. Error**	1.38×10^{-8}	7.14×10^{-14}	1.78
		(Mul.- No Mod.-) center direct	2.2×10^{28}	3.26×10^{25}	1.65×10^{33}
	Exact value	**(Mul.- No Mod.-) Outer appprox.**	510.5	488	512
		Log center approx	242	228	301
Random	Total error	**Mul. Outer Rem. Error**	1.9×10^{-11}	7.51×10^{-14}	19.36
		(Mul.- No Mod.-) center direct	6.15×10^{27}	3.11×10^{24}	3.75×10^{31}
	Exact value	**(Mul. Center- No Mod.-) Center Rem. Error**	435	410	451
		(Bitwise- Mul.- No Mod.-) center direct	239	229	295

Table 8 shows the run-time comparison from the total time taken when calling the respective functions 1,000,000 times. The benchmark was repeated 1000 times, and the means over all tests is reported. For all executions the same argument was provided, and the function signature is the same, fn(double val).

Table 8. Run-time performance of root functions (average of 1,000,000 calls). Our approach is faster Java and nearly matches Langdon and Petkes approach, but can not compete with hardware acceleration.

	Mean (in nanoseconds per call)		
Language	sqrt	cbrt	surt
Hardware Accelerated C	0.88	0.88	0.88*
Hardware Accelerated C++	4.10	21.35	8.10*
Langdon and Petkes cbrt			
Our approach	25.33	27.46	29.58
Java	1.02	69.51	1.03*

*surt implemented as sqrt(sqrt(x))

Our approach is slightly slower than [8]. The difference is likely due to the number of multiplications, which is higher in our approach. It can not compete with the hardware accelerated functions of C and C++. All approaches for cube root perform better than Java. The approach was designed to enable generation of lookup tables for user provided functions, such as trust regions in Genetic Programming [14]. Hardware acceleration is not likely to exist for these cases.

4.2 Limitations

The greatest limitation of our approach is that it will not work on the entire range that the double data type can provide, but rather only for the range generated. As discussed in Sect. 2.2, reference implementations contain additional logic to ensure that algorithms like square root work over the entire double range. Our work concentrates on generating lookup tables for any given function, so these steps cannot be implemented since they would reduce the accuracy of the results when applied to a different function than intended.

The only currently known workarounds are increasing the size of the generated lookup table with the range allows keeping precision intact, while also increasing memory consumption. Alternatively increasing the allowed amount of Newton-Raphson iterations increases the range the lookup table can be generated for, at the cost of run-time performance.

The second limitation of the approach is that, due to Newton-Raphson, it cannot deal with functions that have inflections. While a single inflection point has a strong negative impact on result quality and the time it takes CMA-ES to generate the lookup table, a valid table can still be generated. With multiple inflection points generating a lookup table is not possible anymore.

5   Conclusions and Outlook

Generating lookup tables works well with smooth functions and can achieve double precision accuracy. Nearly all values can be approximated to the closest bit of a double. The run-time performance is in some instances faster than comparable software solutions, but can not compete with hardware accelerated functions.

That it is not able to equal [8] still shows that a well considered algorithm is more important than a good generation of constants with CMA-ES. The combination of robust algorithms with CMA-ES does provide the best results. In smooth functions however the approach consistently provides more accuracy than the reference implementation of C++ and to a lesser extent Java.

The results support the original findings of [8], that the application of genetic improvement techniques can be applied to create or update constants in programs. CMA-ES is especially a good fit as it manages its experiment parameters internally, and can deal with small (1×10^{-14}) differences in the search space. It is not robust against functions with inflection points. Even a single inflection in the function can hinder the approach.

The approach may also be applicable to any approximation function, such Gauss Newton, Aitken Extrapolation or Gradient Descent. Additionally, specializations to the resulting function (such as [10]) should be considered to reduce the range limitation. In the future we also intend to use CMA-ES in Genetic Improvement as an operator to improve constant values in the population.

The source code, scripts and full results for Tables 4, 5, 6 and 7 are available via https://github.com/oliver-krauss/EuroGP2020-LookupTables.

References

1. Carli, R., Notarstefano, G., Schenato, L., Varagnolo, D.: Analysis of Newton-Raphson consensus for multi-agent convex optimization under asynchronous and lossy communications. In: 2015 54th IEEE Conference on Decision and Control (CDC), December 2015. https://doi.org/10.1109/CDC.2015.7402236
2. Gordon, T.G.W.: Exploiting development to enhance the scalability of hardware evolution. Ph.D. thesis, University of London (2005)
3. Hansen, N.: Benchmarking a BI-population CMA-ES on the BBOB-2009 function testbed. In: GECCO 2009. ACM (2009). https://doi.org/10.1145/1570256.1570333
4. Hansen, N., Ostermeier, A.: Completely derandomized self-adaptation in evolution strategies. Evol. Comput. 9(2), 159–195 (2001)
5. IEEE: Standard for Floating-Point Arithmetic. Std 754–2008, August 2008. https://doi.org/10.1109/IEEESTD.2008.4610935
6. Koza, J.R.: Genetic programming: a paradigm for genetically breeding populations of computer programs to solve problems. Technical report (1990)
7. Langdon, W.B.: Genetic improvement of software for multiple objectives. In: Barros, M., Labiche, Y. (eds.) SSBSE 2015. LNCS, vol. 9275, pp. 12–28. Springer, Cham (2015). https://doi.org/10.1007/978-3-319-22183-0_2
8. Langdon, W.B., Petke, J.: Evolving better software parameters. In: Colanzi, T.E., McMinn, P. (eds.) SSBSE 2018. LNCS, vol. 11036, pp. 363–369. Springer, Cham (2018). https://doi.org/10.1007/978-3-319-99241-9_22

9. Lenser, S.R., Tan, D.S.: Genetic algorithms for synthesizing data value predictors. Technical report, Carnegie Mellon University, November 1999
10. Markstein, P.W.: Computation of elementary functions on the IBM RISC System/6000 processor. IBM J. Res. Dev. **34**(1), 111–119 (1990). https://doi.org/10.1147/rd.341.0111
11. Press, W.H., Teukolsky, S.A., Vetterling, W.T., Flannery, B.P.: Numerical Recipes 3rd Edition: The Art of Scientific Computing. Cambridge University Press, Cambridge (2007). http://dl.acm.org/citation.cfm?id=1403886
12. Varagnolo, D., Zanella, F., Cenedese, A., Pillonetto, G., Schenato, L.: Newton-Raphson consensus for distributed convex optimization. IEEE Trans. Autom. Control **61**(4) (2016). https://doi.org/10.1109/tac.2015.2449811
13. Yap, S.Z.Z., Zahari, S.M., Derasit, Z., Shariff, S.S.R.: An iterative Newton-Raphson (NR) method on Lee-Carter parameter's estimation for predicting hospital admission rates. Am. Inst. Phys. (AIP) Conf. Proc. **1974**(1) (2018). https://doi.org/10.1063/1.5041580
14. Z-Flores, E., Trujillo, L., Schütze, O., Legrand, P.: A local search approach to genetic programming for binary classification. In: GECCO 2015, pp. 1151–1158. ACM (2015). https://doi.org/10.1145/2739480.2754797

Optimising Optimisers with Push GP

Michael A. Lones(✉)

School of Mathematical and Computer Sciences,
Heriot-Watt University, Edinburgh, UK
m.lones@hw.ac.uk

Abstract. This work uses Push GP to automatically design both local and population-based optimisers for continuous-valued problems. The optimisers are trained on a single function optimisation landscape, using random transformations to discourage overfitting. They are then tested for generality on larger versions of the same problem, and on other continuous-valued problems. In most cases, the optimisers generalise well to the larger problems. Surprisingly, some of them also generalise very well to previously unseen problems, outperforming existing general purpose optimisers such as CMA-ES. Analysis of the behaviour of the evolved optimisers indicates a range of interesting optimisation strategies that are not found within conventional optimisers, suggesting that this approach could be useful for discovering novel and effective forms of optimisation in an automated manner.

Keywords: Genetic Programming · Optimisation · Metaheuristics

1 Introduction

This work is motivated by two issues. First, due to the innate constraints and biases of human thought, it is likely that manual design of optimisers explores only a subspace of optimiser designs. It is unlikely that this subspace contains optimal optimisers for all optimisation problems. Second, recent attempts to create novel optimisers from models of natural systems have been largely unsuccessful in broadening the scope of optimiser designs, instead tending only to generate variants of existing metaheuristic frameworks [9,16]. This work attempts to address both of these issues by using Genetic Programming (GP) to explore the broader space of optimisation algorithms, with the aim of discovering novel optimisation behaviours that differ from those used by existing algorithms. In order to make the optimiser search space as broad as possible, a Turing-complete language, *Push*, is used to represent the optimisers, and the Push GP system is used to optimise them [17]. In [8], this approach was used to evolve local optimisers that can solve continuous-valued problems. In this work, this approach is extended to the population-based case, using Push GP to automatically design both local and population-based optimisers from primitive instructions.

The paper is organised as follows. Section 2 reviews existing work on the automated design of optimisers. Section 3.1 gives a brief overview of the Push

© Springer Nature Switzerland AG 2020
T. Hu et al. (Eds.): EuroGP 2020, LNCS 12101, pp. 101–117, 2020.
https://doi.org/10.1007/978-3-030-44094-7_7

language and the Push GP system, Sect. 3.2 describes how Push GP has been modified to support the evolution of population-based optimisers, and Sect. 3.3 outlines how the optimisers are evaluated. Section 4 presents results and analysis. Section 5 concludes.

2   Related Work

There is a significant history of using GP to optimise optimisers. This can be divided into two areas: using GP to optimise GP, and using GP to optimise other kinds of optimiser. The former approaches use a GP system to optimise the solution generation operators of a GP framework [4,6,17]. Autoconstructive evolution [17] is a particularly open-ended approach to doing this in which programs contains code that generates their own offspring; also notable is that, like our work, it uses the Push language.

However, more relevant is previous work on using GP to optimise non-GP optimisers. Much of this work has taken place within the context of *hyperheuristics*, which involves specialising existing optimisation frameworks so that they are better suited to solving particular problem classes. In this context, GP has been used to re-design components of evolutionary algorithms, such as their mutation [23], recombination [5] and selection operators [13], with the aim of making them better adapted to particular solution landscapes. Other hyperheuristic approaches have used GP to generate new optimisation algorithms by recombining the high-level building blocks of existing metaheuristic frameworks [3,10,12,15]. Recently, this kind of approach has also been used to explore the design space of swarm algorithms, using grammatical evolution to combine high-level building blocks derived from existing metaheuristics [3]. Our approach differs from this, and previous work in hyperheuristics, in that it focuses on designing optimisers largely from scratch. By not reusing or building upon components of existing optimisers, the intention is to reduce the amount of bias in the exploration of optimiser design space, potentially allowing the exploration of previously unexplored areas.

Another recent development, which has some similarities to our work, is the use of deep learning to optimise optimisers [1,11,21]. So far these approaches have focused on improving the training algorithms used by deep learners, i.e. they are somewhat akin to using GP to optimise GP, though it is plausible that deep learning could be applied to the task of designing optimisers for non-neural domains. However, this is arguably an area in which GP is better suited than deep learning, since the optimisers produced by GP are likely to be far more efficient (in terms of runtime) than those produced by deep learning. Runtime efficiency is an important consideration for optimisers, since the same code is typically called over and over again during the course of an optimisation trajectory. Another advantage of GP is the relative interpretability of its solutions when compared to deep learning, and the potential that more general insights could be made into the design of optimisers by studying the code of evolved solutions.

3   Methods

3.1   Push and Push GP

In this work, optimisation behaviours are expressed using the Push language. Push was designed for use within a GP context, and has a number of features that promote evolvability [17–19]. These include the use of stacks, a mechanism that enables evolving programs to maintain state with less fragility than using conventional indexed memory instructions [7]. However, it is also Turing-complete, meaning that it is more expressive that many languages used within GP systems. Another notable strength is its type system, which is designed so that all randomly generated programs are syntactically valid, meaning that (unlike type systems introduced to more conventional forms of GP) there is no need to complicate the variation operators or penalise/repair invalid solutions. This is implemented by means of multiple stacks; each stack contains values of a particular type, and all instructions are typed, and will only execute when values are present on their corresponding type stacks. There are stacks for primitive data types (booleans, floats, integers) and each of these have both special-purpose instructions (e.g. arithmetic instructions for the integer and float stacks, logic operators for the boolean stack) and general-purpose stack instructions (push, pop, swap, duplicate, rot etc.) associated with them. Another important stack is the execution stack. At the start of execution, the instructions in a Push program are placed onto this stack and can be manipulated by special instructions; this allows behaviours like looping and conditional execution to be carried out. Finally, there is an input stack, which remains fixed during execution. This provides a way of passing non-volatile constants to a Push program; when popped from the input stack, corresponding values get pushed to the appropriate type stack. Push programs are evolved using the Push GP system. Since a Push program is basically a list of instructions, it can be represented as a linear array and manipulated using genetic algorithm-like mutation and crossover operators.

3.2   Evolving Population-Based Optimisers

In order to evolve population-based optimisers, this work uses a modified version of Psh (http://spiderland.org/Psh/), a Java implementation of Push GP. To allow programs to store and manipulate search points, an extra vector type has been added to the Push language. This represents search points as fixed-length floating point vectors, and these can be manipulated using the special-purpose vector instructions shown in Table 2; see [8] for more details about these instructions. Evolutionary parameters are shown in Table 1.

Algorithm 1 outlines the procedure for evaluating evolved Push optimisers. To reduce evolutionary effort, a Push program is only required to carry out a single move, or optimisation step, each time it is called. In order to generate an optimisation trajectory within a given search space, the Push program is then called multiple times by an outer loop until a specified evaluation budget has been reached. After each call, the value at the top of the Push program's

Table 1. Psh parameter settings

Population size = 200

Maximum generations = 50

Tournament size = 5

Program size limit = maximum of 100 instructions

Execution limit = maximum of 100 instruction executions per move

Instructions = boolean/float/integer/vector.{dup flush pop rand
rot shove stackdepth swap yank yankdup}; boolean.{= and fromfloat
frominteger not or xor}; exec.{= do*count do*range do*times if iflt
noop}; float.{% * + - / < = > abs cos erc exp fromboolean frominteger
ln log max min neg pow sin tan}; input.{inall inallrev index};
integer.{% * + - / < = > abs erc fromboolean fromfloat ln log max
min neg pow}; vector.{* / + - apply between dim+ dim* dprod mag pop
scale urand wrand zip}; false; true

Table 2. Vector stack instructions

Instruction	Pop from	Push to	Description
vector.+	vector, vector	vector	Add two vectors
vector.-	vector, vector	vector	Subtract two vectors
vector.*	vector, vector	vector	Multiply two vectors
vector./	vector, vector	vector	Divide two vectors
vector.scale	vector, float	vector	Scale vector by scalar
vector.dprod	vector, vector	float	Dot product of two vectors
vector.mag	vector	float	Magnitude of vector
vector.dim+	vector, float, int	vector	Add float to specified component
vector.dim*	vector, float, int	vector	Multiply specified component by float
vector.apply	vector, code	vector	Apply code to each component
vector.zip	vector, vector, code	vector	Apply code to each pair of components
vector.between	vector, vector, float	vector	Generate point between two vectors
vector.rand		vector	Generate random vector of floats
vector.urand		vector	Generate random unit vector
vector.wrand	float	vector	Generate random vector within bounds
vector.current	integer	vector	Get current point of given pop member
vector.best	integer	vector	Get best point of given pop member

vector stack is popped and the corresponding search point is evaluated. The
objective value of this search point, as well as information about whether it was
an improving move and whether it moved outside the problem's search bounds,
are then passed back to the Push program via the relevant type stacks. Since
the contents of a program's stacks are preserved between calls, Push programs
have the capacity to build up their own internal state during the course of an
optimisation run, and consequently the potential to carry out different types of
moves as search progresses.

Algorithm 1. Evaluating an evolved Push GP optimiser

1: $fitness \leftarrow 0$
2: **for** *repeats* **do**   ▷ Measure fitness over multiple optimisation runs
3:     $pbest \leftarrow \infty$
4:     **for** $p \leftarrow 1, popsize$ **do**   ▷ Initialise population state
5:         $prog_p \leftarrow$ copy of evolved Push program
6:         CLEARSTACKS($prog_p$)
7:         $point_p \leftarrow$ random initial point within search bounds
8:         $value_p \leftarrow$ EVALUATE($point_p$)
9:         PUSH($point_p$, $prog_p$.**vector**)   ▷ Pass initial search point to program
10:        PUSH($value_p$, $prog_p$.**float**)   ▷ Pass initial objective value to program
11:        PUSH(**true**, $prog_p$.**boolean**)
12:        PUSH(bounds, $prog_p$.**input**)   ▷ Put search space bounds on input stack
13:        $bestval_p \leftarrow value_p$
14:        **if** $bestval_p < pbest$ **then**
15:            $pbest \leftarrow bestval_p$, $pbestindex \leftarrow p$
16:        **end if**
17:    **end for**
18:    **for** $m \leftarrow 1, moves$ **do**
19:        **for** $p \leftarrow 1, popsize$ **do**
20:            PUSH(m, $prog_p$.**integer**)   ▷ Pass move number to program
21:            PUSH(p, $prog_p$.**integer**)   ▷ Pass population index to program
22:            PUSH($pbestindex$, $prog_p$.**integer**)   ▷ Pass index of pbest to program
23:            $previous \leftarrow value_p$
24:            EXECUTE($prog_p$)
25:            $point_p \leftarrow$ PEEK($prog_p$.**vector**)   ▷ Get next search point from program
26:            **if** $point_p$ is within search bounds **then**
27:                $value_p \leftarrow$ EVALUATE($point_p$)
28:                **if** $value_p < bestval_p$ **then**
29:                    $bestval_p \leftarrow value_p$, $best_p \leftarrow point_p$
30:                **end if**
31:                **if** $value_p < previous$ **then**
32:                    PUSH(**true**, $prog_p$.**boolean**)   ▷ Tell program it improved
33:                **else**
34:                    PUSH(**false**, $prog_p$.**boolean**)   ▷ Tell program it didn't improve
35:                    PUSH($best_p$, $prog_p$.**vector**)   ▷ and remind it of its best point
36:                **end if**
37:                PUSH($value_p$, $prog_p$.**float**)   ▷ Pass new objective value
38:            **else**
39:                PUSH(**false**, $prog_p$.**boolean**)
40:                PUSH(∞, $prog_p$.**float**)   ▷ Or indicate move was out of bounds
41:            **end if**
42:            **if** $best_p < pbest$ **then** $pbest \leftarrow best_p$
43:        **end for**
44:    **end for**
45:    $fitness \leftarrow fitness + pbest$
46: **end for**
47: $fitness \leftarrow fitness/repeats$ ▷ Mean of best objective values found in each repeat

---

To handle population-based optimisation, multiple copies of the Push program are run in parallel, one for each population member. Each copy of the program has its own stacks, so population members are able to build up their internal state independently. Population members are persistent, meaning there is no explicit mechanism to create or destroy them during the course of an optimisation run. To allow coordination between population members, two extra instructions are provided, vector.current and vector.best. These both look up information about another population member's search state, returning either its current or best seen point of search. The target population member is determined by the value at the top of the integer stack (modulus the population size to ensure a valid number); if this stack is empty, or contains a negative value, the current or best search point of the current population member is returned. This sharing mechanism, combined with the use of persistent search processes, means that the evolved optimisers resemble swarm algorithms in their general mechanics. However, there is no selective pressure to use these mechanisms in any particular way, so evolved optimisers are not constrained by the design space of existing swarm optimisers.

3.3   Evaluation

Evolved optimisers are evaluated using a selection of functions taken from the widely used CEC 2005 real-valued parameter optimisation benchmarks [20]. These are all minimisation problems, meaning that the aim is to find the input vector (i.e. the search point) that generates the lowest value when passed as an argument to the function. The functions used during fitness evaluation, which were selected to provide a diverse range of optimisation landscapes, are:

- F_1, the sphere function, a separable unimodal bowl-shaped function. It is the simplest of the benchmarks, and can be solved by gradient descent.
- F_9, Rastrigin's function, has a large number of regularly spaced local optima whose magnitudes curve towards a bowl where the global minimum is found. The difficulty of this function lies in avoiding the many local optima on the path to the global optimum, though it is made easier by the regular spacing, since the distance between local optima basins can in principle be learnt.
- F_{12}, Schwefel's problem number 2.13, is multimodal and has a small number of peaks that can be followed down to a shared valley region. Gradient descent can be used to find the valley, but the difficulty lies in finding the global mimimum, since it contains multiple irregularly-spaced local optima.
- F_{13} is a composition of Griewank's and Rosenbrock's functions. This composition leads to a complex surface that is highly multimodal and irregular, and hence challenging for optimisers to navigate.
- F_{14}, a version of Schaffer's F_6 Function, comprises concentric elliptical ridges. In the centre is a region of greater complexity where the global optimum lies. It is challenging due to the lack of useful gradient information in most places, and the large number of local optima.

To discourage overfitting to a particular problem instance, random transformations are applied to each dimension of these functions when they are used to measure fitness during the course of an evolutionary run. Random translations (of up to ±50% for each axis) prevent the evolving optimisers from learning the location of the optimum, random scalings (50–200% for each axis) prevent them from learning the distance between features of the landscape, and random axis flips (with 50% probability per axis) prevent directional biases, e.g. learning which corner of the landscape contains the global optimum. Fitness is the mean of 10 optimisation runs, each with random initial locations and random transformations. The 10-dimensional versions of the problems are used for training, with an evaluation budget of 1E+3 fitness evaluations (FEs). For the results tables and figures shown in the following section, the best-of-run optimisers are reevaluated over the CEC 2005 benchmark standard of 25 optimisation runs, and random transformations are not applied.

4   Results

For a population-based optimiser, the 1E+3 evaluation budget can be split between the population size and the number of iterations/generations in different ways. In these experiments, splits of (population size × iterations) 50×20, 25×40, 5×200 and 1×1000 are used. The latter is included to give a comparison against local search, i.e. optimisers which only use a single point of search. Figure 1 shows the fitness distributions over 50 evolutionary runs for each of these configurations, where fitness is the mean error when the best-of-run optimisers are reevaluated over 25 optimisation runs. To give an idea of how these error rates compare to established general purpose optimisers, Fig. 1 also reproduces the mean errors achieved by two algorithms from the original CEC 2005 competition. G-CMA-ES [2] is a variant of the Covariance Matrix Adaptation Evolution Strategy (CMA-ES) with the addition of restarts and an increasing population size at each restart; it is a relatively complex algorithm and is generally regarded as the overall winner of the CEC 2005 competition. Differential Evolution (DE) [14], although less successful than G-CMA-ES in the competition, is another example of a well-regarded population-based optimiser.

Figure 1 compares the ability of Push GP to find optimisers with different trade-offs between population size and number of iterations. The distributions show that this trade-off is more important for some problems than others. For F_1, better optimisers are generally found for smaller population sizes, with the 1×1000 distribution having the lowest mean error. This makes sense, because the unimodal F_1 landscape favours intensification over diversification. For F_{12}, the sweet spot appears to be for 5×200, possibly reflecting the number of peaks in the landscape, i.e. 5. For the other problems, the differences appear relatively minor, and effective optimisers could be evolved for all configurations. In most cases, the best optimiser for a particular problem is an outlier within the distributions, so may not reflect any intrinsic benefit of one configuration

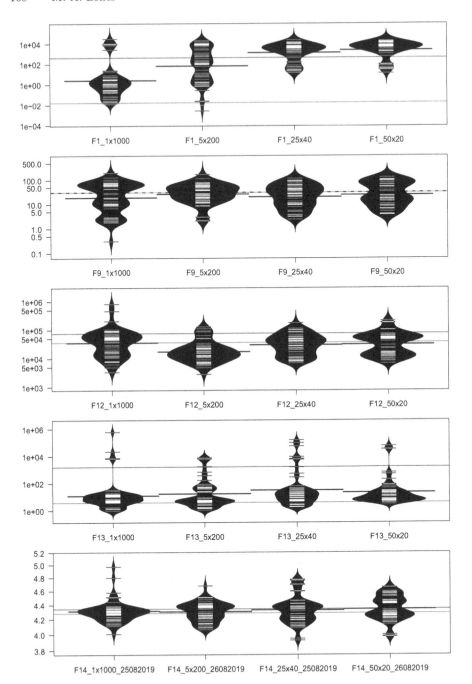

Fig. 1. Fitness distributions of 50 runs for each problem and configuration. The value shown for each run is the mean fitness of the best solution over 25 reevaluations. Published results for CMA-ES (blue) and DE (green) are also shown. (Color figure online)

over another. That said, four of these best-in-problem classifiers used small populations (2 with 1×1000 and 2 with 5×200), so maybe it is easier to find effective optimisers that use small populations than larger ones.

Perhaps more importantly, Fig. 1 shows that the Push GP runs found at least one optimiser that performed better, on average, than CMA-ES and DE. For the simplest problem F_1, there was only one evolved optimiser that beat the general purpose optimisers. For the other problems, many optimisers were found that performed better. This reflects the results in [8], and is perhaps unsurprising given that the capacity to overfit problems is a central motivation for existing work on hyperheuristics. However, an important difference in this paper is the use of random problem transformations during training, since this causes the problems to exhibit greater generality, preventing optimisers from over-learning specific features of the landscape. The results suggest that this does not affect the ability of evolved optimisers to out-perform general purpose optimisers.

This ability to out-perform general purpose optimisers on the problem on which they were trained is arguably not that important. Of more interest is how they generalise to larger and different problems. Table 3 gives an insight into this, showing how well the best evolved optimiser for each training problem generalises to larger instances of the same problem and to the other four problems. Mean error rates are shown both for the 10-dimensional problems with the 1E+3 evaluation budget used in training, and for 30-dimensional versions of the same problems and 1E+4 evaluation budgets. First of all, these figures show that the evolved optimisers do not stop progressing after the 1E+3 solution evaluations on which they were trained, since they make significantly more progress on the same problem when given a budget of 1E+4 solution evaluations. Also, it is evident that most of the optimisers generalise well to 30-dimensional versions of the same problem. The best optimisers evolved on the 10D F_{12}, F_{13} and F_{14} problems do particularly well in this regard, outperforming CMA-ES and DE on both the 10D and 30D versions of the problems. The F_1 optimiser is the only one which generalises relatively poorly, being beaten by CMA-ES, DE and several of the other optimisers on the 30D version.

The most interesting insight from Table 3 is that many of the optimisers also generalise to other problems. For the 10D, 1E+3 evaluations case, all of the optimisers do better than DE when their average rank is taken across all five problems. More surprisingly, the F_{12} optimiser does as well as CMA-ES across all problems, despite only having been trained on one of them. Its average rank does drop slightly when its F_{12} rank is removed from the calculation of its average rank, suggesting it does not generalise quite as well as CMA-ES on the 10D problems. However, the figures for the 30D case are even more surprising, with the F_{12} optimiser doing better across the five problems (even with F_{12} discounted) than CMA-ES. Also notable is that the F_{13} optimiser comes first in three out of the five 30D problems, though this is balanced by coming last in the other two. CMA-ES does do slightly better than the F_{12} optimiser when given a budget of 1E+4 solution evaluations, but the difference is slight, and the best mean error rates for the four most difficult problems are found by the evolved optimisers.

Table 3. Generality of evolved optimisers. For each optimiser, mean errors are shown for 25 optimisation runs on 10D and 30D problems. The mean rank including (and excluding) the problem the optimiser was trained on is also shown, and the best result for each combination of problem dimensionality (D) and fitness evaluation budget (FEs) is underlined for each problem number and ranking.

D	FEs	Optimiser	F_1	F_9	F_{12}	F_{13}	F_{14}	Rank
10	1E+3	CMA-ES	1.70E−2	3.07E+1	3.59E+4	3.84E+0	4.28E+0	<u>3.4</u>
		DE	4.21E+2	3.11E+1	7.48E+4	1.62E+3	4.34E+0	5.0
		F_1 best	<u>2.48E−3</u>	7.28E+1	3.29E+4	5.26E+0	4.47E+0	4.0 (4.8)
		F_9 best	1.32E+4	<u>3.27E−1</u>	9.32E+3	1.18E+0	4.86E+0	3.6 (4.3)
		F_{12} best	3.10E+3	7.28E+0	<u>2.79E+3</u>	2.43E+0	4.52E+0	<u>3.4</u> (4.0)
		F_{13} best	3.56E+4	2.44E+0	4.63E+4	<u>1.05E+0</u>	4.82E+0	4.2 (5.0)
		F_{14} best	4.11E+2	7.76E+1	9.97E+4	2.69E+2	<u>4.04E+0</u>	4.4 (5.3)
	1E+4	CMA-ES	<u>5.20E−9</u>	6.21E+0	2.98E+3	9.71E−1	3.91E+0	<u>2.8</u>
		DE	2.00E+1	<u>5.49E−9</u>	1.64E+4	9.05E+0	4.02E+0	4.2
		F_1 best	2.44E−6	8.05E+1	2.36E+4	3.60E+0	4.50E+0	4.8 (5.5)
		F_9 best	1.45E−3	2.06E−1	7.72E+3	7.04E−1	4.85E+0	3.8 (3.8)
		F_{12} best	5.96E−4	7.47E−2	<u>3.93E+2</u>	4.98E−1	4.21E+0	3.0 (3.5)
		F_{13} best	1.51E−4	3.66E−6	3.07E+4	<u>3.45E−1</u>	4.90E+0	4.0 (4.8)
		F_{14} best	1.37E+1	5.16E+1	3.77E+4	1.62E+1	<u>3.57E+0</u>	5.4 (6.5)
30	1E+3	CMA-ES	<u>8.16E+2</u>	2.53E+2	1.67E+6	1.14E+2	1.42E+1	3.2
		DE	2.06E+4	3.77E+2	1.53E+6	1.62E+5	1.41E+1	4.2
		F_1 best	7.75E+4	4.36E+2	1.07E+6	3.47E+4	1.45E+1	5.2 (5.0)
		F_9 best	7.63E+4	3.24E+2	1.07E+6	4.00E+3	1.45E+1	4.2 (4.3)
		F_{12} best	5.74E+4	1.18E+2	3.46E+5	3.62E+1	1.44E+1	<u>2.8</u> (3.0)
		F_{13} best	1.63E+5	<u>1.00E+2</u>	<u>1.73E+5</u>	<u>1.84E+1</u>	1.47E+1	3.4 (4.0)
		F_{14} best	2.14E+4	4.15E+2	2.19E+6	3.52E+4	<u>1.38E+1</u>	4.6 (5.5)
	1E+4	CMA-ES	<u>5.42E−9</u>	4.78E+1	2.51E+5	3.80E+0	1.38E+1	<u>2.2</u>
		DE	4.71E+0	9.85E+1	9.29E+5	1.02E+2	1.39E+1	4.0
		F_1 best	1.36E+2	3.68E+2	4.08E+5	4.18E+1	1.44E+1	4.8 (5.0)
		F_9 best	6.40E+4	3.27E+2	1.09E+6	3.52E+3	1.46E+1	6.0 (6.3)
		F_{12} best	5.97E−2	5.76E+0	<u>3.43E+4</u>	5.00E+0	1.41E+1	2.4 (2.8)
		F_{13} best	2.44E+4	<u>5.04E−2</u>	1.26E+5	<u>1.42E+0</u>	1.47E+1	3.4 (4.0)
		F_{14} best	1.64E+2	3.33E+2	1.17E+6	3.97E+3	<u>1.33E+1</u>	5.2 (6.3)

Table 4 shows the evolved Push expression used by each best-in-problem optimiser, in each case slightly simplified by removing instructions that have no effect on their fitness. Whilst it is difficult to understand their behaviour by looking at these expressions alone, it is usually possible to gain more insight by observing the interpreter's stack states as they run, and by observing their trajectories on

Table 4. Evolved Push expressions of best-in-problem optimisers

F_1	`(exec.dup float.- vector.- float.pop vector.zip vector.zip`
	`integer.swap float.cos float.- float.cos float.- float.yank`
	`vector.best vector.wrand float.abs float.dup float.frominteger`
	`vector.- vector.dim*)`

F_9	`(input.stackdepth float.frominteger vector.yank vector.wrand`
	`boolean.dup integer.fromboolean vector.swap integer.rot`
	`float.frominteger float.sin vector.yank vector.shove`
	`vector.dim+ vector.yank 0.0 float.> input.inall boolean.not`
	`1 boolean.dup vector.pop boolean.stackdepth)`

F_{12}	`(vector.stackdepth vector.swap float.fromboolean`
	`integer.fromboolean integer.rand vector.dim+ float.+`
	`vector.swap integer.rand 0 vector.swap integer.max`
	`integer.= vector.stackdepth integer.dup vector.- integer.dup`
	`integer.rand vector.- vector.dim+ vector.mag float.frominteger`
	`float.tan integer.rot vector.dim+)`

F_{13}	`(integer.- float.sin vector.wrand integer.yankdup vector.dim*` `vector.- input.inall float.sin vector.-)`

F_{14}	`(float.< float./ vector.best vector.yankdup float.ln float.max`
	`float.stackdepth 0.48999998 float.abs vector.between`
	`vector.wrand vector.scale integer.yank input.index`
	`vector.- float.rand float.neg 0.97999996 float.- 0.97999996`
	`vector.wrand vector.scale vector.-)`

2D versions of the problems on which they were trained. Figure 2 shows examples of the latter; in almost all cases, optimisers generalise well to these easier 2D problems, and it can be seen in each case that the global optimum is found. It can also be seen from the trajectories that the behaviours of the five optimisers are quite diverse, and this is reflected in their program-level behaviours:

- Each particle in the F_1 optimiser looks up the population best and then adds a random vector to this to generate a new search point. Notably, the size of this random vector is determined using a trigonometric expression based on the components of the particle's current and best search points, meaning that the move size carried out by each particle in the population is different.
- The F_9 optimiser (which uses only one point of search) continually switches between searching around the best-seen search point and evaluating a random search point. When searching around the best point, at each iteration it adds the sine of the move number to a single dimension, moving along two dimensions each time; in essence, this causes it to systematically explore the nearby search space, building up the space-filling pattern seen in Fig. 2.
- The F_{12} optimiser is the most complex, and its behaviour at the instruction level is hard to understand. However, it does use the particle's index and the index (but not the vector) of the population best, and both the improvement and out-of-bounds Boolean signals to determine each move. By observing its

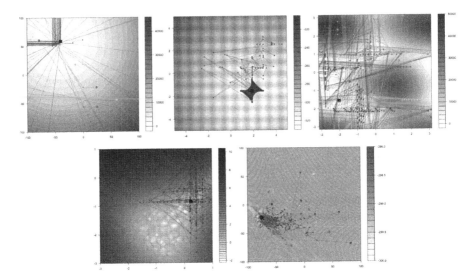

Fig. 2. Example trajectories of the best-in-problem optimisers (F_1, F_9 & F_{12} top, F_{13} & F_{14} bottom) on the 2D versions of the benchmark problems they were trained on. The global minimum is shown as a black circle. The best point reached by the optimiser is shown as a black cross. Each population member's trajectory is shown as a separate colour, with each search point shown as a point. Initial search points are surrounded by small coloured circles. The search landscape is shown in the background as a contour plot. (Color figure online)

search trajectories, it is evident that it builds up a geometric pattern that causes it to explore moves with a power series distribution—in essence, a novel form of variable neighbourhood search.

- The F_{13} optimiser, by comparison, has the simplest program. Each iteration, it adds a random value to one of the dimensions of the best-seen search point, cycling through the dimensions on each subsequent move (hence why it generates a cross-shaped trajectory). The size of the move (the upper bound of the random value) is determined by both the sine of the objective value of the current point and the sine of the maximum dimension size, the former causing it to vary cyclically as search progresses, and the latter allowing it to adapt the move size to the search area.

- The F_{14} optimiser is the only one which uses both a larger population and the `vector.between` instruction. Each iteration, it uses this to generate a new population of search points half-way between the population best and one of each particle's previous positions. Interestingly, which previous position is used for a particular particle is determined by its index; the first particle uses its current position, higher numbered particles go back further in time. This may allow backtracking, which could be useful for landscapes that are deceptive and have limited gradient information (such as F_{14}). A small random vector is added to each half-way point, presumably to inject further diversity.

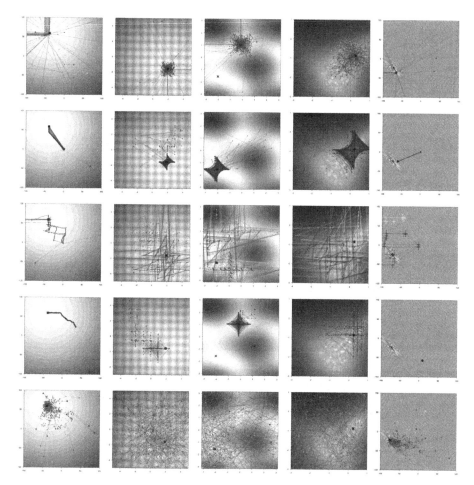

Fig. 3. Examples of the best evolved optimisers for each problem (top to bottom: F_1, F_9, F_{12}, F_{13}, F_{14}) applied to each of the other problems (left-right: F_1, F_9, F_{12}, F_{13}, F_{14}). See caption of Fig. 2 for more information.

Figure 3 shows examples of trajectories when each of these optimisers are applied to 2D versions of the other four problems. These suggest that optimisers may fail to generalise not because of intrinsic assumptions about properties of landscapes, but because they make assumptions about the dimensions of the search area. For example, the F_9 and F_{13} optimisers appear to fail on the F_{14} landscape because they are making moves, or sampling regions, which are only appropriate for a landscape with much smaller overall dimensions. Using a larger range of random scalings during training might help with this.

However, these optimisers were not evolved for generality, so the fact that most of them generalise to other problems is a fortunate bi-product. Furthermore, it is likely that the optimisers that do best on one problem are not likely

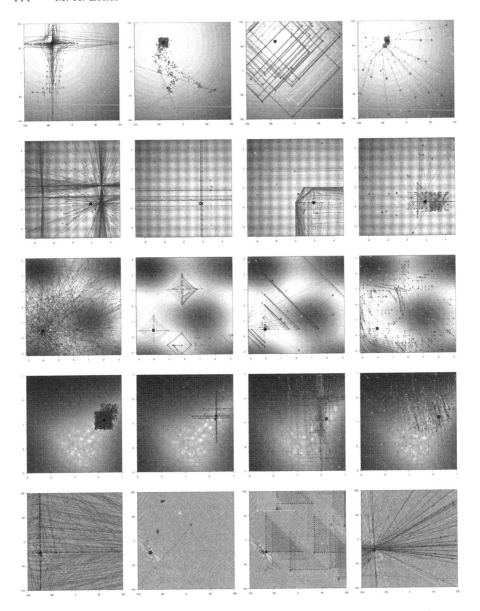

Fig. 4. Trajectories of other evolved optimisers. One example is shown for each combination of problem (top to bottom: F_1, F_9, F_{12}, F_{13}, F_{14}) and population size (left to right: 1, 5, 25, 50). See caption of Fig. 2 for more information.

to be the best in terms of generality. Hence, in practice there is likely to be a benefit to looking at the best optimisers from the other 245 runs depicted in Fig. 1. Figure 4 gives a snapshot of these, showing one example for each combination of training problem and optimiser population size. These illustrate some of the broad diversity seen amongst the solutions. Many of these trajectories look nothing like conventional optimisers, so it is likely that interesting ideas of how to do optimisation could be gained by looking more closely at them. Another interesting direction for future work would be to consider ensembles of optimisers. There are many potential ways of doing this. For example, early results suggest that it may be advantageous, in terms of generality, to form a heterogenous population-based optimiser by combining the best programs from multiple runs.

5   Conclusions

In recent years, there has been a lot of criticism of the *ad hoc* design of new optimisers through mimicry of natural phenomena. Despite early success with evolutionary algorithms and particle swarm optimisation, this trend has increasingly resulted in optimisers that are technically novel, but which differ in minor and often arbitrary ways from existing optimisers. If we are to create new optimisation algorithms (and the no free lunch theorem [22] suggests a need for diverse optimisers), then perhaps it is better to do this in a more systematic, objective and automated manner. This paper contributes towards this direction of research by investigating the utility of Push GP for exploring the space of optimisers. The results show that Push GP can both discover and express optimisation behaviours that are effective, complex and diverse. Encouragingly, the evolved optimisers scale to problems they did not see during training, and often out-perform general purpose optimisers on these previously unseen problems. The behavioural analysis shows that the evolved optimisers use a diverse range of metaheuristic strategies to explore optimisation landscapes, using behaviours that differ significantly from existing local and population-based optimisers. Furthermore, these are only the tip of the iceberg; the evolved optimiser populations appear to contain broad behavioural diversity, and there are many potential ways of combining diverse optimisers to create ensembles.

References

1. Andrychowicz, M., et al.: Learning to learn by gradient descent by gradient descent. In: Advances in Neural Information Processing Systems (2016)
2. Auger, A., Hansen, N.: A restart CMA evolution strategy with increasing population size. In: Proceedings of the IEEE Congress on Evolutionary Computation, IEEE CEC 2005, vol. 2, pp. 1769–1776. IEEE (2005)
3. Bogdanova, A., Junior, J.P., Aranha, C.: Franken-swarm: grammatical evolution for the automatic generation of swarm-like meta-heuristics. In: Proceedings of the Genetic and Evolutionary Computation Conference Companion, GECCO 2019, pp. 411–412. ACM (2019)
4. Edmonds, B.: Meta-genetic programming: Co-evolving the operators of variation. Technical report CPM Report 98–32, Manchester Metropolitan University (1998)

5. Goldman, B.W., Tauritz, D.R.: Self-configuring crossover. In: Proceedings of the Genetic and Evolutionary Computation Conference Companion, GECCO 2011, pp. 575–582. ACM (2011)
6. Kantschik, W., Dittrich, P., Brameier, M., Banzhaf, W.: Meta-Evolution in Graph GP. In: Poli, R., Nordin, P., Langdon, W.B., Fogarty, T.C. (eds.) EuroGP 1999. LNCS, vol. 1598, pp. 15–28. Springer, Heidelberg (1999). https://doi.org/10.1007/3-540-48885-5_2
7. Langdon, W.B.: Genetic Programming And Data Structures: Genetic Programming + Data Structures = Automatic Programming!. Springer, New York (2012). https://doi.org/10.1007/978-1-4615-5731-9
8. Lones, M.A.: Instruction-level design of local optimisers using push GP. In: Proceedings of the Genetic and Evolutionary Computation Conference Companion, GECCO 2019, pp. 1487–1494. ACM (2019)
9. Lones, M.A.: Mitigating metaphors: a comprehensible guide to recent nature-inspired algorithms. SN Comput. Sci. 1(1), 49 (2020)
10. Martin, M.A., Tauritz, D.R.: Evolving black-box search algorithms employing genetic programming. In: Proceedings of the Genetic and Evolutionary Computation Conference Companion, GECCO 2013, pp. 1497–1504. ACM (2013)
11. Metz, L., Maheswaranathan, N., Nixon, J., Freeman, D., Sohl-dickstein, J.: Learned optimizers that outperform SGD on wall-clock and test loss. In: Proceedings of the 2nd Workshop on Meta-Learning. MetaLearn 2018 (2018)
12. Oltean, M.: Evolving evolutionary algorithms using linear genetic programming. Evol. Comput. 13(3), 387–410 (2005)
13. Richter, S.N., Tauritz, D.R.: The automated design of probabilistic selection methods for evolutionary algorithms. In: Proceedings of the Genetic and Evolutionary Computation Conference Companion, GECCO 2018, pp. 1545–1552. ACM (2018)
14. Ronkkonen, J., Kukkonen, S., Price, K.V.: Real-parameter optimization with differential evolution. In: Proceedings of the IEEE Congress on Evolutionary Computation, IEEE CEC 2005, vol. 1, pp. 506–513. IEEE (2005)
15. Ryser-Welch, P., Miller, J.F., Swan, J., Trefzer, M.A.: Iterative cartesian genetic programming: creating general algorithms for solving travelling salesman problems. In: Heywood, M.I., McDermott, J., Castelli, M., Costa, E., Sim, K. (eds.) EuroGP 2016. LNCS, vol. 9594, pp. 294–310. Springer, Cham (2016). https://doi.org/10.1007/978-3-319-30668-1_19
16. Sörensen, K.: Metaheuristics–the metaphor exposed. Int. Trans. Oper. Res. 22(1), 3–18 (2015)
17. Spector, L.: Autoconstructive evolution: push, pushGP, and pushpop. In: Proceedings of the Genetic and Evolutionary Computation Conference, GECCO 2019, vol. 137 (2001)
18. Spector, L., Perry, C., Klein, J., Keijzer, M.: Push 3.0 programming language description. Technical report, HC-CSTR-2004-02, School of Cognitive Science, Hampshire College (2004)
19. Spector, L., Robinson, A.: Genetic programming and autoconstructive evolution with the push programming language. Genet. Program Evolvable Mach. 3(1), 7–40 (2002)
20. Suganthan, P.N., et al.: Problem definitions and evaluation criteria for the CEC 2005 special session on real-parameter optimization, KanGAL report, 2005005 (2005)
21. Wichrowska, O., et al.: Learned optimizers that scale and generalize. In: Proceedings of the 34th International Conference on Machine Learning-Volume 70, ICML 2017, pp. 3751–3760 (2017)

22. Wolpert, D.H., Macready, W.G.: No free lunch theorems for optimization. IEEE Trans. Evol. Comput. **1**(1), 67–82 (1997)
23. Woodward, J.R., Swan, J.: The automatic generation of mutation operators for genetic algorithms. In: Proceedings of the Genetic and Evolutionary Computation Conference, GECCO 2012, pp. 67–74. ACM (2012)

An Evolutionary View on Reversible Shift-Invariant Transformations

Luca Mariot[1(✉)], Stjepan Picek[1], Domagoj Jakobovic[2], and Alberto Leporati[3]

[1] Cyber Security Research Group, Delft University of Technology,
Mekelweg 2, Delft, The Netherlands
{L.Mariot,S.Picek}@tudelft.nl
[2] Faculty of Electrical Engineering and Computing, University of Zagreb,
Unska 3, Zagreb, Croatia
domagoj.jakobovic@fer.hr
[3] DISCo, Università degli Studi di Milano-Bicocca,
Viale Sarca 336/14, 20126 Milano, Italy
alberto.leporati@unimib.it

Abstract. We consider the problem of evolving a particular kind of shift-invariant transformation – namely, Reversible Cellular Automata (RCA) defined by conserved landscape rules – using GA and GP. To this end, we employ three different optimization strategies: a single-objective approach carried out with GA and GP where only the reversibility constraint of marker CA is considered, a multi-objective approach based on GP where both reversibility and the Hamming weight are taken into account, and a lexicographic approach where GP first optimizes only the reversibility property until a conserved landscape rule is obtained, and then maximizes the Hamming weight while retaining reversibility. The results are discussed in the context of three different research questions stemming from exhaustive search experiments on conserved landscape CA, which concern (1) the difficulty of the associated optimization problem for GA and GP, (2) the utility of conserved landscape CA in the domain of cryptography and reversible computing, and (3) the relationship between the reversibility property and the Hamming weight.

Keywords: Shift-invariant transformations · Cellular automata · Reversibility · Genetic Programming · Genetic Algorithms

1 Introduction

The property of *shift-invariance* plays an important role in studying and modeling several types of discrete dynamical systems. In particular, any translation of the input state results in the same translation of the output state in a system governed by a shift-invariant transformation. When the state of the system is described by a finite array, shift-invariant transformations are *cellular automata* (CA), i.e., functions defined by a local update rule which is uniformly applied at

T. Hu et al. (Eds.): EuroGP 2020, LNCS 12101, pp. 118–134, 2020.
https://doi.org/10.1007/978-3-030-44094-7_8

all sites of the array. Due to their simplicity and versatility, CA have been studied as models for simulating a wide variety of dynamical systems (see e.g. [1]).

Reversible shift-invariant transformations, and in particular Reversible CA (RCA) have the additional characteristic of preserving information. Thus, the dynamics of an RCA can be reversed backward in time starting from any state, and the inverse mapping is itself a CA. This makes RCA especially interesting for the design of energy-efficient computing devices since as stated by *Landauer's principle* [2] any *irreversible* logical operation implemented in hardware leads to the dissipation of heat, hence posing a physical lower bound on the miniaturization of devices based on irreversible gates. Another domain of interest is *cryptography*, where RCA can be used to design encryption and decryption algorithms [3].

Despite the extensive body of literature about RCA, up to now only a few classes of reversible CA are known (see [4] for a concise survey). Moreover, although such RCA are characterized in terms of relatively simple combinatorial definitions, there are no straightforward ways to construct them by taking into account further criteria that are of interest for practical applications. In this regard, *Evolutionary Algorithms* (EAs) represent an interesting method to investigate known RCA classes concerning these additional design criteria, since exhaustively searching for all possible RCA becomes unfeasible for large local rule sizes. To the best of our knowledge, this research method has not been pursued before, although some authors employed EA to evolve CA featuring certain properties other than reversibility [5,6].

The aim of this paper is to start the investigation of RCA by means of Genetic Algorithms (GA) and Genetic Programming (GP), focusing in particular on the class of reversible *marker* CA. There, the local update rule flips the state of a cell if its neighbors take on a set of patterns (or *landscapes*), which are *conserved* by the resulting shift-invariant transformation [7]. The motivation of our goal is twofold. First, the local rules of marker CA have a simple description through their *generating functions*, which leads to a natural formulation of the optimization objective for the reversibility property by minimizing the *compatibility* of its flipping landscapes. Second, the *Hamming weight* of a generating function in a marker CA is a good indicator of its *nonlinearity*, a fundamental property in cryptography, as well as of its dynamical behavior, which is relevant in the design of reversible computing devices. Consequently, maximizing the Hamming weight of the generating function can be considered as a further optimization objective in addition to reversibility.

After defining the genotype encodings for GA and GP to represent the candidate marker CA and the fitness function for reversibility, we set up three different research questions which consider the difficulty of the optimization problem for GA and GP, the utility of reversible marker CA for applications, and the relationship between reversibility and Hamming weight. We address this questions by organizing our experiments in three phases. In the first phase, we adopt a *single-objective* approach where only the reversibility of marker CA is optimized. In particular, our results show that both GA and GP always manage to generate reversible marker CA over all considered problem instances, although with different performances. In the second phase, we consider a *multi-objective* (MO) approach with GP, where we optimize both the reversibility and the Hamming weight of marker CA. The Pareto fronts approximated by our MOGP algorithm clearly show that there is a trade-off between these two properties: the higher is the Hamming weight of a generating function, the lower will be the reversibility of the resulting marker CA. Finally, in the third phase, we use a *lexicographic optimization* strategy, where we first use GP to optimize only the reversibility property, and then maximize the Hamming weight when a reversible solution is found. With this approach, we manage to obtain a better coverage of reversible marker CA in terms of the Hamming weights.

The rest of this paper is organized as follows. Section 2 covers the necessary background notions about shift-invariant transformations and reversible CA. Section 3 defines the optimization problem for reversible marker CA with conserved landscapes, discusses the genotype encodings for GA and GP, and defines the fitness function for the reversibility property. Section 4 briefly reviews the existing literature about the use of evolutionary algorithms to design CA for specific purposes, such as in cryptography. Section 5 presents and discusses the results of our experiments organized into three phases. Finally, Sect. 6 sums up the main findings of the paper and sketches some directions for future work.

2   Background

2.1   Shift-Invariant Transformations and Cellular Automata

Let A be a finite alphabet and $A^{\mathbb{Z}}$ be the *full-shift space* of bi-infinite strings over A. In the field of symbolic dynamics, *shift-invariant transformations* are those mappings $F : A^{\mathbb{Z}} \to A^{\mathbb{Z}}$ that commute with the *shift operator*. *Cellular Automata* (CA) are a particular class of shift-invariant transformations whose output is determined by the uniform application of a single *local update rule* over all components (or *cells*) of a bi-infinite string. In this work, we focus only on shift-invariant transformations over finite arrays, which coincide with finite CA; thus, in what follows we will use the term CA and shift-invariant transformation interchangeably.

Various models of CA can be defined depending on the dimension of the lattice, the alphabet of the cells, and the boundary conditions. In this work, we focus on one-dimensional periodic Boolean CA, defined as follows:

Definition 1. *A one-dimensional periodic Boolean CA (for short, a PBCA) of length n, diameter d, offset ω, and local rule $f : \{0,1\}^d \to \{0,1\}$ is defined by a vectorial function $F : \{0,1\}^n \to \{0,1\}^n$ where for all vectors $x \in \{0,1\}^n$ and $0 \le i \le n - 1$ the i-th component of the output is defined as:*

$$F(x)_i = f(x_{[i-\omega,i-\omega+d-1]}) = f(x_{i-\omega}, x_{i-\omega+1}, \cdots, x_{i-1}, x_i, x_{i+1}, \cdots, x_{i-\omega+d-1})$$
(1)

with all indices being computed modulo n. Function F is also called the global rule *of the CA.*

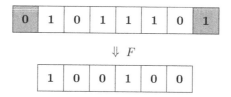

Fig. 1. Example of CA based on rule 150.

In other words, a PBCA is composed of a one-dimensional vector of n cells that can be either in state 0 or 1, where each cell simultaneously updates its state by applying the local rule f on the neighborhood formed by itself, the ω cells on its left and the $d - 1 - \omega$ cells on its right. Here, "periodic" refers to the fact that all indices are computed modulo n: in this way, the leftmost ω cells and the rightmost $d - 1 - \omega$ ones respectively have enough left and right neighboring cells in order to apply the local rule. In particular, the state vector of a PBCA can be seen as a ring, with the first cell following the last one. In the following, we will refer to PBCA simply as CA, since the former is the main CA model considered in this work.

Since the cells of a CA take binary values, the local rule can be seen as a *Boolean function* $f : \mathbb{F}_2^d \to \mathbb{F}_2$ of d variables where $\mathbb{F}_2 = \{0, 1\}$ is the finite field of two elements, and thus it can be represented by its *truth table*, which specifies for each of the possible 2^d input vectors $x \in \mathbb{F}_2^d$ the corresponding output value $f(x) \in \mathbb{F}_2$. Assuming that the input vectors of $\mathbb{F}_2^d$ are sorted lexicographically, one can encode the truth table as a single binary string $\Omega_f \in \mathbb{F}_2^{2^d}$, which is basically the output column of the table. In the CA literature, the decimal encoding of Ω_f is also called the *Wolfram code* of the local rule f [8]. Figure 1 reports an example of CA with $n = 6$ cells, diameter $d = 3$, offset $\omega = 1$, and local rule defined as $f(x_{i-1}, x_i, x_{i+1}) = x_{i-1} \oplus x_i \oplus x_{i+1}$, which corresponds to Wolfram code 150. Hence, each cell looks at itself and its left and right neighbors in order to compute its next state through rule 150. The two cells shaded in grey in Fig. 1 represent "copies" respectively of the first and the last cell, in order to better visualize the neighborhoods of the cells at the boundaries.

2.2   Reversible CA

Reversibility is a particular property featured by certain dynamical systems where the orbits are cycles without transient parts or pre-periods. In particular, the orbits of a reversible system can also be run backward in time, since each state has exactly one predecessor, and the "inverse system" is analogous to the original one. In the CA context, this means that the global rule of a reversible CA must be bijective (to ensure that each global state of the cellular array has exactly one predecessor) and its inverse must also be a CA, that is, F^{-1} must be defined by a local rule.

Hedlund [9] showed that an infinite CA is reversible if and only if its global rule is bijective. On the other hand, the relationship between bijectivity and reversibility is more complicated in the case of finite CA. In particular, if we know that a local rule f induces a bijective global rule on a CA of a certain length $n \in \mathbb{N}$, then the inverse global rule is not necessarily defined by a local rule, nor it is the case, in general, that the global rule remains bijective for different lengths of the CA using the same local rule.

Local rules that generate bijective global rules only for certain lengths $n \in \mathbb{N}$ of the CA array and whose inverses cannot be described by local rules are also called *globally invertible*. An example is the χ transformation used in the KECCAK sponge construction for hash functions [10], which corresponds to a CA of length $n = 5$ and it is defined by the local rule of diameter $d = 3$ with Wolfram code 210. The offset of this CA is $\omega = 0$, which means that each cell applies rule 210 over itself and the two cells to its right to update its state. Daemen [11] showed that rule 210 is globally invertible, since it induces a bijective global rule only for odd CA lengths.

On the other hand, a local rule that induces a bijective global function for all finite lengths $n \in \mathbb{N}$ of the CA array is called *locally invertible*. In this case, the inverse mapping is also defined by a local rule, possibly of a different diameter, and thus the resulting CA is reversible. In what follows, we will consider the search of locally invertible rules as an optimization problem, focusing on the class of marker CA.

2.3   Marker CA

A *marker CA* (or *complementing landscape CA* [7]) is defined by a local rule that always complements the bit of the cell whose state is being updated whenever the cells in its neighborhood form a particular pattern (or *marker*, hence the name). Otherwise, the cell keeps its current state. The set of patterns defining a local rule of a marker CA can be conveniently formalized through the concept of *landscape*, which we define below:

Definition 2. *Let* $d, \omega \in \mathbb{N}$ *with* $\omega < d$. *A landscape of width* d *and center* ω *is a string* $L = l_0 l_1 \cdots l_{\omega-1} \star l_{\omega+1} \cdots l_{d-1}$ *where* $l_i \in \{0, 1, -\}$ *for all* $i \neq \omega$.

The $\star$ symbol in a landscape L is used to indicate the *origin* of the neighborhood in the local rule (that is, the cell whose state is being updated), and thus it occurs at position ω. The $-$ symbol represents a "don't care", meaning that the corresponding cell can be either in state 0 or 1. Hence, landscapes can be considered as a restricted form of regular expressions over the binary alphabet $\{0, 1\}$, where the don't care symbol stands for the regular expression $(0+1)$ (i.e., both 0 and 1 match).

A local rule of a marker CA can be described by one or more landscapes, all having the same width d and center ω. In particular, in the multiple landscape case, a cell is flipped if its neighborhood partakes on any of the patterns included in the union $\bigcup_{i=1}^{k} L_i$ of the landscapes $L_1, \cdots, L_k$ that define the locale rule. Observe that it is possible to define a partial order $\leq_C$ over the set of landscapes.

Namely, given two landscapes $L = l_0 \cdots l_{d-1}$ and $M = m_0 \cdots m_{d-1}$ with the same width d and center ω, we define

$$L \leq_C M \Leftrightarrow l_i = m_i \text{ or } l_i \in \{0,1\} \text{ and } m_i = - \tag{2}$$

for all $0 \leq i \leq d-1$. Intuitively, this partial order describes the "generality" of a landscape: the more don't care symbols it has, the more patterns it contains. The extreme cases are the *atomic landscapes* that do not contain any don't care symbol, which describe only single patterns, and the landscape composed only of don't cares, which includes all possible patterns. In what follows, we will refer to $\leq_C$ as the *compatibility* partial order relation. In particular, we will call two landscapes L_1, L_2 with the same width d and center ω *compatible* if $L_1 \leq_C L_2$ or $L_2 \leq_C L_1$. Otherwise, if L_1 and L_2 are not comparable with respect to the partial order relation $\leq_C$, we will say that they are *incompatible*.

The compatibility order relation can be used to characterize a subset of reversible marker CA, namely those of the *conserved landscape* type. In such CA, a cell that is in a particular landscape L defined by the local rule will still be in the *same* landscape upon application of the global rule. This property can be formalized by requiring that the cells in the neighborhood are in landscapes that are incompatible with L, as shown in the following result proved in [7]:

Lemma 1. *Let $f : \mathbb{F}_2^d \to \mathbb{F}_2$ be a local rule of a marker CA defined by a set of k landscapes $L_1, \cdots, L_k$ of width d and center ω. Further, for all $i \in \{1, \cdots, k\}$ let $M_{i,0}, \cdots, M_{i,\omega-1}, M_{i,\omega+1}, \cdots, M_{i,d-1}$ be the set of $d-1$ landscapes associated to the neighborhood of L_i. Then, if $M_{i,j}$ is incompatible with all landscapes $L_1, \cdots, L_k$ for all $i \in \{1, \cdots, k\}$ and $j \in \{0, \cdots, \omega-1, \omega+1, \cdots, d-1\}$, rule f induces a locally invertible marker CA.*

When the conditions of Lemma 1 are fulfilled, we also say that f is a *conserved landscape* rule. As noted in [7], a conserved landscape local rule induces an *involution*, i.e., the global rule of the resulting marker CA equals its own inverse. This is due to the fact that any cell being in one of the marker landscapes will still be in the same landscape after applying the local rule. After a further application of the local rule, the cell will go back to its initial state.

Hence, conserved landscape rules define a particular type of reversible CA, since all cycles have length 2. Daemen [11] argued that such CA can be useful in those cryptographic applications where both the encryption and decryption functions must be implemented in hardware. As noted in [7], one can relax the conditions of Lemma 1 by allowing the landscapes of the local rule to partially *overlap* one another. In this case, a cell that is in a landscape defined by the local rule will be in any of the other landscapes defined by the local rule after applying the global rule. As a consequence, the resulting marker CA can exhibit more complex behaviors, with longer cycle lengths.

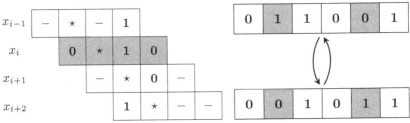

(a) Landscape tabulation for rule $0 \star 10$.   (b) Example of cycle of length 2.

Fig. 2. A locally invertible CA defined by the single landscape $0 \star 10$.

To better illustrate the idea, we conclude this section by showing an example of a single conserved landscape rule of diameter $d = 4$, originally discovered by Patt [12]:

Example 1. Let $d = 4$ and $\omega = 1$, and let $f : \mathbb{F}_2^4 \to \mathbb{F}_2$ be the local rule defined by the single landscape $L = 0 \star 10$. The tabulation depicted in Fig. 2a shows that all three landscapes of the neighboring cells are incompatible with L. In particular, when x_i is in landscape L, then:

- Cell x_{i-1} is in landscape $- \star -1$, which is incompatible with $0 \star 10$ since there is a mismatch in position 3.
- Cell x_{i+1} is in landscape $- \star 0-$, which is incompatible with $0 \star 10$ since there is a mismatch in position 2.
- Cell x_{i+2} is in landscape $1 \star --$, which is incompatible with $0 \star 10$ since there is a mismatch in position 0.

Figure 2b displays an example of cycle starting from the initial state 011001. The two cells shaded in grey are in the landscape $0 \star 10$.

3   Optimizing Landscapes

3.1   Genotype Representation for Marker CA

Lemma 1 states that a conserved landscape CA can be constructed by searching for a set of landscapes $L_1, \cdots, L_k$ such that their associated neighborhood landscapes are incompatible with them. To perform such a search through Evolutionary Algorithms such as GA and GP, the first question is how to encode the genotype of the candidate solutions. In particular, since GA usually works on a bitstring encoding of the candidate solutions while GP relies on a tree representation, directly using the landscape specification of a marker CA rule does not seem a straightforward choice for encoding the genotype.

Let $L_1, \cdots, L_k$ be a set of landscapes of diameter d and center ω defining a local rule $f : \mathbb{F}_2^d \to \mathbb{F}_2$. Additionally, let $\mathcal{L} = \bigcup_{i=1}^k L_i$ be the union of the landscapes, and define $\nu = x_{i-\omega} \cdots x_{i-1} x_{i+1} \cdots x_{i+d-1-\omega}$ be the vector of $d-1$

variables describing the states of the cells in the neighborhood of the cell at position i. Consider now the *generating function* $g : \mathbb{F}_2^{d-1} \to \mathbb{F}_2$ that outputs 1 if and only if the pattern formed by inserting the origin symbol $\star$ in vector ν at position ω belongs to $\mathcal{L}$. Then, the local rule of the marker CA can be defined as:

$$f(x_{i-\omega} \cdots x_{i-1} x_i x_{i+1} \cdots x_{i+d-1-\omega}) = x_i \oplus g(x_{i-\omega} \cdots x_{i-1} x_{i+1} \cdots x_{i+d-1-\omega}) \tag{3}$$

for all neighborhood configuration $x_{i-\omega} \cdots x_{i-1} x_i x_{i+1} \cdots x_{i+d-1-\omega} \in \mathbb{F}_2^d$. Hence, the algebraic expression of the local rule of a marker CA can be expressed as the XOR of the cell in the origin with the generating function g computed on the surrounding cells. This is due to the fact that g evaluates to 1 if and only if the neighborhood takes on any of the landscapes in $\mathcal{L}$.

Consequently, we can reduce the representation of the local rule f of a marker CA to its generating function g. In particular, for GA we take the 2^{d-1}-bit string of the truth table Ω_g as encoding for the candidate solution. For GP, we use a tree where the terminal nodes represent the input variables of g, while the internal nodes are Boolean operators combining the values received from their child nodes and propagating their output to their parent node. The output of the root node will be the output of the whole generating function g.

3.2   Fitness Functions

We can now define the fitness function used to drive the search of conserved landscape CA rules. Suppose that we have the truth table of a generating function g, and let $supp(g) = \{x \in \mathbb{F}_2^{d-1} : g(x) \neq 0\}$ be the *support* of g, i.e., the set of input vectors over which g evaluates to 1. By construction, the elements of $supp(g)$ coincide with all patterns that the cells surrounding the origin must feature to flip the state of the central cell. To obtain the list of atomic landscapes, it just suffices to insert the origin symbol $\star$ in position ω to each vector of the support. The set of atomic landscapes obtained from the support can be used to check if a rule is of the conserved landscape type or not. In fact, it is not difficult to see that two landscapes with don't care symbols in them are incompatible if and only if all the atomic landscapes that they describe are incompatible between themselves. This means that we can directly use the support of the generating function to *count* the number of pairs of landscapes that are compatible.

Given that we want to minimize such number to get a conserved landscape rule, we define the following fitness function. Let $g : \mathbb{F}_2^{d-1} \to \mathbb{F}_2$ be a generating function of a marker CA rule $f : \mathbb{F}_2^d \to \mathbb{F}_2$ of diameter d and offset ω, and let $supp(g)$ be its support. Further, let $L_1, \cdots, L_k$ be the set of atomic landscapes obtained by adding the origin symbol $\star$ in position ω to each vector in $supp(g)$, and for each $i \in \{1, \cdots, k\}$ let $M_{i,0}, \cdots, M_{i,\omega-1}, M_{i,\omega+1}, \cdots, M_{i,d-1}$ be the set of neighborhood landscapes associated to L_i obtained through the tabulation procedure. Then, the *reversibility fitness* value of g is defined as:

$$fit_1(g) = \sum_{i,t \in [k], j \in [d-1]_\omega} comp(M_{i,j}, L_t), \tag{4}$$

where $[k] = \{1, \cdots, k\}$, $[d-1]_\omega = \{0, \cdots, \omega-1, \omega+1, \cdots, d-1\}$, and the function $comp(\cdot, \cdot)$ returns 1 if the two landscapes passed as arguments are compatible, and 0 otherwise. Hence, the fitness function loops over all neighborhood landscapes $M_{i,j}$ induced by each atomic landscape L_i, compares each of these neighborhood landscapes with all atomic landscapes $L_1, \cdots, L_k$ through the function $comp(\cdot, \cdot)$, and adds 1 whenever a compatible pair is found. Therefore, the fitness function fit_1 measures the degree of compatibility of a set of atomic landscapes induced by the support of a generating function g. Consequently, the optimization objective is to *minimize* fit_1, with $fit_1(g) = 0$ corresponding to an optimal solution where all neighborhood landscapes are incompatible with the atomic landscapes, and thus the latter define a conserved landscape rule.

A good indicator of the complexity of the dynamical behavior of a marker CA is the *Hamming weight* of its generating function g, i.e., the cardinality of its support. This can be used both as a utility measure of a marker CA in cryptography (where it is related to the *nonlinearity* of the CA) and in designing reversible computing circuits. Given a generating function g, we thus define a second optimization objective by maximizing the following fitness function:

$$fit_2(g) = |supp(g)|. \tag{5}$$

4   Related Work

As already stated, this work is the first to use Evolutionary Algorithms to evolve reversible shift-invariant transformations. As such, there are no related works on the topic. Still, we mention several characteristic works where EAs are used to evolve shift-invariant transformations or related objects.

Bäck and Breukelaar used genetic algorithms to evolve behavior in CA where the authors explored different neighborhood shapes [6]. Sipper and Tomassini [13] proposed a cellular programming algorithm to co-evolve the rule map of non-uniform CA for designing random number generators. For a somewhat outdated, but very detailed overview of works using GA to evolve CA, we refer readers to [5]. Picek et al. demonstrated that GP can be used to evolve CA rules that then produce S-boxes with good cryptographic properties [14]. Next, Picek et al. used the same technique to further demonstrate that the S-boxes obtained from the CA rules have good implementation properties [15]. Mariot et al. conducted a more detailed analysis of the S-boxes based on CA where they also proved what are the best possible values for relevant cryptographic properties if one uses CA rules of a certain size [3]. There, the authors used GP to experimentally validate their findings but also to reverse engineer a CA rule from a given S-box. Mariot et al. used EA to construct orthogonal Latin squares based on CA [16]. Finally, the evolution of CA rules for cryptographic purposes is connected with the evolution of Boolean functions with good cryptographic properties. There, there are several works considering various evolutionary approaches, see for example [17,18].

5   Experiments

5.1   Research Questions and Experimental Setting

As noted in Sect. 3.1, the local rule of a marker CA of diameter d can be identified with its generating function g of $d - 1$ variables which is computed on the neighborhood cells surrounding the origin, since the state of the central cell is simply XORed with the result of g. Given a diameter $d \in \mathbb{N}$, this means that we can define the phenotype space as the set $\mathcal{P}(d) = \{g : \mathbb{F}_2^{d-1} \to \mathbb{F}_2\}$ of all Boolean functions of $d - 1$ variables. The genotype space, on the other hand, will correspond to the set of all binary strings of length 2^{d-1} specifying the truth tables Ω_g of the generating functions in $\mathcal{P}(d)$, while for GP it will be the space of all Boolean trees whose terminals represent the $d - 1$ input variables and the internal nodes represent Boolean operators. In what follows, we will assume that the offset ω is always fixed to $\lfloor (d - 1)/2 \rfloor$, i.e., when d is odd the neighborhood origin will be the middle cell, while for d even it will be the left middle cell. This does not hinder the scope of our investigation since as shown in [7] reversible marker rules in different offsets are symmetric under rotations and reflection.

Note that, since the number of Boolean functions of $d - 1$ variables is $2^{2^{d-1}}$, the phenotype space $\mathcal{P}(d)$ can be exhaustively searched for reversible marker CA rules up to diameter $d = 6$, since there are at most $2^{32} \approx 4.3 \cdot 10^9$ generating functions to check for the conserved landscape property. As far as we are aware, an exhaustive search of reversible marker CA rules has been carried out only by Patt [12], who considered diameters up to $d = 4$. For completeness, Table 1 reports the numbers of conserved-landscape rules we found by exhaustively searching the sets of generating functions up to $d = 6$, along with the length of the truth table (2^{d-1}), the size of the phenotype space ($\#\mathcal{P}(d)$), and the observed Hamming weights. Recall that the Hamming weight of the generating function corresponds to the number of atomic landscapes over which a cell flips its state. Further, we excluded from the count the identity rule which simply copies the state of the central cell, since it is trivially reversible for any diameter. As a general remark, one can see from Table 1 that the number of conserved landscape rules is much smaller than the size of the whole generating function set. Moreover, the number of observed Hamming weights is quite limited, since for the largest considered instance of diameter $d = 6$ we only found reversible rules defined by at most 3 landscapes, which are thus not very useful for

Table 1. Numbers of conserved landscape rules found by exhaustive search.

d	2^{d-1}	$\#\mathcal{P}(d)$	#REV	Weights
3	4	16	0	–
4	8	256	1	1
5	16	65 536	10	1, 2
6	32	$4.3 \cdot 10^9$	46	1, 2, 3

cryptographic and reversible computing purposes. Nevertheless, these findings prompt us with three interesting research questions:

- **RQ1:** Does the limited number of conserved landscape rules with respect to the search space size imply a difficulty for evolutionary algorithms to find them?
- **RQ2:** Do there exist conserved landscapes rules of a larger diameter which are useful for cryptographic and reversible computing applications, i.e., having larger Hamming weights with respect to the size of the generating function truth table?
- **RQ3:** Is there a trade-off between the reversibility of a marker CA rule (as measured by the fitness function fit_1 defined in Sect. 3.2) and its Hamming weight?

We employed Genetic Algorithms (GA) and Genetic Programming (GP) to investigate the three questions above, by optimizing the fitness functions fit_1 and fit_2. The reason for comparing GA and GP was to assess whether the representation of the solutions as bitstrings or trees affected the convergence to an optimal solution on this particular problem. We considered the spaces of marker CA rules of diameter between $d = 8$ and $d = 13$ as problem instances for our experiments, using the $d = 7$ case for tuning our evolutionary algorithms. Both our GA and GP employed a steady-state tournament selection operator, which randomly samples three individuals from the populations. Next, the crossover is applied to the best two individuals of the tournament to produce a child candidate solution, which is then mutated and inserted into the population by replacing the worst individual of the tournament. For GA, we employed one-point, two-point, and uniform crossover operators (selected at random at each iteration), while we adopted a classic bit-flip operator for mutation. In the case of GP, we used a function set for the Boolean trees composed of the binary operators AND, OR, XOR, XNOR, and the unary operator NOT. Additionally, we included the ternary function IF, which returns the second argument if the first one is true, and the third one otherwise. Although this function set is redundant, since any Boolean function can be formulated with a smaller set, the choice of these elements is based on our previous experience evolving Boolean expressions with GP that define CA [3]. To avoid bloat, we observed through preliminary experiments that setting the maximum tree depth equal to the number of variables of the generating functions $(d-1)$ was a good choice in terms of GP performance. Further, for crossover in GP, we employed five different operators, namely simple subtree crossover, uniform crossover, size fair, one-point, and context preserving crossover, again selected at random at each iteration. Analogously to GA, for mutation we adopted a single operator, namely subtree mutation. Concerning the population size and the mutation probability, we performed a tuning phase over the $d = 7$ problem instance, which resulted in population sizes of 25 and 500 individuals for GA and GP, respectively, and a mutation probability of 0.8 and 0.5 for GA and GP. Similarly to previous works on related optimization problems [16,18], we set a budget of 500 000 fitness evaluations for both GA and GP, and we performed 30 runs for each considered problem instance.

5.2   Single-Objective Approach

As a first attempt to investigate the research questions stated in the previous section, we employed a single-objective approach where GA and GP only minimized the reversibility fitness function fit_1 as an optimization criterion, analyzing the Hamming weights of the best solutions in a second moment. The motivation was to address research question RQ1, i.e., investigate how difficult it is for GA and GP to optimize fit_1, especially considering the scarcity of conserved landscape rules assessed by our exhaustive search experiments.

The first remarkable finding is that *GA and GP achieved a full success rate over all considered problem instances*, i.e., both algorithms always converged to a reversible rule in all 30 experimental runs for each diameter between $d = 8$ and $d = 13$. In particular, using the fitness function fit_1 as defined in Eq. (4), GP always converged to the trivial solution 0, which corresponds to the identity rule. For this reason, we slightly tweaked fit_1 for our GP experiments by adding a penalty factor that punishes a candidate solution having a null Hamming weight. After this modification, GP again obtained a full success rate over all problem instances, thus finding *non-trivial* conserved landscape rules. Interestingly, this finding is analogous to what was observed in [16] for the optimization of orthogonal Latin squares based on cellular automata, where GP always converged to "simple" solutions – which in that context were represented by *linear* local rules – when optimizing only the orthogonality constraint.

The remarks above seem to answer question RQ1 in negative: the limited number of conserved landscape rules as compared to the size of the search space does not seem to pose a problem for GA and GP to converge to an optimal solution. However, the comparison shown in Fig. 3 on the number of fitness evaluations performed by GA and GP tells us a more precise story. As can be seen, the number of fitness evaluations required by GA to find a reversible rule scales exponentially with respect to the rule diameter (note that we adopted a logarithmic scale in Fig. 3 for the sake of comparison). In particular, the median number of fitness evaluations performed by GA approximately doubles every time the diameter increases by 1. On the contrary, GP features a much more stable and slower growth in the number of fitness evaluations that are necessary for converging to an optimal solution. Further, this number is always smaller by at least one order of magnitude than the number of GA fitness evaluations over all problem instances. This observation indicates that GP is a better suited heuristic than GA for this optimization problem, for which reason we employed only GP in our subsequent experiments on multi-objective and lexicographic optimization. The superiority of GP with respect to GA is also reflected in the Hamming weights of the optimal solutions found by the two heuristics: although GA provides a better coverage of distinct weights over all 30 experimental runs for each instance, the maximum weight found by GP is always consistently greater than the maximum achieved by GA. We refer the reader to Table 2 for a comparison of the Hamming weights found by all optimization approaches.

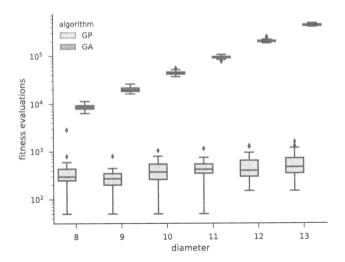

Fig. 3. Comparison of fitness evaluations performed by GA and GP.

5.3 Multi-objective Approach

To investigate the interaction between the reversibility of a marker CA rule and the Hamming weight of its generating function, we adopted a multi-objective strategy as a second optimization approach. In particular, we considered only a multi-objective version of GP (MOGP), since in the single-objective approach we observed that GP outperformed GA in terms of fitness evaluations. The MOGP approach used the well-known NSGA-II algorithm, where we *minimized* the reversibility fitness value fit_1 and *maximized* the Hamming weight as measured by fit_2. For each considered problem instance, we run the MOGP algorithm with the same experimental parameters adopted for the single-objective setting described in Sect. 5.1, and at the end of each run, we recorded all Pareto optimal solutions in the population and added them to a list. Figure 4 plots the Pareto front approximated by MOGP for the instance $d = 8$. The main observation one can draw from the plot is that there is a clear trade-off between reversibility and the Hamming weight, thereby providing an empirical answer to research question RQ3: *the closer a marker CA rule is to being of the conserved landscape type, the lower the Hamming weight of its generating function must be.* Incidentally, the left tail of the Pareto front also provides some hints with respect to research question RQ2. Indeed, there are only a few points aligned on the $fit_1 = 0$ value, all having small Hamming weights with respect to the truth table size of the generating function (which for $d = 8$ equals 128). This finding seems to hinder the applicability of conserved landscape rules in cryptography, and in particular in the design of S-boxes based on CA [3], since a local rule with a low Hamming weight will induce an S-box with low nonlinearity.

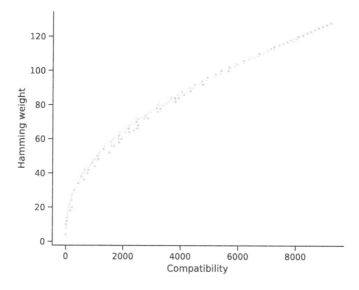

Fig. 4. Pareto front for $d = 8$.

5.4 Lexicographic Optimization

Our third experiment consisted of a *lexicographic optimization* approach, to assess whether a better coverage of the Hamming weights of conserved landscape rules could be obtained. In the first optimization stage, GP minimized only the reversibility fitness value fit_1. After obtaining a conserved landscape solution, in the second stage GP maximized fitness fit_2, logging each new solution that was still reversible and with a higher Hamming weight.

Table 2 compares in terms of solutions diversity the four optimization approaches adopted in our experiments – single-objective GA (SOGA) and GP (SOGP), multi-objective GP (MOGP), and lexicographic GP (LEXGP). In particular, each entry of the table is a triplet of the form (*UHW, MHW, USol*) where *UHW* denotes the number of distinct Hamming weights found, *MHW* is the maximum Hamming weight observed, and *USol* is the number of distinct optimal solutions found. For single-objective GA and GP, we report only the data of the best solutions found over all 30 experimental runs, while for MOGP and lexicographic GP we consider the whole populations after finishing the 30 runs. In particular, one can see that LEXGP is the method achieving the best trade-off in terms of distinct weights coverage, maximum weight, and uniqueness of solutions produced. SOGA is the heuristic that reaches the widest diversity of distinct Hamming weights but its maximum weights are the lowest among all four methods. SOGP, on the other hand, reaches higher maximum weights than GA, but with a quite low variety of the Hamming weights. MOGP further improves on the maximum weights and have similar coverage of distinct weights to SOGP, but the number of distinct solution is quite low (recall that with MOGP we recorded all Pareto optimal solutions in the population

Table 2. Diversity of the solutions produced by all optimization methods.

d	SOGA			SOGP			MOGP			LEXGP		
	UHW	MHW	USol	UHW	MHW	USol	UHW	MHW	USol	UHW	MHW	USol
8	5	6	30	4	8	27	4	10	24	5	10	47
9	6	7	30	4	16	29	2	20	22	8	20	60
10	7	11	30	3	16	30	4	32	48	6	28	65
11	9	15	30	3	32	29	6	56	40	6	56	64
12	11	23	30	4	64	30	4	72	29	7	80	71
13	12	29	30	2	64	29	4	128	50	7	160	73

over all runs). Finally, LEXGP is the one obtaining a good coverage of distinct weights, although not as good as SOGA. This is compensated by the fact that LEXGP achieved the highest maximum weights among all four methods (except for the case $d = 10$ where it was outperformed by MOGP). Moreover, LEXGP generated more distinct reversible solutions than MOGP.

6   Conclusions and Future Work

In this paper, we used GA and GP to study a particular class of reversible shift-invariant transformations – namely CA defined by conserved landscape rules – using three different optimization approaches. We now sum up the main findings of our experiments and suggest some possible future developments in the context of the three research questions that we posed.

Regarding the first research question, the results obtained with the single-objective approach seems to indicate that evolutionary algorithms, and in particular GP, can find relatively easily conserved landscape CA rules, despite the limited size of the optimal solutions set. Although this makes the associated optimization problem unsuitable for benchmark purposes, it would be interesting to investigate the performance difference between GA and GP, for example by analyzing the fitness landscapes induced by fit_1 on the two genotype spaces.

For the second research question, our findings show that the relevance of conserved landscape CA for cryptography and reversible computing is quite limited since their Hamming weights are too low concerning the truth table size of their generating functions. Nevertheless, as remarked in Sect. 2.3, one can easily relax the definition of conserved landscape rules by allowing partial overlapping of the landscapes, and obtain a larger class of reversible CA with more complex behaviors. A possible idea worth exploring in this direction would be to adapt the fitness function fit_1 to allow for this partial overlapping, and use GP to investigate the Hamming weights of the resulting reversible CA, in particular with the lexicographic optimization method that proved to be the best performing one.

References

1. Chopard, B.: Cellular automata and lattice Boltzmann modeling of physical systems. In: Rozenberg, G., Bäck, T., Kok, J.N. (eds.) Handbook of Natural Computing, pp. 287–331. Springer, Heidelberg (2012). https://doi.org/10.1007/978-3-540-92910-9_9
2. Landauer, R.: Irreversibility and heat generation in the computing process. IBM J. Res. Dev. **5**(3), 183–191 (1961)
3. Mariot, L., Picek, S., Leporati, A., Jakobovic, D.: Cellular automata based S-boxes. Cryptogr. Commun. **11**(1), 41–62 (2018). https://doi.org/10.1007/s12095-018-0311-8
4. Kari, J.: Reversible cellular automata: from fundamental classical results to recent developments. New Gener. Comput. **36**(3), 145–172 (2018). https://doi.org/10.1007/s00354-018-0034-6
5. Mitchell, M., Crutchfield, J.P., Das, R., et al.: Evolving cellular automata with genetic algorithms: a review of recent work. In: Proceedings of the First International Conference on Evolutionary Computation and Its Applications (EvCA 1996), vol. 8 (1996)
6. Bäck, T., Breukelaar, R.: Using genetic algorithms to evolve behavior in cellular automata. In: Calude, C.S., Dinneen, M.J., Păun, G., Pérez-Jímenez, M.J., Rozenberg, G. (eds.) UC 2005. LNCS, vol. 3699, pp. 1–10. Springer, Heidelberg (2005). https://doi.org/10.1007/11560319_1
7. Toffoli, T., Margolus, N.H.: Invertible cellular automata: a review. Phys. D **45**(1–3), 229–253 (1990)
8. Wolfram, S.: Statistical mechanics of cellular automata. Rev. Mod. Phys. **55**(3), 601 (1983)
9. Hedlund, G.A.: Endomorphisms and automorphisms of the shift dynamical systems. Math. Syst. Theory **3**(4), 320–375 (1969). https://doi.org/10.1007/BF01691062
10. Bertoni, G., Daemen, J., Peeters, M., Assche, G.V.: The Keccak reference (2011)
11. Daemen, J.: Cipher and hash function design strategies based on linear and differential cryptanalysis. Ph.D. thesis, Doctoral Dissertation, KU Leuven, March 1995
12. Patt, Y.: Injections of neighborhood size three and four on the set of configurations from the infinite one-dimensional tessellation automata of two-state cells. Technical report, Army Electronics Command Fort Monmouth, NJ (1972)
13. Sipper, M., Tomassini, M.: Co-evolving parallel random number generators. In: Voigt, H.-M., Ebeling, W., Rechenberg, I., Schwefel, H.-P. (eds.) PPSN 1996. LNCS, vol. 1141, pp. 950–959. Springer, Heidelberg (1996). https://doi.org/10.1007/3-540-61723-X_1058
14. Picek, S., Mariot, L., Leporati, A., Jakobovic, D.: Evolving S-boxes based on cellular automata with genetic programming. In: Proceedings of the Genetic and Evolutionary Computation Conference Companion, GECCO 2017, pp. 251–252 (2017)
15. Picek, S., Mariot, L., Yang, B., Jakobovic, D., Mentens, N.: Design of S-boxes defined with cellular automata rules. In: Proceedings of the Computing Frontiers Conference, CF 2017, pp. 409–414 (2017)
16. Mariot, L., Picek, S., Jakobovic, D., Leporati, A.: Evolutionary algorithms for the design of orthogonal latin squares based on cellular automata. In: Proceedings of the Genetic and Evolutionary Computation Conference, GECCO 2017, pp. 306–313 (2017)

17. Picek, S., Carlet, C., Guilley, S., Miller, J.F., Jakobovic, D.: Evolutionary algorithms for Boolean functions in diverse domains of cryptography. Evol. Comput. **24**(4), 667–694 (2016)
18. Mariot, L., Jakobovic, D., Leporati, A., Picek, S.: Hyper-bent Boolean functions and evolutionary algorithms. In: Sekanina, L., Hu, T., Lourenço, N., Richter, H., García-Sánchez, P. (eds.) EuroGP 2019. LNCS, vol. 11451, pp. 262–277. Springer, Cham (2019). https://doi.org/10.1007/978-3-030-16670-0_17

Benchmarking Manifold Learning Methods on a Large Collection of Datasets

Patryk Orzechowski[1,2(✉)], Franciszek Magiera[2], and Jason H. Moore[1]

[1] Institute for Biomedical Informatics, University of Pennsylvania,
Philadelphia, PA 19104, USA
`patryk.orzechowski@gmail.com`
[2] Department of Automatics, AGH University of Science and Technology,
al. Mickiewicza 30, 30-059 Krakow, Poland

Abstract. Manifold learning, a non-linear approach of dimensionality reduction, assumes that the dimensionality of multiple datasets is artificially high and a reduced number of dimensions is sufficient to maintain the information about the data. In this paper, a large scale comparison of manifold learning techniques is performed for the task of classification. We show the current standing of genetic programming (GP) for the task of classification by comparing the classification results of two GP-based manifold leaning methods: GP-Mal and ManiGP - an experimental manifold learning technique proposed in this paper. We show that GP-based methods can more effectively learn a manifold across a set of 155 different problems and deliver more separable embeddings than many established methods.

Keywords: Manifold learning · Genetic programming · Machine learning · Dimensionality reduction · Benchmarking

1 Introduction

Dimensionality reduction has been a very important area of research over the past few years because of its pivotal role in machine learning (ML) and related fields. Feature extraction, which is determining the most informative and non-redundant features derived from the original features, reduces the feature space and allows multiple ML methods to be applied to increasingly large datasets. It also allows to create human interpretable visualization of the data in two or three dimensional space and to better understand underlying associations between the features. An extensive review of different dimensionality reduction approaches can be found in the literature [8,9,14,16,18,22,36,48].

Over the years, multiple methods of dimensionality reduction have been developed. The most popular linear dimensionality reduction methods include principal component analysis (PCA) [30,39], linear discriminant analysis (LDA) [12,33], canonical correlations analysis [17] and factor analysis (FA) [37].

© Springer Nature Switzerland AG 2020
T. Hu et al. (Eds.): EuroGP 2020, LNCS 12101, pp. 135–150, 2020.
https://doi.org/10.1007/978-3-030-44094-7_9

Manifold learning is one of the approaches for non-linear dimensionality reduction. The most popular approaches include multidimensional scaling (MDS) [4,40], locally linear embeddings (LLE) [35], Laplacian eigenmaps [2], isomaps [38], local tangent space alignment (LTSA) [47], maximum variance unfolding [44], diffusion maps [7], and t-distributed stochastic neighbor embedding (t-SNE) [25]. Apart from visualization purposes, manifold learning has been also used as a preprocessing step before classification [41,42].

Among multiple dimensionality reduction techniques, a couple of notable methods of feature extraction exist that use genetic algorithms (GA) [34,45] or genetic programming (GP) [6,15]. Over the recent years multiple attempts were also taken to use genetic programming for classification [3,11,20]. The main advantage of GP-based approaches is delivering a fully interpretable model that could be used for describing the data structure. In a recent paper Lensen et al. proposed a manifold learning method based on GP called GP-MaL. The method was shown to outperform other popular manifold learning techniques in terms of accuracy in at least half of 10 datasets considered [23]. This approach inspired us to design a study on separability of data using manifold learning techniques. We designed a GP-based method focusing in optimizing the same goal used in benchmarking the methods, which is providing observable separation of classes in the embedded space.

The major contribution of this paper is performing a large-scale comparison of different manifold learning methods with their sets of parameters on the large collection of 155 datasets from Penn Machine Learning Benchmark (PMLB) [27]. To our knowledge, this is the largest and the most comprehensive comparison of manifold learning techniques on the collection of real world problems. As manifold learning methods are usually applied to create convincing visualizations, we check if manifold learning methods can deliver easily separable embeddings in two dimensional space. To measure the performance of the methods, we used unsupervised clustering algorithm and verified the performance of the methods for the task of classification, for which the ground truth is already known. As some of the considered datasets in PMLB are multi-class problems with different numbers of instances per class, a balanced accuracy score [5] is used in order to account for the class imbalance. Type of the data (e.g. categorical or ordinal) was not taken into account.

The second contribution of the paper is providing a convenient open-source framework for testing new manifold learning methods. All source code for our analysis is available at https://github.com/athril/manigp. An important input here is providing a scikit-learn friendly wrapper for GP-MaL, a GP-based manifold learning method proposed at EuroGP track of EvoStar 2019, which investigated application of genetic programming to manifold learning.

Thirdly, we propose a novel manifold learning technique based on genetic programming called ManiGP which uses a multi-tree representation, a popular k-means clustering [24] and balanced accuracy to verify their integrity. The proposed method could be considered a thought experiment that would answer a question if a method intentionally designed to exploit the benchmark has unfair advantage over its competitors. We show over a large collection of problems that, albeit its extensive running time, a method based on genetic programming can learn a manifold significantly better than multiple other techniques. Therefore, we touch on a broader subject of the fairness of comparisons of the methods which feature GP.

2   Methods

In our study we covered eight well established manifold learning methods and two methods that use GP: GP-MaL, a winner of a best paper award at EvoStar 2019, and ManiGP, which is introduced in this paper. All the methods were benchmarked against the collection of 155 datasets from Penn Machine Learning Benchmark (PMLB). The input data was standardized using RobustScaler and split into training and test set with stratification maintained. Manifold learning method were launched with different combinations of input parameters (apart from GP-MaL, which was launched with default parameters). The embeddings provided by the methods were later clustered using K-Means, a popular clustering algorithm. Hungarian (Kuhn-Munkres) algorithm was used for obtaining optimal assignment of clusters to the actual classes [26]. The distance to the nearest centroid served as a basis for predicting a class label for unseen data points. Balanced accuracy was used as a metric for measuring performance (i.e separability) of the embeddings. As the major application of manifold learning is visualization, we have focused on distinction between the classes in two dimensional space. The detailed information on the design of the experiment is provided in the methodology section.

2.1   Manifold Learning Methods

We have included the methods that are part of scikit-learn [31], a popular machine learning library. We have also adapted the source code GP-MaL and created a Python wrapper.

Isomap is a manifold learning method partly based on MDS [38]. Isomap improves on standard MDS by aiming to preserve geodesic distances between points instead of straight-line distances. This change leads to the creation of more adequate embeddings compared to MDS for manifolds with characteristics akin to the Swiss Roll for which the small euclidean distance between two points does not imply that they are similar. Isomap is computationally efficient and scales well to high-dimensional datasets.

Locally Linear Embedding (LLE) is based on a premise that finding linear transformations preserving local structures and applying them to overlaying neighborhoods can retain a non-linear global structure of a dataset [35]. Local structures are maintained by expressing each data instance as a linear combination of its neighbors using the same weights in high and low-dimensional space. LLE can perform poorly when data is separated and has tendencies to collapse the low-dimensional mapping to a single point.

Hessian Locally Linear Embedding (HLLE) is a variant of LLE that uses quadratic form based on Hessian matrix to preserve the local structure of the data [10]. HLLE was shown to perform better on non-convex manifolds than standard LLE, but it suffers from high computational complexity and does not scale well to large datasets, partly due to the necessity of estimating second order derivatives.

Modified Locally Linear Embedding (MLLE) is a variant of LLE that looks for more than one linear combinations of every point's neighbors to embed the data in a low-dimensional space while maintaining the local structure of a manifold [46]. This change results in a more robust embedding compared to standard LLE.

Local Tangent Space Alignment (LTSA) is a modification of LLE that represents local structures using tangent spaces and aligns them in a global structure to derive a coordinate system to describe manifold [47]. Similarly to LLE, the method is susceptible to the noise.

Mutidimensional Scaling (MDS) is one of the oldest methods which can be applied to non-linear dimensionality reduction [4]. It focuses on maintaining the euclidean distances between the points in the low-dimensional embedding. This approach works well if distance is a good measure of similarity between points, because then related points are grouped together.

Laplacian Eigenmaps - Spectral embedding (SE) is another manifold learning method which focuses on preserving the local structures of the data [2]. This is achieved by representing the dataset as a graph and using the eigenvectors of the Laplacian matrix of that graph for dimensionality reduction. Laplacian Eigenmaps have also been used for data clustering.

t-Distributed Stochastic Neighbor Embedding (t-SNE) is a popular method for visualizing high-dimensional datasets [25]. Similarity of points in the dataset is evaluated using conditional probabilities which measure how likely a certain point would be to choose another point as its neighbor. The method looks for a low-dimensional embedding of the dataset that minimizes the difference between the distributions of high and low-dimensional sets which is expressed by Kullback-Leibler divergence [19]. t-SNE was shown to create high quality visualizations of high-dimensional datasets [25]. In addition, it is a powerful tool for data exploration and can be used after feature extraction to assess what characteristics of the data the extraction really captured. Nonetheless, t-SNE has some disadvantages. Firstly, it is not easily interpretable [43]. Secondly, new points cannot be embedded in low-dimensional space[1].

---

[1] https://lvdmaaten.github.io/tsne/.

GP-MaL is a recently proposed manifold learning method based on genetic programming [23]. The method uses interpretable trees to evolve mappings from high to low dimensional space. The mappings are measured on how well they maintain dataset's structure with a similarity metric based on neighbor ordering. GP-Mal was shown to be a competitive dimensionality reduction technique for the tasks of classification, data visualization and establishing feature importance. The mappings produced by the method while interpretable, suffered from excessive complexity. GP-MaL demonstrated the potential of GP in dimensionality reduction and manifold learning applications.

2.2 ManiGP - A New Manifold Learning Method Based on Genetic Programming

ManiGP is a manifold learning method which, similar to GP-MaL, uses a multi-tree representation of an individual and focuses on delivering highly separable mappings of distinct classes.

Motivation. The intuition behind the method is as follows. As manifold learning techniques are primarily used for creating convincing visualizations, our aim was to provide a highly interpretable method, which would clearly distinguish classes for the task of classification and also have potential for being adapted to unsupervised data analysis. Thus, despite its susceptibility to outliers and noise, a k-means clustering [24] was chosen as a base for finding groupings of the instances in the embedded space. The number of clusters is always set to the number of classes in the data. Each of the clusters was later assigned to the closest classes using Hungarian algorithm. Finally, a balanced accuracy metric is used as a fitness score for each of the individual in order to become independent of the size of each class in the original data. The goal of the method is maximizing the fitness score, which should lead to higher separability of the classes and thus to more convincing visualizations. The predictions for the unseen instances were made based on the distance to the closest centroid.

Allowable Operators. The primitive set of a GP syntax tree for ManiGP comprises various mathematical operations, random ephemeral constants and terminals equal to 0 or 1. The allowable operations are addition, subtraction, multiplication, safe division (to prevent division by 0), modulo, modulo-2 summation; equal, not equal, less than, greater than comparisons; logical and, or, xor and not; bitwise and, or and xor; abs, factorial, power, logarithm a of b, permutation, choose; left, right, min and max. A maximal permissible height is used as a bloat control to prevent the excessive growth of trees.

The Method. The concept of the method is visualized on the example of the appendicitis dataset in Fig. 1. Each point represents an instance of the original dataset, which was mapped into a new space. The color of the point corresponds to its original class. The coordinates of the new space are determined by syntax

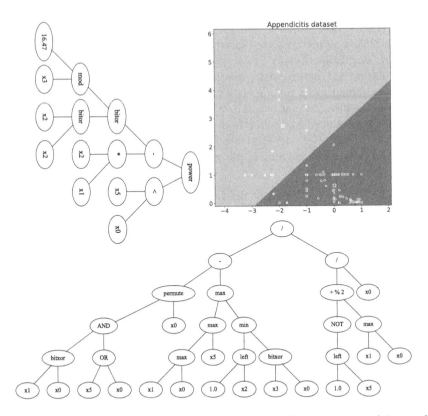

Fig. 1. A concept of ManiGP. A population of the algorithm contains evolving tuples of trees that create a manifold to separate classes.

trees which were evolved using GP. Each of the trees is responsible for constructing a single embedding in a low-dimensional space. This means that the number of trees in the individual is equal to the dimensionality of the reduced dataset. In this example, the balanced accuracy on the training dataset is equal to 93.7%, whereas on the testing data 80.9% (both were plotted in the same chart).

The evolution process in ManiGP is set up as follows.

1. A number of best individuals from the previous population is selected to the next generation. The selection operator sorts the individuals by their fitness function values in descending order and then chooses the ones from the beginning of the list. The number of individuals chosen is equal to the size of the initial population.
2. The population is randomly shuffled and individuals are assigned to pairs based on their position in the population. Specifically, the first individual on the list is paired with the second one, the third one with the fourth one and so on.
3. A crossover operator is applied on each pair of individuals with a certain probability. Corresponding coordinates of the trees are crossed over using a

one point crossover operator which chooses random nodes in each of the two trees and swaps the subtrees that have a root in that randomly chosen node creating two new trees. In this way, two new individuals are created. If all of the trees comprising the new individual are of admissible height, then the individual is added to the population. The resulting population contains both parents and children.

4. Each individual in the population - including the children created with a crossover operator - is mutated with a certain probability. Each tree of an individual is mutated using the mutation operator. Within each of the trees, the operator chooses randomly a subtree and swaps it with a randomly generated one.

5. A bloat control check (i.e. verification of the height of the tree) is performed before admitting it to the population.

6. Each of the instances is mapped into the new space using trees. On the reduced space, a k-means clustering is run to find groupings of instances. The number of clusters used in k-means is equal to the number of classes. As clustering does not use information on the class labels, an additional assignment needs to be made in order to match clusters to classes. This is performed using Hungarian algorithm [26].

7. The fitness function of each individual is defined as a balanced accuracy across all classes.

8. The evolution stops after a predefined number of iterations. If the predefined number of iterations is not met, the next population is created using selection of best individuals[2]. Otherwise, the instances of the data are transformed using the individual with the highest fitness.

Implementation. ManiGP was implemented in Python using Distributed Evolutionary Algorithms in Python (DEAP) framework [13,32] and other popular Python libraries such as NumPy, pandas, and sklearn.

Related Work. GP and nearest centroid classifiers were shown to be powerful tools for improving classification accuracy and feature selection [1]. Although in some ways similar, the approach taken in this study applies GP and K-means in a different context than in the research conducted by Al-Madi et al., which focused more on improving classification results derived from GP with a k-means based algorithm. The design of the method used in this paper is very closely related to M4GP, the method of dimensionality reduction by La Cava et al. [20] with four major differences. Firstly, the representation of the individual is different. ManiGP represents individual as multi-tree structure, whereas M4GP use a stack-based representation. Secondly, ManiGP uses the simplest possible strategies (e.g. selection of best individuals), whereas M4GP uses advanced selection operators, such as epsilon lexicase selection and Age-fitness Pareto survival.

---

[2] Empirical tests have surprisingly shown the superior performance of this technique in comparison to tournament selection.

Thirdly, the fitness objective is different [20]. Finally, ManiGP presets the resulting dimensionality, whereas M4GP dynamically determines it in the course of evolution.

It needs to be emphasized, that ManiGP by no means was designed to be a fully fledged classifier. It emerged as an experiment during designing a fair methodology for the comparison of the methods. Our hypothesis was that it is possible to design a method that would work at least as well as the state-of-the-art methods for a large set of problems, if it is given a leverage and optimizes the same metric used later in benchmarking. This, in our opinion, not only puts the method in favourable position over the others, but also adds an interesting layer in the discussion on existence of the objective comparison methodology.

2.3   Datasets

Penn Machine Learning Benchmark (PMLB) is one of the largest available collections of publicly available dataset for classification and regression. Multiple problems included in the benchmark suite were pulled from popular repositories, such as UCI, OpenML or Kaggle and transformed into a machine learning friendly format [27]. In this paper our focus was classification task, for which we pulled 166 classification datasets. The following 11 datasets were excluded from the comparison because of issues with convergence or running times exceeding 168 h for at least 2 methods: 'adult', 'connect-4', 'fars', 'kddcup', 'krkopt', 'letter', 'magic', 'mnist', 'poker', 'shuttle', and 'sleep'. As the result, the collection included in this analysis contained 155 different datasets.

2.4   Methodology of Comparison

One of the greatest challenges in benchmarking manifold learning methods is the fact that not every method supports mapping of the previously unseen data. For example a very popular t-SNE learns a non-parametric mapping, which means there is no function learned that would map the point from the input space to the embedded one. A similar issue involves also MDS and Spectral Embeddings, two other popular manifold learning techniques. This has far-reaching consequences, as the performance of the methods on test data can't be reported for the method. It also means that cross-validation can't be used for finding the optimal setting of the input parameters.

There are two potential ways of getting around this fact, but none of them could be considered a good strategy. First, a regressor could be proposed which for each of the samples in the test data finds the closest sample (or samples) and assigns its score (or performs a form of majority voting). Unfortunately, this may be erroneous for some of the datasets, which contain categorical, or ordinal values. The second approach is learning manifold on full data and reporting the score only for the test points. In this scenario, however, testing data is used in training, which creates additional bias. After consideration we have decided not to report the performance of aforementioned methods on test data. This resulted in abandoning k-fold cross validation in favor of running method with 5 different random seeds with a grid of the parameters and using the best performance within training data for testing.

The second challenge was proposing an objective metric for assessing performance. After learning the manifold, multiple existing classifiers could be adapted and trained on the data with reduced dimensionality. Our choice was using k-means, a popular clustering technique. This unsupervised technique could be considered as unbiased measure of separability of the classes as it does not use real class labels for the analysis. The correct assignments to the classes are handled using Hungarian algorithm in similar way as in Orzechowski and Boryczko [28]. Although we are aware that k-means isn't perfect, as doesn't handle well clusters of different densities, irregular shapes as well as outliers, the simplicity and linear division of the classes in the embedded space were the reasons why k-means was chosen as the base for the analysis.

The workflow for benchmarking manifold learning method was constructed as follows:

1. For each of the datasets 5 different randomly initialized seeds were selected. The seeds were used for splitting each of the dataset to train and testing sets with proportion 75%–25%. Stratified split was used to maintain the proportion of the representatives of each class in both training and testing set and RobustScaler was used for preprocessing data.
2. Each manifold learning method was initialized with the same random seed. For each of the methods we have used a grid of input parameters. The methods with their parameters are presented in Table 1.
3. In order to better understand separability of the classes, the resulting two dimensional embedding from each manifold learning methods served as a base for performing k-means clustering with the number of clusters equal to the number of classes.
4. Hungarian algorithm [26] was used to assign class label to the clusters.
5. For the methods that allow projection of a test set, the distance to the center of the nearest cluster was used to assign label to the point.
6. As class imbalance is an issue with different datasets, a popular metric called balanced accuracy was used as a measure of performance.
7. For each of the methods and a given seed the highest balanced accuracy score was considered across a grid of the parameters.

3   Results

For benchmarking we have included all of the manifold learning methods described in the previous chapter. For the sake of clarity, we have narrowed down our analysis to manifold learning methods only and decided not to include linear dimensionality reduction techniques, as they remain out of scope for this paper. The detailed results of the analysis have been added to our project repository[3].

---

[3] https://github.com/athril/manigp/.

Table 1. Parameters settings of the analyzed methods. The names of the parameters refer to scikit-learn implementation.

Algorithm	Parameter	Values
ManiGP	'(xover rate, mut rate)'	{(0.9,0.1), (0.5,0.5), (0.1,0.9)}
	'generations'	500
	'pop_size'	100
GP-MaL	'generations'	1000
	pop_size	1024
Isomap	'n_neighbors'	[5,6,7,8,9,10,15,20],
	'eigen_solver'	['arpack','dense'],
LLE	'reg'	[1e−4, 1e−3, 0.001, 0.1, 1, 10]
	'n_neighbors'	[5,6,7,8,9,10,15,20]
	'eigen_solver'	['dense']
Hessian	'reg'	[1e−4, 1e−3, 0.001, 0.1, 1, 10]
	'n_neighbors'	[5,6,7,8,9,10,15,20]
	'eigen_solver'	['dense']
Modified LLE	'reg'	[1e−4, 1e−3, 0.001, 0.1, 1, 10]
	'n_neighbors'	[5,6,7,8,9,10,15,20]
	'eigen_solver'	['dense']
LTSA	'reg'	[1e−4, 1e−3, 0.001, 0.1, 1, 10]
	'n_neighbors'	[5,6,7,8,9,10,15,20]
	'eigen_solver'	['dense']
MDS	'max_iter'	[300,500]
	'metric'	[True,False]
	'dissimilarity'	['euclidean']
Spectral	'affinity'	['nearest_neighbors']
	'n_neighbors'	[5,6,7,8,9,10]
	'eigen_solver'	[None, 'arpack', 'lobpcg','amg']
	or	
	'affinity'	['rbf']
	'eigen_solver'	[None, 'arpack', 'lobpcg','amg']
t-SNE	'perplexity'	[5,10,15,20,25,30,35,40,45,50]
	'n_iter'	[1000,5000]

All of the methods were run starting from 5 different seeds on a reduced PMLB benchmark suite with grid of the parameters presented in Table 1. For each of the seeds, the setting with the highest balanced accuracy score on the training data was chosen for the subsequent analysis. The median score across the seeds served for ranking the methods.

The performance for the task of classification on the training dataset is presented in Fig. 2. This analysis compares the methods on separating labeled data, what makes it a good benchmark for providing clarity of visualization.

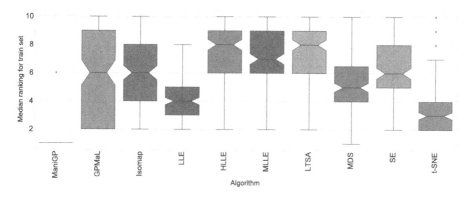

Fig. 2. The ranking of the manifold learning on the training dataset. The lower, the better.

Three of the methods, namely MDS and SE and t-SNE are not suitable for making predictions for the unseen data. Thus, they were removed from the assessment in the test data, which is presented in Fig. 3. This analysis shows the potential of the methods to be used as dimensionality reduction techniques.

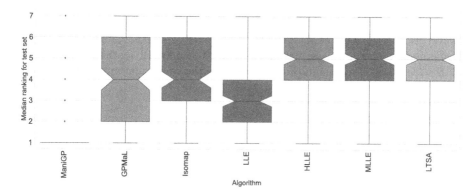

Fig. 3. The ranking of the manifold learning on the testing dataset. The lower, the better. Some of the methods (PCA, t-SNE and SE) had to be excluded as they don't provide the mapping that would allow to make predictions for unseen data.

To inspect the significant differences, we ran a Friedman test using balanced accuracy scores for the test data. As the number of datasets is large, the analysis has higher statistical power. P-values less than 0.005 suggest significant differences between the methods. Post-hoc pairwise tests are presented in Table 2.

Summary. Ranking the methods on the training data shows ManiGP as the leader, followed by t-SNE and LLE. The other methods performed visibly worse, with a few exceptions of MDS and GP-MaL.

Table 2. Friedman's asymptotic general symmetry test. P-values lower than 0.005 were boldfaced.

	GPMaL	Isomap	LLE	HLLE	MLLE	LTSA
ManiGP	**2.2e−16**	**2.2e−16**	**3.3e−14**	**2.2e−16**	**2.2e−16**	**2.2e−16**
GPMaL	–	0.99	2.0e−02	6.6e−03	4.1e−02	2.9e−02
Isomap	–	–	**4.8e−03**	0.02	0.12	0.09
LLE	–	–	–	**4.6e−10**	**3.5e−09**	**2.0e−09**
HLLE	–	–	–	–	0.99	0.99
MLLE	–	–	–	–	–	0.99

Considering the results on testing data, the clear leader is again ManiGP, which statistically outperformed each of the considered methods. The runner up is LLE, which significantly outperformed all methods, but ManiGP and GP-MaL. The remaining comparisons showed no significant differences.

Considering running times, both GP methods were a couple of orders of magnitude slower than the rest of approaches. Additionally, ManiGP was far slower than GP-MaL. GP-MaL was run for 1000 iterations with population of 1024 and was faster than ManiGP, which was run for 500 iterations with population of 100. The other methods had comparable running times, counted in seconds/minutes instead of hours/dozens of hours, as was the case with GP approaches. Notice however, that for the fairness all the methods were run with a single thread and GP methods could be run in parallel. Among the non-GP methods, MDS and t-SNE were an order of magnitude slower than the remaining approaches.

4   Conclusions

In this paper a comparison of 10 different manifold learning methods was performed on a large collection of real world datasets. The comparison was performed using rigorous machine learning standards [21,29] over a large collection of 155 datasets from PMLB [27]. The study aimed at empirical verification of how well the manifold learning approaches separate instances for the task of classification. All the source code of our analysis is open source and publicly available. Two of the methods included in the study were based on genetic programming: GP-MaL and ManiGP. To perform this study, we have created an open source framework for benchmarking of manifold learning techniques, as well as created a wrapper for GP-MaL.

Due to the nature of some of the manifold learning methods, such as MDS, SE and t-SNE, which are unable to transform an unseen instance, our benchmark is split into two parts: the training part, which could be considered benchmarking of potential of manifold learning techniques for visualization, and the testing part, in which the potential of the methods to serve as dimensionality reduction techniques could be more thoroughly assessed.

As for the visualization purposes, we have confirmed that ManiGP – an experimental technique proposed in this paper – delivers the most separable charts in comparison to any other manifold learning technique for the vast majority of datasets. Due to its excessive time however, its practical use remains highly limited. Among the methods with reasonable execution time, t-SNE can be considered the first choice and LLE the second.

Taking into account potential of using the methods toward further data analysis, ManiGP provides by far more separable results than any other manifold learning technique included in the comparison. The obtained results of ManiGP in terms of balanced accuracy were also significantly better compared to any other method included in the study. Another advantage of the method is interpretability, as it uses two (or more) syntax trees with arithmetic-logical operations. This makes the method easily adaptable to an unseen data. The greatest downside of the method is excessive running time, which we consider not feasible for larger datasets. On the other hand, the method wasn't optimized for the purpose of this study and a couple possible improvements might be taken out of the box. The further experiments suggest that the results are also comparable with some of the leading machine learning classifiers in the field. Once again, we would emphasize that the development of a method wasn't the major goal of this study and this method shouldn't be considered a valid classifier, which could be used in production.

Our analysis showed that GP-based approaches are capable of delivering fully interpretable, better separable and even significantly better results than multiple well established manifold learning approaches. Despite its excessive run times for larger datasets, ManiGP proposed in this paper outperformed other methods, although it used only very basic evolutionary techniques and evaluated over 20 times less individuals than GP-MaL. Among non-GP methods, considering potential of using a method to predict an unseen data, we believe that LLE remains a good trade off between the speed and performance, as it offers superior results to multiple other manifold learning methods within reasonable time frame. For the pure aspect of visualization, t-SNE remains a convenient approach, as it provides better separation.

Finally, we would like to elaborate more on the fairness of the presented comparison. One of the aspects of our study was proposing a method that deliberately optimizes the same score used later for evaluation. We have discovered that this approach performed statistically better than the approaches based on other merits. The question that should be asked is how objective could any comparison be considered, assuming that one method intentionally used the evaluation metric. The answer is not straightforward; it is necessary however that the designers of the study put as much effort as possible into designing as objective a comparison as possible with support for their results from multiple tests.

In summary, we believe that this paper set new standards in benchmarking manifold learning techniques and addresses not only their visualization potential, but far beyond. An important findings in this study are as follows: (1) not every manifold learning method provides the possibility to analyze unseen data, (2) the advantage of GP in manifold learning lies in providing interpretable results, (3) because of excessive running time of GP-based methods, their potential of creating convincing visualizations is highly limited, (4) application of GP in manifold learning is justified if the focus of the study is interpretability of the model and excessive running time will later be rewarded by instantaneous testing, (5) the fairness of benchmarking requires further research. Even those benchmarks that seem to be objective may be exploited by the methods that purposefully exploit the design of the study.

Acknowledgements. This research was supported in part by PL-Grid Infrastructure and by National Institutes of Health (NIH) grant LM012601. The authors would like to thank Dr. Andrew Lensen from Victoria University of Wellington for his help in running GP-MaL.

References

1. Al-Madi, N., Ludwig, S.A.: Improving genetic programming classification for binary and multiclass datasets. In: 2013 IEEE Symposium on Computational Intelligence and Data Mining (CIDM), pp. 166–173. IEEE (2013)
2. Belkin, M., Niyogi, P.: Laplacian eigenmaps and spectral techniques for embedding and clustering. In: Advances in Neural Information Processing Systems, pp. 585–591 (2002)
3. Bhowan, U., Zhang, M., Johnston, M.: Genetic programming for classification with unbalanced data. In: Esparcia-Alcázar, A.I., Ekárt, A., Silva, S., Dignum, S., Uyar, A.Ş. (eds.) EuroGP 2010. LNCS, vol. 6021, pp. 1–13. Springer, Heidelberg (2010). https://doi.org/10.1007/978-3-642-12148-7_1
4. Borg, I., Groenen, P.: Modern multidimensional scaling: theory and applications. J. Educ. Meas. **40**(3), 277–280 (2003)
5. Brodersen, K.H., Ong, C.S., Stephan, K.E., Buhmann, J.M.: The balanced accuracy and its posterior distribution. In: 2010 20th International Conference on Pattern Recognition, pp. 3121–3124. IEEE (2010)
6. Cano, A., Ventura, S., Cios, K.J.: Multi-objective genetic programming for feature extraction and data visualization. Soft. Comput. **21**(8), 2069–2089 (2015). https://doi.org/10.1007/s00500-015-1907-y
7. Coifman, R.R., Lafon, S.: Diffusion maps. Appl. Comput. Harmonic Anal. **21**(1), 5–30 (2006)
8. Cunningham, J.P., Ghahramani, Z.: Linear dimensionality reduction: survey, insights, and generalizations. J. Mach. Learn. Res. **16**(1), 2859–2900 (2015)
9. De Backer, S., Naud, A., Scheunders, P.: Non-linear dimensionality reduction techniques for unsupervised feature extraction. Pattern Recogn. Lett. **19**(8), 711–720 (1998)
10. Donoho, D.L., Grimes, C.: Hessian eigenmaps: locally linear embedding techniques for high-dimensional data. Proc. Nat. Acad. Sci. **100**(10), 5591–5596 (2003)
11. Espejo, P.G., Ventura, S., Herrera, F.: A survey on the application of genetic programming to classification. IEEE Trans. Syst. Man Cybern. Part C (Appl. Rev.) **40**(2), 121–144 (2009)
12. Fisher, R.A.: The use of multiple measurements in taxonomic problems. Ann. Eugen. **7**(2), 179–188 (1936)

13. Fortin, F.A., De Rainville, F.M., Gardner, M.A., Parizeau, M., Gagné, C.: DEAP: evolutionary algorithms made easy. J. Mach. Learn. Res. **13**, 2171–2175 (2012)
14. Gisbrecht, A., Hammer, B.: Data visualization by nonlinear dimensionality reduction. Wiley Interdiscip. Rev.: Data Min. Knowl. Discov. **5**(2), 51–73 (2015)
15. Guo, H., Zhang, Q., Nandi, A.K.: Feature extraction and dimensionality reduction by genetic programming based on the fisher criterion. Expert Syst. **25**(5), 444–459 (2008)
16. Guyon, I., Gunn, S., Nikravesh, M., Zadeh, L.A.: Feature Extraction: Foundations and Applications. STUDFUZZ, vol. 207. Springer, Heidelberg (2006). https://doi.org/10.1007/978-3-540-35488-8
17. Hotelling, H.: Relations between two sets of variates. In: Kotz, S., Johnson, N.L. (eds.) Breakthroughs in Statistics. SSS, pp. 162–190. Springer, New York (1992). https://doi.org/10.1007/978-1-4612-4380-9_14
18. Khalid, S., Khalil, T., Nasreen, S.: A survey of feature selection and feature extraction techniques in machine learning. In: 2014 Science and Information Conference, pp. 372–378. IEEE (2014)
19. Kullback, S., Leibler, R.A.: On information and sufficiency. Ann. Math. Stat. **22**(1), 79–86 (1951)
20. La Cava, W., Silva, S., Danai, K., Spector, L., Vanneschi, L., Moore, J.H.: Multidimensional genetic programming for multiclass classification. Swarm Evol. Comput. **44**, 260–272 (2019)
21. La Cava, W., Williams, H., Fu, W., Moore, J.H.: Evaluating recommender systems for AI-driven data science. arXiv preprint arXiv:1905.09205 (2019)
22. Lee, J.A., Verleysen, M.: Nonlinear Dimensionality Reduction. Springer, New York (2007). https://doi.org/10.1007/978-0-387-39351-3
23. Lensen, A., Xue, B., Zhang, M.: Can genetic programming do manifold learning too? In: Sekanina, L., Hu, T., Lourenço, N., Richter, H., García-Sánchez, P. (eds.) EuroGP 2019. LNCS, vol. 11451, pp. 114–130. Springer, Cham (2019). https://doi.org/10.1007/978-3-030-16670-0_8
24. Lloyd, S.: Least squares quantization in PCM. IEEE Trans. Inf. Theory **28**(2), 129–137 (1982)
25. van der Maaten, L., Hinton, G.: Visualizing data using t-SNE. J. Mach. Learn. Res. **9**(Nov), 2579–2605 (2008)
26. Munkres, J.: Algorithms for the assignment and transportation problems. J. Soc. Ind. Appl. Math. **5**(1), 32–38 (1957)
27. Olson, R.S., La Cava, W., Orzechowski, P., Urbanowicz, R.J., Moore, J.H.: PMLB: a large benchmark suite for machine learning evaluation and comparison. BioData Min. **10**(1), 36 (2017)
28. Orzechowski, P., Boryczko, K.: Parallel approach for visual clustering of protein databases. Comput. Inform. **29**(6+), 1221–1231 (2012)
29. Orzechowski, P., La Cava, W., Moore, J.H.: Where are we now?: a large benchmark study of recent symbolic regression methods. In: Proceedings of the Genetic and Evolutionary Computation Conference, pp. 1183–1190. ACM (2018)
30. Pearson, K.: LIII. On lines and planes of closest fit to systems of points in space. Lond. Edinb. Dublin Philos. Mag. J. Sci. **2**(11), 559–572 (1901)
31. Pedregosa, F., et al.: Scikit-learn: machine learning in Python. J. Mach. Learn. Res. **12**, 2825–2830 (2011)
32. Rainville, D., Fortin, F.A., Gardner, M.A., Parizeau, M., Gagné, C., et al.: DEAP: a python framework for evolutionary algorithms. In: Proceedings of the 14th Annual Conference Companion on Genetic and Evolutionary Computation, pp. 85–92. ACM (2012)

33. Rao, C.R.: The utilization of multiple measurements in problems of biological classification. J. Roy. Stat. Soc.: Ser. B (Methodol.) **10**(2), 159–203 (1948)
34. Raymer, M.L., Punch, W.F., Goodman, E.D., Kuhn, L.A., Jain, A.K.: Dimensionality reduction using genetic algorithms. IEEE Trans. Evol. Comput. **4**(2), 164–171 (2000)
35. Roweis, S.T., Saul, L.K.: Nonlinear dimensionality reduction by locally linear embedding. Science **290**(5500), 2323–2326 (2000)
36. Sorzano, C.O.S., Vargas, J., Montano, A.P.: A survey of dimensionality reduction techniques. arXiv preprint arXiv:1403.2877 (2014)
37. Spearmen, C.: General intelligence objectively determined and measured. Am. J. Psychol. **15**, 107–197 (1904)
38. Tenenbaum, J.B., De Silva, V., Langford, J.C.: A global geometric framework for nonlinear dimensionality reduction. Science **290**(5500), 2319–2323 (2000)
39. Tipping, M.E., Bishop, C.M.: Probabilistic principal component analysis. J. Roy. Stat. Soc.: Ser. B (Stat. Methodol.) **61**(3), 611–622 (1999)
40. Torgerson, W.S.: Multidimensional scaling: I. Theory and method. Psychometrika **17**(4), 401–419 (1952). https://doi.org/10.1007/BF02288916
41. Vural, E., Guillemot, C.: Out-of-sample generalizations for supervised manifold learning for classification. IEEE Trans. Image Process. **25**(3), 1410–1424 (2016)
42. Vural, E., Guillemot, C.: A study of the classification of low-dimensional data with supervised manifold learning. J. Mach. Learn. Res. **18**(1), 5741–5795 (2017)
43. Wattenberg, M., Viégas, F., Johnson, I.: How to use t-SNE effectively. Distill (2016). https://doi.org/10.23915/distill.00002. http://distill.pub/2016/misread-tsne
44. Weinberger, K.Q., Saul, L.K.: An introduction to nonlinear dimensionality reduction by maximum variance unfolding. In: AAAI, vol. 6, pp. 1683–1686 (2006)
45. Yao, H., Tian, L.: A genetic-algorithm-based selective principal component analysis (GA-SPCA) method for high-dimensional data feature extraction. IEEE Trans. Geosci. Remote Sens. **41**(6), 1469–1478 (2003)
46. Zhang, Z., Wang, J.: MLLE: modified locally linear embedding using multiple weights. In: Advances in Neural Information Processing Systems, pp. 1593–1600 (2007)
47. Zhang, Z., Zha, H.: Principal manifolds and nonlinear dimensionality reduction via tangent space alignment. SIAM J. Sci. Comput. **26**(1), 313–338 (2004)
48. Zhao, D., Lin, Z., Tang, X.: Laplacian PCA and its applications. In: 2007 IEEE 11th International Conference on Computer Vision, pp. 1–8. IEEE (2007)

Ensemble Genetic Programming

Nuno M. Rodrigues[(✉)][ID], João E. Batista[ID], and Sara Silva[ID]

LASIGE, Faculdade de Ciências, Universidade de Lisboa, Lisbon, Portugal
{nmrodrigues,jebatista,sara}@fc.ul.pt

Abstract. Ensemble learning is a powerful paradigm that has been used in the top state-of-the-art machine learning methods like Random Forests and XGBoost. Inspired by the success of such methods, we have developed a new Genetic Programming method called Ensemble GP. The evolutionary cycle of Ensemble GP follows the same steps as other Genetic Programming systems, but with differences in the population structure, fitness evaluation and genetic operators. We have tested this method on eight binary classification problems, achieving results significantly better than standard GP, with much smaller models. Although other methods like M3GP and XGBoost were the best overall, Ensemble GP was able to achieve exceptionally good generalization results on a particularly hard problem where none of the other methods was able to succeed.

Keywords: Genetic Programming · Ensemble learning · Binary classification · Machine Learning

1 Introduction

Genetic Programming (GP) [25] is one of the most proficient Machine Learning (ML) methods. It is capable of addressing multiple tasks such as classification and regression, using a variety of techniques from the most classical [17] to the most recent, like the geometric semantic approaches [28] and the cluster-based multiclass classification [22].

Ensemble learning [9] is a powerful ML paradigm where multiple models are induced and their predicted outputs are combined in order to obtain predictions that are more accurate than the individual ones. Some of the most successful ML methods are based on ensemble learning, like Random Forests (RF) [4] and XGBoost (XG) [7]. On the other hand, their performance may vary substantially depending on the setting of some crucial parameters, like the number of trees and their maximum depth, which in turn depend on the properties of each dataset.

Inspired by the success of such methods, and motivated by the need to automatically find the right settings for these parameters, we have developed a new GP method called Ensemble GP (eGP). The evolutionary cycle of eGP follows the same steps as other GP systems, but with differences in the population structure, fitness evaluation and genetic operators. In particular, the population

T. Hu et al. (Eds.): EuroGP 2020, LNCS 12101, pp. 151–166, 2020.
https://doi.org/10.1007/978-3-030-44094-7_10

is composed of two subpopulations, trees and forests, where each subpopulation uses its own fitness function and genetic operators. The approach can be described as co-evolutionary, cooperative and compositional, and involves subsampling of both observations and features.

The rest of the paper is organized as follows. Section 2 describes related work, while Sect. 3 provides the details of the eGP method. Section 4 specifies the experimental setup, and Sects. 5 and 6 report and discuss the results obtained. Finally, Sect. 7 contains the conclusions and future work.

2   Related Work

Evolutionary computation and other bio-inspired methods have been linked to ensemble learning from early on (see [11] and references therein). An obvious way to build ensembles is to combine different individuals of a population, whether they are GP individuals (*e.g.* [31]) or other types, like neural networks (review in [15]). Many other types of ensembles have been built using evolutionary and other bio-inspired methods, like ensembles of clustering algorithms [8], Decision Trees [5], Support Vector Machines [1], or a mix of different types [10]. Diversity is important among ensemble members, and multiobjective evolutionary approaches have been often used to address this issue (*e.g.* [2,6,24] and references therein).

A multitude of publications focus on single specific aspects of ensemble learning, like selecting and combining the members of the ensemble (*e.g.* [10] and references therein), or evolving the functions that combine the different members (*e.g.* [10,16,19]). Others focus on building complete ensembles from scratch, but even if we limit ourselves to the ones that use GP exclusively (*e.g.* [3,13,29]), we find a large diversity of designs, goals and scales of application. A systematic review of this extremely vast and diverse literature is much needed in both evolutionary and ensemble learning communities.

3   Ensemble GP

Now, we describe the method we call ensemble GP (eGP) with all the variants we implemented and tested. The evolutionary cycle of eGP follows the same steps as other GP systems, but with differences in the population structure, fitness evaluation and genetic operators. In particular, the population is composed of two subpopulations, where each subpopulation uses its own fitness function and genetic operators. The approach can be described as co-evolutionary, cooperative and compositional, and involves subsampling of both observations and features. Algorithm 1 describes the main steps of eGP.

Before describing the details regarding the population, fitness and genetic operators of eGP, we briefly describe a GP system called M3GP [22] (Multidimensional Multiclass GP with Multidimensional Populations), not only because it is one of the baselines in our experiments, but also because some elements of eGP are highly inspired in M3GP.

Algorithm 1. eGP

---

procedure EGP($Dataset(D_s), n_t, n_f$)

    $Split\ D_s\ into\ training,\ testing\ and\ sub\ samples\ \Phi$

    $T_{list} \leftarrow Generate\ Trees(\Phi, n_t)$

    $F_{list} \leftarrow Generate\ Forests(n_f)$

    while $generation(g) < max\ generations$ **do**

        $T_{parents} \leftarrow Selection(T_{list})$

        $F_{parents} \leftarrow Selection(F_{list})$

        $T_{offspring} \leftarrow Breeding(T_{parents})$

        $F_{offspring} \leftarrow Breeding(F_{parents})$

        $F_{list} \leftarrow Prune(F_{offspring})$ ▷ Prune only the best forest

        $g++$

    end while

end procedure

3.1 M3GP

In terms of representation of the solutions, the main difference between M3GP and standard tree-based GP is the number of trees that are part of the same individual. While a standard GP individual is a single tree, a M3GP individual may be composed of several trees, called dimensions. Originally developed for performing multiclass classification [14,22], M3GP evolves each individual as a set of hyperfeatures, each one represented by a different tree/dimension. After remapping the input data into this new multidimensional feature space, it calculates the accuracy by forming clusters based on the data labels and classifying each observation as the class of the closest centroid according to the Mahalanobis distance. M3GP has also been used for evolving hyperfeatures for regression [23] and for classification in other GP systems [18].

Starting with only one tree/dimension per individual, M3GP uses standard subtree crossover and mutation between individuals, and three other operators designed for removing a tree/dimension from an individual, adding a randomly created tree/dimension to an individual, and swapping trees/dimensions between individuals. Additionally, a pruning operator is applied to the best individual of each generation, removing the trees/dimensions that do not improve its accuracy.

3.2 eGP Population Structure

The population is composed of two types of individuals: trees and forests. A tree is not the output model, but only a part of it. The output model is a forest, built as an ensemble of trees. Each tree may be part of many different forests, and some trees may be part of none.

Trees have the same structure as those used in standard GP, but instead of having access to all the observations and features of the training dataset, each individual only sees a subset of observations, and in many cases also a subset of features. Different variants of eGP use different sampling options: (1) 60% of all observations, all features included; (2) between one and all observations, one to all features included, these numbers being randomly chosen before each sampling. In both options, the sampling is done uniformly without replacement, and repeated whenever a new subset of training data is required for allocating to a new tree.

Forests have the same structure as the M3GP individuals, with each dimension being a tree from the subpopulation of trees.

3.3   eGP Fitness Functions

The subpopulation of trees uses a standard fitness function based on the error between expected and predicted outputs, like the Root Mean Squared Error (RMSE). In classification problems, the class labels are interpreted as the numeric expected outputs. The fitness of each tree is calculated using only the subset of observations allowed for this tree.

The subpopulation of forests uses a fitness function based on the accuracy obtained on all the observations of the training set. Each forest gathers, for each observation, a vote (on a class) from each of the trees that compose its ensemble. This vote is obtained by adopting the class label that is closer to the predicted output. The votes from the different trees of the ensemble can be combined by normal majority voting or by weighted voting.

In normal voting, for each observation the class that receives more votes wins, and ties are solved by randomly choosing one of the classes. In weighted voting (Algorithm 2), for each observation a certainty value is calculated for each class prediction of each tree, based on the vector of predicted values by all the trees of the ensemble (1). The sum of certainty values for each class is then calculated, and divided by the sum of certainty values for both classes. The class with highest results is chosen as the prediction.

We chose to use L2 normalization (2) for consistency with the cosine similarity used for the eCrossover (described next), which also uses L2. Other normalization methods were considered. Min-Max was discarded due to its inability for dealing with outliers; Z-Score was discarded because the resulting array was not contained in the $[0, 1]$ range.

$$certainty = 1 - l_2(X), X = \begin{pmatrix} x_1 \\ x_2 \\ \vdots \\ x_n \end{pmatrix} \tag{1}$$

$$l_2\ normalization = \sqrt{\sum_{k=1}^{n} |x_k|^2} \tag{2}$$

3.4   eGP Genetic Operators

The trees and forests of eGP use different genetic operators. Trees use what can be described as protected versions of the standard subtree crossover and mutation, designated here as eCrossover and eMutation, respectively. The protection

Algorithm 2. Weighted Voting

---

procedure WEIGHTED_VOTING(*predictions, certainties*)
    votes ← [ ]
    for *row in predictions* **do**
        zeros, ones ← 0
        for *col in certainties* **do**
            if *predictions*[*row*][*col*] == 1
                ones+ = *certainties*[*row*][*col*]
            else
                zeros+ = *certainties*[*row*][*col*]
        end for
        votes.append(0 **if** *zeros*/(*zeros* + *ones*) ≥ *ones*/(*zeros* + *ones*) **else** 1)
    end for
end procedure

---

is needed when parent trees are not allowed to see all the features due to feature sampling (see Sect. 3.2). In this case, the offspring must inherit feature restrictions from their parents, otherwise after a number of generations all the trees will be using all the features. Without feature sampling, these operators behave the same as the standard ones.

eMutation simply has to ensure that the new subtree created to replace a random branch of the parent is restricted to the same subset of features as the parent. eCrossover must guarantee that each swapped branch is also restricted to the subset of features inherited by the receiving offspring. Each of the two offspring inherits from one of its two parents. Instead of relying on a careful choice of compatible couples and branches to swap, eCrossover relies on a repair procedure that replaces features on the received branches whenever these features are not allowed by the inherited restrictions (Algorithm 3). Each illegal feature is compared to all the legal ones on the complete training set, using the cosine similarity measure (3). The chosen replacement is the most similar feature to the one that was removed. Unlike the euclidean distance, the cosine similarity can compare and recognize two vectors of similar meaning even if they have very different magnitudes.

$$S(X,Y) = \frac{\sum_{k=1}^{n} |x_k||y_k|}{\sqrt{\sum_{k=1}^{n} |x_k|^2}\sqrt{\sum_{k=1}^{n} |y_k|^2}} \tag{3}$$

Regarding the subpopulation of forests, it uses the same genetic operators as M3GP, namely two mutation operators to add and remove trees from the ensemble, and one crossover operator to swap trees between different ensembles.

4   Experimental Setup

This section describes our experimental setup for the eGP methods, comparing them against two baselines, standard GP and M3GP, and two state-of-the-art

---

Algorithm 3. eCrossover

---

procedure SUBTREE CROSSOVER($parent_1, parent_2$)
  $cp_1, cp_2 \leftarrow$ *choose crossover points*   ▷ crossover point 1 and 2
  $refact\ tree(parent_1, parent_2, cp_1, cp_2, bag_1, bag_2, Data_{Training})$
end procedure

procedure REFACT TREE($parent_1, parent_2, cp_1, cp_2, bag_1, bag_2, Data_{Training}$)
  $parent_1, parent_2 \leftarrow swap\ branches(cp_1, cp_2)$
  $fix\ terminals(p_1, bag_1, bag_2, Data_{Training})$
  $fix\ terminals(p_2, bag_2, bag_1, Data_{Training})$
end procedure

---

classifiers, Random Forests (RF) and XGBoost (XG). Six different variants of eGP were tested, and the results were analysed in terms of training and test accuracy, number of trees and number of nodes of the final solutions. When comparing accuracy, statistical significance is determined using the non-parametric Kruskal-Wallis test at $p < 0.01$. Next, we describe all the 10 methods tested, their main parameter settings, and the eight datasets used for obtaining the reported results.

4.1 Methods

Table 1 contains the acronyms and descriptions of all the methods used, and will serve as a memory aid for the remainder of this paper. The six eGP variants are eGP-N and eGP-W (normal and weighted voting with sampling of features and observations); eGP-N5 and eGP-W5 (same as previous but with populations of 500 trees and 500 forests, instead of 250 each); eGPn and eGPw (same as eGP-N and eGP-W but without feature sampling).

Table 1. Acronyms and descriptions of the methods

GP	Standard Genetic Programming
M3GP	Multidimensional Multiclass GP with Multidimensional Populations
eGP-N	Ensemble GP, feature sampling, normal voting
eGP-W	Ensemble GP, feature sampling, weighted voting
eGP-N5	Ensemble GP, feature sampling, normal voting, larger population
eGP-W5	Ensemble GP, feature sampling, weighted voting, larger population
eGPn	Ensemble GP, no feature sampling, normal voting
eGPw	Ensemble GP, no feature sampling, weighted voting
RF	Random Forests
XG	XGBoost

Table 2. Main parameter settings

Runs	30
Generations	100
Population size	GP/M3GP = 500, eGP = {250 + 250, 500 + 500}
Function set	$\{+, -, \times, /, \log, \sqrt{}\}$ (protected)
Fitness	GP = RMSE, M3GP/eGP = Accuracy
Selection	Tournament size 5 (GP/M3GP = Double Tournament)
Crossover/Mutation	GP = 0.95/0.05, M3GP/eGP = 0.5/0.5
Number of estimators	{50, 100, 150, 200}
Maximum depth	{2, 4, 6, 8}
Impurity measure	RF = {Gini, Entropy}

4.2   Parameters

Table 2 summarizes the main parameters used in the GP-based methods and in
the RF and XG methods. Each experiment is performed 30 times, with each
run using a different partition of the dataset in 70% training and 30% test.
The GP-based methods run for 100 generations. GP and M3GP use populations
of 500 individuals, while eGP initializes each subpopulation with 250 (or 500)
individuals, for a total of 500 (or 1000) trees + forests. Trees are initialized using
Ramped Half-and-Half, as suggested by Koza [17], while forests are initialized
in a similar fashion to M3GP, with only one tree per forest [22]. The arithmetic
operators of the function set are protected in the following way: when dividing a
value by zero, we return the numerator; when trying to square root or logarithm
a negative number, we return the number untouched. Therefore, the protection
is to ignore the presence of the operator whenever it raises an exception. No
constants are used. The fitness guiding the evolution is the RMSE in GP, and
the accuracy in M3GP and eGP. In order to obtain the accuracy from GP, the
predicted outputs are transformed into the closest numeric class labels. Selection
for breeding is made with Double Tournament [21] in GP and M3GP, and regular
tournament in eGP, size 5. Regarding genetic operators, the crossover/mutation
probabilities are 0.95/0.05 for GP, and 0.5/0.5 for both M3GP and eGP. This
means choosing between crossover and mutation with equal probability, but for
M3GP and eGP forests the specific type of crossover or mutation must then be
chosen, also with equal probability. Elitism guarantees that the best parent is
copied into the new population.

Regarding RF and XG (last three rows of the table), both were 10-fold cross-
validated for number of estimators and maximum depth, and RF was also cross-
validated for the impurity criterion.

4.3   Datasets

Table 3 describes the main characteristics of the datasets used in our experiments. We have selected eight problems from various domains, all being binary
classification tasks, with a different number of features and observations.

Table 3. Number of features, observations and negative/positive ratio on each dataset.

Datasets	BCW	BRAZIL	GAMETES	HEART	IONO	PARKS	PPI	SONAR
Features	11	8	1000	13	33	23	3	61
Observations	683	4872	1600	270	351	195	31320	208
Neg/Pos Ratio	35/65	42/58	50/50	45/55	65/35	75/25	52/48	46/54

BCW, HEART, IONO, PARKS. *Breast Cancer Wisconsin, Heart Disease, Ionosphere* and *Parkinsons* are datasets included in the UCI ML repository [20].

BRAZIL. *Brazil* is a dataset for detecting burned areas in satellite imagery, containing the radiance values of a set of pixels from a Landsat 8 OLI image over Brazil, and corrected unburned/burned labels [26].

GAMETES. *GAMETES_Epistasis_2-Way_1000atts_0.4H_EDM-1_EDM-1_1* is a simulated Genome-Wide Association Studies (GWAS) dataset generated using the GAMETES tool [18], available in OpenML [12].

PPI. *GRID/HPRD-unbal-HS* is a dataset built from a Protein-Protein Interaction benchmark of the human species [30], containing the $Resnik_{Max}$ semantic similarity measure between each pair of proteins on three different semantic aspects [27].

SONAR. *sonar.all-data* is a dataset for binary classification of sonar returns, available in Kaggle [32].

5   Results

Figures 1, 2, 3, 4, 5, 6, 7 and 8 show boxplots of the training and test accuracy obtained by all the methods on all the problems. For each problem there are two whiskered boxes, the left one for training and the right one for test. On the BRAZIL problem, five outliers were removed for visualization purposes, two on training (90.97% and 67.92%, both for GP) and three on test (90.70% and 68.95% for GP, 77.29% for eGP-N5).

Between the two baselines, as expected M3GP is better than standard GP, achieving significantly better training accuracy on all eight problems, and also significantly better test accuracy on five of them (BRAZIL, IONO, PARKS, PPI and SONAR). In fact, in all pairwise comparisons with the other methods in all the problems, standard GP is significantly worse in 96% of the cases on training, and 46% on test. The only exception where it performs significantly better is on the HEART problem, against RF on the test data.

Regarding the two proposed methods eGP-N and eGP-W, a comparison between them reveals that the weighted voting (eGP-W) does not seem to improve performance over the normal voting (eGP-N), as the weighted voting resulted in one significantly worse training accuracy in the PARKS problem (and another borderline worse in IONO), all other results being equal to the ones of normal voting. Also between eGP-N5 and eGP-W5 the weighted voting resulted in one significantly worse training accuracy in the IONO problem, all other results showing no significant differences.

Increasing the population size from 250 to 500 proved to be only marginally beneficial, more to weighted than to normal voting. eGP-N5 achieved significantly better results than eGP-N on four problems (GAMETES, IONO, PARKS and SONAR) on training, and none on test, all other results being statistically equal. eGP-W5 was significantly better than eGP-W on five problems (BCW, HEART, IONO, PARKS and SONAR) on training, and on one problem (IONO) on test, all other results equal.

Regarding the eGP methods without feature sampling (eGPn and eGPw), in several cases they revealed to be significantly better than their feature sampling counterparts (eGP-N and eGP-W), more often on training but also on two test cases, on problems IONO and PARKS. Even when compared to the 500 individual counterparts, they were often better on training and never worse on test. The weighted voting did not improve or worsen the obtained accuracy.

When comparing the eGP methods with the M3GP baseline, we realize that on training accuracy M3GP is better than all eGP methods on four problems (GAMETES, HEART, PARKS and SONAR), worse than all eGP methods on two problems (BCW and PPI), and on the remaining problems it is better or equal to most eGP methods, except one case where it is worse (than eGPw, on BRAZIL). On test accuracy M3GP is better than all eGP methods on four problems (IONO, PARKS, PPI and SONAR), statistically the same as all eGP methods on three problems (BCW, GAMETES, HEART), and on the remaining problem M3GP is better than all eGP feature sampling methods and statistically the same as eGPn and eGPw.

When comparing the eGP methods with the state-of-the-art RF and XG, on training both are significantly better than practically all eGP methods on all problems (except SONAR, where RF is significantly worse than all except eGP-N and eGP-W). On test accuracy, on two problems (BCW and GAMETES) there are few significant differences (XG is better than eGP-N and eGP-W), on two other problems (IONO, PARKS) both RF and XG are better than all eGP methods, and on the remaining problems RF is either the same (BRAZIL and PPI), worse (HEART) or better (SONAR) in most cases, while XG is better in all except a few cases (eGPn and eGPw on BRAZIL, eGP-N on HEART, with no significant differences).

6   Discussion

In order to better understand how each of the 10 methods scored relatively to each other, we have counted how many significantly better results each one obtained among all $72 + 72 = 144$ (training + test) pairwise comparisons on all problems. Table 4 shows the counting (totals are the sum of all problems) and ranks the methods according to the test totals (training + test in case of tie).

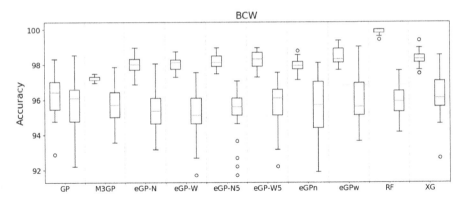

Fig. 1. Boxplot for the training (left) and test (right) accuracy of each method in the BCW dataset.

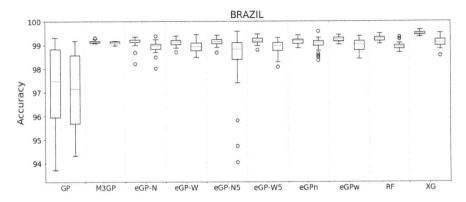

Fig. 2. Boxplot for the training (left) and test (right) accuracy of each method in the BRAZIL dataset. Outliers removed for visualization purposes: on training, 90.97% and 67.92%, both for GP; on test, 90.70% and 68.95% for GP, and 77.29% for eGP-N5.

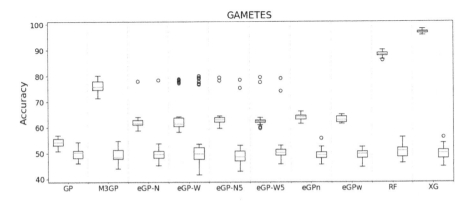

Fig. 3. Boxplot for the training (left) and test (right) accuracy of each method in the GAMETES dataset.

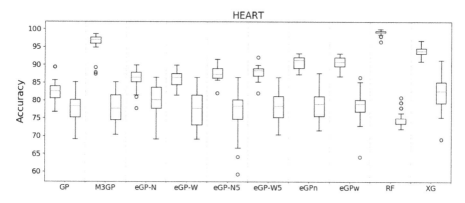

Fig. 4. Boxplot for the training (left) and test (right) accuracy of each method in the HEART dataset.

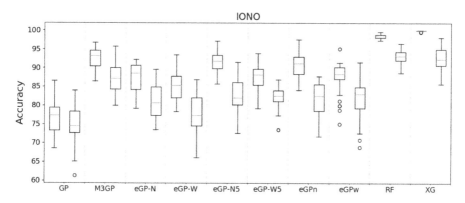

Fig. 5. Boxplot for the training (left) and test (right) accuracy of each method in the IONO dataset.

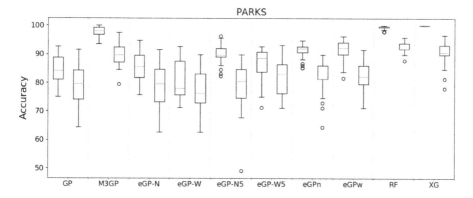

Fig. 6. Boxplot for the training (left) and test (right) accuracy of each method in the PARKS dataset.

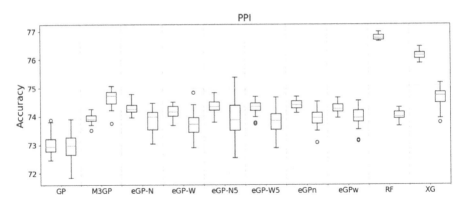

Fig. 7. Boxplot for the training (left) and test (right) accuracy of each method in the PPI dataset.

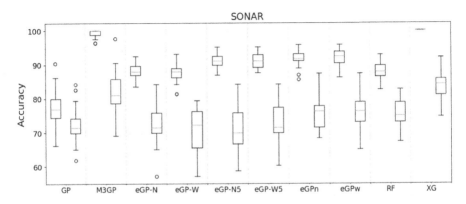

Fig. 8. Boxplot for the training (left) and test (right) accuracy of each method in the SONAR dataset.

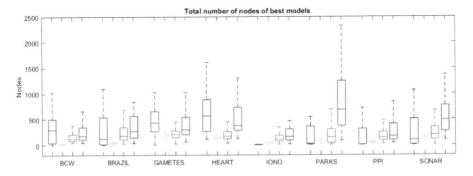

Fig. 9. Number of nodes of final models. For each problem, the four boxes are: GP (black), M3GP (cyan), eGP-N + eGP-W + eGP-N5 + eGP-W5 all together (magenta), and eGPn + eGPw together (blue). All outliers removed for visualization purposes. (Color figure online)

Table 4. Counting of how many significantly better results each method obtained among all pairwise comparisons. The totals are the sum for all problems. Order of the problems: BCW, BRAZIL, GAMETES, HEART, IONO, PARKS, PPI, SONAR.

Method	Training	Test
XG	$3+9+9+7+9+9+8+9=\mathbf{63}$	$2+6+0+8+8+7+8+8=\mathbf{47}$
M3GP	$1+1+7+8+5+7+1+8=\mathbf{38}$	$0+6+0+1+7+7+8+8=\mathbf{37}$
RF	$9+6+8+9+8+8+9+1=\mathbf{58}$	$0+1+0+0+8+8+2+4=\mathbf{23}$
eGPw	$5+5+3+5+1+4+2+4=\mathbf{29}$	$0+1+0+1+2+1+1+0=\ \mathbf{6}$
eGPn	$2+1+5+5+5+4+3+4=\mathbf{29}$	$0+1+0+1+2+0+1+0=\ \mathbf{5}$
eGP-N5	$2+1+2+2+5+3+3+4=\mathbf{22}$	$0+1+0+1+2+0+1+0=\ \mathbf{5}$
eGP-W5	$4+1+1+3+2+1+2+4=\mathbf{18}$	$0+1+0+1+2+0+1+0=\ \mathbf{5}$
eGP-N	$2+1+1+1+2+1+2+1=\mathbf{11}$	$0+1+0+1+1+0+1+0=\ \mathbf{4}$
eGP-W	$2+1+1+1+1+0+2+1=\ \mathbf{9}$	$0+1+0+0+0+0+1+0=\ \mathbf{2}$
GP	$0+0+0+0+0+0+0+0=\ \mathbf{0}$	$0+0+0+1+0+0+0+0=\ \mathbf{1}$

These numbers confirm what had already been observed in the boxplots: (1) the eGP methods, although better than standard GP, were not able to outperform M3GP or the state-of-the-art RF and XG, (2) the eGP variants without feature sampling (eGPn and eGPw) are better than the other eGP methods, and (3) normal voting is generally better than weighted voting.

Not being an ensemble method, it is noteworthy how well M3GP scored, better than RF and all other methods except XG. It is also important to emphasize that the only methods where the running parameters were tuned by cross-validation were RF and XG (see Sect. 4.2). Therefore, we have no doubt regarding the superiority of M3GP over RF, and raise the question of whether it could surpass XG had its parameters also been tuned.

Regarding the ranking of the eGP methods, it is possible that feature sampling is not necessary for a GP ensemble, due to the feature selection that most GP trees naturally do. We must also consider that the feature replacement performed by eCrossover may have highly destructive effects on the fitness of the offspring. Another thing to consider is the possible inadequacy of our certainty measure to weight the voting of the ensembles.

Although the results of the eGP methods seem disappointing, they are no doubt a viable alternative to standard GP, not only in terms of fitness but also in terms of the size of the evolved models. Figure 9 shows the total number of nodes of the best models found by the GP-based methods, grouped in four sets: (1) GP only (black); (2) M3GP only (cyan); (3) eGP methods with feature sampling (eGP-N + eGP-W + eGP-N5 + eGP-W5 all together, magenta); (4) eGP methods without feature sampling (eGPn + eGPw together, blue), results per problem.

The variants with feature sampling exhibit values with much less dispersion than the ones produced by GP (except on the IONO problem), and significantly lower on three problems (BCW, GAMETES, HEART). This result becomes even more important when we recall that GP used Double Tournament for bloat control (see Sect. 4.2) and is composed of a single tree, while eGP did not use any bloat control and is composed of an ensemble of trees. M3GP produced the smallest solutions of all GP-based methods, however it also used Double Tournament. Regarding the number of trees that form the evolved ensembles (not shown), the eGP methods revealed a remarkable consistency among the different problems, with different runs always using between $2(\pm1)$ and $13(\pm2)$ trees on the best forest. This is in sharp contrast to the number of dimensions used by M3GP, with some problems using as few as 1–4 (BCW) and others using as many as 11–24 (SONAR), 13–30 (HEART) and 20–36 (GAMETES).

The GAMETES problem posed the largest difficulties to all the methods, but special attention must be given to the results obtained by some of the eGP methods, precisely the ones that scored worse in general: eGP-N, eGP-W, eGP-N5, eGP-W5. Looking back at Fig. 3, we observe a large amount of outliers of much higher accuracy than normal. On the test data, these are by far the best results achieved, similar to the ones reported in [18], and only the four mentioned eGP methods were able to achieve them. Although out of the scope of this paper, these methods were indeed the only ones able to find, among the 1000 features of this problem, the right combinations that allowed such a big "jump" in accuracy. Therefore, they deserve more investigation, despite their apparent modest performance.

7   Conclusions and Future Work

We have developed a new GP method called Ensemble GP (eGP) and tested it on eight binary classification problems from various domains, with a different number of features and observations. Different variants of eGP were compared to standard GP and M3GP baselines, and to the Random Forests and XGBoost state-of-the-art methods. The results show that eGP consistently evolves smaller and more accurate models than standard GP. M3GP and XGBoost were the best methods overall, but on a particularly hard problem the eGP variants were able to reach exceptionally good generalization results, way above all the other methods.

As future work, we will investigate ways to improve eGP in different fronts, making it more competitive with M3GP and XGBoost while maintaining the characteristics that granted its current success. For example, bloat control and some parameter tuning are two elements that other methods are benefiting from, and that we will incorporate also in eGP. Different voting schemes may also prove beneficial, as well as alternative ways to sample features and observations. Additionally, we will also work towards extending eGP in order to give it the ability to address also regression problems and multiclass classification problems.

Acknowledgement. This work was partially supported by FCT through funding of LASIGE Research Unit UIDB/00408/2020 and projects PTDC/CCI-INF/29168/2017, PTDC/CCI-CIF/29877/2017, DSAIPA/DS/0022/2018, PTDC/ASP-PLA/28726/2017 and PTDC/CTA-AMB/30056/2017.

References

1. Okayama,de Araújo Padilha, C.A., Barone, D.A.C., Neto, A.D.D.: A multi-level approach using genetic algorithms in an ensemble of least squares support vector machines. Knowl.-Based Syst. **106**, 85–95 (2016). https://doi.org/10.1016/j.knosys.2016.05.033
2. Bhowan, U., Johnston, M., Zhang, M., Yao, X.: Evolving diverse ensembles using genetic programming for classification with unbalanced data. IEEE Trans. Evol. Comput. **17**(3), 368–386 (2013). https://doi.org/10.1109/TEVC.2012.2199119
3. Brameier, M., Banzhaf, W.: Evolving teams of predictors with linear genetic programming. Genet. Program Evolvable Mach. **2**(4), 381–407 (2001). https://doi.org/10.1023/A:1012978805372
4. Breiman, L.: Random forests. Mach. Learn. **45**, 5–32 (2001). https://doi.org/10.1023/A:1010933404324
5. Cantu-Paz, E., Kamath, C.: Inducing oblique decision trees with evolutionary algorithms. IEEE Trans. Evol. Comput. **7**(1), 54–68 (2003)
6. Chandra, A., Yao, X.: Ensemble learning using multi-objective evolutionary algorithms. J. Math. Model. Algorithms **5**(4), 417–445 (2006). https://doi.org/10.1007/s10852-005-9020-3
7. Chen, T., Guestrin, C.: XGBoost: a scalable tree boosting system. ArXiv abs/1603.02754 (2016)
8. Coelho, A.L.V., Fernandes, E., Faceli, K.: Multi-objective design of hierarchical consensus functions for clustering ensembles via genetic programming. Decis. Support Syst. **51**(4), 794–809 (2011). https://doi.org/10.1016/j.dss.2011.01.014
9. Dietterich, T.G.: Ensemble methods in machine learning. In: Kittler, J., Roli, F. (eds.) MCS 2000. LNCS, vol. 1857, pp. 1–15. Springer, Heidelberg (2000). https://doi.org/10.1007/3-540-45014-9_1
10. Escalante, H.J., Acosta-Mendoza, N., Morales-Reyes, A., Gago-Alonso, A.: Genetic programming of heterogeneous ensembles for classification. In: Ruiz-Shulcloper, J., Sanniti di Baja, G. (eds.) CIARP 2013. LNCS, vol. 8258, pp. 9–16. Springer, Heidelberg (2013). https://doi.org/10.1007/978-3-642-41822-8_2
11. Gagné, C., Sebag, M., Schoenauer, M., Tomassini, M.: Ensemble learning for free with evolutionary algorithms? In: Proceedings of the 9th Annual Conference on Genetic and Evolutionary Computation (GECCO 2007), pp. 1782–1789. ACM, New York (2007). https://doi.org/10.1145/1276958.1277317
12. Gijsbers,P.:Gametes_epistasis_2-way_1000atts_0.4h_edm-1_edm-1_1(2017).https://www.openml.org/d/40645
13. Iba, H.: Bagging, boosting, and bloating in genetic programming. In: Proceedings of the 1st Annual Conference on Genetic and Evolutionary Computation (GECCO 1999), vol. 2, pp. 1053–1060. Morgan Kaufmann Publishers Inc., San Francisco (1999). http://dl.acm.org/citation.cfm?id=2934046.2934063
14. Ingalalli, V., Silva, S., Castelli, M., Vanneschi, L.: A multi-dimensional genetic programming approach for multi-class classification problems. In: Nicolau, M., et al. (eds.) EuroGP 2014. LNCS, vol. 8599, pp. 48–60. Springer, Heidelberg (2014). https://doi.org/10.1007/978-3-662-44303-3_5

15. Islam, M.M., Yao, X.: Evolving artificial neural network ensembles. IEEE Comput. Intell. Mag. **3**, 31–42 (2008)
16. Johansson, U., Lofstrom, T., Konig, R., Niklasson, L.: Building neural network ensembles using genetic programming. In: The 2006 IEEE International Joint Conference on Neural Network Proceedings, pp. 1260–1265, July 2006. https://doi.org/10.1109/IJCNN.2006.246836
17. Koza, J.R.: Genetic Programming (1992)
18. La Cava, W., Silva, S., Vanneschi, L., Spector, L., Moore, J.: Genetic programming representations for multi-dimensional feature learning in biomedical classification. In: Squillero, G., Sim, K. (eds.) EvoApplications 2017. LNCS, vol. 10199, pp. 158–173. Springer, Cham (2017). https://doi.org/10.1007/978-3-319-55849-3_11
19. Langdon, W.B., Buxton, B.F.: Genetic programming for combining classifiers. In: Proceedings of the Genetic and Evolutionary Computation Conference (GECCO 2001), pp. 66–73. Morgan Kaufmann (2001)
20. Lichman, M.: UCI Machine Learning Repository (2013). https://archive.ics.uci.edu/ml/index.php
21. Luke, S., Panait, L.: Fighting bloat with nonparametric parsimony pressure. In: Guervós, J.J.M., Adamidis, P., Beyer, H.-G., Schwefel, H.-P., Fernández-Villacañas, J.-L. (eds.) PPSN 2002. LNCS, vol. 2439, pp. 411–421. Springer, Heidelberg (2002). https://doi.org/10.1007/3-540-45712-7_40
22. Muñoz, L., Silva, S., Trujillo, L.: M3GP – multiclass classification with GP. In: Machado, P., et al. (eds.) EuroGP 2015. LNCS, vol. 9025, pp. 78–91. Springer, Cham (2015). https://doi.org/10.1007/978-3-319-16501-1_7
23. Muñoz, L., Trujillo, L., Silva, S., Castelli, M., Vanneschi, L.: Evolving multidimensional transformations for symbolic regression with M3GP. Memetic Comput. **11**(2), 111–126 (2018). https://doi.org/10.1007/s12293-018-0274-5
24. de Oliveira, D.F., Canuto, A.M.P., de Souto, M.C.P.: Use of multi-objective genetic algorithms to investigate the diversity/accuracy dilemma in heterogeneous ensembles. In: 2009 International Joint Conference on Neural Networks, pp. 2339–2346 (2009)
25. Poli, R., Langdon, W.B., McPhee, N.F.: A Field Guide to Genetic Programming. Lulu Enterprises, UK Ltd., Essex (2008)
26. Silva, S., Vanneschi, L., Cabral, A.I., Vasconcelos, M.J.: A semi-supervised genetic programming method for dealing with noisy labels and hidden overfitting. Swarm Evol. Comput. **39**, 323–338 (2018). https://doi.org/10.1016/j.swevo.2017.11.003
27. Sousa, R.T., Silva, S., Pesquita, C.: Evolving knowledge graph similarity for supervised learning in complex biomedical domains. BMC Bioinform. **21**, 6 (2020). https://doi.org/10.1186/s12859-019-3296-1
28. Vanneschi, L.: An introduction to geometric semantic genetic programming. In: Schütze, O., Trujillo, L., Legrand, P., Maldonado, Y. (eds.) NEO 2015. SCI, vol. 663, pp. 3–42. Springer, Cham (2017). https://doi.org/10.1007/978-3-319-44003-3_1
29. Veeramachaneni, K., Arnaldo, I., Derby, O., O'Reilly, U.M.: FlexGP. J. Grid Comput. **13**, 391–407 (2015)
30. Yu, J., Guo, M., Needham, C.J., Huang, Y., Cai, L., Westhead, D.R.: Simple sequence-based kernels do not predict protein-protein interactions. Bioinformatics **26**(20), 2610–2614 (2010). https://doi.org/10.1093/bioinformatics/btq483
31. Zhang, B., Joung, J.G.: Enhancing robustness of genetic programming at the species level. In: Genetic Programming Conference (GP 1997), pp. 336–342. Morgan Kaufmann (1997)
32. Zhang, S.: sonar.all-data (2018). https://www.kaggle.com/ypzhangsam/sonaralldata

SGP-DT: Semantic Genetic Programming Based on Dynamic Targets

Stefano Ruberto[1(✉)], Valerio Terragni[2], and Jason H. Moore[1]

[1] Institute for Biomedical Informatics, University of Pennsylvania,
Philadelphia, USA
stefano.ruberto@pennmedicine.upenn.edu, jhmoore@upenn.edu
[2] Faculty of Informatics, Universitá della Svizzera italiana USI, Lugano, Switzerland
valerio.terragni@usi.ch

Abstract. Semantic GP is a promising approach that introduces semantic awareness during genetic evolution. This paper presents a new Semantic GP approach based on Dynamic Target (SGP-DT) that divides the search problem into multiple GP runs. The evolution in each run is guided by a new (dynamic) target based on the residual errors. To obtain the final solution, SGP-DT combines the solutions of each run using linear scaling. SGP-DT presents a new methodology to produce the offspring that does not rely on the classic crossover. The synergy between such a methodology and linear scaling yields to final solutions with low approximation error and computational cost. We evaluate SGP-DT on eight well-known data sets and compare with ϵ-LEXICASE, a state-of-the-art evolutionary technique. SGP-DT achieves small RMSE values, on average 23.19% smaller than the one of ϵ-LEXICASE.

Keywords: Semantic GP · Genetic Programming · Natural selection · Symbolic Regression · Residuals · Linear scaling · Crossover · Mutation

1 Introduction

Recently, researchers successfully applied Semantic methods to Genetic Programming (SGP) on different domains, showing promising results [1–3]. While the classic GP operators (e.g., selection, crossover and mutation) act at the syntactic level, blindly to the semantic (behavior) of the individuals (e.g., programs), the key idea of SGP is to apply semantic evaluations [1]. More specifically, classic GP operators ignore the behavioral characteristic of the offspring, focusing only on improving the fitness of the individuals. Differently, SGP uses a richer feedback during the evolution that incorporates semantic awareness, which has the potential to improve the power of genetic programming [1].

In this paper, we are considering the Symbolic Regression domain, and thus assuming the availability of training cases (defined as m pairs of inputs and desired output). Following the most popular SGP approaches [1], we intend *"semantics"* as the set of output values of a program on the training cases [4].

© Springer Nature Switzerland AG 2020
T. Hu et al. (Eds.): EuroGP 2020, LNCS 12101, pp. 167–183, 2020.
https://doi.org/10.1007/978-3-030-44094-7_11

Such an approach obtains a richer feedback during the evolution relying on the evaluation of the individuals on the training cases. More formally, the semantics of an individual $\mathcal{I}$ is a vector $sem(\mathcal{I}) = \langle y_1, y_2, \cdots, y_m \rangle$ of responses to the m inputs of the training cases. Let $sem(\hat{y}) = \langle \hat{y_1}, \hat{y_2}, \cdots, \hat{y_m} \rangle$ denote the semantic vector of the target (as defined in the training set), where $\hat{y_1}, \hat{y_2}, \cdots, \hat{y_m}$ are the desired outputs. SGP defines *semantic space* [1] with a metric that characterizes the distance between the semantic vectors of the individuals $sem(\mathcal{I})$ and the target $sem(\hat{y})$. SGP often relies on such a distance to compute the fitness score, inducing a unimodal fitness landscape, which avoids local optima by construction [5].

The effectiveness of SGP depends on the availability of GP operators that can move in the semantic space towards the global optimum. An example of semantic operator is the geometric crossover proposed by Moraglio et al. [5]. It produces an offspring with a semantic vector that lies on the line connecting the parents in the semantic space. Thus, it guarantees that the offspring is no worse than the worst of the parents [5]. However, such crossover operator has the major drawback of producing individuals with an exponentially increasing size (i.e., *exponential bloat*) [1,5]. To avoid the exponential bloat, researchers proposed variants of this operator that minimize bloating [2] but at the cost of dropping the important guarantee of non-worsening crossover operations.

In this paper, we present a new SGP approach called **SGP-DT** (*S*emantic *G*enetic *P*rogramming based on *D*ynamic *T*argets) that minimizes the exponential bloat problem and at the same time gives a bound on the worsening of the offspring. SGP-DT divides the search problem into multiple GP runs. Each run is guided by a different dynamic target, which SGP-DT updates at each run based on the residual errors of the previous run. Then, SGP-DT combines the results of each run into a *"optimized"* final solution.

In a nutshell, SGP-DT works as follows. SGP-DT runs the GP algorithm (see Algorithm 1) a fixed number of times (N_{ext}) depending on the available budget. We call these runs *external* iterations. As opposed to the *internal* iterations (i.e., generations) that the GP algorithm performs to evolve the individuals. Each GP run performs a fixed number of internal iterations and returns a model (i.e., the best solution) that we call *partial model*. The next external iteration runs the GP algorithm with a modified training set, where SGP-DT replaces the m desired outputs $\hat{y}_i = \langle \hat{y_1}, \hat{y_2}, \cdots, \hat{y_m} \rangle$ with the residual errors of the partial model returned by the previous iteration. That is, the difference between $sem(\mathcal{I}_i)$ and $sem(\hat{y}_{i-1})$, where $\mathcal{I}_i$ is the partial model at the ith iteration. Thus, at each external iteration, the fitness function evaluates differently the individuals (because the fitness functions predicates on different training sets). As such, each partial model focuses on a different portion of the problem, the one that most influences the fitness value. As a result, our approach leads to dynamic targets that change at each external iteration incorporating the semantic information. SGP-DT obtains the final solution after N_{ext} iterations with a linear combination in the form $\sum_{i=0}^{N_{ext}} a_i + b_i \cdot \mathcal{I}_i$, where a_i and b_i are computed with the well-known *linear scaling* [6]. There is a key advantage of using linear scaling.

Keijzers showed that linear scaling gives a bound on the error of those generated individuals that are linear scaled [6]. Therefore, SGP-DT entails a bound on the worsening of the offspring at each internal and external iteration.

To reduce the exponential bloat problem, SGP-DT performs the internal GP iterations relying on classic mutation operators only. It does not rely on any form of crossover, neither geometric nor classic, and thus avoiding their fundamental limitations. Geometric crossover leads to exponential bloat and classic crossover decreases the chance to obtain a fitness improvement because it exchanges random functionalities at random points [7]. Despite the absence of crossovers, SGP-DT implicitly recombines different functionalities, similarly to a geometric crossover [5]. This is because, each partial model focuses on a different characteristic of the problem that the fitness function recognized as important (at that iteration). This makes the search more efficient because the evolution focuses on a single characteristic at a time leaving unaltered other (already optimized) characteristics.

We evaluated our approach on eight well-known regression problems. We compared SGP-DT with two baselines: LASSO a least square regression technique by Efron et al. [8]; and ϵ-LEXICASE a state-of-the-art SGP approach by La Cava et al. [9]. The results show that our approach obtains a median RMSE on 50 runs that is, on average, 51.47% and 23.19% smaller than the one of LASSO and ϵ-LEXICASE, respectively. Moreover, SGP-DT requires as much as 9.26$\times$ fewer tree computations than ϵ-LEXICASE (4.81$\times$ on average).

The remainder of this paper is organized as follows. Section 2 describes our approach. Section 3 discusses the related work. Section 4 reports our experimental evaluation and discusses the results. Section 5 concludes the paper.

2   Methodology

Algorithm 1 overviews the SGP-DT approach. Given the values of the independent ($\overline{x}$) and dependent ($\hat{y}$) variables of the training cases, and the number of external (N_{ext}) and internal (N_{int}) iterations, it returns the final solution (*finalModel*).

SGP-DT considers tree-like individuals with the usual non-terminal symbols: $+, -, \cdot, /$ (the protected division), *ERC* (between -1 and 1). In addition, SGP-DT considers the functions *Min* and *Max* that returns the minimum and maximum between two numbers, respectively. The rationale of adding the two latter symbols is to inject *discontinuity* to make the linear combinations more adaptable. Although also the protected division adds discontinuity in the form of asymptotes, such discontinuity often promotes overfitting [6,10]. With *Min* and *Max* functions, we introduce valid discontinuities alternatives that do not suffer from the limitation of the protected division.

Algorithm 1 holds out a portion of the training cases for validation (lines 1–3). SGP-DT will use such validation sets to construct the final solution (line 22). Lines 4–5 initialize the current target with $\hat{y}$ and the lists of the best models with the empty list. Line 6 starts the external loop, which re-assigns $\mathcal{P}$

Algorithm 1: SGP-DT

---

input : $\overline{x}$: values of the independent variables of the training cases
$\hat{y}$: values of the dependent variables of the training cases
N_{ext} : number of external iterations
N_{int} : number of internal iterations

output : $finalModel$: final regression model

1   $\langle \overline{x}_{\text{val}}, \hat{y}_{\text{val}} \rangle \leftarrow \text{SPLIT}(\overline{x}, \hat{y})$

2   $\overline{x} \leftarrow \{\overline{x} \backslash \overline{x}_{\text{val}}\}$

3   $\hat{y} \leftarrow \{\hat{y} \backslash \hat{y}_{\text{val}}\}$

4   $target \leftarrow \hat{y}$

5   $models \leftarrow \emptyset$

6   **for** $ext\text{-}iter\ 1 \ldots N_{ext}$ **do**

7     $\mathcal{P} \leftarrow \text{GET-RANDOM-INITIAL-POPULATION}()$

8   **for** $int\text{-}iter\ 1 \ldots N_{int}$ **do**

9   **for** $each\ \mathcal{I} \in \mathcal{P}$ **do**

10        $\mathcal{I}_{\text{ls}} \leftarrow \text{COMPUTE-LS}(\mathcal{I}, \overline{x}, target)$ // linear scaling

11        $fitness(\mathcal{I}) \leftarrow \sigma^2(sem(\mathcal{I}_{\text{ls}}(\overline{x})) - target)$ // σ^2 variance

12       $\mathcal{I}_{ls}^{\star} \leftarrow \text{GET-BEST-INDIVIDUAL}(\mathcal{P})$

13       $error \leftarrow target - sem(\mathcal{I}_{ls}^{\star}(\overline{x}))$

14   add $\mathcal{I}_{ls}^{\star}$ to $models$

15       $\mathcal{P}' \leftarrow \emptyset$

16   add $\text{ELITE}(\mathcal{P})$ to $\mathcal{P}'$

17   **while** $\mathcal{P}'$ *is not full* **do**

18        $\mathcal{I} \leftarrow \text{TOURNAMENT-SELECTION}(\mathcal{P})$

19   add $\text{MUTATE}(\mathcal{I})$ to $\mathcal{P}'$

20       $\mathcal{P} \leftarrow \mathcal{P}'$

21     $target \leftarrow error$ // update the target

22   $bestModels \leftarrow \text{VALIDATE-AND-SELECT}(\overline{x}_{\text{val}}, \hat{y}_{\text{val}}, models)$ // best MSE models on val

23   $finalModel \leftarrow \sum_{model \in bestModels} model$

24   **return** $finalModel$

---

to a fresh randomly generated population with the *ramped-half-and-half* approach (function GET-RANDOM-INITIAL-POPULATION of Algorithm 1). Starting every external iteration with a new population alleviates the overfitting problem. Indeed, the syntactic structures of already evolved individuals can be too complex to adapt to a new fitness landscape or to generalize on unseen data. To further reduce overfitting and the cost of fitness evaluation, SGP-DT generates the initial population with individuals with low complexity (i.e., a few nodes).

At line 8, SGP-DT starts the N_{int} internal iterations, which resembles the classic GP but with the addition of linear scaling and the absence of crossover. Before line 11 computes the fitness of each individual $\mathcal{I}$ in $\mathcal{P}$, line 10 performs the linear scaling of $\mathcal{I}$ [6]. Linear scaling has the advantage of transforming the semantic of individuals so that their potential fit with the current target is immediately given: we do not need to wait for GP to produce a partial model that reaches the same result [6]. And thus, linear scaling reduces the number of both external and internal iterations. Fewer iterations means populations with simpler structural complexity and less computational cost. Reducing the complexity of the solutions may reduce overfitting [11].

Linear scaling has another important property: it gives an upper bound on the error [6]. Recall that SGP-DT considers errors on dynamic targets, which change at each iteration (at the first iteration the dynamic target is $\hat{y}$). To exploit such a situation, we propose a fitness function based on this upper bound. Following Keijzer [6], we compute the linear scaling of an individual $\mathcal{I}$ as follows:

$$\mathcal{I}_{ls} = a + b \cdot \mathcal{I} \tag{1}$$

$$\text{where} \quad a = \bar{\hat{y}} - b \cdot \bar{y} \quad \text{and} \quad b = \frac{\sum_{i=1}^{n}[(\hat{y}_i - \bar{\hat{y}}) \cdot (y_i - \bar{y})]}{\sum_{i=1}^{n}[(y_i - \bar{y})^2]} \tag{2}$$

We define the following fitness function of an individual $\mathcal{I}$:

$$\text{fitness}(\mathcal{I}) = \sigma^2(\text{sem}(\mathcal{I}_{ls}(\overline{x})) - \hat{y}) \tag{3}$$

The rationale of this function is that the Mean Square Error (MSE) of $\mathcal{I}_{ls}$ has the variance (σ^2) of the current target as an upper bound [12]:

$$MSE = \frac{\sum_{i=0}^{m}(y_i - \hat{y}_i)^2}{m} \leq \sigma^2(\hat{y}) \tag{4}$$

where m is the number of training cases (y).

At each new external iteration the residual error becomes the new target (line 21).

$$\text{target} = \hat{y} - \text{sem}(\mathcal{I}_{ls}^{\star}(\overline{x})) \tag{5}$$

where $\text{sem}(\mathcal{I}_{ls}^{\star}(\overline{x}))$ is the evaluation of the best individual at the current iteration, which we call *partial model*.

The inequality 4 does not guarantee that the external iterations converge to a lower MSE because we do not know if $\sigma^2(\text{error}) \leq \sigma^2(\hat{y})$, where $\text{error} = \text{target} - \text{sem}(\mathcal{I}_{les}^{\star}(\overline{x}))$. Thus, by optimizing the variance of the error shown in Eq. 3, we act directly on the minimization of the upper bound, so that the next external iteration can benefit from a lower bound.

At lines 17–19, Algorithm 1 runs a classic GP algorithm without crossovers, using only mutations. We use a tree-based mutation operator because SGP-DT uses trees as syntactic structures for the individuals. The operator randomly generates a subtree from a randomly chosen node. To increase the synergy with linear scaling, we set two constraints during mutation. First, the node selection is biased towards the leaves of the tree, so that the mutated tree does not diverge too much from the original semantic (*locality principle*). Producing a mutation that is close to the original semantic of the tree preserves the validity of the selection performed after the linear scaling. And thus, we only allow minor changes to improve the fitness. Second, for the same reason, the mutation is biased towards replacing the selected node with a sub-tree of limited depth. Note that, we decided not to limit the maximum size (number of nodes in the tree) or depth of an individual. By doing so, GP can grow and choose the right solution complexity for the problem at hand. These two constraints help us to mitigate the overfitting and bloat problem without preventing the SGP-DT to effectively search for competitive individuals. As linear scaling helps GP to find useful individuals (thanks to the upper bound). Moreover, additional external iterations will further refine other aspects of the problem not yet addressed.

We decided to exclude the classic crossover operator in the internal iterations, as several researchers argued about the effectiveness of crossover in relation to the problem of modularity of GP [13]. There is a consensus that an effective GP algorithm needs a crossover that preserves the semantics of the parts swapped among individuals respecting the boundaries of a useful functionality within the individual's structure [2,7,14]. According to McPhee et al. [4] and Ruberto et al. [11] most classic crossover operators do not obtain a meaningful variation (or any variation at all) in the program semantics, when dealing with Boolean and real value symbolic regression domains. The main issue is that classic crossover operators do not preserve a *common context* [4] among the building blocks of the individuals exchanged during crossover, which is important to increase the chance of obtaining a semantically meaningful offspring [14]. The idea of determining a common context has been introduced by Poli and Langdon with the one-point crossover operator [7]. But how to identify a meaningful common context among trees structures is still an open problem.

Instead, SGP-DT exchanges functionalities among individuals by relying on the linear combination of the *partial models* (i.e., the fittest individuals at each external iteration, line 12 Algorithm 1) and on a specific mechanism for selecting and mutating the individuals during the GP runs. In light of this, we exclude the crossover operators in the presence of these semantic recombination alternatives. To have an effective exchange of functionalities among individuals we need to: (i) preserve building blocks semantics (ii) preserve the context of building blocks (iii) make the exchange of functionalities directed towards producing new and interesting semantics. SGP-DT achieves these objectives by (i) mapping each building block to a single partial model (this would avoid arbitrary fragmentations of the blocks); (ii) preserving the context of the building blocks because in our scenario the partial models obtained at previous iterations represent the context; and (iii) using mutation only, which promotes diversity in the population. Despite the absence of crossover, SGP-DT exchanges building blocks because each partial model is a building block. Differently from the classical crossover that exchanges random fragments, SGP-DT obtains the final model by summing the linear scaled partial models. This approach makes the exchange of functionalities more effective, as each partial model (building block) characterizes a specif functionality.

The for-loop at line 6 terminates when SGP-DT concludes all external iterations. We decide not to introduce a different stopping criterion based on the stagnation of fitness improvement. This is because it is difficult to predict if the fitness will not escape stagnation in future iterations. After all the external iterations, the function VALIDATE-AND-SELECT at line 22 of Algorithm 1 returns the partial models that will be combined into the final solution. Such models are selected as follows. The validation takes in input the ordered sequence of best individuals (*models*) collected after each internal iteration (line 14 Algorithm 1) and the validation sets ($\overline{x}_{val}$ and $\hat{y}_{val}$) obtained at line 1. Note that, SGP-DT saves the computed linear scaling parameters (a and b Eq. (2)) at line 10 and do not recompute them during the validation and test phases. Internally, the validation scans the sequence *models* and progressively computes the MSE evaluating the individuals on the validation set to find the point in the sequence where MSE is the smallest. SGP-DT finds the smallest MSE using the rolling mean of the validation set error at a fixed window size to minimize the short-term fluctuations. The function VALIDATE-AND-SELECT returns the sequence (*bestModels*) of the partial models that were produced before the smallest MSE. Such sequence represents the transformation chain of the dynamic targets. In case SGP-DT obtained the model with the smallest MSE during the internal iterations, it appends this individual at the end of *bestModels*. Line 23 of Algorithm 1 computes the final model by summing all the models in *bestModels*.

3 Related Work

This section divides the related work of SGP-DT in three groups. Each group refers to techniques that are relevant to a main characteristic of SGP-DT: (i) having dynamic or semantic objectives, (ii) using linear combinations or geometric operators, (iii) using an iterative approach on residual errors.

Dynamic or Semantic Objectives. The GP techniques proposed by Krawiec et al. [15] and Liskowski et al. [16] present semantic approaches that consider interactions between individuals and the training set. These approaches cluster such interactions to derive new targets for a multi-objective GP.

Otero et al. proposed an approach with dynamic objectives that combines intermediate solutions in a final Boolean tree [17]. This technique progressively eliminates from the training cases the ones perfectly predicted from the current intermediate solution and operates exclusively in a Boolean domain.

Krawiec and O'Reilly [18] proposed a GP approach that explicitly models the semantic behavior of a solution during the computation of training cases.

BPGP by Krawiec and O'Reilly [18] explicitly models the semantic behavior of a solution during the computation of training cases. BPGP proposes an operator that mutates an individual by replacing a randomly selected sub-tree with a random one. According to Krawiec and O'Reilly this "mutation-like" [18] operator is intended as a "form of crossover". We think that this is similar in principle to our design choice of dropping crossover altogether and instead choosing among mutated alternatives in the population. However, Krawiec and O'Reilly still use the traditional crossover alongside with this new mutation [18].

We differ from all of these techniques because we build our solution progressively crystallizing the intermediate achievements. Most of these approaches use auxiliary objectives during their search and use a single GP run. Conversely, SGP-DT uses a non-predetermined number of objectives in subsequent GP runs.

The approach of Otero et al. [17] is the only one that progressively builds the solution but it uses a strategy that works for Boolean trees only.

Linear Combinations. MRGP [19] uses multiple linear regression to combine the semantics of sub-programs (subtrees) to form the semantic of an individual.

Ruberto et al. proposed ESAGP [20], which derives the target semantics by relying on a specific linear combination between two "optimally aligned" individuals in the error space. Leveraging such geometric alignment property, Vanneschi et al. proposed NA-GP [21], which performs linear combinations between two aligned chromosomes belonging to the same individual.

Gandomi et al. proposed MGGP [22], where each individual is composed of multiple trees. MGGP produces the final solution with a linear combination of the tree's semantics, deriving the values of the coefficients from the training data with a classic least squares method. However, the number of trees in the linear combination is fixed and the fitness landscape is not dynamic.

Moraglio et al. proposed the Geometric Semantic GP (GSGP) crossover operator [5], which uses linear combinations to guarantee offspring that is not worse than the worst of the parents. Unfortunately, GSGP suffers from the exponential bloat problem and requires many generations to converge, especially if the target is not in the convex hull spanned by the initial population [5].

Notably, all the approaches described in this second group use a single run to search for the final solution. Differently from SGP-DT, they fix the number of components in advance (the only exception is GSGP but it suffers from the exponential bloat problem [5]). In addition, all of the techniques in the first and second groups have a static target, and thus they continuously evolve a population without re-initialization. This limits the diversity of the genetic alternatives when the population converges at later generations. Conversely, SGP-DT has a dynamic target and it starts with a fresh population at each internal iteration (see Algorithm 1).

Iterative Approaches Based on Residual Errors. Sequential Symbolic Regression (SSR) [23] uses the crossover operator GSGP [5] to iteratively transform the target using a semantic distance that resembles the classical residual approach. However, no statistical difference (on the errors) from the classical GP approach was found [23]. Differently from SGP-DT, SSR considers residuals that do not optimize the linear combinations with a least square method. Although SSR overcomes the exponential bloat, it weakens the advantage of using residuals.

Medernach et al. presented the WAVE technique [24,25] that similarly to SGP-DT, executes multiple GP runs using the same definition of residual errors (Eq. 5) and obtains the final model by summing the intermediate models. WAVE produces a sequence of short and heterogeneous GP runs, obtained by "fuzzing" the settings of system parameters (e.g, population size, number of internal iterations) and by alternating the use of linear scaling. However, SGP-DT drastically differs from WAVE. The heterogeneity nature of WAVE emulates this dynamic evolutionary environment by simulating periods of a rapid change [24,25]. The effectiveness of such an approach requires specif combinations of system parameters that converges to a fitter solution. Due to the huge space of possible system parameters, finding such combinations often requires a large number of iterations [24,25]. Conversely, SGP-DT steers the evolution with a novel approach that gradually evolves the building blocks of the final solution without exploring the huge space of possible combinations of system parameters.

All the techniques of this group use residuals differently from SGP-DT. Moreover, they rely on the classic or geometric crossover. Conversely, one of the key novel aspects of SGP-DT is to avoid crossover altogether.

Table 1. Data sets of regression problems.

Name	# attributes	# instances	Source	Name	# attributes	# instances	Source
airfoil	5	1,503	UCI [26]	housing	14	506	UCI [26]
concrete	8	1,030		tower	25	3,135	
enc	8	768		yacht	6	309	
enh	8	768		uball5d	5	6,024	[27]

4 Evaluation

Data Sets. We performed our experiments on eight well-known data sets of regression problems that have been used to evaluate most of the techniques discussed in Sect. 3 [9,19,21,22,24,25]. Table 1 shows the name, number of attributes, and number of instances for each data set. For *uball5d*[1] we followed the same configuration used by Cava et al. [28].

4.1 Methods

We compared SGP-DT with two techniques (LASSO [8] and ϵ-LEXICASE [9]) and two variants of SGP-DT (DT-EM and DT-NM).

LASSO. Both SGP-DT and LASSO [8] use the least square regression method to linearly combine solution components. More specifically, LASSO incorporates a regularization penalty into least-squares regression using an ℓ_1 norm of the model coefficients and uses a tuning parameter λ to specify the weight of this regularization [8]. We relied on the LASSO implementation by Efron et al. [8], which automatically chooses λ using cross-validation.

ϵ-LEXICASE. This evolutionary technique adapts the *lexicase* selection operator for continuous domains [9]. The idea behind ϵ-LEXICASE selection is to promote candidate solutions that perform well on unique subsets of samples in the training set, and thereby maintain and promote diverse building blocks of solutions [9]. Each parent selection begins with a randomized ordering of both

---

[1] $f(x) = 10/(5 + \sum_{i=1}^{5}(x_i - 3)^2)$.

the training cases and the solutions in the selection pool (i.e., population). Individuals are iteratively removed from the selection pool if they are not within a small threshold (ϵ) of the best performance among the pool on the current training sample. The selection procedure terminates when all but one individual is left in the pool, or until all individuals have tied performance. In the latter case, a random one is chosen. The recent study of Orzechowski et al. shows that ϵ-LEXICASE [9] outperforms many GP-inspired algorithms [29]. We relied on the publicly available implementation of ϵ-LEXICASE, *ellyn*[2], which uses stochastic hill climbing to tune the scalar values of each generated individual. It also relies on a 25% validation hold-out from the training data to choose the final model from a bi-dimensional *Pareto archive*, which *ellyn* constantly updates during the evolution. The two dimensions are the number of nodes and the fitness.

DT-EM. We considered a variant of SGP-DT (called DT-EM) with a modified fitness function as the only difference with SGP-DT:

$$fitness(\mathcal{I}) = MSE = \frac{\sum_{i=0}^{m}(y_i - \hat{y}_i)^2}{m} \tag{6}$$

While the original fitness of SGP-DT minimizes the upper bound of the MSE in Eq. 3, this function directly minimizes the MSE in Eq. 6. This variant helps to evaluate the impact of a direct error minimization with respect to a more qualitative and indirect measure of the error, such as the variance (σ^2).

DT-NM. We considered another variant, called DT-NM, that excludes the *Min* and *Max* non-terminal symbols (as the only difference with SGP-DT), and thus evaluating the advantage of different discontinuity types during the evolution.

4.2 Evaluation Setup

Following the setup of Orzechowski et al. [29] for ϵ-LEXICASE, we set for all the four GP techniques (SGP-DT, ϵ-LEXICASE, DT-EM, and DT-NM) a population size of 1,000 and a budget of 1,000 generations. We ran 50 trials for every technique on each data set using 25% of the data for testing and 75% for training.

SGP-DT and its two variants share the same configuration: We divided the 1,000 generations in 20 external iterations ($N_{\text{ext}} = 20$), and thus the number of internal iterations (N_{int}) is 50. We used ramped half&half initialization up to a maximum depth of four (function GET-RANDOM-INITIAL-POPULATION at line 7 of Algorithm 1). The probability of mutation is 100% and the maximum depth of the sub-trees generated by the mutation operators is five. The probability of a sub-tree mutation happening at the leaf level is 70%. We set no limits on the number of nodes in the trees and on the depth of the trees. We set the Elitism to keep only the best individual at each internal iteration (function ELITE at line 16 of Algorithm 1). We obtained the validation set by extracting 10% of the training cases (function SPLIT at line 1 of Algorithm 1). The fixed window size for the rolling-mean is 20. We chose this configuration after a preliminary tuning phase and kept uniform for all the eight data sets.

---

[2] https://github.com/EpistasisLab/ellyn.

4.3   Results and Discussion

Errors' Comparison. Following previous work we use the Root Mean Square Error (RMSE) to evaluate the final solution with the test set. The first five columns of Table 2 show for each technique the median RMSE of the 50 trials. The last four columns of Table 2 indicate the percentage decrease of the RMSE medians with respect to the competitor techniques[3]. A positive percentage value means that the RMSE median of SGP-DT is lower (i.e., better), while a negative value means a worst median RMSE. Figure 1 shows the box plots of the RMSE values of the 50 trials[4]. When comparing the RMSE values we performed a non-parametric pairwise Wilcoxon rank-sum test with Holm correction for multiple-testing, with a confidence level of 95% (p-value <0.05).

Table 2. Median RMSE of the 50 trials.

Data set	Root mean square error (RMSE)					Median RMSE % decrease of SGP-DT over:			
	SGP-DT	lasso	ε-lexicase	DT-EM	DT-NM	lasso	ε-lexicase	DT-EM	DT-NM
airfoil	2.4634	4.8484	3.6505	2.5643	2.9237	49.19%	32.52%	3.94%	15.75%
concrete	6.5123	10.5383	7.0707	6.4476	6.4132	38.20%	7.90%	−1.00%	−1.55%
enc	1.4838	3.2498	1.8647	1.4993	1.4584	54.34%	20.43%	1.03%	−1.75%
enh	0.5560	2.9645	1.2952	0.5714	0.5410	81.25%	57.07%	2.70%	−2.76%
housing	4.4700	4.9155	4.2785	4.4377	4.5273	9.06%	−4.48%	−0.73%	1.26%
tower	0.2606	0.2953	0.2975	0.2900	0.2900	11.75%	12.39%	10.12%	10.12%
uball5d	0.0402	0.1939	0.0618	0.0430	0.0372	79.29%	35.00%	6.63%	−7.87%
yacht	1.0221	9.0237	1.3577	1.2849	1.1786	88.67%	24.72%	20.45%	13.28%
Average RMSE % decrease:						51.47%	23.19%	5.39%	3.31%

SGP-DT achieves a smaller RMSE than LASSO for all the data sets, obtaining always statistical significance. The decrease of the RMSE medians ranges from 9.06% for *housing* to 88.67% for *yacht* (51.47% on average). SGP-DT has smaller RMSE medians than ε-LEXICASE for all data sets but *housing* (decrease −4.48%). This is the only comparison of SGP-DT and ε-LEXICASE without statistically significance. The decrease of the RMSE medians ranges from −4.48% for *housing* to 57.07% for *ench* (23.19% on average). This is a remarkable result considering that ε-LEXICASE outperforms many GP-inspired algorithms [29]. Comparing with the variant DT-EM, SGP-DT achieves the only statistically significant differences with DT-EM on the data sets *uball5d* and *yacht*, with percentage decreases of 6.63% and 20.45%, respectively. For such datasets SGP-DT performs better than DT-EM indicating that our fitness function that minimizes the upper bound achieves a better final solution. SGP-DT has statistically significant differences of the median RMSE with DT-NM only with the data sets

---

[3] calculated with $((M_T - M_D)/M_T) \cdot 100$, where M_D is the median RMSE of SGP-DT and M_T is the one of the competing technique.

[4] for readability reasons we omitted 4 out-layers for LASSO, 13 for ε-LEXICASE, 30 for SGP-DT, 30 for DT-NM and 35 for DT-EM.

airfoil, tower and *uball5d*. SGP-DT performs better than DT-NM on the *airfoil* and *tower* datasets: 3.94% and 10.12% of percentage decrease, respectively. This means that the *Min* and *Max* non-terminal symbols provide an advantage only in these two datasets. However, Fig. 1 indicates that using such non-terminal symbols does not penalize the outcome in any other dataset, except for *uball5d* where the difference is statistically significant (the decrease is −7.87%).

Error Comparison with Related Work. Unfortunately, the implementation of WAVE [24,25] is not publicly available, and thus a direct comparison would be difficult. We extracted the median RMSE from the GECCO 2016 paper [25] for our two common subjects: 4.1 (*concrete*) and 8.7 (*yacht*). SGP-DT achieves a median RMSE percentage decrease of 25.17% (*concrete*) and 75.12% (*yacht*), see Table 2 for the reference values. Note that, the computational cost reported in the GECCO paper has the same order of magnitude with the one of SGP-DT.

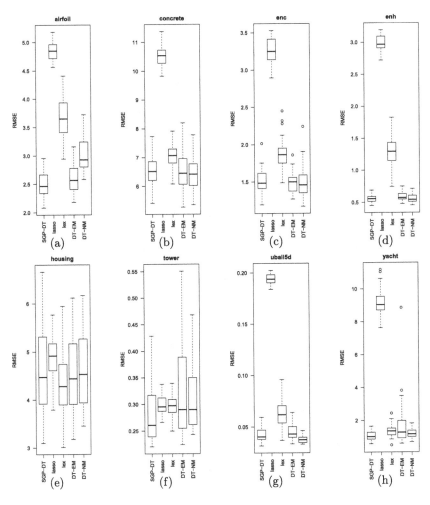

Fig. 1. RMSE of test set for all the techniques and for all the eight data sets.

From the paper of Vanneschi et al. [21], we extracted the median RMSE on the data set *concrete* of the following GP techniques: 10.44 (NA-GP [21]), 8.1 (NA-GP-50 [21]), 12.50 (GSGP [5]), and 9.43 (GSGP-LS [30]). SGP-DT has a percentage decrease of 37.64%, 19.62%, 47.92% and 30.96%, respectively. These results are only indicative because their evaluation setup differs from ours.

Computational Effort. To evaluate the computational effort of the evolutionary techniques we decided not to rely on execution time because it depends on implementation details. Instead, we relied on the total number of evaluated nodes (being not a GP technique this metric is not applicable to LASSO). Both SGP-DT and ϵ-LEXICASE operate on nodes, SGP-DT on tree-like data structures, while ϵ-LEXICASE on stack-based ones. Following Ruberto et al. [11], we count a node operation every time a technique evaluates a node regardless the purpose of the operation (e.g., mutation, fitness computation). We excluded the computational effort of linear scaling because it does not perform operations on nodes. However, it has a linear computational cost of $\mathcal{O}(m \cdot P)$, where m is the size of the training set and P the population size. For comparing the number of evaluated nodes, we used the Wilcoxon rank-sum test with Holm correction for multiple-testing, with a confidence level of 95% (p-value < 0.05). The test show that all the comparisons between each pair of techniques are statically significance, except the comparison with SGP-DT and DT-NM on subject *uball5d*.

Table 3. Median number of evaluated nodes and reduction ratio of SGP-DT.

Data set	Median number of evaluated nodes				Reduction ratio of SGP-DT over		
	SGP-DT	ϵ-lexicase	DT-EM	DT-NM	ϵ-lexicase	DT-EM	DT-NM
airfoil	1.00E+10	9.28E+10	1.00E+10	9.03E+09	9.26×	1.00×	0.90×
concrete	1.14E+10	6.43E+10	1.14E+10	8.82E+09	5.64×	1.00×	0.77×
enc	1.18E+10	4.99E+10	1.17E+10	9.37E+09	4.25×	0.99×	0.80×
enh	1.18E+10	5.08E+10	1.17E+10	9.27E+09	4.30×	0.99×	0.78×
housing	7.70E+09	3.09E+10	7.63E+09	6.03E+09	4.02×	0.99×	0.78×
tower	7.21E+10	1.94E+11	7.12E+10	4.45E+10	2.69×	0.99×	0.62×
uball5d	9.83E+10	3.94E+11	9.76E+10	7.50E+10	4.01×	0.99×	0.76×
yacht	4.62E+09	2.00E+10	4.58E+09	3.47E+09	4.34×	0.99×	0.75×
Average reduction ratio:					**4.81×**	**0.99×**	**0.77×**

Table 3 reports the median number of nodes (of the 50 runs) that the GP techniques evaluate to produce the final solution. The last three columns of Table 3 report the ratio between the number of node evaluations of SGP-DT with those of ϵ-LEXICASE, DT-EM and DT-NM. A ratio greater (lower) than one means that SGP-DT evaluates a lower (higher) number of nodes. Comparing with ϵ-LEXICASE, SGP-DT reduces the amount of node evaluations by a factor between 4.01× and 9.26×, obtaining statistically significant better RMSE values than ϵ-LEXICASE for seven out of eight data sets. This result can be explained by (i) SGP-DT computes only a fraction of the entire solution (partial models) at a time; (ii) the size of the individuals is kept at minimum (see Sect. 2).

The number of evaluated nodes of SGP-DT and DT-EM are almost identical (0.99× on average). This indicates that guiding the evolution with the fitness function of SGP-DT and with the one of DT-EM yield to the same computational cost but SGP-DT achieves better median RMSE (5.39% on average). DT-NM always evaluated less nodes than SGP-DT (0.77× on average).

Size of the Final Solutions. SGP-DT has no limits on the maximum complexity of the individuals, while ε-LEXICASE has a limit of 50 nodes because at higher limits the computational effort of ε-LEXICASE becomes prohibitively expensive [9]. SGP-DT produces solutions with size ranging from 442 to 1,184 nodes (760 on average), which is on average 15× larger than the one produced by ε-LEXICASE and is not large enough to be considered (exponential) bloat. This extra complexity of the final solutions positively contributes at the performance of the algorithm. We are investigating a post-processing phase to simplify the final solutions.

On average, DT-EM produces solutions with 806 nodes and DT-NM with 591. DT-NM generates smaller solutions than DT-EM, this could be due to the fact that DT-NM has a smaller search space (DT-NM omits the *Min* and *Max* symbols). Evaluating smaller solutions require less computation, this explains why DT-NM requires less computation than SGP-DT and DT-EM (see Table 3).

Overfitting. Figure 2 plots for each data set the median of the best RMSE by computational effort (number of evaluated tree nodes) for SGP-DT and its two variants. Unfortunately, the implementation of ε-LEXICASE that we used does not report the intermediate RMSE on test. We use the computational effort, rather the number of generations, for a fair comparison of the three techniques. This is because the number of evaluated nodes is not uniform across the generations.

The eight plots indicate that SGP-DT slightly overfits on the data sets *tower* and *yacht*, while on *housing* produces a substantial overfitting, which is comparable to the one of DT-EM but less severe than the one of DT-NM. DT-EM overfits four data sets: *airfoil* (Fig. 2a), *housing* (Fig. 2e), *tower* (Fig. 2f), *yacht* (Fig. 2h). The worst performance is from DT-NM that shows severe overfitting on *airfoil* (Fig. 2a), *housing* (Fig. 2e), *tower* (Fig. 2f) and *yacht* (Fig. 2h). Note that all three techniques overfit for the data sets *yacht* (Fig. 2h) and *housing* (Fig. 2e). This can be explain by their relatively low number of instances (see Table 1).

For the data sets *concrete* (Fig. 2b), *enc* (Fig. 2c) and *enh* (Fig. 2d) all three techniques do not manifest overfitting (yet). Interestingly, in these three cases DT-NM arrives to a low RMSE with less computations than SGP-DT and DT-EM. We conjecture that this is because *concrete*, *enc* and *enh* are problems that do not need the additional expressiveness of the *Min* and *Max* symbols.

DT-NM is the technique that yields to the smallest individuals, as such we would expect less overfitting. Surprisingly, this is not the case. We believe that, to compensate the absence of discontinuity that *Max* and *Min* introduce, DT-NM

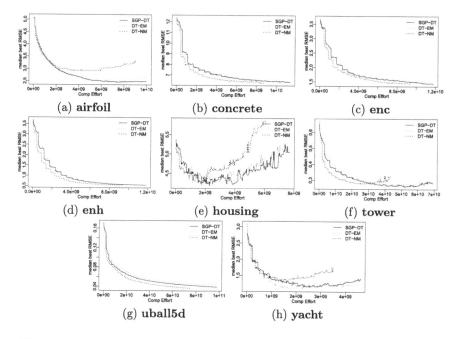

Fig. 2. Median RMSE of the best so far on the test set by computational effort.

used the protected divisions more frequently. This may lead to many asymptotic discontinuities, which are known to increase the overfitting [6].

When considering each data set individually, SGP-DT and DT-EM mostly manifest similar overfitting, while DT-NM manifests overfitting much earlier. This suggests that (i) the non-terminal symbols *Max* and *Min* help to alleviate the overfitting problem; and (ii) relying on the variance (SGP-DT) rather than MSE (DT-EM) in the fitness function indeed contributes to reduce RMSE (5.39% on average, see Table 2) but not to influence overfitting.

5 Conclusion

In this paper, we proposed SGP-DT, a new evolutionary technique that dynamically discovers and resolves intermediate dynamic targets. Our key intuition is that the synergy of the linear scaling and mutation helps to exchange good genetic materials during the evolution. Notably, SGP-DT does not rely on any form of crossover, and thus without suffering from its intrinsic limitations [2,7]. Our experimental results confirm our intuitions and show that SGP-DT outperforms ε-LEXICASE in both lower RMSE and less computational cost. This is a promising result as ε-LEXICASE outperforms many GP-inspired algorithms [29].

This paper sparks interesting future work:

We do not perform any type of post-processing of the final solutions to reduce their size. Indeed, the solutions may contain redundant elements. We are currently investigating a post-processing step to minimize the size of the final solutions.

A possible future research direction is to automatically identify the proper number of iterations of SGP-DT. Indeed, problems with different complexity and nature may require a different number of external and internal iterations.

References

1. Vanneschi, L., Castelli, M., Silva, S.: A survey of semantic methods in genetic programming. Genet. Program. Evolvable Mach. **15**(2), 195–214 (2014). https://doi.org/10.1007/s10710-013-9210-0
2. Pawlak, T.P., Wieloch, B., Krawiec, K.: Review and comparative analysis of geometric semantic crossovers. Genet. Program. Evolvable Mach. **16**(3), 351–386 (2015). https://doi.org/10.1007/s10710-014-9239-8
3. O'Neill, M.: Semantic methods in genetic programming. Genet. Program. Evolvable Mach. **17**(1), 3–4 (2016). https://doi.org/10.1007/s10710-015-9254-4
4. McPhee, N.F., Ohs, B., Hutchison, T.: Semantic building blocks in genetic programming. In: O'Neill, M., et al. (eds.) EuroGP 2008. LNCS, vol. 4971, pp. 134–145. Springer, Heidelberg (2008). https://doi.org/10.1007/978-3-540-78671-9_12
5. Moraglio, A., Krawiec, K., Johnson, C.G.: Geometric semantic genetic programming. In: Coello, C.A.C., Cutello, V., Deb, K., Forrest, S., Nicosia, G., Pavone, M. (eds.) PPSN 2012. LNCS, vol. 7491, pp. 21–31. Springer, Heidelberg (2012). https://doi.org/10.1007/978-3-642-32937-1_3
6. Keijzer, M.: Improving symbolic regression with interval arithmetic and linear scaling. In: Ryan, C., Soule, T., Keijzer, M., Tsang, E., Poli, R., Costa, E. (eds.) EuroGP 2003. LNCS, vol. 2610, pp. 70–82. Springer, Heidelberg (2003). https://doi.org/10.1007/3-540-36599-0_7
7. Poli, R., Langdon, W.B.: Schema theory for genetic programming with one-point crossover and point mutation. Evol. Comput. **6**(3), 231–252 (1998)
8. Efron, B., Hastie, T., Johnstone, I., Tibshirani, R., et al.: Least angle regression. Ann. Stat. **32**(2), 407–499 (2004)
9. La Cava, W., Spector, L., Danai, K.: Epsilon-Lexicase selection for regression. In: Proceedings of the Conference on Genetic and Evolutionary Computation (GECCO 2016), pp. 741–748 (2016)
10. Nicolau, M., Agapitos, A.: On the effect of function set to the generalisation of symbolic regression models. In: Proceedings of the Companion of the Conference on Genetic and Evolutionary Computation (GECCO 2018), pp. 272–273 (2018)
11. Ruberto, S., Vanneschi, L., Castelli, M.: Genetic programming with semantic equivalence classes. Swarm Evol. Comput. **44**, 453–469 (2019)
12. Keijzer, M.: Scaled symbolic regression. Genet. Program. Evolvable Mach. **5**(3), 259–269 (2004). https://doi.org/10.1023/B:GENP.0000030195.77571.f9
13. Gerules, G., Janikow, C.: A survey of modularity in genetic programming. In: the IEEE Congress on Evolutionary Computation (CEC 2016), pp. 5034–5043 (2016)
14. Krawiec, K., Pawlak, T.: Locally geometric semantic crossover: a study on the roles of semantics and homology in recombination operators. Genet. Program. Evolvable Mach. **14**(1), 31–63 (2013). https://doi.org/10.1007/s10710-012-9172-7

15. Krawiec, K., Liskowski, P.: Automatic derivation of search objectives for test-based genetic programming. In: Machado, P., et al. (eds.) EuroGP 2015. LNCS, vol. 9025, pp. 53–65. Springer, Cham (2015). https://doi.org/10.1007/978-3-319-16501-1_5
16. Liskowski, P., Krawiec, K.: Online discovery of search objectives for test-based problems. Evol. Comput. **25**(3), 375–406 (2017)
17. Otero, F.E.B., Johnson, C.G.: Automated problem decomposition for the boolean domain with genetic programming. In: Krawiec, K., Moraglio, A., Hu, T., Etaner-Uyar, A.Ş., Hu, B. (eds.) EuroGP 2013. LNCS, vol. 7831, pp. 169–180. Springer, Heidelberg (2013). https://doi.org/10.1007/978-3-642-37207-0_15
18. Krawiec, K., O'Reilly, U.M.: Behavioral programming: a broader and more detailed take on semantic GP. In: Proceedings of the Conference on Genetic and Evolutionary Computation (GECCO 2014), pp. 935–942 (2014)
19. Arnaldo, I., Krawiec, K., O'Reilly, U.M.: Multiple regression genetic programming. In: Proceedings of the Conference on Genetic and Evolutionary Computation (GECCO 2014), pp. 879–886 (2014)
20. Ruberto, S., Vanneschi, L., Castelli, M., Silva, S.: ESAGP – a semantic GP framework based on alignment in the error space. In: Nicolau, M., et al. (eds.) EuroGP 2014. LNCS, vol. 8599, pp. 150–161. Springer, Heidelberg (2014). https://doi.org/10.1007/978-3-662-44303-3_13
21. Vanneschi, L., Castelli, M., Scott, K., Trujillo, L.: Alignment-based genetic programming for real life applications. Swarm Evol. Comput. **44**, 840–851 (2019)
22. Gandomi, A.H., Alavi, A.H.: A new multi-gene genetic programming approach to nonlinear system modeling. Neural Comput. Appl. **21**(1), 171–187 (2012)
23. Oliveira, L.O.V.B., Otero, F.E.B., Pappa, G.L., Albinati, J.: Sequential symbolic regression with genetic programming. In: Riolo, R., Worzel, W.P., Kotanchek, M. (eds.) Genetic Programming Theory and Practice XII. GEC, pp. 73–90. Springer, Cham (2015). https://doi.org/10.1007/978-3-319-16030-6_5
24. Medernach, D., Fitzgerald, J., Azad, R.M.A., Ryan, C.: Wave: a genetic programming approach to divide and conquer. In: Proceedings of the Companion of the Conference on Genetic and Evolutionary Computation. (GECCO 2015), pp. 1435–1436 (2015)
25. Medernach, D., Fitzgerald, J., Azad, R.M.A., Ryan, C.: A new wave: a dynamic approach to genetic programming. In: Proceedings of the Conference on Genetic and Evolutionary Computation (GECCO 2016), pp. 757–764 (2016)
26. Asuncion, A., Newman, D.: UCI Machine Learning Repository (2007)
27. White, D.R., Mcdermott, J., Castelli, M., et al.: Better GP benchmarks: community survey results and proposals. Genet. Program. Evolvable Mach. **14**(1), 3–29 (2013). https://doi.org/10.1007/s10710-012-9177-2
28. Cava, W.L., Helmuth, T., Spector, L., Moore, J.H.: A probabilistic and multi-objective analysis of Lexicase selection and ε-Lexicase selection. Evol. Comput. **27**, 1–28 (2018)
29. Orzechowski, P., Cava, W.L., Moore, J.H.: Where are we now?: A large benchmark study of recent symbolic regression methods. In: Proceedings of the Conference on Genetic and Evolutionary Computation (GECCO 2018), pp. 1183–1190 (2018)
30. Castelli, M., Trujillo, L., Vanneschi, L., Silva, S. Geometric semantic genetic programming with local search. In: Proceedings of the Conference on Genetic and Evolutionary Computation (GECCO 2015), pp. 999–1006 (2015)

Effect of Parent Selection Methods on Modularity

Anil Kumar Saini[1(✉)] and Lee Spector[1,2,3]

[1] University of Massachusetts, Amherst, MA 01002, USA
aks@cs.umass.edu
[2] Hampshire College, Amherst, MA 01002, USA
lspector@hampshire.edu
[3] Amherst College, Amherst, MA 01002, USA

Abstract. The effects of various genetic operators and parent selection algorithms on the performance of a genetic programming system on different problems have been well studied. In this paper, we analyze how different selection algorithms influence modularity in the population of evolving programs. In particular, we observe how the number of individuals with some form of modular structure, i.e., the presence of code blocks executed multiple times, changes over generations for various selection algorithms.

Keywords: Parent selection algorithms · Reuse metric · Lexicase selection

1 Introduction

In genetic programming, a parent selection method is employed to select individuals from the current generation that can be used to produce individuals for the next generation. All selection methods take into account the performance of individuals on a set of test cases to determine which individuals would be selected as parents. Although the selection algorithms use only errors on the test cases, they can influence other properties of the evolving population, which in turn can influence the chances of that population producing a successful individual program.

In this paper, we look at how the number of modular individuals changes over generations. For the purpose of this paper, we define a modular individual as the one containing at least one code block, which is executed multiple times while appearing only once in the program code. In other words, the program should have some form of loops or other control structures that allow for a group of instructions to be executed multiple times. We compare three parent selection methods—lexicase, tournament, and fitness proportionate—on a number of software synthesis problems. We observe that, in general, lexicase selection leads to a high number of modular individuals in a given generation. Although we are

© Springer Nature Switzerland AG 2020
T. Hu et al. (Eds.): EuroGP 2020, LNCS 12101, pp. 184–194, 2020.
https://doi.org/10.1007/978-3-030-44094-7_12

using stack-based genetic programming, the experiments can be easily repeated for tree-based genetic programming as well.

We believe the analysis presented in the paper can offer insights into why some selection algorithms are better at producing solutions than others, and whether there is a connection between an individual being modular and the chances of it solving a particular problem.

We start with some related work in Sect. 2. The parent selection algorithms used in our analysis are described in Sect. 3. While Sect. 4 discusses the features of Push language that allow for the evolution of modularity, Sect. 5 describes the metric used to calculate the modularity in the evolving programs. Section 6 describes the experimental set-up, and the results of the experiments are given in Sect. 7. We analyze the results in detail in Sect. 8 and conclude our discussion in Sect. 9.

2   Related Work

Population dynamics in terms of different kinds of diversity during evolution have been well studied in genetic programming. In [1], the authors list various types of diversity measures—measuring the number of unique individuals based on their genotype, phenotype, edit distance from the best individual in the population, etc.—and analyses their relationship with the best fitness in the population. Mean behavioral diversity, i.e., the number of unique individuals with respect to outputs on the test cases, has been studied in [6]; the authors present the mean behavioral diversity of the population of various software synthesis problems for different selection algorithms. In the field of genetic algorithms, [8] analyzes how the genotypic diversity in the population is different for different selection algorithms. Although our analysis looks similar to the ones described above, instead of measuring the number of unique individuals, we measure the number of individuals in the population with a specific property.

Other works in evolutionary computation analyze the evolving populations at the level of modules. While [14] looks at how different modules are used—how often they are used and how fit the individual using them are—during evolution for grammatical evolution, [7] analyzes the role of explicit loops for some simple problems in genetic programming. In the analysis presented in this paper, we only consider whether an individual has modules and do not focus on individual modules and how they are used.

3   Parent Selection Algorithms

In this section, we describe three parent selection algorithms that are used in our experiments. These algorithms are used widely in the genetic programming literature and differ significantly in how they use the errors on the test cases.

3.1 Lexicase Selection

Lexicase selection, introduced in [11] and [6], is a parent selection method, whereby for each selection event, the pool of prospective parents is winnowed down based on their error on a set of test cases ordered randomly. In other words, whenever a parent is needed, the set of test cases is ordered randomly, and then for each test case, only the individuals which perform best on that test case are kept, and the rest are removed from the pool. This winnowing down continues until only one individual remains; if there are multiple individuals remaining after going over all the test cases, one individual is randomly selected. The pseudo-code for this method is given in Algorithm 1. Note that unlike other parent selection algorithms, lexicase selection does not aggregate errors on all test cases into a single value.

Input: All individuals in the population
Result: A parent individual
candidates := all individuals in the population;
test_cases := test cases ordered randomly;
for *t in test_cases* **do**
    candidates := those individuals from *candidates* that perform best on *t* ;
    if *candidates contain only one individual* **then**
      | **return** *candidates*
    end
end
return one individual randomly from *candidates*;

Algorithm 1: Lexicase Selection

3.2 Tournament Selection

Tournament selection is a popular parent selection method used in evolutionary computation. With a given tournament size s, for each selection event, s number of individuals are randomly chosen, and then the individual with the least total error is selected as a parent. Algorithm 2 describes the exact procedure to select one parent from the population of evaluated individuals.

Input: All individuals in the population;
       tournament size
Result: A parent individual
tour_size := tournament size;
candidates := select *tour_size* individuals from the population randomly;
return the individual from *candidates* with the least total error;

Algorithm 2: Tournament Selection

3.3 Fitness-Proportionate Selection

In this method, all individuals in the population have a certain probability of getting selected as a parent. The probability for a given individual is calculated as:

$$fitness_i = \frac{1}{1 + totalError_i}$$

$$probability_i = \frac{fitness_i}{\sum_{j=1}^{n} fitness_j},$$

where $fitness_i$ is the fitness of ith individual in the population containing n individuals, $totalError_i$ is the sum of its errors on all test cases, and $probability_i$ is the probability of ith individual getting selected as a parent.

4 Push and the Evolution of Modularity

In this paper, we evolve programs in Push programming language. Push [12, 13] is a stack-based programming language in which a program consists of instructions that can take their inputs from and place their outputs on different stacks. Each data type has a separate stack. Program code is placed on the :exec stack, and in each step, the top item of the :exec is executed. Code itself is a data type with a dedicated stack, which allows programs to manipulate code blocks while running: code blocks can be repeated a certain number of times, they can be executed in a different order than the one specified in the program code, etc. This allows for the evolution of loop-like control structures in the push programs. Some example :exec instructions are given in Table 1.

Table 1. Examples of looping instructions in Push.

Instruction	Explanation
exec_do * range	while the counter moves from the second item of :integer stack to the first item of :integer stack by 1 (+ or −), keep executing the top item of :exec stack
exec_dup	execute the top item of :exec stack twice

Push has been used in the experiments because it allows for the evolution of the kind of modularity we are trying to measure; it contains certain instructions which allow a group of instructions to execute multiple times.

Although there are different kinds of modularity in natural systems like morphological, evolutionary, developmental, etc. [2], the modularity used in this paper is defined in a specific sense. It relates to modules, which are chunks of code being executed multiple times but appearing only once in the program code. This means that even if a program has looping instructions, but the loop only executes once, it will not be considered in our analysis.

5   Reuse Metric

We use the reuse metric introduced in [9] to calculate the modularity of a given program. It measures how many times a group of instructions gets executed. Specifically, for modules of different sizes appearing only once in the program, it measures how frequently they appear in the execution trace of the program. Note that if a group of instructions appears twice in the program code at different locations and the instructions at those locations execute only once, it will not be considered as reuse despite the fact that the group of instructions appears twice in the execution trace.

A module is defined in a simple way. A group of instructions in a program is considered a module if it is executed multiple times. In other words, a group of instructions appearing at least twice in the execution trace is considered a module provided the order in which the instructions appearing in the execution trace is the same as the order in which they appear in the program code. The subset of a module is also a module. For example, if the group of instructions 'ABC' appears twice in the execution trace, 'A', 'B', 'C', 'AB', 'BC', 'ABC' all are modules, provided 'ABC' appears in the program code. The reuse is calculated from the execution trace using the following formulation:

$$Reuse = \frac{\sum_{i=1}^{m} l_i \cdot 2^{f_i}}{2^u}, \tag{1}$$

where there are m modules such that the length of the ith module is l_i, and it appears f_i number of times in the execution trace. The term u is the number of the instructions of the program that are actually executed; the instructions which are present in the program but not executed are not counted.

A given program will have higher reuse if it has any of the following types of control structures:

1. *Loop-like*: instructions falling in this category takes a group of instructions as input and execute those instructions multiple times.
2. *Function-like*: instructions of this category label a group of instructions with some identifier. Whenever that label is called, the same set of instructions are executed.

Although for the purpose of this paper, we only need to check whether or not an individual has reuse which can be computed quite easily—if there is any code block that is repeated more than once in the execution trace of a given program, it has non-zero reuse—we use the full reuse measure given in Eq. 1 so as to get additional insights for future work.

We follow the procedure given in [10] to calculate the reuse metric from Push programs. Additionally, since we are measuring modularity in the programs by calculating their reuse values, we will use terms 'reuse' and 'modularity' interchangeably in this paper.

6   Experimental Set-Up

We conduct experiments on some of the problems from the benchmark suite of [5]. The description of the problems is reproduced here:

1. **Last Index of Zero**: Given a vector of integers, at least one of which is 0, return the index of the last occurrence of 0 in the vector.
2. **Digits**: Given an integer, print that integer's digits each on their own line, starting with the least significant digit. A negative integer should have a negative sign printed before the most significant digit.
3. **Compare String Lengths**: Given three strings $n1$, $n2$, and $n3$, return true if $length(n1) < length(n2) < length(n3)$, and false otherwise.

We use Clojush[1], a genetic programming system written in Clojure that evolves programs in Push language.

We use three selection algorithms in this analysis: lexicase, tournament, and fitness proportionate. The results presented in [6] suggest that tournament sizes between 4 and 10 perform better than other smaller tournament sizes. Therefore, a tournament size of 7 has been chosen for the experiments conducted in this paper.

The genetic programming parameters used in the experiments are given in Table 2. We do not perform crossover and only use a mutation operator called Uniform Mutation by Addition and Deletion, introduced in [4]. UMAD leads to an increase in the success rates for many software synthesis problems in the benchmark suite of [5]. For each combination of software synthesis problem and selection algorithm, 50 independent runs were launched. All other parameters use standard values found in the literature.

For every generation in all the runs, we calculate the reuse value as described in Sect. 5 for every individual in the population. For each individual, we first choose one test case randomly from the set of test cases, run the program on that test case to obtain the execution trace, and use that execution trace to calculate the reuse metric. Note that while calculating errors, the individual is run on all test cases, but while calculating reuse, it is run only on one test case. This is done to make sure that the evaluation time per individual does not increase considerably since calculating the reuse metric can be computationally expensive.

7   Results

The results of the experiments are shown in Fig. 1. Each line represents a single run and denotes the number of individuals, out of 1000 in a given generation, which have non-zero value of the reuse metric. The incomplete lines are the ones that produced a successful solution before hitting the generation limit of 300. (The data for the digits problem with lexicase selection include only 49 runs,

---

[1] https://github.com/lspector/Clojush.

Table 2. Common genetic programming parameters.

Parameter	Value
Population size	1000
Number of generations	300
Parent selection algorithms	Lexicase, tournament, fitness proportionate
Mutation rate	Uniform Mutation by Addition and Deletion (UMAD)
Mutation rate	0.09
Number of runs per selection algorithm	50

since one run was terminated for system-related reasons. The general results hold regardless of how that run would have turned out.)

From the plots, it is evident that with lexicase selection, most of the lines are concentrated in the upper half, whereas with tournament selection, there is a much broader distribution of the number of modular individuals across all generations. With fitness proportionate selection, the lines are concentrated in the lower half for all problems.

Table 3 shows the number of individuals with non-zero reuse averaged over all generations of all runs for a given problem. The numbers are calculated in the following way. For each run of a given problem under a specific condition (for example, with lexicase selection), we calculate the average number of modular individuals across all generations in that run. Note that, if a run succeeds before hitting the generation limit of 300, we do not consider the generations after the generation at which it succeeded. After we have one number for each run, we calculate the average over all the runs. In each row of the table, we also mark the value, which is significantly higher than the other two values in the same row.

To give a sense of the success rate under each condition presented in Table 3, we report the number of successful runs out of 50 for all problems in Table 4. The successful run is the one that evolves a program having zero error on all test cases. To test statistical significance in Tables 3 and 4, we use pairwise chi-square test at 0.05 significance level.

There seems to be a relation between the number of individuals with non-zero reuse in the population with the number of successful runs. But do solution programs themselves have any reuse? Table 5 shows the number of solution programs that have non-zero values of the reuse metric. Each solution program has also been simplified for 5000 steps to remove unnecessary instructions, and the reuse metric is again calculated on the simplified program. Simplification [3] is a technique whereby, in every step, a small number of instructions or a parenthesis pair chosen randomly are removed from the program as long as the errors on the test cases do not change. Note that the value of the reuse metric can be different for the solutions programs before and after simplification due to two reasons:

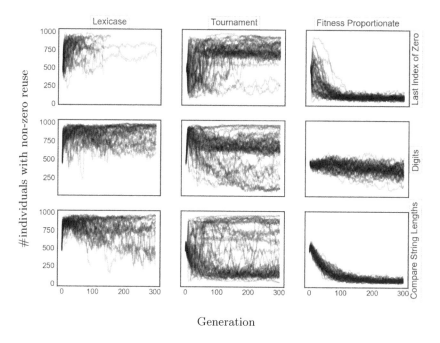

Fig. 1. The number of individuals in a given generation with a non-zero value of reuse. Each line represents one single run on the problem specified in the respective row using the parent selection method specified in the respective column.

some instructions may be removed from the program during simplification, and we choose a test case randomly each time we calculate the reuse metric. Hence, a program can have zero value of reuse before simplification and non-zero value after simplification and vice-versa. We observe that the number of such individuals is very low, and hence there is no significant effect on the analysis presented in this paper.

It is clear from the table that almost all of the solutions have a non-zero value of reuse. This means that most of the solution programs make use of the looping instructions provided by the system.

8   Discussion

While we do not investigate why the selection methods produce the plots given in Fig. 1, they certainly have some features which might be responsible for this behavior.

While tournament and fitness proportionate selection methods aggregate errors of an individual on all the test cases to produce a single value and use that value as input, lexicase selection, by virtue of its design, does not need to aggregate the errors. This allows lexicase selection to choose 'specialists', the individuals which are best on some test cases, but might not be good on others.

Table 3. The average number of individuals with non-zero reuse in a generation averaged over all runs for different problems. Underline indicates that the value is significantly higher ($p > 0.05$) than the other two values in the same row. The value of 'NA' indicates the absence of any successful run.

Problem	Condition	Lexicase	Tournament	Fitness proportionate
Last Index of Zero	Successful	<u>744.68</u>	655.19	195.22
	Non-successful	<u>743.65</u>	675.59	153.02
	All	<u>744.64</u>	671.51	153.86
Digits	Successful	<u>845.05</u>	713.62	NA
	Non-successful	<u>846.86</u>	640.95	403.92
	All	<u>846.28</u>	643.86	403.92
Compare String Lengths	Successful	<u>820.90</u>	441.88	NA
	Non-successful	<u>778.07</u>	444.06	140.18
	All	<u>803.77</u>	443.98	140.18

Table 4. The number of successful runs out of 50 under various treatments. Underline indicates that the value is significantly higher than the other two values in the same row.

Problem	Lexicase	Tournament	Fitness proportionate
Last Index of Zero	<u>48</u>	10	1
Digits	<u>16</u>	2	0
Compare String Lengths	<u>30</u>	2	0

Table 5. The number of simplified and non-simplified solution programs with non-zero reuse under various treatments. For each solution program, we calculate the reuse metric on both simplified and non-simplified version.

Problem	Condition	Lexicase	Tournament	Fitness proportionate
Last Index of Zero	Non-simplified	46	8	0
	Simplified	47	9	1
Digits	Non-simplified	16	2	0
	Simplified	16	1	0
Compare String Lengths	Non-simplified	27	0	0
	Simplified	25	0	0

The selection methods considered in this paper also show different levels of tolerance towards individuals having high values of total error. In fitness proportionate selection, if an individual has a very high error on one test case or high values of errors on multiple cases, its probability of getting selected reduces drastically. In contrast, in lexicase selection, if an individual is best on even one test case, the magnitude of errors on all other test cases does not matter. Tournament selection falls midway between these two extremes: an individual with high total error can be selected as a parent if it gets selected in a tournament and has a slightly better fitness than other individuals in the population.

Although the number of individuals with non-zero reuse in the population is highly correlated with the success rates for different selection methods, whether there is a causal relationship between the two is not yet clear. Two possibilities arise: having some form of reuse is essential if we want to increase success rate above a certain threshold, or, some other property of individuals or populations is essential to having high success rate and that property indirectly also causes individuals to have reuse.

9   Conclusions and Future Work

From our experiments, it is clear that in addition to affecting the fitness of individuals in the population, parent selection methods also influence their modularity. In particular, we have shown how the number of individuals with non-zero reuse in their execution traces is affected by different parent selection algorithms. Our analysis also shows that the number of individuals with non-zero reuse is highly correlated with the success rates for different selection methods. For example, lexicase selection, which has the highest success rate among the selection methods considered in the study, also has the highest number of individuals with non-zero reuse. Whether having more modular individuals in the population is responsible for the high success rate can be taken up as future work. Similarly, what aspects of lexicase selection lead to more modular individuals can also be considered in a future study.

While we have only considered whether or not an individual has a non-zero value of the reuse metric in this paper, analyzing the magnitude of reuse can shed some more light on the relationship between modularity and different selection methods. Finally, other metrics of modularity—like the repetition metric of [9]—can also be analyzed for evolving populations.

Acknowledgements. We would like to thank Michael Garcia and other members of Hampshire College Institute for Computational Intelligence for their valuable inputs.

This material is based upon work supported by the National Science Foundation under Grant No. 1617087. Any opinions, findings, and conclusions or recommendations expressed in this publication are those of the authors and do not necessarily reflect the views of the National Science Foundation.

This work was performed in part using high performance computing equipment obtained under a grant from the Collaborative R&D Fund managed by the Massachusetts Technology Collaborative.

References

1. Burke, E.K., Gustafson, S., Kendall, G.: Diversity in genetic programming: an analysis of measures and correlation with fitness. IEEE Trans. Evol. Comput. **8**(1), 47–62 (2004)

2. Callebaut, W., Rasskin-Gutman, D., Simon, H.A.: Modularity: Understanding the Development and Evolution of Natural Complex Systems. MIT Press, Cambridge (2005)
3. Helmuth, T., McPhee, N.F., Pantridge, E., Spector, L.: Improving generalization of evolved programs through automatic simplification. In: Proceedings of the Genetic and Evolutionary Computation Conference, pp. 937–944. ACM (2017)
4. Helmuth, T., McPhee, N.F., Spector, L.: Program synthesis using uniform mutation by addition and deletion. In: Proceedings of the Genetic and Evolutionary Computation Conference, pp. 1127–1134. ACM (2018)
5. Helmuth, T., Spector, L.: General program synthesis benchmark suite. In: Proceedings of the 2015 Annual Conference on Genetic and Evolutionary Computation, pp. 1039–1046. ACM (2015)
6. Helmuth, T., Spector, L., Matheson, J.: Solving uncompromising problems with lexicase selection. IEEE Trans. Evol. Comput. **19**(5), 630–643 (2014)
7. Li, X., Ciesielski, V.: An analysis of explicit loops in genetic programming. In: 2005 IEEE Congress on Evolutionary Computation, vol. 3, pp. 2522–2529. IEEE (2005)
8. Metevier, B., Saini, A.K., Spector, L.: Lexicase selection beyond genetic programming. In: Banzhaf, W., Spector, L., Sheneman, L. (eds.) Genetic Programming Theory and Practice XVI. GEC, pp. 123–136. Springer, Cham (2019). https://doi.org/10.1007/978-3-030-04735-1_7
9. Saini, A.K., Spector, L.: Modularity metrics for genetic programming. In: Proceedings of the Genetic and Evolutionary Computation Conference Companion, pp. 2056–2059. ACM (2019)
10. Saini, A.K., Spector, L.: Using modularity metrics as design features to guide evolution in genetic programming. In: Genetic Programming Theory and Practice XVII. Springer (2020)
11. Spector, L.: Assessment of problem modality by differential performance of lexicase selection in genetic programming: a preliminary report. In: McClymont, K., Keedwell, E. (eds.) 1st workshop on Understanding Problems (GECCO-UP), pp. 401–408. ACM, Philadelphia, Pennsylvania, USA, 7–11 July 2012 (2012). https://doi.org/10.1145/2330784.2330846, http://hampshire.edu/lspector/pubs/wk09p4-spector.pdf
12. Spector, L., Klein, J., Keijzer, M., Keijzer, M.: The push3 execution stack and the evolution of control. In: Proceedings of the 7th Annual Conference on Genetic and Evolutionary Computation, pp. 1689–1696. ACM (2005)
13. Spector, L., Robinson, A.: Genetic programming and autoconstructive evolution with the push programming language. Genet. Program. Evolvable Mach. **3**(1), 7–40 (2002). https://doi.org/10.1023/A:1014538503543, http://hampshire.edu/lspector/pubs/push-gpem-final.pdf
14. Swafford, J.M., Hemberg, E., O'Neill, M., Brabazon, A.: Analyzing module usage in grammatical evolution. In: Coello, C.A.C., Cutello, V., Deb, K., Forrest, S., Nicosia, G., Pavone, M. (eds.) PPSN 2012. LNCS, vol. 7491, pp. 347–356. Springer, Heidelberg (2012). https://doi.org/10.1007/978-3-642-32937-1_35

Time Control or Size Control? Reducing Complexity and Improving Accuracy of Genetic Programming Models

Aliyu Sani Sambo[1]([✉])[iD], R. Muhammad Atif Azad[1][iD],
Yevgeniya Kovalchuk[1][iD], Vivek Padmanaabhan Indramohan[2],
and Hanifa Shah[3]

[1] School of Computing and Digital Technology, Birmingham City University,
Birmingham, UK
aliyu.sambo@mail.bcu.ac.uk,
{atif.azad,yevgeniya.kovalchuk}@bcu.ac.uk
[2] School of Health Science, Birmingham City University, Birmingham, UK
vivek.indramohan@bcu.ac.uk
[3] Faculty of Computing, Engineering and the Built Environment,
Birmingham City University, Birmingham, UK
hanifa.shah@bcu.ac.uk

Abstract. Complexity of evolving models in genetic programming (GP) can impact both the quality of the models and the evolutionary search. While previous studies have proposed several notions of GP model complexity, the size of a GP model is by far the most researched measure of model complexity. However, previous studies have also shown that controlling the size does not automatically improve the accuracy of GP models, especially the accuracy on out of sample (test) data. Furthermore, size does not represent the functional composition of a model, which is often related to its accuracy on test data. In this study, we explore the *evaluation time* of GP models as a measure of their complexity; we define the evaluation time as the time taken to evaluate a model over some data. We demonstrate that the evaluation time reflects both a model's size and its composition; also, we show how to measure the evaluation time reliably. To validate our proposal, we leverage four well-known methods to size-control but to control evaluation times instead of the tree sizes; we thus compare size-control with *time-control*. The results show that time-control with a nuanced notion of complexity produces more accurate models on 17 out of 20 problem scenarios. Even when the models have slightly greater times and sizes, time-control counterbalances via superior accuracy on both training and test data. The paper also argues that time-control can differentiate functional complexity even better in an identically-sized population. To facilitate this, the paper proposes Fixed Length Initialisation (FLI) that creates an identically-sized but functionally-diverse population. The results show that while FLI particularly suits time-control, it also generally improves the performance of size-control. Overall, the paper poses evaluation-time as a viable alternative to tree sizes to measure complexity in GP.

© Springer Nature Switzerland AG 2020
T. Hu et al. (Eds.): EuroGP 2020, LNCS 12101, pp. 195–210, 2020.
https://doi.org/10.1007/978-3-030-44094-7_13

Keywords: Genetic Programming · Complexity · Evaluation time

1   Introduction

Motivations for controlling the complexity of machine learning (ML) models vary and so does the notion of complexity [3]. One reason for managing the complexity of ML models is to attain models that are only complex enough to explain the phenomenon generating the given data but not too complex to reflect noise in the data. Doing so means that the predictions produced by the models on previously unseen data are accurate [18]; in other words, the model *generalises* well. However, the challenge in this goal is determining when the complexity is just enough. Another incentive for managing complexity is the requirement for models to use computational resources efficiently. For example, some computational environments such as the *Internet of Things* (IoT) devices constrain the evaluation time of an acceptable model even if this compromises its accuracy [13]. In Genetic Programming (GP), preventing the models from growing too complex is also necessary to prevent the evolutionary search from becoming ineffective [11]. A further motivation for managing complexity is the demand for interpretable models: simple models can be more interpretable [14], and the interpretability of ML models is now important. For example, the EU General Data Protection Regulation (GDPR) stipulates a *right to explanation* where ML algorithms are applied to make a decision affecting a person.

The challenge of defining a notion of complexity is compounded in the context of Genetic programming (GP). For example, while ridge regression penalises the growth in the magnitude of numeric coefficients in an otherwise fixed regression model, this penalty does not necessarily work in GP because GP evolves the model itself. Moreover, GP is a versatile tool that can also evolve compilable programs; therefore, minimising the coefficients does not automatically make sense. Also, since during evolution the GP models grow in size, controlling this growth (bloat control) has dominated the landscape of complexity control in GP. However, some previous work [21] shows that controlling the size alone does not automatically produce models that generalise as might have been expected. Moreover, [2] shows that size does not indicate functional composition (or complexity): after all, a very large GP tree may compose a simple linear function; likewise, a small GP tree can compose a highly non-linear function. Together the above challenges show that universally defining complexity is difficult.

This paper uses the *evaluation time* – the computational time required to evaluate a model on the given data – to indicate its complexity. Due to different functional and syntactic compositions of models in the evolving populations, the evaluation time of the models varies. For example, the models made up of computationally expensive functions or exceptionally large syntactic structures take long to evaluate. Unlike size, the evaluation time thus indicates both the syntactic and functional complexity; Sect. 2.2 expands further on that. However, since evaluation times vary from one measurement to another, Sect. 2.3 shows how to measure them reliably.

To control evaluation times, we use four well-known techniques for bloat-control to control evaluation time. However, instead of controlling size, we control evaluation times using the same mechanisms; the techniques thus effect *time-control*. We then compare the effect of time-control with that of size (or bloat) control on the composition, size and accuracy of the evolving models.

The results of our experiments suggest that time-control with a nuanced notion of complexity outperforms size-control in model-accuracy on 17 out of 20 problem scenarios. Even when time-control produces models with slightly greater times and sizes, it counterbalances via superior accuracy on both training and test data. The paper also shows that time-control can differentiate functional complexity even better in an identically-sized population. To facilitate this, the paper proposes Fixed Length Initialisation (FLI) that creates an identically-sized but functionally-diverse population. The results show that while FLI particularly suits time-control, it also generally improves the performance of size-control.

Following this introductory part, Sect. 2 of this paper provides some background; Sect. 3 details the experiments; Sect. 4 presents the results; and Sect. 5 covers future works and concludes the paper.

2   Background

2.1   Complexity in Genetic Programming

Traditionally, controlling complexity in GP means controlling structural complexity such as the size (bloat control) of the evolved expressions, or the number of encapsulated sub-trees and layers, while ignoring the underlying functional or computational complexity [6,7,9,17,21]. For example, bloat control penalises a large yet linear expression $4x+8x+2x+x+x$, which is functionally and computationally less complex than a smaller expression $sin(x)$ [2], which is equivalent to its Taylor series expansion $\sum_{n=0}^{\infty}(-1)^n \frac{x^{2n+1}}{(2n+1)!}$. Clearly, the smaller expression $sin(x)$ needs more computational resources than its linear counterpart. Thus, complexity in GP is more than merely the expression size.

Approaches based on functional complexity recognise that small structures may be more complex than larger ones and hence focus on the functionality of structures. To elicit functional complexity, one approach approximates the evolving expressions by polynomials [23]; complex expressions are approximated by polynomials of a high degree owing to large oscillations in the response of the function. This degree of approximating polynomials is thus minimised in [23]. However, the minimisation requires the evolving expressions to be twice differentiable, a property that is not always guaranteed. To alleviate this constraint, Vanneschi et al. [21] defined a less rigorous measure of functional complexity, whereby the slope of an expression is approximated by a simpler but error prone measure. As such Vanneschi et al. did not control the complexity; instead, they only measured the complexity of evolving expressions. Another approach [1] used the variance of the outputs of the evolving expressions to measure the functional complexity; this approach explicitly minimised the variance and maximised accuracy using a multi-objective optimisation approach. Note, however, that slope of the evolving functions can not indicate complexity when evolving compilable programs for tasks such as robot navigation.

Similarly, statistical learning theory measures the complexity of a space of functions that can be learned using statistical classification. The main techniques include generalisation error bound VC theory and VC dimensions [12,22].

As the discussion highlights, the above techniques are either specialised to various domains or challenging to implement. In contrast, the present study simply measures the complexity of a model with its evaluation time.

2.2   Evaluating Time Is More Than Measuring Size

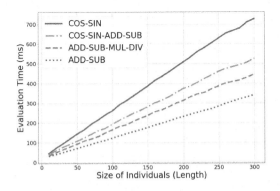

Fig. 1. Relationship between evaluation time, size and the composition of models is shown. Individuals made up of COS and SIN operators have higher average evaluation times than the same-sized individuals from other functions sets. Also, note that size correlates with evaluation time.

While the previous section argues why measuring size is fundamentally different to evaluating time, it is also important to empirically verify that. After all, the evaluation time also increases when the expression size increases; however, we must also ascertain if the evaluation time also practically increases with the functional complexity. Otherwise, measuring time becomes simply a proxy for measuring size. Clearly, that is undesirable.

To this end, we used four different *functions sets* to generate symbolic regression models of different complexities; Fig. 1 details the functions sets. For each functions set, we generated differently sized individuals (10, 20, 30, ..., 300), and in turn for each size we generated 30 random expressions. All the models were then evaluated 50 times, each with the same data. Figure 1 presents the average evaluation times of individuals according to their size and complexity.

Two trends are clearly visible in Fig. 1: (1) given the same size, the evaluation times of functionally complex individuals are consistently higher than those for their counterparts; and (2) evaluation times are also strongly correlated with the expression sizes, as expected. Hence, the evaluation times indeed differentiate between functional complexities; however, if a simple function is inefficiently coded as an excessively large expression, it evaluates slower. Therefore, evaluation time control impacts conditionally: it prefers functional simplicity if the sizes of a competing set of individuals are within a certain tolerance (or range); otherwise, it prefers smaller sizes. Note, this tolerance increases as the size of individuals increases. For example, the evaluation time of size 75 with functions set COS-SIN is the same as that for size 175 with the functions set ADD-SUB.

The above findings also predict the limiting behaviour of evaluation time control in GP. In a functionally diverse but a size-converged population – where bloat control is impotent – evaluation times discriminate between functional complexities, whereas in a functionally converged but a size-diverse population, evaluation times discriminate between sizes.

The idea that time control discriminates between functional complexities when sizes have converged prompted us to try a new initialisation scheme. The new scheme starts with a population of identically sized but functionally diverse individuals. We tested the impact of this new initialisation on all methods before applying it to our experiments. Section 3.4 details this scheme and its impact.

2.3 Stabilising Evaluation Time Measurements

A problem with measuring evaluation times is that they vary across multiple executions, and if this variability is high, one cannot reliably estimate the complexity of a given model from a single evaluation. Since this variation results from CPU scheduling that is under the control of the operating system, we can not eliminate this variation totally. However, we found ways to significantly minimise this variation across evaluations.

We found that CPU management options can help minimise this variation. These options include: (1) stopping all background services, (2) locking the CPU speed to prevent the operating system power management from interfering, (3) executing the experiments on dedicated processors and (4) assigning the experimental tasks a high priority. Figure 2 illustrates the impact of these changes. Each box-plot represents multiple evaluation times for an individual of a given size. Clearly the variation decreases significantly after CPU management. Thus, we were able to use a single evaluation to measure the evaluation time.

3 Experiments

We used four existing bloat control techniques to compare size-control with time-control. When controlling time, the evaluation time replaces size in each of the bloat control techniques.

3.1 Bloat Control Techniques

(a) **Death by Size (DS)** [16] is a steady state replacement method that replaces the larger individuals from the present population with a given probability

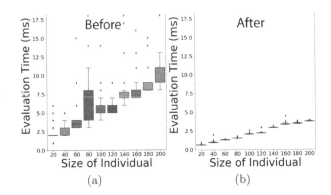

Fig. 2. Using CPU management options decreases variability in evaluation times.

(typically 0.7; we use the same). To replace an individual, DS selects two individuals randomly and replaces the larger one probabilistically. By necessity, DS uses steady-state GP.

(b) Double Tournament (DT) [15,16] increases the probability of choosing smaller individuals as parents to encourage the reproduction of similarly small offspring. DT runs two rounds of tournaments. In the first round, it runs n probabilistic tournaments each with a tournament of size 2 to select a set of n individuals. Each of these tournaments selects the smaller individual with a probability of 0.7. Then, in the second round, DT selects the fittest out of the n individuals. We implemented the DT experiments using steady-state GP.

(c) Operator Equalisation (OpEq) [4,20] allows the sizes of individuals to grow only when fitness is improving. It controls the distribution of the population by employing two core functions. The first determines the target distribution (by size) of individuals in the next generation; the second ensures that the next generation matches the target distribution. To define the target distribution, OpEq puts the current individuals into bins according to their sizes and calculates the average fitness score of each bin. This average score is then used to calculate the number of individuals to be allowed in a corresponding bin in the next generation (target distribution). Thus, from one generation to the next the target distribution changes to favour the sizes that produce fit individuals. The width of the bins can vary and thus is a parameter. Bin width of 1 to 10 has been successfully used previously [20]. In our experiments we used the better performing Dynamic OpEq variant [20] and used *bin width* = 5. Note, OpEq uses generational replacement.

To adapt OpEq to control evaluation time, we had to estimate the time equivalent of the bin width. This value is then used to create bins to classify individuals according their evaluation times in the same way as bin width size is used to create bins to classify individuals by their sizes. To get a reliable estimate we used multiple samples, evaluated multiple times and used the median of several estimates. This is done only once at the beginning of the GP run.

(d) The Tarpeian (TP) [19] method controls size-growth by assigning the worst fitness to a fraction W (recommended $W = 0.3$; we use the same) of the individuals that have above-average size. TP uses generational replacement and calculates the average size of the population at every generation.

To adapt this method to control evaluation time we simply replaced the average size with the average evaluation time.

3.2   Test Problems

We use five tough problems to compare the results in this paper. The problems are tough because the results in Sect. 4 show that the accuracy scores are low (less than 41%). Hence, these problems require GP to run long and thus present a good test bed for complexity control because at least the size-complexity in GP grows with long runs. Four of these problems are multi-dimensional (with five or more input variables). The data set for problems 1–4 are available at [5]; Problem 5 is a bi-variate version of the function used in [8]. A summary of the data sets is available in Table 1.

Table 1. Overview of test problems

ID	Problem label	No. of variables	No. of instances
1	Airfoil	5	1503
2	Boston housing	13	506
3	Concrete strength	8	1030
4	Energy efficiency	8	768
5	$y^2x^6 - 2.13y^4x^4 + y^6x^2$	2	250 (x = min:−0.3, step: 0.012; y = x + 0.03)

3.3   Configuration and Parameters

The basic parameters for all the methods are summarised in Table 2. The other key experimental decisions are as follows. First, the individuals with divide-by-zero errors were assigned the worst fitness; as discussed in [10], the protected operators commonly used in GP lead to poor generalisation. Next, the datasets were randomly split (without replacement) into 80% for training and 20% testing. Finally, the fitness was computed as the normalised mean squared error (MSE) and maximised as follows: $\frac{1}{1+\frac{1}{n}\Sigma_{i=1}^{n}(y_i-\hat{y_i})^2}$.

The experiments were run on Windows 10 (64-bit) with 32 GB RAM, and Intel Core i7-6700 CPU @ 3.40 GHz (Quad-Core).

3.4   Initialising the Population

Section 2.2 motivated the need for an initialisation scheme that produces functionally diverse but identically sized individuals; such a scheme can increase

Table 2. Summary of Parameters

Parameter	Setting
Number of runs	50
Population size	500
Run terminates	After 35,000 evaluations ($\equiv$ 70 generations)
Random tree/subtree generation	Ramped half-and-half($1 =< depth =< 4$); and Fixed Length Initialisation (see Sect. 3.4)
Operators & probabilities	One point crossover = 0.9; Point mutation = 0.1
Depth Limit	17
Function set	$+, -, *, /, \sin, \cos,$ neg
Constants (ERC)	$|ERC| = 100$ (min = 0.05, step: 0.05)
Terminal set	{Input variables} U ERC
Selection	tournament size = 3
Replacement	steady state/generational as per each method

the focus of the time-control on differentiating functional complexity. Therefore, we created a *Fixed-Length Initialisation scheme (FLI)* for these experiments. Henceforth, we call the Ramped-Half-and-Half initialisation the Variable Length Initialisation (VLI).

For the present study, we used the FLI to produce an initial population of unique individuals each having the same length (or size) of 10 nodes. Given the functions set size, a fixed length of 10 can easily produce populations of a few hundred unique individuals; we leave studying the impact of varying the lengths to future work. To encourage functional diversity, we do not consider two individuals different if they only differ by numeric constants.

Before applying FLI to our experiments, we examined its impact on all the methods. The charts in Fig. 3 show the mean test fitness accuracy by generation for all the methods and problems. The significance of the differences of the final populations as established by the Mann-Whitney U test are captured in Fig. 4. The figure is colour coded so that green indicates where the accuracy of the final populations produced by FLI are significantly higher, brown where VLI is higher, and yellow where the difference is not significant. FLI produced better results in 16 out of 20 for Time-control and 11 out of 20 for size-control.

We observed that when using OpEq, size-control with VLI was better than size-control with FLI on all the problems. Therefore, for OpEq we compare time-control with the result of size-control with VLI (the better result). For all other methods we used the proposed FLI.

4 Results

We compare the accuracy, complexity and compositions of the models produced by each method to controlling size and time. For accuracy, although our key measure is test fitness (accuracy on out-of-sample data), we also report training fitness; the higher the value the better. For complexity we report both the size and evaluation times of the models; the lower the values the better. Finally, to give further insight into the complexity of the evolved models, we report the composition of final populations as to what percentage of the genetic material comprised of more or less complex mathematical functions.

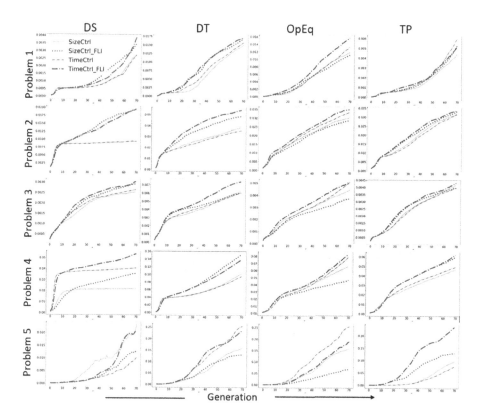

Fig. 3. Comparing the test fitness of initialisation schemes, VLI and FLI. The mean test fitness values are plotted by generation. The thick lines represent FLI and the thin VLI; the green and red lines represent time-control and size-control respectively. (Color figure online)

Figures 6, 7, 8 and 9 show how the test set accuracy, size and evaluation times of both time-control and size-control evolve with each of DS, DT, OpEq and TP. The figures show that for all the methods the values of all the measures increase continuously through to the final generations. Therefore, we evaluate the statistical significance of the differences in the performances in the final generations and report it in Fig. 5. Also, unless stated otherwise, henceforth, the discussion of results concerns Fig. 5.

Statistical Significance: Figure 5 shows the colour-coded results of the Mann-Whitney U statistical test comparing the final populations of time-control and size-control. The table contains results for all the test problems and techniques. The attributes tested include the evaluation time, size, training and test fitness (accuracy on out-of-sample data). The p-values included in Fig. 5 statistically compare the metrics of time-control against those of size-control. The rows are green when time-control is significantly better (more for accuracy, and less for both size and evaluation time), brown when it is significantly worse, and yellow when the difference is not significant.

	DEATH BY SIZE			DOUBLE TOURNAMENT			OPERATOR EQUALISATION			TARPEIAN		
	VLI Fitness (mean)	FLI Fitness (mean)	p-values	VLI Fitness (mean)	FLI Fitness (mean)	p-values	VLI Fitness (mean)	FLI Fitness (mean)	p-values	VLI Fitness (mean)	FLI Fitness (mean)	p-values
	Problem 1			Problem 1			Problem 1			Problem 1		
SizeCtrl	0.00278	0.00349	2.96E-66	0.01501	0.01691	3.60E-40	0.01206	0.01124	1.25E-16	0.00449	0.00534	4.27E-61
TimeCtrl	0.00278	0.00397	1.57E-267	0.01576	0.01718	6.21E-122	0.01336	0.01578	1.64E-91	0.00609	0.00529	1.04E-29
	Problem 2			Problem 2			Problem 2			Problem 2		
SizeCtrl	0.00958	0.01957	0	0.03836	0.04855	0	0.03032	0.02887	1.59E-11	0.03203	0.03338	1.89E-35
TimeCtrl	0.00961	0.01966	0	0.03765	0.05424	0	0.03347	0.035	1.19E-20	0.03176	0.03416	6.85E-59
	Problem 3			Problem 3			Problem 3			Problem 3		
SizeCtrl	0.00266	0.00306	1.70E-168	0.00628	0.00606	3.99E-07	0.00469	0.00392	4.50E-188	0.00438	0.00418	9.43E-23
TimeCtrl	0.00282	0.00322	4.53E-200	0.00607	0.00743	0	0.00515	0.00515	0.29144419	0.00417	0.0045	1.31E-77
	Problem 4			Problem 4			Problem 4			Problem 4		
SizeCtrl	0.02207	0.03611	0	0.10185	0.15296	0	0.06802	0.04706	0	0.0468	0.05983	0
TimeCtrl	0.04099	0.05381	0	0.09512	0.13909	0	0.07845	0.08261	6.99E-08	0.0495	0.0621	0
	Problem 5			Problem 5			Problem 5			Problem 5		
SizeCtrl	0.02323	0.01316	5.60E-10	0.16036	0.13006	6.13E-41	0.16036	0.06566	0	0.09681	0.13006	0
TimeCtrl	0.01032	0.0204	0.400547	0.25417	0.23543	1.34E-08	0.25417	0.18866	0	0.07608	0.23543	0

☐ = Difference not significant   ☐ = Significant and in favour of FLI   ☐ = Significant and in favour of VLI

Fig. 4. Testing the significance of the impact of the new FLI initialisation scheme. In the final populations, FLI test fitness accuracy improved 16 of 20 for time-control and 11 of 20 for size-control. (Color figure online)

Accuracy of Models: Time-control produced significantly more accurate models (on both training and test data) across all problems and all control techniques except on three occasions. The exceptions are problem 1 on TP (the difference is not significant), and problem 2 on DS and problem 5 on TP where size-control outperformed time-control. Overall, time-control outperformed size-control on training and test accuracy on 17 of the 20 occasions and matched size-control on one occasion.

Complexity of Models: Time-control produced less complex (evaluation time and size) models with 2 out of the 4 control techniques; the techniques are DS and DT. As seen in Fig. 5, DS produced simpler models on all the problems except on problem 2 where the difference in evaluation times is not significant.

Likewise, DT produced simpler models on 4 out of 5 problems, the exception being problem 3.

Composition of Models: Table 3 counts and differentiates the nature of nodes constituting the GP trees in the final populations to understand the composition of the genetic material therein. Consistent with the results on evaluation times and sizes, time-control with DS and DT used smaller percentages of complex mathematical functions: the percentages of tree nodes containing SIN and COS with time-control are smaller than the respective figures for size-control. Likewise, OpEq and TP – much like their results on evaluation times and sizes – use greater percentages of SIN and COS.

	DEATH BY SIZE			DOUBLE TOURNAMENT			OPERATOR EQUALIZATION			TARPEIAN		
	Size Ctrl (Mean)	Time Ctrl (Mean)	p-values	Size Ctrl (Mean)	Time Ctrl (Mean)	p-values	Size Ctrl (Mean)	Time Ctrl (Mean)	p-values	Size Ctrl (Mean)	Time Ctrl (Mean)	p-values
Problem 1	**AIRFOIL**											
Evln_time	0.00619	0.005	4.7E-300	0.00943	0.00864	2.67E-245	0.01629	0.02737	0	0.00796	0.00745	2.7E-102
Length	91.53	80.97	2.26E-96	143	135.25	1.04E-97	80.03	120.75	0.00E+00	116.42	107.01	2.05E-128
Train_Fitness	0.00319	0.00359	2.03E-04	0.0148	0.01488	7.81E-23	0.01051	0.0137	8.21E-205	0.00476	0.00478	2.16E-01
Test_Fitness	0.00349	0.00397	5.85E-05	0.01691	0.01718	8.413E-38	0.01206	0.01578	2.84E-209	0.00534	0.00529	1.03E-01
Problem 2	**BOSTON**											
Evln_time	0.00154	0.00154	1.13E-106	0.00425	0.00343	0.00E+00	0.00839	0.0145	0.00E+00	0.00778	0.00787	2.52E-09
Length	9.44	9.41	7.30E-12	95.94	83.9	1.99E-147	57.28	91.48	0.00E+00	90.13	91.49	1.26E-12
Train_Fitness	0.00678	0.00674	0.00157	0.03419	0.03769	0.00E+00	0.02213	0.02558	9.7E-230	0.02346	0.02417	2E-32
Test_Fitness	0.00958	0.00944	2.65E-05	0.04855	0.05424	2.16E-294	0.03032	0.035	8.72E-139	0.03336	0.03416	1.71E-02
Problem 3	**CONCRETE**											
Evln_time	0.00397	0.00366	2.95E-59	0.00619	0.0068	1.994E-67	0.01629	0.02666	0.00E+00	0.00782	0.00956	3.56E-188
Length	44.06	41.98	1.18E-36	74.77	89.1	2.81E-163	60.51	87.03	0.00E+00	86.19	88.13	6.74E-11
Train_Fitness	0.00344	0.00357	3.18E-07	0.007	0.00841	0	0.00527	0.00593	2.99E-95	0.0047	0.005	2.08E-46
Test_Fitness	0.00306	0.00322	7.91E-11	0.00606	0.00743	0	0.00469	0.00515	1.10E-58	0.00418	0.0045	9.19E-54
Problem 4	**ENERGY**											
Evln_time	0.00443	0.00193	0.00E+00	0.00763	0.0063	2.84E-221	0.01806	0.02931	0.00E+00	0.009	0.00956	5.06E-21
Length	40.98	13.69	0	78.39	69.19	8.254E-87	60.79	89.22	0	93.28	97.27	2.91E-08
Train_Fitness	0.038	0.05655	0	0.15619	0.14312	2.086E-51	0.06819	0.08433	4.8E-149	0.06214	0.06431	1.91E-31
Test_Fitness	0.03611	0.05381	0	0.15296	0.13909	4.375E-80	0.06602	0.08261	3.4E-161	0.05983	0.0621	4.79E-34
Problem 5	**X2Y6..**											
Evln_time	0.00153	0.00148	8.54E-53	0.00164	0.00153	1.115E-21	0.00149	0.00954	0.00E+00	0.00308	0.00298	3.29E-26
Length	28.54	27.86	3.28E-28	32.94	30.21	1.41E-119	28.16	77.04	0.00E+00	87.72	81.39	7.07E-79
Train_Fitness	0.01765	0.02694	2.76E-05	0.18468	0.28112	0	0.21448	0.22432	1.53E-295	0.11117	0.11028	3.61E-02
Test_Fitness	0.01316	0.0204	5.15E-09	0.13006	0.23543	0	0.16036	0.18866	5.36E-274	0.08636	0.08446	2.67E-02

☐=Difference Not Significant   ▨ = Significant and Favourable to Time-Ctrl.   ▨ = Significant and Favourable to Size-Ctrl.

Fig. 5. Results of Mann-WhitneyU test for significance in the differences between the final populations of time-control and size-control. Time-control produced more accurate training and test scores in 17 out of 20 tests. While time-control with the steady-state methods (DS and DT) produced simpler (smaller sizes and evaluation times) models than size-control in 9 out of 10 tests, time-control with the generational methods (OpEq and TP) produced more complex models in 8 out of 10 tests. (Color figure online)

4.1   Discussion

Section 1 argued that sensible management of complexity should produce models that are only complex enough to explain the phenomenon generating the given data but not too complex. The results show that time control almost consistently delivers superior accuracy despite splitting results on complexity measures. Even so, the increased complexity with time-control with OpEq and TP is not off the scale as is typically the case with the standard, unrestrained GP.

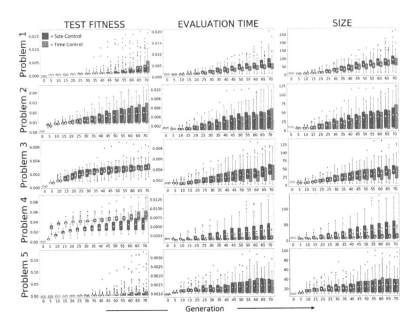

Fig. 6. Death By Size: Comparing changes in metrics by generation between time-control and size-control using DS.

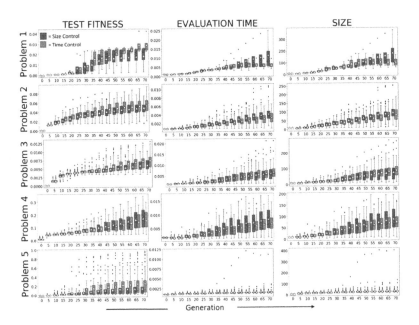

Fig. 7. Double Tournament: Comparing changes in metrics by generation between time-control and size-control using DT.

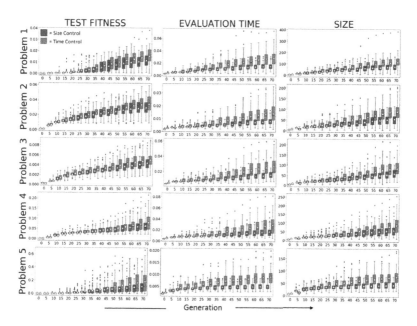

Fig. 8. Operator Equalisation: Comparing changes in metrics by generation between time-control and size-control using OpEq.

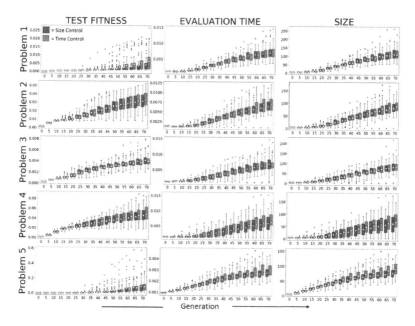

Fig. 9. Tarpeian: Comparing changes in metrics by generation between time-control and size-control using TP.

Table 3. Composition of the final populations.

	Component Type:	Problem 1		Problem 2		Problem 3		Problem 4		Problem 5	
		Size Ctrl	Time Ctrl	Size Ctrl	Time Ctrl	Size Ctrl	Time Ctrl	Size Ctrl	Time Ctrl	Size Ctrl	Time Ctrl
DT	SIN & COS Operators:	19.15%	17.55%	17.67%	9.15%	10.38%	6.82%	18.90%	13.14%	8.02%	5.23%
	ADD & SUB Operators:	33.28%	34.27%	27.80%	30.17%	27.24%	29.72%	24.40%	27.94%	14.84%	12.11%
	Component Type:	Size Ctrl	Time Ctrl	Size Ctrl	Time Ctrl	Size Ctrl	Time Ctrl	Size Ctrl	Time Ctrl	Size Ctrl	Time Ctrl
DS	SIN & COS Operators:	15.29%	8.89%	11.25%	10.42%	9.78%	7.69%	16.88%	5.16%	6.66%	4.42%
	ADD & SUB Operators:	36.31%	37.95%	30.80%	28.77%	32.82%	36.03%	26.17%	30.77%	14.45%	14.55%
	Component Type:	Size Ctrl	Time Ctrl	Size Ctrl	Time Ctrl	Size Ctrl	Time Ctrl	Size Ctrl	Time Ctrl	Size Ctrl	Time Ctrl
OpEq	SIN & COS Operators:	11.95%	15.85%	12.06%	16.64%	9.42%	13.28%	18.26%	20.73%	9.38%	12.11%
	ADD & SUB Operators:	27.18%	24.98%	24.82%	23.23%	23.53%	21.71%	22.76%	21.46%	19.14%	18.04%
	Component Type:	Size Ctrl	Time Ctrl	Size Ctrl	Time Ctrl	Size Ctrl	Time Ctrl	Size Ctrl	Time Ctrl	Size Ctrl	Time Ctrl
TP	SIN & COS Operators:	14.05%	15.70%	17.29%	17.34%	15.81%	15.21%	18.07%	20.31%	8.47%	9.90%
	ADD & SUB Operators:	29.86%	30.46%	26.49%	25.01%	25.02%	24.03%	23.16%	23.29%	20.04%	19.26%

As to why time-control with OpEq and TP produces greater complexity is not exactly clear at present; however, it is worth noting that these two methods require generational replacement where the size (or time) distributions of the entire generations must be computed before allowing new individuals in. In contrast, DT and DS are steady state methods where a new individual replaces the loser of a tournament.

Interestingly, Fixed Length Initialisation (FLI) improved the results with not only time control but more often than not even with size control. The results encourage further investigation into this initialisation technique. FLI is designed to promote compositional (functional) diversity and thus allow time-control to distinguish complexity based more on composition than on size. However, FLI can not enforce size similarity beyond the initial generation; therefore, further work must investigate the effects of promoting size similarity in the remaining evolution and see if that further intensifies the effect of time-control.

5   Conclusions and Future Work

This paper asks the question - why not use time instead of size to measure complexity in GP? Unlike model size, evaluation time is a function of both syntactic and computational characteristics of a model. This measure is broadly applicable, and although this paper studies regression problems, in principle, evaluation time can represent complexity in other domains as well.

A criticism of evaluation time is the variability in its repeated measurements; therefore, this paper shows how to minimise this variability.

The results indicate that the nuanced notion of complexity in time-control almost consistently produces superior accuracy on both training and test data. Even when time-control produces slightly greater sizes or times, the correspondingly superior accuracy counter-weighs these increases. After all, the complexity-control is not the end-goal alone; instead, it should also accompany better accuracy. Even so, the increase in complexity is not off the scale as is typically the case with unrestrained GP.

The paper also shows that time-control can differentiate functional complexity especially when the population has identically-sized individuals. To facilitate this, the paper proposes Fixed Length Initialisation (FLI) that creates an identically-sized but functionally-diverse population. The results show that while FLI particularly suits time-control, it also generally improves the performance of size-control.

Overall, the paper poses evaluation time as a promising alternative to counting nodes in GP.

References

1. Azad, R.M.A., Ryan, C.: Variance based selection to improve test set performance in genetic programming. In: Proceedings of the 13th Annual Conference on Genetic and Evolutionary Computation, pp. 1315–1322. ACM, Dublin (2011). http://dl. acm.org/citation.cfm?id=2001754

2. Azad, R.M.A., Ryan, C.: A simple approach to lifetime learning in genetic programming based symbolic regression. Evol. Comput. **22**(2), 287–317 (2014). https://doi.org/10.1162/EVCO_a_00111. http://www.mitpressjournals.org/doi/abs/10.1162/EVCOa00111

3. Couture, M.: Complexity and chaos-state-of-the-art; formulations and measures of complexity. Technical report, Defence research and development Canada Valcartier, Quebec (2007)

4. Dignum, S., Poli, R.: Operator equalisation and bloat free GP. In: O'Neill, M., et al. (eds.) EuroGP 2008. LNCS, vol. 4971, pp. 110–121. Springer, Heidelberg (2008). https://doi.org/10.1007/978-3-540-78671-9_10

5. Dua, D., Karra Taniskidou, E.: UCI machine learning repository (2017). http://archive.ics.uci.edu/ml

6. Falco, I.D., Iazzetta, A., Tarantino, E., Cioppa, A.D., Trautteur, G.: A kolmogorov complexity-based genetic programming tool for string compression. In: Proceedings of the 2nd Annual Conference on Genetic and Evolutionary Computation, pp. 427–434. Morgan Kaufmann Publishers Inc., Las Vegas (2000)

7. Griinwald, P.: Introducing the minimum description length principle. Adv. Minimum Description Length: Theory Appl. **3**, 3–22 (2005)

8. Gustafson, S., Burke, E.K., Krasnogor, N.: On improving genetic programming for symbolic regression. In: Corne, D., et al. (eds.) Proceedings of the 2005 IEEE Congress on Evolutionary Computation, vol. 1, pp. 912–919. IEEE Press, Edinburgh, 2–5 September 2005. http://ieeexplore.ieee.org/servlet/opac?punumber=10417&isvol=1

9. Iba, H., de Garis, H., Sato, T.: Genetic programming using a minimum description length principle. In: Kinnear, Jr., K.E. (ed.) Advances in Genetic Programming, chap. 12, pp. 265–284. MIT Press, Cambridge, MA, USA (1994). http://cognet.mit.edu/sites/default/files/books/9780262277181/pdfs/9780262277181_chap12.pdf

10. Keijzer, M.: Improving symbolic regression with interval arithmetic and linear scaling. In: Ryan, C., Soule, T., Keijzer, M., Tsang, E., Poli, R., Costa, E. (eds.) EuroGP 2003. LNCS, vol. 2610, pp. 70–82. Springer, Heidelberg (2003). https://doi.org/10.1007/3-540-36599-0_7

11. Koza, J.R.: Genetic Programming: On the Programming of Computers by Means of Natural Selection. MIT Press, Cambridge (1992). http://mitpress.mit.edu/books/genetic-programming

12. Kulkarni, S.R., Harman, G.: Statistical learning theory: a tutorial. Wiley Interdisc. Rev.: Comput. Stat. **3**(6), 543–556 (2011). https://doi.org/10.1002/wics.179

13. Kumar, A., Goyal, S., Varma, M.: Resource-efficient machine learning in 2 KB RAM for the internet of things. In: Precup, D., Teh, Y.W. (eds.) Proceedings of the 34th International Conference on Machine Learning. Proceedings of Machine Learning Research, PMLR, International Convention Centre, vol. 70, pp. 1935–1944. Sydney, 06–11 August 2017

14. Lipton, Z.C.: The mythos of model interpretability. Commun. ACM **61**(10), 36–43 (2018). https://doi.org/10.1145/3233231

15. Luke, S., Panait, L.: Fighting bloat with nonparametric parsimony pressure. In: Guervós, J.J.M., Adamidis, P., Beyer, H.-G., Schwefel, H.-P., Fernández-Villacañas, J.-L. (eds.) PPSN 2002. LNCS, vol. 2439, pp. 411–421. Springer, Heidelberg (2002). https://doi.org/10.1007/3-540-45712-7_40. http://www.springerlink.com/openurl.asp?genre=article&issn=0302-9743&volume=2439&spage=411

16. Luke, S., Panait, L.: A comparison of bloat control methods for genetic programming. Evol. Comput. **14**(3), 309–344 (2006). https://doi.org/10.1162/evco.2006.14.3.309. http://cognet.mit.edu/system/cogfiles/journalpdfs/evco.2006.14.3.309.pdf

17. Mei, Y., Nguyen, S., Zhang, M.: Evolving time-invariant dispatching rules in job shop scheduling with genetic programming. In: McDermott, J., Castelli, M., Sekanina, L., Haasdijk, E., García-Sánchez, P. (eds.) EuroGP 2017. LNCS, vol. 10196, pp. 147–163. Springer, Cham (2017). https://doi.org/10.1007/978-3-319-55696-3_10

18. Paris, G., Robilliard, D., Fonlupt, C.: Exploring overfitting in genetic programming. In: Liardet, P., Collet, P., Fonlupt, C., Lutton, E., Schoenauer, M. (eds.) EA 2003. LNCS, vol. 2936, pp. 267–277. Springer, Heidelberg (2004). https://doi.org/10.1007/978-3-540-24621-3_22

19. Poli, R.: A simple but theoretically-motivated method to control bloat in genetic programming. In: Ryan, C., Soule, T., Keijzer, M., Tsang, E., Poli, R., Costa, E. (eds.) EuroGP 2003. LNCS, vol. 2610, pp. 204–217. Springer, Heidelberg (2003). https://doi.org/10.1007/3-540-36599-0_19. http://www.springerlink.com/openurl.asp?genre=article&issn=0302-9743&volume=2610&spage=204

20. Silva, S., Dignum, S., Vanneschi, L.: Operator equalisation for bloat free genetic programming and a survey of bloat control methods. Genet. Program Evolvable Mach. **13**(2), 197–238 (2012). https://doi.org/10.1007/s10710-011-9150-5

21. Vanneschi, L., Castelli, M., Silva, S.: Measuring bloat, overfitting and functional complexity in genetic programming. In: GECCO 2010: Proceedings of the 12th Annual Conference on Genetic and Evolutionary Computation, pp. 877–884. ACM, Portland, 7–11 July 2010. https://doi.org/10.1145/1830483.1830643

22. Vapnik, V.N.: Statistical Learning Theory. Adaptive and Learning Systems for Signal Processing, Communications, and Control. Wiley, New York (1998). OCLC: 845016043

23. Vladislavleva, E.J., Smits, G.F., Den Hertog, D.: Order of nonlinearity as a complexity measure for models generated by symbolic regression via pareto genetic programming. IEEE Trans. Evol. Comput. **13**(2), 333–349 (2009). https://doi.org/10.1109/TEVC.2008.926486. http://ieeexplore.ieee.org/document/4632147/

Challenges of Program Synthesis
with Grammatical Evolution

Dominik Sobania$^{(\boxtimes)}$ and Franz Rothlauf

Johannes Gutenberg University, Mainz, Germany
{dsobania,rothlauf}@uni-mainz.de

Abstract. Program synthesis is an emerging research topic in the field of EC with the potential to improve real-world software development. Grammar-guided approaches like GE are suitable for program synthesis as they can express common programming languages with their required properties. This work uses common software metrics (lines of code, McCabe metric, size and depth of the abstract syntax tree) for an analysis of GE's search behavior and the resulting problem structure. We find that GE is not able to solve program synthesis problems, where correct solutions have higher values of the McCabe metric (which means they require conditions or loops). Since small mutations of high-quality solutions strongly decrease a solution's fitness and make a high percentage of the solutions non-executable, the resulting problem constitutes a needle-in-a-haystack problem. To us, one of the major challenges of future GP research is to come up with better and more adequate fitness functions and problem specifications to turn the current needle-in-a-haystack problems into problems that can be solved by guided search.

Keywords: Program synthesis · Genetic programming · Grammatical evolution · Software engineering · Needle-in-a-haystack

1 Introduction

Program synthesis, a technique to generate source code in a high-level programming language that meets a certain specification [9], is a relevant research topic in the field of evolutionary computation (EC) with the potential to improve real-world software development. An example showing this potential is the work by Harman et al. [10] in which a translation feature was synthesized by using EC and automatically integrated into the Pidgin instant messaging system.

Grammatical evolution (GE) [22] is a variant of genetic programming (GP) that is suitable for program synthesis, because the used Backus-Naur-Form (BNF) grammar allows GE to express high-level programming languages or subsets of these languages with all their required properties (e.g., conditions, loops, or typing constraints). Inspired by the benchmark suite by Helmuth et al. [13,14], which contains several program synthesis problems selected from introductory programming tasks, some recent work uses grammar-guided approaches for solving program synthesis problems [5,6,15]. For example, Forstenlechner et al. [7]

© Springer Nature Switzerland AG 2020
T. Hu et al. (Eds.): EuroGP 2020, LNCS 12101, pp. 211–227, 2020.
https://doi.org/10.1007/978-3-030-44094-7_14

sorted and classified the problems of the benchmark suite according to the success of G3P, a grammar-guided approach. They found that some problems were easy, whereas others could not be solved a single time. As the reasons for these huge differences in performance are unclear, the next logical step is to study the complexity of the problems and what makes difficult problems difficult for GE.

This work analyzes the behavior of GE as well as the structure of a representative set of program synthesis benchmark problems with common metrics from the EC and software development domains. In a first step, we analyze how robust human-designed reference implementations (solutions that correctly solve a given benchmark problem) are with respect to small modifications of its genotype. In the second step, we analyze by using common and standard software metrics the functions generated by GE during search as well as the resulting problem structure and problem complexity.

Section 2 presents work relevant to the domain of program synthesis with GE. In Sect. 3, we describe the used software metrics, the selected program synthesis problems from the benchmark suite, and the structure of the used GE approach. Following this, in Sect. 4, we describe our experimental setting and discuss the findings. Section 5 concludes the paper.

2   Related Work

There are two major trends for the synthesis of source code with EC: grammar-guided approaches [5–7,15,24] in contrast to approaches based on the stack-based programming language Push [11,12,17]. Both types of methods support the use of multiple data types (e.g., Boolean, integer, float, or string). Grammar-guided approaches, like GE [22], enforce syntax rules and the typing of a programming language by using a BNF grammar, whereas Push [25] ensures correct typing by using separate stacks for each required data type.

For program synthesis with EC, Krawiec [18] already identified some challenges. The most obvious challenge is the large search space. Every additional programming language construct (e.g., a control structure, or a function) leads to a dramatic increase of possible combinations. Even worse, the influence of a programming language construct on the program's behavior is context-dependent as the same instruction in a different setting may lead to completely different results. Furthermore, in a programming language, desired functionality can be expressed in multiple ways (see the multiple-attractor problem [1]). This makes it hard for guided evolutionary search to find a program with the desired functionality and structure. This is also relevant if the evolved program should be improved or maintained by human software developers as they expect human-readable code and not overly complex, but correct, synthesized program code. Therefore, evolved code should not only have the desired functionality but also follow a human-like coding style [24]. Another unsolved problem is how to measure whether a program has the desired functionality. For example, the well-known benchmark suite for program synthesis [13,14] checks the correctness of a program with large sets of test cases. Unfortunately, the use of test cases does not allow to appropriately measure generalization as even Dijkstra [2, p. 864] pointed out that *"program testing can be a very effective way to show the presence of bugs, but it is hopelessly inadequate for showing their absence"*.

A variety of GE papers analyzed different aspects of the algorithm, like the influence of grammars [16,20], the genotype-phenotype mapping [4,21], or the initialization method [3,24]. However, to our knowledge, there is no work so far that performs a systematic analysis of GE's behavior on a representative set of program synthesis benchmark problems using standard and common software metrics.

3   Methodology

This section presents the software metrics required for analysis, the selected benchmark problems, and the structure of the GE approach.

3.1   Software Metrics

In our experiments, we use software metrics that are directly applied to a function's source code as well as metrics that measure properties of a function's abstract syntax tree (AST). For generating the AST from a given Python function, we use the Python module astdump[1]. We use the following software metrics:

- **Lines of code (LOC)**: the number of lines of a function's source code including the function's signature. Comments and empty lines are not relevant in this work because the used grammar does not support them.
- **McCabe metric**: the number of decision branches defined by a piece of code added to the minimum value which is one [19]. Decision branches arise in source code, e.g., through conditions and loops. For calculating the McCabe metric, we use the Python module radon[2].
- **AST depth**: the number of edges on the path from an AST root node to its deepest leaf node.
- **AST nodes**: the number of nodes in an AST.

3.2   Program Synthesis Problems

For our experiments, we selected four problems from the 29 problems defined in the program synthesis benchmark suite [13,14]. To obtain a representative subset of test problems, we selected problems with different complexity and different data types necessary for a correct solution. We selected the following problems:

- **Number IO**: return the sum of a given integer and a float.
- **Small or Large**: for a given integer n, return "small" if $n < 1,000$, "large" if $n \geq 2,000$, and an empty string if $1,000 \leq n < 2,000$.

---

[1] https://pypi.org/project/astdump/.
[2] https://pypi.org/project/radon/.

– **Count Odds**: return the number of odds in a given vector of integers.
– **Smallest**: return the smallest of four given integers.

The training sets consist of 100 cases for each problem, except for Number IO where it consists of 25 and Count Odds where it consists of 200. The test sets consist of 1,000 cases for each problem, except for Count Odds (2,000).

```
def count_odds(numlist0):
    num0 = num1 = num2 = num3 = num4 = 0    # Initialization
    for num1 in numlist0:
        if num1 % 2 == 1:
            num0 = num0 + 1
    return num0
```

Fig. 1. The reference implementation for the Count Odds problem. We shortened the initialization part.

For each of the considered benchmark problems, we defined a hand-written reference implementation that correctly solves the problem and which resembles a solution written by a human software developer. Figure 1 exemplarily shows the reference implementation for the Count Odds problem. Since the reference implementations are consistent with the BNF grammar used in the experiments (see Sect. 3.3), they also contain an initialization part for all possible variables (shortened for readability in the figure). For reproducibility, all reference implementations are available online[3].

Table 1. Properties of the reference implementations. The values in brackets are without the not required part of the initialization.

Benchmark problem	LOC	McCabe metric	AST depth	AST nodes
Number IO	12 (3)	1 (1)	5 (5)	74 (19)
Small or Large	18 (9)	3 (3)	6 (6)	92 (35)
Count Odds	13 (6)	3 (3)	7 (7)	84 (34)
Smallest	12 (3)	1 (1)	7 (7)	85 (34)

To assess the structure and complexity of the problems, Table 1 shows the calculated software metrics (see Sect. 3.1) for our reference implementations. The values in brackets show the software metrics without the not required part of the variable initialization.

As we can see, the selected benchmark problems cover a range from 12 to 18 LOC, respectively 3 to 9 LOC without the not required part of the initialization.

---

[3] https://gitlab.rlp.net/dsobania/ge-program-synthesis/tree/master/reference.

The complexity, measured by the McCabe metric, ranges from 1 to 3. The AST-based metrics are distributed in a similar way. As expected, the initialization part has no influence on the McCabe metric and the AST depth.

3.3   GE Grammar and Fitness Function

For our experiments, we use a standard GE approach with a BNF grammar. Since the GE only uses the training set during a run (which means that we make no assumptions on the type of problem), we created a very expressive grammar which supports all 29 problems from the program synthesis benchmark suite [13,14]. The resulting BNF grammar consists of 31 production rules and supports conditions, loops, numbers, strings, Booleans, and lists. Slicing of strings and lists is also possible. Figure 2 shows an excerpt of the used BNF grammar. For reproducibility, the complete grammar is available online[4].

```
<main>  ::= def small_or_large(num0): NEWLINE INDENT num1 = num2 =
            num3 = num4 = 0 NEWLINE bool0 = bool1 = bool2 = False
            NEWLINE numlist0 = [] NEWLINE numlist1 = [] NEWLINE
            numlist2 = [] NEWLINE str0 = str1 = str2 = "" NEWLINE
            strlist0 = [] NEWLINE strlist1 = [] NEWLINE
            strlist2 = [] NEWLINE <stmt> return <expr_string>
<stmt>  ::= <stmt> <stmt> | <var_numeric> = <expr_numeric> NEWLINE |
            <var_bool> = <expr_bool> NEWLINE | ...
```

Fig. 2. An excerpt of the used BNF grammar. The shown first production rule is designed for the Small or Large benchmark problem.

The only problem-specific adaptation of the BNF grammar is the first production rule, which defines – for each considered problem – the function arguments, ensures an initialization of all variables, and defines the return type. For example, Fig. 2 lists inter alia the first production rule for the Small or Large benchmark problem. The rest of the grammar is identical for all problems. The indentation style, which is mandatory in the Python programming language, is realized by newline, indent, and dedent markers in the grammar. These markers are replaced before the evaluation.

For the evaluation of a solution (function), we use the same fitness function for all benchmark problems defined as

$$f(S, T, p_{inv}, p_{err}) = \begin{cases} p_{inv}\,|T| & \text{if } S \text{ is invalid,} \\ p_{err}\,|T| & \text{if } S \text{ causes a run-time error,} \\ \sum_{t_i \in T} d(S, t_i) & \text{else,} \end{cases} \tag{1}$$

where S is a candidate solution (a generated Python function), T is the training set, t_i is the ith element of T, p_{inv} is the penalty for invalid solutions, p_{err}

---

[4] https://gitlab.rlp.net/dsobania/ge-program-synthesis/tree/master/grammar.

is the penalty for candidate solutions causing a run-time error, and $d(S, t_i)$ is a function that returns 0 if the candidate solution produces the correct output and 1 otherwise. Thus, the fitness of a candidate solution is increased by 1 for every element of the training set that is not correctly solved. If a candidate solution is invalid, because the genotype-phenotype mapping is not successful, we assign the penalty p_{inv} to all elements of the training set. If a candidate solution causes a run-time error (e.g., an index error, a division by zero error, or an endless loop), we apply analogously the penalty p_{err}.

4   Experiments and Discussion

Sections 4.1 and 4.2 analyze the neighborhood (fitness and structure) of the reference implementations for the selected program synthesis problems. Section 4.3 analyzes the properties of the Python functions evolved during a GE run. In Sect. 4.4, we study how the fitness of solutions depend on the number of AST nodes, the AST depth, and the McCabe metric.

4.1   Robustness of Reference Implementations: Part I

We use random walks to study how robust the reference implementations are with respect to small modifications of the genotype. A problem (or more precise, the GE genotype of a reference implementation of a problem) is robust if small modifications of the genotype have only low effect on the properties and fitness of the corresponding phenotype. We use robustness in the sense of locality [21], where small changes of a genotype should correspond to small changes of the phenotype.

For our study, we created a corresponding GE genotype for each of the reference implementations (phenotypes). Then, we iteratively apply random mutations to the active codons of the GE genotype. After each mutation, we calculate the fitness (Eq. 1) of the solution, the number of not correctly solved training cases as well as the percentage of invalid solutions, solutions that cause a run-time error, and solutions that are still executable.

Since we have defined a large and expressive BNF grammar, we use an integer-based genome with a length of 250 (number of codons) and a codon size of 1,000. As we do not need all codons of the genotype for encoding a reference implementation, we fill all non-used (inactive) codons with random integers. As the mutations may introduce endless loops, we limit the fitness evaluation to 3 s. If the evaluation is not completed within this time, it will be aborted and the solution counts as a run-time error. In all experiments, we set the invalid penalty $p_{inv} = 2$ and the run-time error penalty $p_{err} = 1.5$. Furthermore, we use no wrapping in the genotype-phenotype mapping process.

Figures 3, 4, 5, 6, 7, 8, 9 and 10 show results for all four benchmark problems. The plots on the left show the average fitness as well as the average number of not correctly solved training cases (denoted as wrong cases) over the number of random mutations. For the fitness plot, we consider all solutions including the ones that cause a run-time error or are invalid. For the plots showing the number of not correctly solved training cases, we consider only solutions that are executable. We average results over 5,000 runs. In each run, we iteratively apply a finite number of random mutation steps starting from the (correctly working) reference implementation. As intended, the reference implementations always have a fitness of zero. The worst solutions, which are functions that are invalid, have a fitness of p_{inv} times the number of training cases. The plots on the right show the percentage of invalid solutions, solutions causing a run-time error, and executable solutions over the number of random mutations (averaged over 5,000 runs).

The fitness plots (left) show similar behavior for all problems. Even very few changes of the GE genotype of only one or two mutations strongly decrease the fitness of a solution. For example, one or two mutations applied to the reference implementation of the Small or Large problem reduces the average fitness from 0 (reference implementation) to 85 or 128, respectively. After a few more mutations, the average fitness is close to 200, which indicate invalid solutions. There are small differences in how fast the solutions become infeasible depending on the considered problem. For example, the fitness slope for the Smallest problem (Fig. 9) is slightly lower compared to the other benchmark

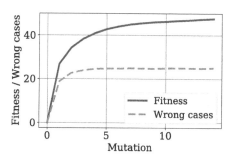

Fig. 3. Fitness/wrong cases over mutations for the Number IO problem.

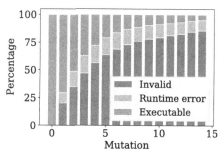

Fig. 4. Percentage of result types over mutations for the Number IO problem.

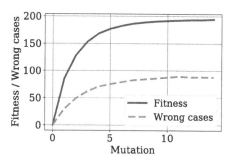

Fig. 5. Fitness/wrong cases over mutations for the Small or Large problem.

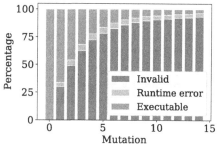

Fig. 6. Percentage of result types over mutations for the Small or Large problem.

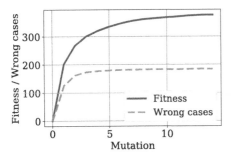

Fig. 7. Fitness/wrong cases over mutations for the Count Odds problem.

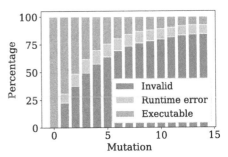

Fig. 8. Percentage of result types over mutations for the Count Odds problem.

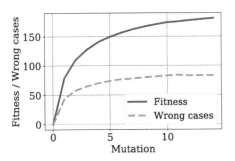

Fig. 9. Fitness/wrong cases over mutations for the Smallest problem.

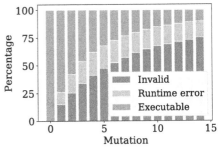

Fig. 10. Percentage of result types over mutations for the Smallest problem.

problems. Since the number of invalid solutions and run-time errors strongly influence a solution's fitness, we also plot the average number of wrongly solved training cases (denoted as wrong cases). For the Number IO (Fig. 3) and the Count Odds problem (Fig. 7), only a few mutations strongly increase the number of wrongly solved training cases; for the Small or Large (Fig. 5) and the Smallest problem (Fig. 9), the mutations have a slightly lower negative influence.

The figures on the right side plotting the percentage of invalid solutions, solutions with a run-time error, and executable solutions confirm the findings and show that after only a few mutations, a large percentage of the solutions are non-executable. For example, for the Small or Large problem, two random mutations of the genotype lead to an average percentage of less than 50% executable solutions. One reason for this high percentage of invalids is the large grammar with many non-terminals. To make the grammar more robust, Schweim et al. [23] suggest to reduce the grammar's average branching factor, e.g., by a lower arity of the functions or adding more terminals to the grammar. Another way to downsize the grammar is the use of domain knowledge, e.g. the textual problem description of the program to be synthesized (cf. Hemberg et al. [15]).

In summary, the reference solutions are not robust against small changes of the genotype. Step-wise random mutations strongly reduce the percentage of executable functions. After about 10 mutations, less than 20% of the solutions are executable. We expect that the high percentage of non-executable solutions in the neighborhood of the reference implementations make it difficult for guided search approaches like GE to find correct solutions.

4.2 Robustness of Reference Implementations: Part II

We also present results for the robustness of the reference implementations with respect to the software metrics defined in Sect. 3.1. For the same experimental setting and identical experimental runs as described in the previous section, we now present results on how the structure and complexity (measured by the software metrics presented in Sect. 3.1) of the reference implementations change when applying subsequent mutations.

Figures 11, 12, 13 and 14 present the average LOC, McCabe metric, number of AST nodes, and AST depth over the number of random mutations. The software metrics are calculated for the complete functions including the variable initialization part (e.g., for Number IO the smallest possible value of LOC is 12). For the analysis, we excluded invalid solutions because for such solutions no well-formed phenotype exists.

The results show only small changes of LOC and McCabe metric over the number of mutations. We observe a slight difference between the Number IO problem (Fig. 11) and Smallest Problem (Fig. 14) on the one hand, where the reference implementations have low LOC and McCabe metric values, and the more complex Small or Large problem (Fig. 12) and Count Odds problem (Fig. 13) on the other hand, where the reference implementations have slightly higher values for LOC and McCabe metric. For the easier problems (Number IO and Smallest), iterative mutations do not significantly change the LOC and McCabe metric values; for the more complex problems (Small or Large and Count Odds), mutations slightly decrease LOC and McCabe metric. For example, for the Small or Large problem, the average LOC decreases from 18 to around 15. Thus, on

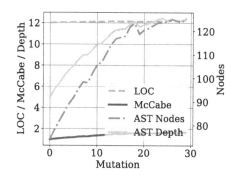

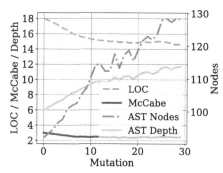

Fig. 11. Software metrics over mutations for the Number IO problem.

Fig. 12. Software metrics over mutations for the Small or Large problem.

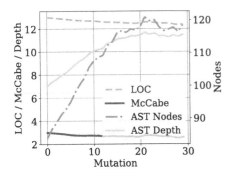
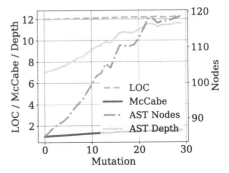

Fig. 13. Software metrics over mutations for the Count Odds problem.

Fig. 14. Software metrics over mutations for the Smallest problem.

average small iterative random changes of the genotype of the reference implementations tend to either reduce or keep constant a solution's size measured by LOC and complexity measured by the McCabe metric.

In contrast, iterative random mutations of the reference implementation strongly increase the average number of AST nodes as well as AST depth for all benchmark problems. 20 random mutations increase the average number of AST nodes by more than 25 nodes; analogously, average AST depth goes up by about 4 nodes. For example, the largest AST depth values of the reference implementations is 7 (Count Odds and Smallest), which increases to more than 10 after about 18 mutations.

Thus, random mutations do not significantly increase the number of lines of code of a function but strongly increase the average length and complexity of each line of code. This leads to more complex and long lines of code. The resulting programs (with high complexity and length of a line of code) are difficult to understand (and not really maintainable) by human programmers.

4.3 Search Behavior of GE

Human programmers that develop correct solutions for the existing benchmark problems often make use of conditions and loops (compare Table 1 for the resulting properties of our – human-coded – reference implementations). This section studies the metrics of functions evolved during a GE run.

The GE uses a population of 25,000 individuals, an integer-based genome of length 250 with a codon size of 1,000. As before, we use no wrapping. We use tournament selection of size 7 and set the crossover probability to 0.7 and the mutation probability to 0.03. As before, we stop the evaluation of a solution after 3 s and set $p_{inv} = 2.0$ and $p_{err} = 1.5$. We stop each GE run after 50 generations.

Table 2 shows the number of test cases, the average and the standard deviation of correctly solved test cases, and the success rate (number of runs that found a correct solution) for the benchmark problems. Results are averaged over 100 runs. We show results for the best solution found during a run.

Table 2. GE performance for the benchmark problems.

Benchmark problem	#Test cases	#Correctly solved cases		Success rate
		Average	Std. dev.	
Number IO	1000	1000.0	0.0	100
Small or Large	1000	531.5	20.2	0
Count Odds	2000	243.9	81.6	0
Smallest	1000	805.5	106.2	14

For the Number IO problem, all GE runs find a correct solution; for the Smallest problem, only 14% of the runs find a correct solution. For the two other benchmark problems, GE does not find a correct solution, nevertheless, evolves solutions that solve some of the test cases. Thus, GE finds correct solutions only for relatively simple problems (Number IO and Smallest), where the reference implementation has a McCabe metric value of one (see Table 1). For the two other, more difficult, problems, where the reference solutions implemented by a human programmer have a McCabe metric of three (see Table 1), GE is not able to evolve a single solution that solves the problem.

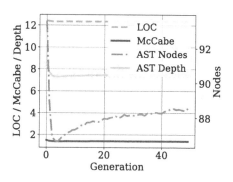

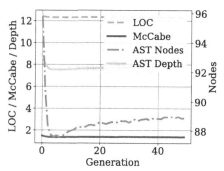

Fig. 15. Software metrics over generations for the Smallest problem.

Fig. 16. Software metrics over generations for the Small or Large problem.

To better understand the differences in GE performance, we analyze the development of the software metrics during a GE run. Figures 15 and 16 plot the average LOC, McCabe metric, number of AST nodes, and AST depth of the solutions evolved by the GE over the number of generations for the Smallest and the Small or Large problem. For both problems, LOC, McCabe metric, and AST depth slightly decrease in the first generations. Afterwards, these values remain about constant. More interestingly, the average number of AST nodes slightly decreases in the first generations (from around 95 down to 87) followed by a slight increase approaching a value lower than the initial one. Comparing these findings with the metrics of the reference implementations (Table 1), the GE finds solutions with similar values of LOC, AST depth, and number of AST nodes. A major difference lies in the McCabe metric, where the GE only evolves solutions with average McCabe metrics of around one. However, to solve the (more difficult) Small or Large problem, higher McCabe metric values would be necessary. For the Smallest problem, the reference implementation has a McCabe metric of only one, which makes the problem easy and allows GE to sometimes solve the problem. The results for the other studied benchmark problems are similar, but are omitted due to space limitations.

The results indicate that evolutionary search is not able to generate more complex solutions with a higher McCabe metric. Thus, GE has problems to correctly use conditions and loops within a solution. Indeed, to evolve a solution with high fitness that uses a condition or loop, many elements of a programming language must fit together and the parameters of the condition or loop must be appropriately set.

```
def smallest(num1, num2, num3, num4):
    # Initialization
    numlist0.append(5)
    return min((num1), min(min((num4), num3), num2))
```

Fig. 17. Correct solution found for the Smallest problem (initialization part is omitted).

```
def small_or_large(num0):
    num1 = num2 = num3 = num4 = 0    # Initialization
    numlist0 = list(reversed(list(range(num0 + num2 + (-1000), 2))))
    return "small"[:len(numlist0)]
```

Fig. 18. Best solution found for the Small or Large problem (shortened initialization).

Consequently, we perform a visual inspection of the source code of the solutions found by GE. Figure 17 shows an example of a (correct) solution found for the Smallest problem. A solution for this problem should return the smallest of four given integers. Unfortunately, the BNF grammar only contains a minimum function $min(a, b)$ that accepts two inputs a and b. Thus, the solutions evolved by GE combines $min()$ multiple times with the four input variables as parameters. The solution found by GE is similar to the reference implementation.

Figure 18 shows the best found solution for the Small or Large problem. To solve this problem, a human programmer would use conditions. GE is not able to solve the problem, but only finds solutions that are correct for some cases. In none of the solutions returned by the GE, conditions have been used in some useful way. Instead, GE finds solutions that mimic conditions by performing many nested simple operations on inputs. For example, the shown example solution uses string slicing and the length of a generated list to return either "small" or an empty string solving correctly around two thirds of the test cases.

In summary, problems are difficult for evolutionary search if they require the usage of conditions and loops (solutions with a higher McCabe metric). Finding such structures is difficult for GE as correct solutions with conditions and loops are difficult to construct (many variables and programming language constructs have to be set correctly to get a useful condition or loop) and solutions using loops easily become non-executable when applying mutations.

4.4 Search for the Needle in a Haystack

To better understand what makes a problem difficult for GE, we study how the fitness of solutions depend on the number of AST nodes, the AST depth, and the McCabe metric. For the Smallest problem, Figs. 19, 20 and 21 plot the average as well as the absolute best fitness of all visited solutions of all 100 runs over the number of AST nodes, AST depth, and McCabe metric, respectively. Figures 22, 23 and 24 show results for the Small or Large problem. We also plot the position of the reference implementation (with fitness 0). The plots include all non-invalid solutions that have been generated during the 100 GE runs.

For the Smallest problem, the reference implementation has a McCabe metric of only 1, an AST size of 85, and an AST depth of 7. The plots show that GE finds many solutions that have similar metric values compared to the reference implementation and high fitness (relevant is the best solution found for a given number of AST nodes, depth, or McCabe metric). Solutions with lower or higher values of AST nodes and depth tend to be worse (higher fitness values). Analogously, a higher value of the McCabe metric leads to worse solutions.

The situation is different for the more difficult Small or Large problem, where the reference implementation has a McCabe metric of 3, an AST size of 92, and an AST depth of 6. GE finds solutions with similar values for AST size and depth as well as McCabe metric, but none of the found solutions has high fitness. Instead, for a given value of a metric, all best found solutions have relatively high fitness values independently of the value of the McCabe metric, number of AST nodes, and AST depth. Thus, the fitness landscape (with respect to metrics

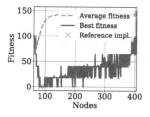

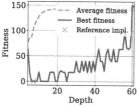

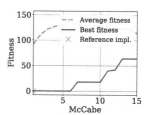

Fig. 19. Fitness over AST nodes (Smallest problem).   **Fig. 20.** Fitness over AST depth (Smallest problem).   **Fig. 21.** Fitness over McCabe metric (Smallest p.).

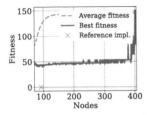

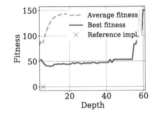

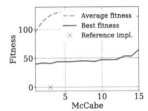

Fig. 22. Fitness over number of AST nodes (Small or Large problem).

Fig. 23. Fitness over AST depth (Small or Large problem).

Fig. 24. Fitness over McCabe metric (Small or Large problem).

measuring size, complexity, or structure of a solution) does not guide (in contrast to the Smallest problem) evolutionary search towards promising solutions but the problem of finding a correct solution is a needle-in-a-haystack problem [8]. When searching through the search space, GE cannot exploit relevant information on where promising solutions are, but finding a correct solution becomes the task of finding a solution with fitness 0 (the needle) in a search space where all other solutions have a fitness of around 50 or worse (the haystack).

5   Conclusions

Program synthesis is an emerging EC research topic with the potential to improve real-world software development. Grammar-guided approaches like GE are suitable for program synthesis as they can express high-level programming languages or subsets of these languages with all their required properties like conditions, loops, or typing constraints. However, program synthesis is a complex problem and researchers as well as practitioners should know about the challenges of this domain. Therefore, this work analyzed the behavior of GE on a representative set of program synthesis benchmark problems using standard and common software metrics like LOC, McCabe metric, or the number of nodes and depth of an AST.

First, we analyzed how robust reference implementations – where each of the hand-written implementations is a correct solution for a benchmark problem – are with respect to small modifications of its genotype. We found that small changes strongly decrease a solution's fitness, make a high percentage of the solutions non-executable, and also have a negative impact on a solution's structure measured by the software metrics. Iterative mutations generate solutions with sometimes a lower number of LOC and McCabe metric but simultaneously strongly increase the number of AST nodes and AST depth. Such solutions do not make use of conditions or loops but contain complex and long code lines.

Second, we studied the properties of functions generated during a GE run. We found that GE is not able to solve program synthesis problems, where correct solutions have higher values of the McCabe metric (which means they require conditions or loops). Evolving such high-quality solutions with higher values of the McCabe metric is a difficult task for GE, as a reasonable use of conditions or loops requires the correct and simultaneous setting of many variables and programming language constructs. Our analysis shows that finding high-quality solutions with a McCabe metric larger than one becomes the task of finding a solution with fitness 0 (the needle) in a search space where all other solutions have a worse fitness value (the haystack).

We conclude that program synthesis is a highly relevant problem and the collection and formulation of program synthesis benchmark problems provides the EC researchers relevant goals. However, the current problem specification and especially the definition of the fitness functions do not allow guided search as the resulting problem constitutes a needle-in-a-haystack problem. The structure of the search space provides no meaningful information for heuristic search to evolve more complex optimal solutions that require conditions or loops. Therefore, we see one of the main challenges for future GP research to come up with better fitness functions and problem specifications to turn the current needle-in-a-haystack problems into problems that can be solved by guided search.

References

1. Altenberg, L.: Open problems in the spectral analysis of evolutionary dynamics. In: Menon, A. (ed.) Frontiers of Evolutionary Computation. GENA, vol. 11, pp. 73–102. Springer, Boston (2004). https://doi.org/10.1007/1-4020-7782-3_4
2. Dijkstra, E.W.: The humble programmer. Commun. ACM **15**(10), 859–866 (1972)
3. Fagan, D., Fenton, M., O'Neill, M.: Exploring position independent initialisation in grammatical evolution. In: IEEE Congress on Evolutionary Computation, pp. 5060–5067. IEEE (2016)
4. Fagan, D., O'Neill, M., Galván-López, E., Brabazon, A., McGarraghy, S.: An analysis of genotype-phenotype maps in grammatical evolution. In: Esparcia-Alcázar, A.I., Ekárt, A., Silva, S., Dignum, S., Uyar, A.Ş. (eds.) EuroGP 2010. LNCS, vol. 6021, pp. 62–73. Springer, Heidelberg (2010). https://doi.org/10.1007/978-3-642-12148-7_6
5. Forstenlechner, S., Fagan, D., Nicolau, M., O'Neill, M.: A grammar design pattern for arbitrary program synthesis problems in genetic programming. In: McDermott, J., Castelli, M., Sekanina, L., Haasdijk, E., García-Sánchez, P. (eds.) EuroGP 2017. LNCS, vol. 10196, pp. 262–277. Springer, Cham (2017). https://doi.org/10.1007/978-3-319-55696-3_17
6. Forstenlechner, S., Fagan, D., Nicolau, M., O'Neill, M.: Extending program synthesis grammars for grammar-guided genetic programming. In: Auger, A., Fonseca, C.M., Lourenço, N., Machado, P., Paquete, L., Whitley, D. (eds.) PPSN 2018. LNCS, vol. 11101, pp. 197–208. Springer, Cham (2018). https://doi.org/10.1007/978-3-319-99253-2_16
7. Forstenlechner, S., Fagan, D., Nicolau, M., O'Neill, M.: Towards understanding and refining the general program synthesis benchmark suite with genetic programming. In: IEEE Congress on Evolutionary Computation. IEEE (2018)
8. Goldberg, D.E.: Genetic algorithms as a computational theory of conceptual design. In: Rzevski, G., Adey, R.A. (eds.) Applications of Artificial Intelligence in Engineering VI, pp. 3–16. Springer, Dordrecht (1991). https://doi.org/10.1007/978-94-011-3648-8_1

9. Gulwani, S., Polozov, O., Singh, R., et al.: Program synthesis. Found. Trends® Program. Lang. **4**(1–2), 1–119 (2017)
10. Harman, M., Jia, Y., Langdon, W.B.: Babel Pidgin: SBSE can grow and graft entirely new functionality into a real world system. In: Le Goues, C., Yoo, S. (eds.) SSBSE 2014. LNCS, vol. 8636, pp. 247–252. Springer, Cham (2014). https://doi.org/10.1007/978-3-319-09940-8_20
11. Helmuth, T., McPhee, N.F., Pantridge, E., Spector, L.: Improving generalization of evolved programs through automatic simplification. In: Proceedings of the Genetic and Evolutionary Computation Conference, pp. 937–944. ACM, New York (2017)
12. Helmuth, T., McPhee, N.F., Spector, L.: Program synthesis using uniform mutation by addition and deletion. In: Proceedings of the Genetic and Evolutionary Computation Conference, pp. 1127–1134. ACM, New York (2018)
13. Helmuth, T., Spector, L.: Detailed problem descriptions for general program synthesis benchmark suite. Technical report, University of Massachusetts Amherst, School of Computer Science (2015)
14. Helmuth, T., Spector, L.: General program synthesis benchmark suite. In: Proceedings of the Genetic and Evolutionary Computation Conference, pp. 1039–1046. ACM, New York (2015)
15. Hemberg, E., Kelly, J., O'Reilly, U.M.: On domain knowledge and novelty to improve program synthesis performance with grammatical evolution. In: Proceedings of the Genetic and Evolutionary Computation Conference, pp. 1039–1046. ACM (2019)
16. Hemberg, E., McPhee, N., O'Neill, M., Brabazon, A.: Pre-, in-and postfix grammars for symbolic regression in grammatical evolution. In: IEEE Workshop and Summer School on Evolutionary Computing 2008, pp. 18–22 (2008)
17. Jundt, L., Helmuth, T.: Comparing and combining lexicase selection and novelty search. In: Proceedings of the Genetic and Evolutionary Computation Conference, pp. 1047–1055. ACM, New York (2019)
18. Krawiec, K.: Behavioral Program Synthesis with Genetic Programming, vol. 618. Springer, Cham (2016). https://doi.org/10.1007/978-3-319-27565-9
19. McCabe, T.J.: A complexity measure. IEEE Trans. Softw. Eng. **SE-2**(4), 308–320 (1976)
20. O'Neill, M., Ryan, C., Nicolau, M.: Grammar defined introns: an investigation into grammars, introns, and bias in grammatical evolution. In: Proceedings of the Genetic and Evolutionary Computation Conference, pp. 97–103. Morgan Kaufmann Publishers Inc., San Francisco (2001)
21. Rothlauf, F., Oetzel, M.: On the locality of grammatical evolution. In: Collet, P., Tomassini, M., Ebner, M., Gustafson, S., Ekárt, A. (eds.) EuroGP 2006. LNCS, vol. 3905, pp. 320–330. Springer, Heidelberg (2006). https://doi.org/10.1007/11729976_29
22. Ryan, C., Collins, J.J., Neill, M.O.: Grammatical evolution: evolving programs for an arbitrary language. In: Banzhaf, W., Poli, R., Schoenauer, M., Fogarty, T.C. (eds.) EuroGP 1998. LNCS, vol. 1391, pp. 83–96. Springer, Heidelberg (1998). https://doi.org/10.1007/BFb0055930
23. Schweim, D., Thorhauer, A., Rothlauf, F.: On the non-uniform redundancy of representations for grammatical evolution: the influence of grammars. In: Ryan, C., O'Neill, M., Collins, J.J. (eds.) Handbook of Grammatical Evolution, pp. 55–78. Springer, Cham (2018). https://doi.org/10.1007/978-3-319-78717-6_3

24. Sobania, D., Rothlauf, F.: Teaching GP to program like a human software developer: using perplexity pressure to guide program synthesis approaches. In: Proceedings of the Genetic and Evolutionary Computation Conference, pp. 1065–1074. ACM, New York (2019)
25. Spector, L., Robinson, A.: Genetic programming and autoconstructive evolution with the push programming language. Genet. Program Evolvable Mach. **3**(1), 7–40 (2002). https://doi.org/10.1023/A:1014538503543

Detection of Frailty Using Genetic Programming

The Case of Older People in Piedmont, Italy

Adane Tarekegn[1]([⊠]) [ID], Fulvio Ricceri[2,3] [ID], Giuseppe Costa[2,3], Elisa Ferracin[3], and Mario Giacobini[4]([⊠]) [ID]

[1] Department of Mathematics "Andrea Peano", University of Turin, Turin, Italy
adanenega.tarekegn@unito.it
[2] Department of Clinical and Biological Sciences, University of Turin, Turin, Italy
{fulvio.ricceri,giuseppe.costa}@unito.it
[3] Unit of Epidemiology, Regional Health Service ASL TO3, Grugliasco, TO, Italy
elisa.ferracin@epi.piemonte.it
[4] Data Analysis and Modeling Unit, Department of Veterinary Sciences, University of Turin, Turin, Italy
mario.giacobini@unito.it

Abstract. Frailty appears to be the most problematic expression of elderly people. Frail older adults have a high risk of mortality, hospitalization, disability and other adverse outcomes, resulting in burden to individuals, their families, health care services and society. Early detection and screening would help to deliver preventive interventions and reduce the burden of frailty. For this purpose, several studies have been conducted to detect frailty that demonstrates its association with mortality and other health outcomes. Most of these studies have concentrated on the possible risk factors associated with frailty in the elderly population; however, efforts to identify and predict groups of elderly people who are at increased risk of frailty is still challenging in clinical settings. In this paper, Genetic Programming (GP) is exploited to detect and define frailty based on the whole elderly population of the Piedmont, Italy, using administrative databases of clinical characteristics and socio-economic factors. Specifically, GP is designed to predict frailty according to the expected risk of mortality, urgent hospitalization, disability, fracture, and access to the emergency department. The performance of GP model is evaluated using sensitivity, specificity, and accuracy metrics by dividing each dataset into a training set and test set. We find that GP shows competitive performance in predicting frailty compared to the traditional machine learning models. The study demonstrates that the proposed model might be used to screen future frail older adults using clinical, psychological and socio-economic variables, which are commonly collected in community healthcare institutions.

Keywords: Frailty · Prediction · Genetic Programming · Imbalanced data

T. Hu et al. (Eds.): EuroGP 2020, LNCS 12101, pp. 228–243, 2020.
https://doi.org/10.1007/978-3-030-44094-7_15

1 Introduction

An increase in longevity results in older people struggling with age-related diseases and functional conditions [1]. This presents enormous challenges towards establishing new approaches for maintaining health at a higher age. An essential aspect of age-related health problems of the general patient condition is the onset of frailty. Even though there are a wide number of studies that have been developed to conceptualize and operationalize frailty, a gold standard definition of frailty still lacks [3–5]. Frailty in elderly people was first characterized as a physical phenotype by Fried et al. [6]. According to this study, frailty is defined on the basis of five physical components: exhaustion, weight loss, slow gait speed, weakness, and low levels of physical activity. People who meet three or more of the above mentioned physical components are classified as frail. Those people who meet one or two criteria as pre-frail and people who meet none of these criteria are classified as not frail. This research was only phenotypic and didn't consider other causes such as psychological and cognitive factors to measure frailty. On the other hand, Rockwood et al. [7] developed a model to detect frailty based on accumulated deficits. In [9,10], the comparison of the frailty phenotype and the frailty index models were also widely discussed. As indicated in the literature, several frailty scores based on different frailty concepts have been developed. However, each of the available tools intended to detect frailty poorly agrees with each other when applied to the same population [11].

The frailty syndrome is associated with a high risk for injurious falls, urgent hospitalization, preventable hospitalization, disability, fracture, access to emergency admissions with red code, and mortality. Using predictive modeling, administrative data allows the detection of potential risk factors and can be used as a clinical decision support system, which provides health professionals with information on the probable clinical patient outcome. This enables the physicians to react quickly and to avoid the likely adverse effects in advance. The identification of elderly people at risk of frailty is essential to provide appropriately tailored care and effectively manage healthcare resources [2].

Most existing studies in the relevant literature for detection of frailty rely on clinical information to investigate the effects of frailty outcomes in the elderly, although these detailed and accurate clinical data may not be adequately available [29]. Models that incorporated patient-level factors such as medical comorbidities and basic demographic data with variables from clinical assessment scores and included numerous social factors have gained good explanatory results. However, prediction remains a poorly understood and complex endeavor, especially when it comes to using available large administrative data. Administrative databases can be used as a better source to implement models able to define, detect, and measure frailty [12]. In [13,14] retrospective studies based on logistic regression models are proposed to develop frailty risk index and validate their content using health record data. There are also few models that are derived from a single source of information, like primary care electronic health record data and only insurance claims data [15]. More recent work on frailty was proposed by F. Bertini et al. [16] using logistic regression. In this paper, they proposed a frailty prediction model using a broad set of socio-clinical and socio-economic variables. Their model was designed to detect and categorize frailty according to the expected risk of hospitalization or death. In general, the frailty indexes proposed in most literature have focused on the possible risk factors associated with frailty in the elderly population, but predicting who is at risk of frailty problems is still requires further investigation. In our work, we proposed a frailty prediction model using Genetic Programming (GP) to detect frailty based on different outcomes of frailty conditions, including mortality, disability, hospitalization, fracture, and access to the emergency department with red code.

To date, various literature on frailty pays particular attention to the statistical methods to detect and predict frailty. However, evolutionary algorithms, such as GP, could also have the capability to address the frailty problems. The ability of GP to produce high performance results depends on the nature of the problem as there is no single algorithm that works best for every problem. As a result, we compared the results of GP with the other commonly used machine learning models in terms of prediction performance on the six different problems of frailty: mortality, access to the emergency department with red code, disability, fracture, urgent hospitalization and preventable hospitalization. On each of the six problems, the results of GP were compared with support vector machine, random forest, artificial neural network and decision tree. The detailed descriptions of these machine learning methods can be found in [8].

2   Methods

2.1   Data Source

We used medical administrative data, which capture patient demographics, healthcare utilization, chronic conditions, and recorded diagnoses to develop predictive models for frailty. The data is based on the Piedmontese Longitudinal Study, an individual record linkage that is available for about 4 millions of Piedmont (Italy) inhabitants between the Italian 2011 census and the administrative and health databases (enrollees registry, hospital discharges, drug prescriptions, outpatient clinical investigation database, and health exemptions) and that is included in the Italian Statistical National Plan. About one million patients aged 65 and above are included in the study. For each patient, a total of 64 different variables are recorded describing histories of frailty related conditions and outcomes. 58 different input variables and 6 different output variables for each subject are included in the dataset. All outcomes and comorbidity variables are represented by Boolean values. The demographic variables such as age, marital status, citizenship, education level, income status, family size, and others are specified using the dummy variables. The 'age' variable is grouped into six categories, with 65–69 used as the first category. The output variables are described as outcomes or measurable changes in the health status of patients. All the 58 input variables were collected in 2016, while the 6 output variables were collected in 2017. So, GP model development was based on using the 2016 variables as input and the 2017 variables as unwanted output. Table 1 presents the description of the 6 output variables in the dataset.

2.2   Data Transformation

The dataset is large in volume and multidimensional, consisting of 58 input variables and 6 different output variables that are assigned simultaneously to each elderly person. This type of data is what we call 'multi-output' dataset. The way the data set is organized is such that one patient can have multiple outcomes. In particular, we identified 6 different outcomes that are associated with frailty conditions namely, mortality, disability, urgent hospitalization, fracture, preventable hospitalization, and access to the emergency department (ED) with red code. This multi-output dataset is transformed into six single-output problems associated with each output variable. Decomposing the original data into six independent datasets helps to study each output independently for the given number of similar risk factors. Transforming the original problem into single independent problems is a straightforward way to implement using GP since it involves transforming the data rather than the algorithm. Additionally, with this method, we can take full advantage of GP since it considers learning problems that contain only one output, i.e., each instance is associated with one single nominal target variable characterizing its property. The six problems with their respective datasets are analysed independently. The descriptive statistics of each dataset are presented in Table 1.

Table 1. Descriptive statistics of datasets in each problem.

Problem (variable)	Category	Code	Number	Percent
Mortality	No	0	1,053,790	96.18
	Yes	1	41,823	3.82
Access to ED with red code	No	0	1,088,124	99.32
	Yes	1	7,489	0.68
Disability	No	0	1,064,186	97.13
	Yes	1	31,427	2.87
Fracture	No	0	1,088,530	99.35
	Yes	1	7,083	0.65
Urgent hospitalization	No	0	1,056,695	96.45
	Yes	1	38,918	3.55
Preventable hospitalization	No	0	1,076,541	98.26
	Yes	1	19,072	1.74

2.3 Learning from Imbalanced Data

Imbalanced data sets are common in medicine and other domains, such as fraud detection [25]. The issue of imbalanced datasets has gathered wide attention from researchers during the last several years [25, 34]. It occurs when the samples represented in a problem show a skewed distribution, i.e., when there is a majority (or negative samples) and a minority (or positive samples). Analyzing such a complex nature of the dataset becomes an issue in the machine learning community including genetic programming [24] and it is observed that most of the traditional machine learning algorithms are very sensitive with imbalanced data [26, 27]. Usually, accurate classification of minority class samples is more important than majority class samples especially in medical diagnosis [24]. The datasets of the six problems in Table 1 (mortality, access to ED with red code, disability, fracture, urgent hospitalization and preventable hospitalization) are imbalanced because the negative class (class '0') contains more samples than the other (class '1'). For all datasets, the imbalanced rate ranges approximately between 1%–4% (that is, the percent range of the data samples that belong to the positive class). In such cases, it is challenging to create an appropriate testing and training datasets for the GP, given that GP is built with the assumption that the test dataset is drawn from similar distribution as the training dataset [17]. Providing imbalanced data to a classifier will produce undesirable results such as much lower performance and increasing the number of false negatives. Among the techniques that deal with imbalanced data, we used the data-level approach to rebalance the class distribution. This is done by either employing under-sampling or oversampling to reduce the imbalance ratio in the dataset [18]. Under-sampling balances the dataset by reducing the size of the abundant class [19, 20], while over-sampling duplicates samples from the minority class [21, 22]. This would possibly improve the performance of classification, as long as the re-sampling does not cause information loss. The oversampling technique is used when the data set is quite small in size. In our case, since the amount of collected data is sufficient, we adopted under-sampling to rebalance the sample distribution. We applied this strategy for all problems with their respective dataset. After performing the undersampling of the majority class, we found a balanced proportion between the positive and negative classes for each dataset, as shown in Table 2.

Table 2. Positive and negative classes in each dataset

Dataset	Class category			
	Positive class		Negative class	
	Count	Percent	Count	Percent
Mortality	41823	50%	41823	50%
Access to ED with red code	7489		7489	
Disability	31427		31427	
Femur fracture	7083		7083	
Urgent hospitalization	38918		38918	
Preventable hospitalization	19072		19072	

3   Experiments

In the present study, we investigated the applicability of GP in the prediction of frailty among patients in elderly people, as explained in the previous section. The experiments include learning a binary classification of the data to frail and non-frail classes by considering the profiles of each individual patient over two years. In analysing the data for prediction, the output variables represent an occurrence in the next year, and the GP predictive model is proposed to detect and classify frailty according to the expected risk of urgent hospitalization, preventive hospitalization, disability, fracture, emergency admissions with a red code and death within a year. The GP model is trained using the training dataset (70%) and tested using test dataset (30%). The training dataset was used for building the model, and the test dataset was used to evaluate the prediction capabilities.

To build an effective predictive model, it is essential to train the model and perform testing using a dataset that comes from the same target distribution. All the six different datasets were randomly split into training and testing using the following steps.

1. Split the samples with negative class into 70% training and 30% testing.
2. Split the samples with positive class into 70% training and 30% testing set.
3. Combine the 70% samples with negative class obtained from step 1 and the 70% samples with positive class obtained from step 2.
4. Combine the 30% samples with negative class obtained from step 1 and the 30% samples with positive class obtained from step 2.
5. Perform a chi-square test with a significance level of 0.05 between the training set obtained from step (3) and the test set obtained from step (4). A statistical test was needed to check if the training set and testing set are representative of each other. A Chi-square independence test is used to determine if there is evidence of a difference between the training set (70%) and the test set (30%) with respect to the 58 categorical input variables. The produced test results are assessed based on the chi-square statistic, and statically significant results were found with respect to all variables.

3.1   GP Parameter Setup

In GP, setting the control parameters is an important first step to manipulate data and to obtain good results. In our datasets, we tried several experiments for classification tasks by using the control parameters of GP proposed in HeuristicLab [33], such as population size, selection method, number of elite individuals, initialization method, number of generations, crossover probability rates, and mutation probability rates. Due to the stochastic nature of GP, 30 runs were performed in all problems, each with a different random number generator seed. For our frailty problem, we specifically focused on the two common parameters of GP: Maximum number of generations and Population size. In order to investigate the effect of few generation over larger population and small population over more generations and also to get an advantage from either of these

GP parameter settings, we run two different algorithms of GP (GP1 and GP2) under varying population size and the maximum number of generations, keeping all other parameters set to default. The maximum number of generations and population size for GP1 is set to be 1000 and 100, respectively. In GP2, we set a maximum number of generations to be 100 and population size 1000. For all frailty problems, GP1 and GP2 were applied, and for each experiment, 30 runs were performed with the same initial configurations of parameters. We clearly observed that the runs with a population size of 1000 and generation 100 are related to the immense runtime requirements, comparing with the runs of population size 100 and generation 1000. In fitness, it is apparent that a large population running for a small number of generations behaves differently from the small population running for a large number of generations. The fitness of GP1 and GP2 across generations were compared for mortality and fracture problems using mean squared error (MSE). The MSE is used as fitness to compare the quality of the two models (GP1 and GP2), and it was observed that GP2 produced lower error rates, which is ranging from 0.18 to 0.25 for mortality and from 0.19 to 0.25 for fracture problems. While for GP1 the MSE is much higher, which is ranging from 0.20 to 0.30 for mortality problem and from 0.22 to 0.29 for fracture problem. The results show that a large population is more likely than a small population to make more significant improvements in fitness from one generation to the next, given that it generates more new trees in each generation. Generally, for frailty problems, it seems that results with GP2 are more stable and that larger population is a better choice than many generations. As a result of this, we preferred GP with larger population size and smaller number of generations for the prediction of frailty conditions. The summary of parameters used for running GP2 experiments is presented in Table 3.

Table 3. GP parameters used in the experiment.

Parameter Name	Value
Algorithm	GP2
Maximum number of generations	100
Population size	1000
Mutation rate	15%
Crossover rate	90%
Solution creator	Ramped Half-and-Half
Maximum tree depth	10
Maximum tree length	100
Elites	1
Terminal set	Constant, variables

4   Results

In this section, we investigated the performance of GP for the prediction of frailty status in terms of the six problems or outcomes. The predictors common to all problems and which were also included in the final model produced by GP were the age, the number of urgent hospitalization, charlson comorbidity index, dementia and mental disease. The final prediction model of each problem generated by GP is a binary parse tree representing the classification model.

4.1   GP Prediction Performance

The different frailty prediction models obtained from GP were evaluated in terms of overall accuracy, sensitvity and specificity on the training and test dataset. In the context of this study, sensitivity measures the frail subjects who are correctly identified as having the event and specificity refers to the nonfrail subjects who are correctly identified as not having the event. The three performance measures were considered for mortality, urgent hospitalization, preventable hospitalization, disability, fracture, and access to ED with a red code. Detecting these adverse outcomes among a large number of subjects is important when applied in real-world practice. Hence, the true positive rate (TPR), also called sensitivity, was the main metric to consider. The overall accuracy (Acc) and true negative rate (TNR), also called specificity, were measured as additional performance metrics. The accuracy, TPR, and TNR were formulated using the true positives (TP), false positives (FP), true negatives, and false negatives (FN) [28].

In analysing GP for classification, the most important aspect is to know the number of samples that are classified correctly and those, which are classified incorrectly. The results averaged from 30 runs of GP experiments are presented in Table 4 on the training set and Table 5 on the testing set. In these problems, using sensitivity and specificity allows to correctly identify those with the disease condition (frail people) and to correctly identify those without the disease (non frail people), respectively. The standard deviation (SD) for mean sensitivity, specificity and accuracy are also calculated, since each problem is run 30 times, as shown in Tables 4 and 5. For mortality problem GP produced the best performance in all measurements. For access to ED with red code, the overall

Table 4. Performance of GP on the training set.

Problem	Sensitivity (SD)	Specificity (SD)	Accuracy (SD)
Mortality	0.75(0.05)	0.75(0.06)	0.75(0.02)
Access to ED with red code	0.76(0.24)	0.45(0.37)	0.58(0.09)
Disability	0.72(0.04)	0.69(0.05)	0.72(0.02)
Fracture	0.71(0.04)	0.67(0.14)	0.74(0.08)
Urgent Hosptalization	0.65(0.22)	0.63(0.29)	0.64(0.13)
Preventable Hosptalization	0.71(0.18)	0.63(0.33)	0.67(0.11)

Table 5. Performance of GP on the testing set.

Problem	Sensitivity (SD)	Specificity (SD)	Accuracy (SD)
Mortality	0.75(0.05)	0.76(0.06)	0.75(0.02)
Access to ED with red code	0.73(0.24)	0.43(0.36)	0.58(0.08)
Disability	0.70(0.04)	0.73(0.05)	0.71(002)
Fracture	0.71(0.14)	0.67(0.08)	0.72(0.04)
Urgent Hosptalization	0.66(0.22)	0.62(0.29)	0.63(0.13)
Preventable Hosptalization	0.73(0.18)	0.64(0.33)	0.68(0.11)

accuracy and specificity of GP are slightly lowered. For the remaining problems the performance of GP is at an acceptable level. These results confirmed the predictive capability of GP on frailty problems.

4.2 Performance of Other Non-GP Classifiers

In this section, we assessed the theoretical and performance comparison of GP with the statistical and machine learning methods. In the literature, there are some studies which compare GP with other statistical and machine learning methods [23,35]. The studies suggest that GP may be better at representing the potentially non-linear relationship of (a smaller subset of) the strongest predictors, although the complexity of the GP-derived model was found to be much higher. The fact that GP required fewer predictors to achieve similar performance may have an advantage in practical application of the developed cliniccal prediction models. Therefore, a prediction model that requires fewer inputs, especially if the information relating to these inputs is in practice recorded easily and to a good quality, would considerably increase adoption and utility. Comparison of GP with statistical models, such as cox regression techniques, was attempted by [30] in terms of the performance of a cardiovascular risk score using a prospective cohort study of patients with symptomatic cardiovascular disease. The predictive ability of cox regression model and GP was evaluated in terms of their risk discrimination and calibration using the validation set. Their findings indicated that the discrimination of both models was comparable. Using the calibration of these models, which was assessed based on calibration plots and the generalization of the Hosmer-Lemeshow test statistic, was also similar, but with the Cox model is better calibrated to the validation data. In [36], a comparison of GP and NN in metamodeling of discrete-event simulation was studied. The results of this study concluded that GP provides greater accuracy in validation tests, demonstrating a better generalization capability than NN, despite the fact that GP when compared to NN requires more computation in model development. Most machine learning methods are usually straightforward to implement and work well with minimum resources; however their blackbox nature makes them non user friendly. On the other hand, GP results are often human friendly and provide an explicit mathematical formula as its output, although developing such an efficient algorithm and realizing its full potential to solve real-world problems can be challenging. GP algorithms are expected to require a computing time that grows exponentially with the size of the problem [32]. In this study, GP prediction capability was compared with the well-known machine learning classifiers on mortality, disability, fracture, access to ED with red code and hospitalization problems.

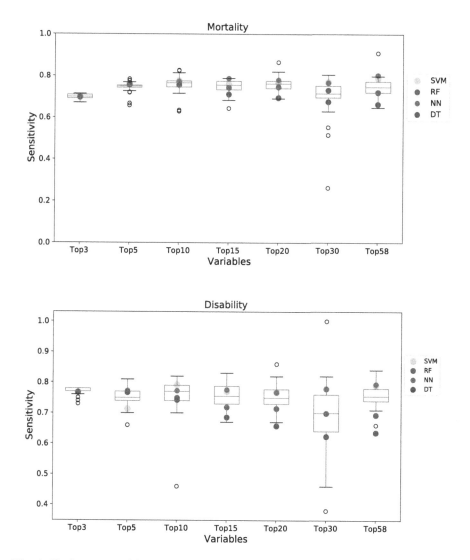

Fig. 1. Performance of GP on Mortality (upper plot) and Disability (lower plot) problems compared to the performance of SVM, RF, NN and DT. The box plots represent the 30 runs of GP with performance measured using sensitivity and the coloured points represent the sensitivity of SVM, RF, NN and DT. Top3 represents the top three variables and so on for each problem.

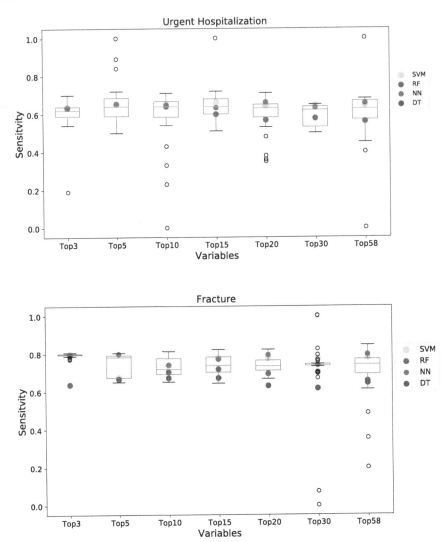

Fig. 2. Performance of GP on Urgent hospitalization (upper plot) and Fracture (lower plot) problems compared to the performance of SVM, RF, NN and DT. The box plots represent the 30 runs of GP with performance measured using sensitivity and the coloured points represent the sensitivity of SVM, RF, NN and DT. Top3 represents the top three variables and so on for each problem.

The most commonly used classifiers such as support vector machines (SVM), artificial neural networks (NN), random forests (RF) and decision trees (DT) were applied in all problems. The results obtained in each problem using the non-GP classifiers are compared with the results of GP using sensitivity. The comparison is based on the ability to identify the positive subjects in the frailty problems using their respective datasets. The performance of predictions by the different classifiers is shown in Figs. 1 and 2. The figures depict the performance of all classifiers using sensitivity on the testing part of the data. From the figures, the performance values were obtained using different subset of ranked features, the boxplots represent the performance at every 30 runs of GP, and the different colored dots represent the performance of the other machine learning algorithms. In all plots, the x-axis represents the number of features and y-axis represents the performance of GP using sensitivity.

Looking at each box plot of GP in Figs. 1 and 2, we can observe that some runs are outliers in each problem due to the stochastic nature of GP. For example, in urgent hospitalization, there are three runs beyond the whiskers for the top 5 and top 10 variables. These runs are outliers of the 30 runs of GP, plotted as points. In all problems with all variables, the performance of SVM, RF, NN, and DT are displayed under the upper quartile of the GP box plots, indicating the maximum performance obtained from the 30 runs of GP is always greater than the performance of the machine learning models. Comparing all algorithms, decision tree followed by random forest has the lowest performance in all problems for the number of variables greater 10. The average sensitivity of GP overlaps with the performance of NN. However, the accuracy of GP is lowered compared to SVM and NN.

For making the fairest comparison possible between GP and other machine learning models, a pairwise statistical test between the 30 runs of GP and each individual machine learning model was also performed. The statistical test used was the Wilcoxon signed rank test. The Wilcoxon statistical test is a nonparametric test that ranks the differences in performances of GP and other algorithms over each frailty problem. The test was based on the sensitivity score of each algorithm in each problem on the test data at the significance level of 0.01. From the test results, it is found that the results between SVM and GP are statistically significant only in disability, urgent hospitalization and preventable hospitalization problems. Combining the experimental results (Figs. 1 and 2) and Wilcoxon-rank test results, it is concluded that for mortality and fracture problems SVM outperforms GP in sensitivity score, while for access to ED with a red code SVM performs lower than GP. GP outperforms DT in all problems except for urgent hospitalization. NN has a similar performance with GP for all problems excluding mortality and femur fracture.

4.3 Feature Selection Comparison of GP and Chi-Square

The performance of GP feature selection is compared with the well-known Chi-Square feature selection method. The top three variables (age, Charlson index, and the number of urgent hospitalization) selected by GP are also selected by chi-square as top three variables in the mortality problem. After three variables, there is slightly a little difference in the position of variables. Table 6 presents the prediction accuracy of the classification model using the features selected by GP and Chi-square for all problems. For each problem, the best average accuracy of the 30 runs of GP is taken to compare the classification performance of GP and Chi-square feature selection methods. From this table, Chi-square performed the best in the mortality problem with an accuracy of 76% followed by GP with an accuracy of 75%, a difference of only 1%. This condition holds also for disability and fracture problems. For urgent hospitalization, both GP and chi-square produce a similar performance. The results show that GP can perform the feature selection task with competitive results.

Table 6. Prediction accuracy via feature selection of GP and Chi-square

Problem	GP feature selection	Chi-Square feature selection
Mortality	0.75	0.76
Urgent hospitalization	0.64	0.64
Disability	0.72	0.73
Preventable hospitalization	0.68	0.71
Red code emergency	0.58	0.68
Fracture	0.71	0.73

5   Discussions and Conclusions

The goals of this study were to develop models to predict the risk of hospitalization, disability, mortality, fracture and emergency admissions among the older people in Piedmont, Italy. In this study, we inspected the possibility of using an administrative dataset to detect frailty in older adults using Genetic programming (GP), which was used as a potential tool for developing a prediction model. Six different models were developed, and the performance of each model relies on the input data provided to the learning algorithm. The performances of models created by GP were assessed by splitting the data into training set and test set. The test set was untouched during the entire training and model selection process and only used for the final model evaluation.

To find what works for our frailty problems, we performed several experiments by varying the parameter values of genetic programming. Typically, we tried to discover the optimal parameter choice between two genetic parameters: the population size and the number of generations. In order to get the efficient GP algorithm that best fits our data, many runs of small populations over many generations and large populations over a few generations are compared. For classification problems, the results demonstrated that large populations running for a small number of generations achieve better fitness than small population running for a large number of generations. After selecting the best GP algorithm for our data, several experiments with 30 runs of GP are conducted by adjusting the remaining parameters. The performance of the models obtained by GP is evaluated using sensitivity, specificity, and accuracy. From the results obtained, it is evident that GP algorithms perform well in separating the positive cases from the negative cases of frailty outcomes. The overall classification performance for both training and testing are comparable with the existing machine learning techniques like artificial neural network, random forest and support vector machines. Overall, the results are encouraging, and further studies on frailty can be investigated to extend the findings on multiple outcomes simultaneously using evolutionary algorithms.

Overall, GP demonstrated substantial potential as a method for the automated development of clinical prediction models for diagnostic and prognostic purposes. The experiments of GP on administrative data acquired from different hospital discharges and drug prescriptions provide comparable accuracy to conventional models in the assessment of the risk of mortality, disability, fracture, access to the emergency department with red code and hospitalization.

References

1. Kojima, G., Liljas, A., Iliffe, S.: Frailty syndrome: implications and challenges for health care policy. Risk Manag. Healthc. Policy **12**, 23–30 (2019). https://doi.org/10.2147/RMHP.S168750
2. Comans, T.A., Peel, N.M., Hubbard, R.E., Mulligan, A.D., Gray, L.C., Scuffham, P.A.: The increase in healthcare costs associated with frailty in older people discharged to a post-acute transition care program. Age Ageing **45**, 317–320 (2016). https://doi.org/10.1093/ageing/afv196
3. Clegg, A., Young, J., Iliffe, S., Rikkert, M.O., Rockwood, K.: Frailty in elderly people. Lancet **381**, 752–762 (2013). https://doi.org/10.1016/S0140-6736(12)62167-9
4. Wennberg, D., Siegel, M., Darin, B., Filipova, N.: Combined predictive model: final report and technical documentation (2006)
5. Lally, F., Crome, P.: Understanding frailty (2007). https://doi.org/10.1136/pgmj.2006.048587
6. Fried, L.P., et al.: Frailty in older adults: evidence for a phenotype. J. Gerontol. Ser. A Biol. Sci. Med. Sci. **56**, M146–M157 (2001). https://doi.org/10.1093/gerona/56.3.M146
7. Rockwood, K., et al.: A global clinical measure of fitness and frailty in elderly people. CMAJ **173**, 489–495 (2005). https://doi.org/10.1503/cmaj.050051
8. Kotsiantis, S.B., et al.: Machine learning: a review of classification and combining techniques. Artif. Intell. Rev. **26**, 159–190 (2006). https://doi.org/10.1007/s10462-007-9052-3
9. Rockwood, K., Andrew, M., Mitnitski, A.: A comparison of two approaches to measuring frailty in elderly people. J. Gerontol. Ser. A Biol. Sci. Med. Sci. **62**, 738–743 (2007). https://doi.org/10.1093/gerona/62.7.738
10. Blodgett, J., Theou, O., Kirkland, S., Andreou, P., Rockwood, K.: Frailty in NHANES: comparing the frailty index and phenotype. Arch. Gerontol. Geriatr. **60**, 464–470 (2015). https://doi.org/10.1016/j.archger.2015.01.016
11. Theou, O., Brothers, T.D., Mitnitski, A., Rockwood, K.: Operationalization of frailty using eight commonly used scales and comparison of their ability to predict all-cause mortality. J. Am. Geriatr. Soc. **61**, 1537–1551 (2013). https://doi.org/10.1111/jgs.12420
12. Katz, A., Wong, S., Williamson, T., Taylor, C., Peterson, S.: Identification of frailty using EMR and admin data: a complex issue. Int. J. Popul. Data Sci. **3** (2018). https://doi.org/10.23889/ijpds.v3i4.832

13. Chen, C.-Y., Wu, S.-C., Chen, L.-J., Lue, B.-H.: The prevalence of subjective frailty and factors associated with frailty in Taiwan. Arch. Gerontol. Geriatr. **50**, S43–S47 (2010). https://doi.org/10.1016/s0167-4943(10)70012-1

14. Lee, D.H., Buth, K.J., Martin, B.J., Yip, A.M., Hirsch, G.M.: Frail patients are at increased risk for mortality and prolonged institutional care after cardiac surgery. Circulation **121**, 973 (2010). https://doi.org/10.1161/CIRCULATIONAHA.108.841437

15. Homer, M.L., Palmer, N.P., Fox, K.P., Armstrong, J., Mandl, K.D.: Predicting falls in people aged 65 years and older from insurance claims. Am. J. Med. **130**, 744.e17–744.e23 (2017). https://doi.org/10.1016/j.amjmed.2017.01.003

16. Bertini, F., Bergami, G., Montesi, D., Veronese, G., Marchesini, G., Pandolfi, P.: Predicting frailty condition in elderly using multidimensional socioclinical databases. Proc. IEEE **106**, 723–737 (2018). https://doi.org/10.1109/JPROC.2018.2791463

17. Amari, S.: Machine learning. In: Amari, S. (ed.) Information Geometry and Its Applications. AMS, vol. 194, pp. 231–278. Springer, Tokyo (2016). https://doi.org/10.1007/978-4-431-55978-8_11

18. Japkowicz, N., Stephen, S.: The class imbalance problem: a systematic study. Intell. Data Anal. **6**, 429–449 (2018). https://doi.org/10.3233/ida-2002-6504

19. Barandela, R., Sánchez, J.S., García, V., Rangel, E.: Strategies for learning in class imbalance problems. Pattern Recogn. **36**, 849–851 (2003). https://doi.org/10.1016/S0031-3203(02)00257-1

20. McCarthy, K., Zabar, B., Weiss, G.: Does cost-sensitive learning beat sampling for classifying rare classes? In: Proceedings of the 1st International Workshop on Utility-based Data Mining - UBDM 2005, pp. 69–77. ACM Press, New York (2005). https://doi.org/10.1145/1089827.1089836

21. Chen, J.X., Cheng, T.H., Chan, A.L.F., Wang, H.Y.: An application of classification analysis for skewed class distribution in therapeutic drug monitoring - the case of vancomycin. In: Proceedings - IDEAS Workshop on Medical Information Systems: The Digital Hospital, IDEAS 2004-DH (2005)

22. Orriols, A., Bernadí-Mansilla, E.: Class imbalance problem in UCS classifier system: fitness adaptation. In: 2005 IEEE Congress on Evolutionary Computation, IEEE CEC 2005, Proceedings (2005)

23. Azimlu, F., Rahnamayan, S., Makrehchi, M., Kalra, N.: Comparing genetic programming with other data mining techniques on prediction models. In: 2019 14th International Conference on Computer Science & Education (ICCSE), pp. 785–791. IEEE (2019). https://doi.org/10.1109/ICCSE.2019.8845381

24. Amal, S., Periwal, V., Scaria, V.: Predictive modeling of anti-malarial molecules inhibiting Apicoplast formation. BMC Bioinf. **14**, 55 (2013). https://doi.org/10.1186/1471-2105-14-55

25. Haixiang, G., Yijing, L., Shang, J., Mingyun, G., Yuanyue, H., Bing, G.: Learning from class-imbalanced data: review of methods and applications. Expert Syst. Appl. **73**, 220–239 (2017). https://doi.org/10.1016/j.eswa.2016.12.035

26. Kang, Q., Chen, X.S., Li, S.S., Zhou, M.C.: A noise-filtered under-sampling scheme for imbalanced classification. IEEE Trans. Cybern. **47**, 4263–4274 (2017). https://doi.org/10.1109/TCYB.2016.2606104

27. Leevy, J.L., Khoshgoftaar, T.M., Bauder, R.A., Seliya, N.: A survey on addressing high-class imbalance in big data. J. Big Data **5**(1), 1–30 (2018). https://doi.org/10.1186/s40537-018-0151-6

28. Han, J., Kamber, M., Pei, J.: Data Mining. Elsevier, Amsterdam (2012). https://doi.org/10.1016/C2009-0-61819-5

29. Volrathongchai, K., Brennan, P.F., Ferris, M.C.: Predicting the likelihood of falls among the elderly using likelihood basis pursuit technique. In: AMIA Annual Symposium, Proceedings (2005)
30. Bannister, C.A., Halcox, J.P., Currie, C.J., Preece, A., Spasić, I.: A genetic programming approach to development of clinical prediction models: a case study in symptomatic cardiovascular disease. PLoS One (2018). https://doi.org/10.1371/journal.pone.0202685
31. Bannister, C.A., Currie, C.J., Preece, A., Spasic, I.: Automatic development of clinical prediction models with genetic programming: a case study in cardiovascular disease. Value Health **17**, A200–A201 (2014). https://doi.org/10.1016/j.jval.2014.03.1171
32. Poli, R., Koza, J.: Genetic programming. In: Burke, E., Kendall, G. (eds.) Search Methodologies, pp. 143–185. Springer, Boston (2014). https://doi.org/10.1007/978-1-4614-6940-7_6
33. HeuristicLab homepage. https://dev.heuristiclab.com/trac.fcgi/wiki
34. Vluymans, S.: Learning from imbalanced data. In: Studies in Computational Intelligence, pp. 81–110 (2019). https://doi.org/10.1007/978-3-030-04663-7_4
35. Ulloa-Cazarez, R.L., López-Martín, C., Abran, A., Yáñez-Márquez, C.: Prediction of online students performance by means of genetic programming. Appl. Artif. Intell. **32**, 858–881 (2018). https://doi.org/10.1080/08839514.2018.1508839
36. Can, B., Heavey, C.: A comparison of genetic programming and artificial neural networks in metamodeling of discrete-event simulation models. Comput. Oper. Res. **39**, 424–436 (2012). https://doi.org/10.1016/j.cor.2011.05.004

Is k Nearest Neighbours Regression Better Than GP?

Leonardo Vanneschi[1,2]([✉]), Mauro Castelli[1], Luca Manzoni[3], Sara Silva[2], and Leonardo Trujillo[4]

[1] NOVA Information Management School (NOVA IMS),
Universidade Nova de Lisboa, Campus de Campolide, 1070-312 Lisboa, Portugal
{lvanneschi,mcastelli}@novaims.unl.pt
[2] LASIGE, Departamento de Informática, Faculdade de Ciências,
Universidade de Lisboa, 1749-016 Lisboa, Portugal
{lvanneschi,sara}@fc.ul.pt
[3] Department of Mathematics and Geosciences, University of Trieste,
Via Valerio 12/1, 34127 Trieste, Italy
lmanzoni@units.it
[4] Tecnológico Nacional de México/IT de Tijuana, Tijuana, BC, Mexico
leonardo.trujillo@tectijuana.edu.mx

Abstract. This work starts from the empirical observation that k nearest neighbours (KNN) consistently outperforms state-of-the-art techniques for regression, including geometric semantic genetic programming (GSGP). However, KNN is a memorization, and not a learning, method, i.e. it evaluates unseen data on the basis of training observations, and not by running a learned model. This paper takes a first step towards the objective of defining a learning method able to equal KNN, by defining a new semantic mutation, called random vectors-based mutation (RVM). GP using RVM, called RVMGP, obtains results that are comparable to KNN, but still needs training data to evaluate unseen instances. A comparative analysis sheds some light on the reason why RVMGP outperforms GSGP, revealing that RVMGP is able to explore the semantic space more uniformly. This finding opens a question for the future: is it possible to define a new genetic operator, that explores the semantic space as uniformly as RVM does, but that still allows us to evaluate unseen instances without using training data?

1 Introduction

Geometric Semantic Genetic Programming (GSGP) [1,2] is a variant of Genetic Programming (GP) [3] that uses Geometric Semantic Operators (GSOs) instead of the standard crossover and mutation. It induces a unimodal fitness landscape for any supervised learning problem; so it is an extremely powerful optimizer and, at the same time, it can limit overfitting [4]. The popularity of GSGP has steadily grown in the last few years, and it is nowadays a well established Machine Learning (ML) method. Nevertheless, GSGP generates very large predictive models,

T. Hu et al. (Eds.): EuroGP 2020, LNCS 12101, pp. 244–261, 2020.
https://doi.org/10.1007/978-3-030-44094-7_16

which are extremely hard to read and understand [1,2]. Even though several implementations have been introduced, that make GSGP usable and efficient [5–7], the lack of interpretability of the model is still an issue. Aware that in GSGP the most important GSO is mutation, and that GSGP without crossover can often outperform GSGP that uses crossover [8,9], in this paper, we introduce a mutation intending to ease a model's interpretability.

The mutation traditionally used by GSGP, called Geometric Semantic Mutation (GSM) uses two random trees. The evaluation of those random trees on training instances is used to obtain a different (random) value for each observation, which is subsequently used to calculate the modification caused by mutation to the outputs of the individual. The operator we introduce in this work, called Random Vectors-based Mutation (RVM), replaces the random trees with a vector of random numbers of the same length as the number of training instances. In this way, for each observation, one different random number is used to decide the modification of the output. GP using RVM as the sole genetic operator will be called RVMGP. Clearly, at the end of a RVMGP evolution, we do not have a real "model" (intended as a program that can be executed on unseen data), and so a different strategy has to be designed for generalizing. In this paper, we adopt a method that is very similar to the one used by k Nearest Neighbours (KNN) [10,11]: the output on an unseen instance is calculated using the similarity between the unseen instance and the training observations. Given that RVMGP works similarly to KNN on unseen data, it makes sense to compare RVMGP not only to GSGP, but also to KNN itself. To make the experimental comparison more complete, we also compare these methods to Random Forest (RF) regression [12], that is currently considered by several researchers as the state of the art for regression with ML, at least for "non-big data" problems [13,14]. The outcome of this experimental study, carried on six real-life regression problems, paves the way to fundamental questions on the relevance itself of using GP, a discussion that is tackled at the end of this paper.

The manuscript is organized as follows: Sect. 2 introduces GSGP. Section 3 introduces RVM. Section 4 presents our experimental study; after presenting the test problems and the employed experimental settings, the comparison between RVMGP and GSGP is presented in Sect. 4.2 and the one between RVMGP, KNN and RF regression in Sect. 4.3. Finally, Sect. 5 concludes the paper.

2   Geometric Semantic Genetic Programming

Let $\mathbf{X} = \{\vec{x_1}, \vec{x_2}, ..., \vec{x_n}\}$ be the set of input data (training instances, observations or fitness cases) of a symbolic regression problem, and $\vec{t} = [t_1, t_2, ..., t_n]$ the vector of the respective expected output or target values (in other words, for each $i = 1, 2, ..., n$, t_i is the expected output corresponding to input $\vec{x_i}$). A GP individual (or program) P can be seen as a function that, for each input vector $\vec{x_i}$ returns the scalar value $P(\vec{x_i})$. Following [2], we call *semantics* of P the vector $\vec{s_P} = [P(\vec{x_1}), P(\vec{x_2}), ..., P(\vec{x_n})]$. This vector can be represented as a point in a n-dimensional space, that we call *semantic space*. Remark that the target vector $\overrightarrow{t}$ itself is a point in the semantic space.

As explained above, GSGP is a variant of GP where the standard crossover and mutation are replaced by new operators called Geometric Semantic Operators (GSOs). The objective of GSOs is to define modifications on the syntax of GP individuals that have a precise effect on their semantics. More in particular: geometric semantic crossover generates one offspring, whose semantics stands in the line joining the semantics of the two parents in the semantic space and geometric semantic mutation, by mutating an individual i, allows us to obtain another individual j such that the semantics of j stands inside a ball of a given predetermined radius, centered in the semantics of i. One of the reasons why GSOs became popular in the GP community is probably related to the fact that GSOs induce an unimodal error surface (on training data) for any supervised learning problem, where fitness is calculated using an error measure between outputs and targets. In other words, using GSOs the error surface on training data is guaranteed to not have any locally optimal solution. This property holds, for instance, for any regression or classification problem, independently on how big and how complex data are (reference [1] contains a detailed explanation of the reason why the error surface is unimodal and its importance). The definitions of the GSOs are, as given in [2], respectively:

Geometric Semantic Crossover (GSC). Given two parent functions $T_1, T_2 : \mathbb{R}^n \to \mathbb{R}$, the geometric semantic crossover returns the real function $T_{XO} = (T_1 \cdot T_R) + ((1 - T_R) \cdot T_2)$, where T_R is a random real function whose output values range in the interval $[0, 1]$.

Geometric Semantic Mutation (GSM). Given a parent function $T : \mathbb{R}^n \to \mathbb{R}$, the geometric semantic mutation with mutation step ms returns the real function $T_M = T + ms \cdot (T_{R1} - T_{R2})$, where T_{R1} and T_{R2} are random real functions.

The reason why GSM uses two random trees T_{R1} and T_{R2} is that the amount of modification caused by GSM must be centered in zero. In other words, a random expression is needed that has the same probability of being positive or negative. Even though this is not in the original definition of GSM, later contributions [1,4,9] have clearly shown that limiting the codomain of T_{R1} and T_{R2} in a predefined interval (for instance $[0, 1]$, as it is done for T_R in GSC) helps to improve the generalization ability of GSGP. As in several previous works [1,5], we constrain the outputs of T_R, T_{R1}, and T_{R2} by wrapping them in a logistic function. Only the definitions of the GSOs for symbolic regression problems are given here, since they are the only ones used in this work. For the definition of GSOs for other domains, the reader is referred to [2].

As reported in [1,2], the property of GSOs of inducing a unimodal error surface has a price. The price, in this case, is that GSOs always generate larger offspring than the parents, and this entails a rapid growth of the size of the individuals in the population. To counteract this problem, in [5–7] implementations of GSOs were proposed, that make GSGP not only usable in practice, but also significantly faster than standard GP. This is possible through a smart representation of GP individuals, that allows us to not store their genotypes during the evolution. The implementation presented in [5] is the one used here. Even though this implementation is efficient, it does not solve the problem of the size of the final model: the genotype of the final solution returned by GSGP can be reconstructed, but it is so large that it is practically impossible to understand it. This turns GSGP into a "black-box" system, as many other popular ML systems are, including deep neural networks.

Several previous contributions (see for instance [8]) have clearly demonstrated that, in GSGP, the most important genetic operator is GSM and in many cases a GSGP system using only GSM, and no GSC, can obtain comparable (or even better) results to the ones of a system using both these operators. Even though GSM limits the problem of the rapid growth of code inside the population (this growth is exponential for GSC, but slower for GSM), the issue remains. In other words, even using only GSM, the final model is often so large that it is hardly readable and practically impossible to understand. Trying to solve this issue is one of the motivations for introducing the novel mutation operator presented in the next section.

3   Random Vector Based Mutation

The rapid code growth caused by GSM can be explained by the fact that the offspring (T_M in the definition of GSM given in Sect. 2) contains the genotype of the parent (T), plus the genotype of two random trees (T_{R1} and T_{R2}) and 4 further nodes. Replacing the two random trees with a random number (i.e. a scalar constant) would vastly limit the code growth. Nevertheless, as explained in [1], this would not allow us to implement ball mutation on the semantic space, which is the objective. Such a mutation would, in fact, modify the semantics of parent T *of the same constant amount* for all its coordinates. On the other hand, the optimization power of GSM is given by the fact that GSM can modify the semantics of T by a *different* amount for each one of its coordinates, since T_{R1} and T_{R2} typically return different values when evaluated on the different training observations. To understand the importance of this, one may consider the case in which one coordinate of T is extremely "close" to the corresponding target, while another coordinate is extremely "far". Modifying both these coordinates of the same quantity would never allow us to transform T into the global optimum.

In this work, we propose to use a *vector* of random numbers $\vec{v}$, of the same length as the number of training observations, to modify the semantics of the individuals by different quantities for each one of its coordinates. Each element $\vec{v}[i]$ of vector $\vec{v}$ stores the particular modification that mutation apports to the ith coordinate of the semantics of T. In GSM, if the codomain of T_{R1} and T_{R2} is constrained in $[0, 1]$ (as it is customary [1, 4, 9]), then, for each coordinate of the semantic vector, the modification is given by a random number included in $[-ms, ms]$. To simulate as closely as possible this behaviour of GSM, in this work each coordinate $\vec{v}[i]$ of vector $\vec{v}$ will contain a random number extracted with uniform distribution from $[-ms, ms]$.

The functioning should be clarified by the following example. Let us assume that we have the following training set D, composed by 3 observations (lines) and 2 features (columns), and the following corresponding target vector $\vec{t}$:

$$D = \begin{bmatrix} 1 & 2 \\ 3 & 4 \\ 40 & 20 \end{bmatrix} \qquad \vec{t} = \begin{bmatrix} 4 \\ 10 \\ 100 \end{bmatrix}$$

Let us also assume that we have a GP individual $P = x_1 + x_2$. The semantics of P is equal to: $\vec{s_P} = [3, 7, 60]$. Let us also assume, for simplicity, that $ms = 1$. All we have to do to mutate P is to generate a vector $\vec{v}$ of random numbers in $[-1, 1]$, of the same length as the number of training observations; for instance: $\vec{v} = [0.75, -0.25, 0.4]$. In this way, the offspring P_M of the mutation of P will be an individual whose semantics is:

$$\vec{s_{P_M}} = \vec{s_P} + \vec{v} \qquad (1)$$

or, in other words: $\vec{s_{P_M}} = [3.75, 6.75, 60.4]$. As we can see, each coordinate of $\vec{v}$ has been used to update the corresponding coordinate of $\vec{s_P}$. We call this type of mutation Random Vector based Mutation (RVM), and GP that uses RVM as the unique genetic operator RVMGP. Both GSM and RVM can be defined as follows:

$$T_M = T + \Delta T \qquad (2)$$

where the only difference between GSM and RVM is given by a different ΔT: ΔT is equal to $ms \cdot (T_{R1} - T_{R2})$ for GSM (as in the definition of Sect. 2) and it is equal to a *different* random number in $[-ms, ms]$ for each training observation for RVM.

At this point, a question comes natural: how can RVMGP be used to calculate the output on unseen observations? The idea proposed in this work is inspired by the KNN algorithm. In particular, given that only regression applications will be used as test problems, the inspiration is taken from KNN regression [10]. It consists in calculating the average of the outputs of the model on the k nearest training observations. Considering the previous example again, let us consider an unseen observation like, for instance: $\vec{u} = [2, 3]$. What is the output of individual P_M on observation $\vec{u}$? If we assume, for instance, that $k = 2$, all we have to do is to calculate the two closest instances to $\vec{u}$ in the training set D and calculate the average of the outputs of P_M on those instances. Considering, for instance, Euclidean distance as the metric used to calculate the k nearest training observations, the two observations that are closer to $\vec{u}$ in D are the first and the second observations, i.e. $[1, 2]$ and $[3, 4]$. Considering the output values of P_M on those two observations, i.e. the first two coordinates of s_{P_M}, the output of P_M on unseen instance $\vec{u}$ is equal to:

$$P_M(\vec{u}) = \frac{3.75 + 6.75}{2} = 5.25 \qquad (3)$$

Let us now take a moment to ponder what is the final model (i.e. the minimum amount of information to calculate the output on unseen instances) for RVMGP.

Actually, the model can be seen from two different viewpoints: the first one is to consider the initial tree, plus the vector of random numbers used to translate its semantics, plus the training set. For instance, for the previous example, if P_M was the final individual returned by RVMGP, one may say that the model is given by:

$$P = x_1 + x_2, \quad \vec{v} = [0.75 \quad -0.25 \quad 0.4], \quad D = \begin{bmatrix} 1 & 2 \\ 3 & 4 \\ 40 & 20 \end{bmatrix} \tag{4}$$

It should be noticed that, if a new generation is executed by RVMGP, P_M will probably be mutated, generating a new individual P'_M, where the semantic of P'_M can be obtained by summing the semantics of P_M to a vector of random trees:

$$\overrightarrow{s_{P'_M}} = \overrightarrow{s_{P_M}} + \overrightarrow{v_1} \tag{5}$$

But, replacing Eq. (1) into Eq. (5), we obtain: $\overrightarrow{s_{P'_M}} = \overrightarrow{s_P} + \vec{v} + \overrightarrow{v_1}$, and if we define $\vec{w} = \vec{v} + \overrightarrow{v_1}$, we obtain: $\overrightarrow{s_{P'_M}} = \overrightarrow{s_P} + \vec{w}$. In other words, also $s_{P'_M}$ can be defined using the semantics of the initial individual P and a vector of random numbers. This reasoning can be generalized to any number of generations. So, independently from the number of generations performed by RVMGP, it will always be possible to interpret the final model as an individual from the initial population, plus a vector of random numbers, plus the training set (as in Eq. (4)).

A second possible way of interpreting the model returned by RVMGP is to consider the semantics of the final individual, plus the training set. Considering the previous example, and assuming that P_M is the final solution returned by RVMGP, the model would be:

$$\overrightarrow{s_{P_M}} = [3.75 \quad 6.75 \quad 60.4], \quad D = \begin{bmatrix} 1 & 2 \\ 3 & 4 \\ 40 & 20 \end{bmatrix} \tag{6}$$

It should be noticed that this second way of interpreting the RVMGP model (reported in Eq. (6)) is completely equivalent to the first one (reported in Eq. (4)), since s_{P_M} can be obtained directly by evaluating P on each line of D, and summing $\vec{v}$. It is only a different way of presenting the same information: while the first interpretation (Eq. (4)) still contains a GP tree, and so vaguely reminds a traditional GP model, the second interpretation (Eq. (6)) allows us to save memory space and to calculate the output on unseen instances faster. If the model is stored as in Eq. (4), to calculate the output on an unseen instance $\vec{u}$ we have to evaluate $o = P(\vec{u})$, calculate the k nearest instances to $\vec{u}$ in D, and sum to o the average of the corresponding coordinates in $\vec{v}$. On the other hand, if the model is stored as in Eq. (6), all we have to do is to calculate the k nearest instances to $\vec{u}$ in D and return the average of the corresponding coordinates in $\overrightarrow{s_{P_M}}$. It is not hard to convince oneself that these two processes lead exactly to the same result, but the second one is faster because it does not involve the evaluation of a program on the unseen instance. We are aware that, in the presence of vast training sets, this could be a large amount of information to store (as vastly discussed in the literature as a drawback of KNN [10]). However, this is still convenient, in terms of memory occupation, compared to storing the huge models generated by GSGP, when GSM is employed.

Finally, it is worth pointing out that the only difference between RVMGP and KNN regression is that KNN regression uses the target values corresponding to the k nearest training observations, instead of the corresponding output of an individual. In other words, considering the previous example, the output of KNN regression for observation $\overrightarrow{u}$ would have been equal to: $\text{KNN}(\overrightarrow{u}) = \dfrac{4 + 10}{2} = 14$.

4   Experimental Study

This section is organized as follows: Sect. 4.1 presents the test problems used for our experimental study and the employed parameter settings. Section 4.2 contains an experimental comparison between GSGP using GSM and RVMGP using RVM (no crossover is considered in this study). Finally, Sect. 4.3 extends the experimental comparison, by including also KNN regression and RF regression. From now on, for simplicity, GP using only GSM will be indicated as GSGP. The notation GSGP-log will be used to indicate the variant of GSGP in which the codomain of random trees T_{R1} and T_{R2} used by GSM are constrained in $[0, 1]$ by wrapping them with a logistic function, as in [1,4,9]. The notation GSGP-nolog will be used to indicate the variant in which the codomains of T_{R1} and T_{R2} are not constrained at all. Finally, to indicate the variant of RVMGP using a particular value $k = x$, we will use the notation RVM-kx.

4.1   Test Problems and Experimental Settings

The six real-life datasets used as test problems are described in Table 1. The table shows, for each dataset, the number of features, the number of observations, and a reference where more information about the data and the application can be found. The six datasets have already been used as test problems for GP before.

Table 1. Description of the test problems. For each dataset, the number of features (independent variables) and the number of instances (observations) are reported.

Dataset	# Features	# Instances
Bioavailability [15]	241	359
Concrete [16]	8	1029
Energy [17]	8	768
Park Motor [18]	18	5875
Park Total [18]	18	5875
PPB [15]	628	131

Table 2. Parameter setting used in our experiments for the studied GP variants.

Parameter	Setting
Population size	100
Max. # of generations	2000
Initialization	Ramped H-H
Crossover rate	0
Mutation rate	1
Max. depth for initialization	6
Tournament selection, size	4

Previous contributions, including the ones referenced in Table 2, clearly show that GSGP outperforms standard GP (i.e. GP using the standard Koza's genetic operators [3]) on all these test problems. For this reason, standard GP is not studied here. For each one of these datasets, 30 independent runs of each one of the studied methods where performed. For each run, a different partition of the dataset into training and test set was used, where 70% of the instances, randomly selected with uniform distribution, form the training set and the remaining 30% were used as a test set.

Table 2 reports the values of the parameters that were used in our GP experiments. Besides, elitism was applied by copying the best individual in the next population at each generation. The mutation step, for all the studied methods, was a random number, extracted with uniform distribution from $[0, 1]$, as proposed in [9]. Concerning RVMGP, different values of k were studied ($k = 1, 5, 10, 20, 50$) and experimentally compared. Concerning KNN, the same values of k as for RVMGP were studied. For both algorithms, the measure used to calculate the similarity between instances was the Euclidean distance, calculated using all the features in the dataset. Concerning RF, least-squares boosting was used, with a maximum of 10 splits per tree and 100 trees.

4.2   Experimental Results: RVMGP vs GSGP

Figure 1 reports the results on the training set obtained by RVMGP, GSGP-log and GSGP-nolog. On training data, RVMGP clearly outperforms both GSGP-log and GSGP-nolog for all the studied test problems. Figure 2 reports the results on the test set. Concerning RVMGP, to avoid cluttering the plots, only the best and worse values of k for each test problem are reported. Concerning GSGP, only the curve of GSGP-log is reported, because, for each studied problem, GSGP-nolog returns results on the test set that are so much worse than the other studied methods that reporting the curve of GSGP-nolog would not allow us to appreciate the mutual differences between the other methods. The fact that GSGP-nolog has a poor generalization ability, hence the need of constraining the output of the random trees generated by GSM, was already known in the literature [1, 4], and our study is a further confirmation of this finding.

Concerning Fig. 2, let us not consider, for the moment, the horizontal straight lines, that represent the results returned by KNN regression. Those results will be discussed in Sect. 4.3. Figure 2 clearly shows that RVMGP with the best-studied k consistently outperforms GSGP on all the studied test problems, while RVMGP with the worst studied k outperforms GSGP in 4 cases over 6. To assess the statistical significance of these results, a set of tests has been performed. The Lilliefors test has shown that the data are not normally distributed and hence a rank-based statistic has been used. The Wilcoxon rank-sum test for pairwise data comparison with Bonferroni correction has been used, under the alternative hypothesis that the samples do not have equal medians at the end of the run, with a significance level $\alpha = 0.05$. The p-values are reported in Table 3, where statistically significant differences are highlighted with p-values in bold. As we can observe, all the differences are statistically significant, except the

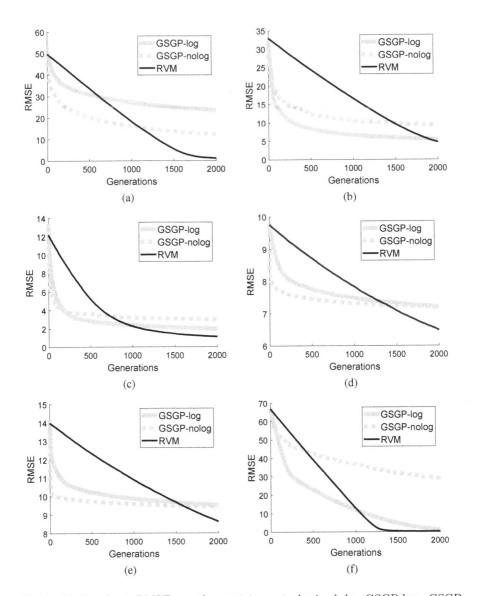

Fig. 1. Median best RMSE on the *training set* obtained by GSGP-log, GSGP-nolog and RVM. (a) = Bioavailability; (b) = Concrete; (c) = Energy; (d) = ParkMotor; (e) = ParkTotal; (f) = PPB.

difference between GSGP and RVMGP with the worst k for the Concrete and PPB datasets. The fact that, for different problems, the best value of k changes is an issue that has been already discussed in the literature for KNN regression [19]. The experimental results reported here seem to confirm that this issue also exists for RVMGP.

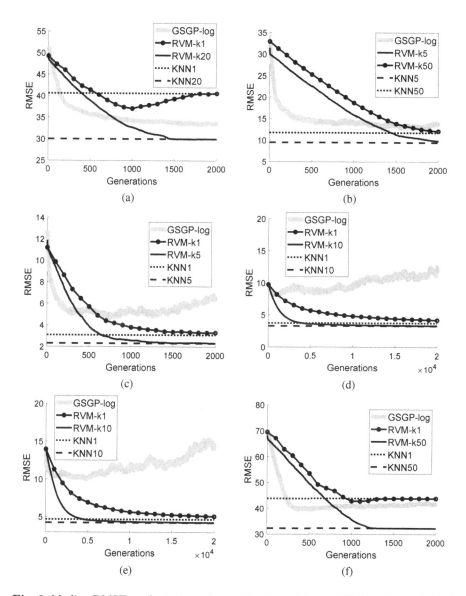

Fig. 2. Median RMSE on the *test set* obtained by GSGP-log and RVMGP. For RVMGP, only the values of k that have allowed us to obtain the best and the worse results are reported. The best is represented with a black-continuous line, the worst with a black line annotated with points. For KNN, the same k values as for RVMGP are reported. The results of KNN are shown as horizontal straight lines. (a) = Bioavailability; (b) = Concrete; (c) = Energy; (d) = Park Motor; (e) = Park Total; (f) = PPB.

Table 3. p-values of the Wilcoxon rank-sum test on unseen data for the experiments of Fig. 2, under the alternative hypothesis that the samples do not have equal medians. Bold denotes statistically significant values.

	GSGP-log vs best RVM	GSGP-log vs worst RVM	best RVM vs worst RVM
Bioavailability	$\mathbf{7.70 \times 10^{-8}}$	$\mathbf{1.46 \times 10^{-10}}$	$\mathbf{3.02 \times 10^{-11}}$
Concrete	$\mathbf{3.82 \times 10^{-9}}$	0.0933	$\mathbf{3.34 \times 10^{-11}}$
Energy	$\mathbf{3.02 \times 10^{-11}}$	$\mathbf{4.08 \times 10^{-5}}$	$\mathbf{3.02 \times 10^{-11}}$
Park Motor	$\mathbf{7.39 \times 10^{-11}}$	$\mathbf{6.12 \times 10^{-10}}$	$\mathbf{4.62 \times 10^{-10}}$
Park Total	$\mathbf{3.02 \times 10^{-11}}$	$\mathbf{2.19 \times 10^{-8}}$	$\mathbf{3.02 \times 10^{-11}}$
PPB	$\mathbf{1.33 \times 10^{-10}}$	0.1154	$\mathbf{3.16 \times 10^{-10}}$

All this considered, we can state that RVMGP, once the best value of k is discovered, is preferable to GSGP for the quality of the returned solutions. An attempt to motivate this result is given in Fig. 3. In this figure, the amounts of modification of the different studied mutation operators (i.e. the quantities ΔT in Eq. (2)) are reported. More in particular, for each individual in the population to which mutation was applied, the used value of ΔT for each fitness case was stored. Given that there is no reason why the values of ΔT should change along the evolution, only the values at the first generation are reported. The scatterplots of Fig. 3 have the fitness cases (i.e. the training instances) on the horizontal axis, ordered randomly. In other words, the values on the horizontal axis are discrete and they consist in the integer values $1, 2, ..., N$, where N is the number of training instances. For each one of the values on the horizontal axis (i.e. for each fitness case) a "column" of points is reported, one for each individual in the population. For each one of those points, the value on the vertical axis corresponds to the ΔT value that mutation applied to that individual. To save space, only the results concerning one of the studied test problems are reported here (specifically, Fig. 3 reports the results on the Concrete dataset), but on the other five test problems, the situation is qualitatively the same, leading to the same conclusions.

Figure 3 offers a clear picture of the differences between the mutation operators used by RVMGP (plot (a)), GSGP-log (plot (b)) and GSGP-nolog (plot (c)). Let us begin by discussing the case of GSGP-nolog (plot (c)). Since the codomain of the random trees is not limited, ΔT often assumes very large (positive and negative) values (up to 10^{16}). As a consequence, GSGP-nolog can cause huge modifications in the semantics of the individuals. This may be the cause for an unstable search process, and thus the poor generalization ability of GSGP-nolog.

Let us now focus on the ΔT values of RVMGP (Fig. 3(a)) and GSGP-log (Fig. 3(b)). First of all, it is worth pointing out that, observing the scatterplots, one should not be surprised by the concentration of points around $\Delta T = 0$. In fact, the mutation step ms is a different random number in $[0, 1]$ at each mutation event, and not a constant value. Given that $\Delta T \in [-ms, ms]$, the interval of variation of ΔT changes at each mutation event, and it is expected

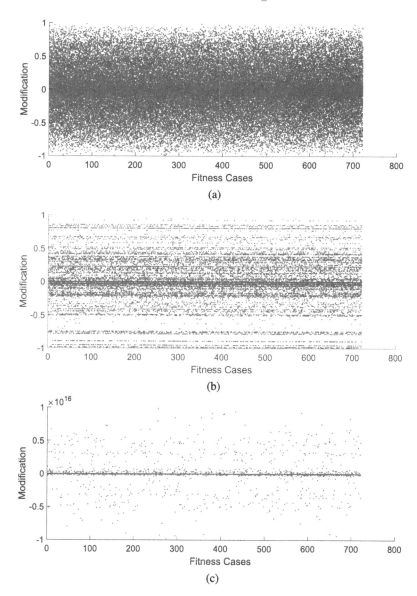

Fig. 3. The modifications ΔT (see Eq. (2)) made by the studied mutations on each training case for each one of the individuals in the population at the first generation for the Concrete dataset. (a) = RVMGP, (b) = GSGP-log, (c) = GSGP-nolog.

that more points are concentrated around zero, while a smaller number of points appear close to the values $\Delta T = 1$ and $\Delta T = -1$. Secondly, one important difference between the scatterplot of RVMGP and the one of GSGP-log is visible: the scatterplot of RVMGP is clearly more "dense" and "uniform". In other words, practically all possible values of ΔT have been achieved for each fitness case. On the other hand, observing the scatterplot of GSGP-log, we can see that it is less uniform, which makes us hypothesize that some values of ΔT are harder to obtain than others. This depends on the data and on the particular random trees that were generated. From this observation, it is straightforward to infer that there are some points (or even "regions") in the semantic space that are harder than others to reach by GSM, while this is not the case for RVM. We could say that RVM induces a *dense* and regular semantic space, while GSM induces a *sparse* and irregular semantic space. Also, more diverse semantic values appear in a RVMGP population than in a GSGP-log population. In other words, more semantic diversity is offered by RVMGP than by GSGP-log. Given that semantic diversity has been demonstrated as one of the factors promoting generalization ability [20], we hypothesize that the better results achieved by RVMGP in Fig. 2 can be motivated by the different behaviour highlighted in Fig. 3.

4.3   Experimental Results: RVMGP vs KNN Regression vs RF Regression

It is now time to look back at Fig. 2, and consider the horizontal lines, that correspond to the median value of the RMSE achieved by KNN regression on the test set (the same values of k as for RVMGP are reported). Of course, this value is a constant (there is no evolution in KNN), but reporting that value as a horizontal line in the plots helps visibility. Two facts can be observed: first of all, KNN consistently outperforms GSGP on all studied problems; as a consequence, KNN also outperforms standard GP, given that GSGP was able to obtain better results than standard GP on all these problems, as discussed above. Secondly, the evolution of RVMGP approximates KNN, until a point in which it obtains practically identical results, without being able to significantly improve them. That point arrives within generation 2000 for all the studied test problems, except Park Motor and Park Total (Fig. 2(d) and (e), respectively). To see the same behaviour, for those two problems we have extended the runs until generation 20000. Table 4 reports, for each studied problem, the numeric values of the median errors for the worst and best KNN and the worst and best RVMGP. To have a more complete vision of how these results compare with other ML algorithms, also the results obtained by RF regression [12] are reported, since RF regression is often considered the ML state of the art for regression. The interested reader is referred to [13,14] to support the use of RF. To assess the statistical significance of these results, once again the Wilcoxon rank-sum test for pairwise data comparison with Bonferroni correction has been used, under the alternative hypothesis that the samples do not have equal medians, with a significance level $\alpha = 0.05$. The p-values are reported in Table 5, where statistically significant differences are highlighted with p-values in bold.

As we can observe, RF regression outperforms the other studied methods only on two of the six studied problems. Discussing the results of RF is beyond the scope of this paper, nevertheless it is worth pointing out the RF outperforms the other methods for the two problems that have the smaller dimensionality of

Table 4. Median error over 30 independent runs returned by the worst and best KNN, the worst and best RVM and RF regression. The best result for each test problem is highlighted in bold.

	worst KNN	best KNN	worst RVM	best RVM	RF Regr.
Bioavailability	40.64	30.01	40.61	**29.99**	36.45
Concrete	12.13	9.86	11.76	9.48	**5.84**
Energy	3.31	2.33	3.08	2.31	**0.40**
Park Motor	3.75	**3.29**	4.20	3.34	3.80
Park Total	4.69	**4.23**	5.10	4.28	4.62
PPB	43.85	**32.29**	43.88	**32.29**	42.0

Table 5. p-values of the Wilcoxon rank-sum test on unseen data for the experiments of Table 4, under the alternative hypothesis that the samples do not have equal medians. Bold denotes statistically significant values.

	best RVM vs best KNN	best RVM vs RF Regr.	best KNN vs RF Regr.
Bioavailability	0.95	**5.49×10^{-11}**	**6.70×10^{-11}**
Concrete	0.92	**3.02×10^{-11}**	**3.02×10^{-11}**
Energy	0.34	**3.02×10^{-11}**	**3.02×10^{-11}**
Park Motor	0.02	**4.50×10^{-11}**	**3.02×10^{-11}**
Park Total	0.23	**4.20×10^{-10}**	**1.33×10^{-10}**
PPB	0.92	**8.99×10^{-11}**	**8.99×10^{-11}**

the feature space. For the other problems, that are characterized by a larger dimensionality of the feature space, RFs are consistently outperformed both by KNN and by RVMGP. All the differences are statistically significant, with the only exception of the differences between RVMGP and KNN, that are not statistically significant for any of the studied problems.

These observations lead to questions that may look dramatic for the GP community: is KNN better than GP? Are we missing the boat by using GP, while KNN, that is a simpler algorithm, can achieve better results?

Answering these questions is not straightforward, and possibly a single answer does not even exist. It is worth pointing out that the excellent generalization ability of KNN, when compared to other ML algorithms, was already known [21], and has recently been discussed in [22]. In the latter contribution, Cohen and colleagues offer an interesting discussion about the difference between learning and memorizing. It is clear that KNN is memorizing, and not learning. KNN, in fact, does not even have a learning phase, and does not have a real model, intended as a program that can be executed on observations. The model is replaced by the training set and generalization is achieved only by comparing an unseen instance to the training observations. However, as pointed out by Cohen *et al.*, memorization and generalization, which are traditionally considered to be contradicting to each other, are compatible and complementary in ML, and this explains the excellent generalization ability of KNN.

On the other hand, having a model of the data can be convenient in many cases. First of all, because a model, if readable, can be interpreted by a domain expert. If a model can be understood and "makes sense" to a domain expert, she will also more likely trust the predictions. Secondly, KNN bases its functioning on the similarity between training and unseen data, which implies that the functioning of KNN is strongly dependent on the distance metric used to quantify this similarity. This dependence can be avoided, in principle, if we have a model, that can potentially make predictions based on concepts that go beyond the immediate similarity between data.

All this considered, instead of answering the previous questions, one may ask another question: is it possible to obtain the same results as KNN, but by means of learning instead of memorization? Our answer is that, in some senses, this is exactly what RVMGP is doing. Furthermore, although only on two test problems, RF regression was able to outperform KNN, and RF regression is learning and not memorizing.

RVMGP is obtaining the same results as KNN, but after a learning process. However, what leaves us unsatisfied with RVMGP is that, as for KNN, also with RVMGP we need the training data to be able to generalize. But *why* does RVMGP need the training data? Simply because RVM uses a vector of random numbers, one for each training observation, and there is no other available element, unless data similarity, that can let us have the appropriate corresponding number to use on unseen data.

From these considerations, a new and final question comes to our mind: is it possible to simulate the behaviour of RVM using random trees, so that generalization can be obtained simply evaluating the final expression? In the end, as explained in Sect. 4.2, our interpretation of what makes RVMGP able to outperform GSGP comes from the difference in the scatterplots of the ΔTs reported in Fig. 3. So, what if we were able to obtain a "dense" and "regular" scatterplot as the one of Fig. 3(a), but using random trees, instead of vectors of random numbers? We hypothesize that this would allow us to obtain results that are comparable to the ones of KNN, but with the big advantage of having a final, executable, expression, that can be evaluated on unseen data.

These ideas open to new and exciting research questions: why is the scatterplot of the ΔTs of GSM different from the one in Fig. 3(a)? Does it depend on the way we are normalizing data? Does it depend on the primitive operators we are using to build the random trees? Does it depend on their size and shape? Is there any way to obtain a behaviour like the one of Fig. 3(a) using random trees, or is it impossible after all? And even further: can we use trained expressions, instead of random expressions, to obtain a scenario like the one in Fig. 3(a)? Can novelty search [23] help learn such expressions? In the end, from Fig. 3(b) it is clear that GSM is sampling similar values of ΔT several times, while disregarding others. Can we simply reward diversity in the creation of the random expressions used by GSM? Is it enough to obtain an algorithm that works like KNN, but learns instead of memorizing? All these questions deserve future work and answering those questions is one of the main interests of our current research.

5   Conclusions and Future Work

A new geometric semantic mutation, called Random Vector-based Mutation (RVM) was presented in this paper. It has the advantage of reducing the size of the model compared to traditional geometric semantic mutation, and it clearly outperforms it on six real-life regression problems. On the other hand, as for the k Nearest Neighbors (KNN), the only way to evaluate unseen instances is by using the similarity with the training observations, which forces us to include the training set in the model. Furthermore, RVM can approximate KNN, until a point in which it is able to return practically identical results, but it is not able to outperform it significantly. The presented results highlighted an excellent generalization ability of KNN, often better than a state-of-the-art method like Random Forest regression. Furthermore, KNN is a much simpler algorithm than GP. These considerations force GPers to a basic reflection on the reason why we are using GP, questioning whether it even makes sense at all. We conclude that learning, as GP does, can be more important than memorizing, as KNN. This puts our future research in front of a clear and ambitious challenge: obtaining the same results as KNN through a GP-based learning process. The first attempt will come from a deeper analysis of the density of the semantic space, induced by different mutation operators.

Acknowledgments. This work was partially supported by FCT, Portugal, through funding of LASIGE Research Unit (UIDB/00408/2020) and projects BINDER (PTDC/CCI-INF/29168/2017), GADgET (DSAIPA/DS/0022/2018), AICE (DSAIPA/DS/0113/2019), INTERPHENO (PTDC/ASP-PLA/28726/2017), OPTOX (PTDC/CTA-AMB/30056/2017) and PREDICT (PTDC/CCI-CIF/29877/2017), and by the Slovenian Research Agency (research core funding No. P5-0410). We also thank Reviewer 2 for the interesting comments, and apologize for not having had enough time to follow all the helpful suggestions.

References

1. Vanneschi, L.: An introduction to geometric semantic genetic programming. In: Schütze, O., Trujillo, L., Legrand, P., Maldonado, Y. (eds.) NEO 2015. SCI, vol. 663, pp. 3–42. Springer, Cham (2017). https://doi.org/10.1007/978-3-319-44003-3_1

2. Moraglio, A., Krawiec, K., Johnson, C.G.: Geometric semantic genetic programming. In: Coello, C.A.C., Cutello, V., Deb, K., Forrest, S., Nicosia, G., Pavone, M. (eds.) PPSN 2012. LNCS, vol. 7491, pp. 21–31. Springer, Heidelberg (2012). https://doi.org/10.1007/978-3-642-32937-1_3

3. Koza, J.R.: Genetic Programming: On the Programming of Computers by Means of Natural Selection. MIT Press, Cambridge (1992)

4. Gonçalves, I., Silva, S., Fonseca, C.M.: On the generalization ability of geometric semantic genetic programming. In: Machado, P., et al. (eds.) EuroGP 2015. LNCS, vol. 9025, pp. 41–52. Springer, Cham (2015). https://doi.org/10.1007/978-3-319-16501-1_4

5. Castelli, M., Silva, S., Vanneschi, L.: A C++ framework for geometric semantic genetic programming. Genetic Program. Evolvable Mach. **16**(1), 73–81 (2015)

6. Moraglio, A.: An efficient implementation of GSGP using higher-order functions and memoization. In: Semantic Methods in Genetic Programming, Workshop at Parallel Problem Solving from Nature (2014)

7. Martins, J.F.B.S., Oliveira, L.O.V.B., Miranda, L.F., Casadei, F., Pappa, G.L.: Solving the exponential growth of symbolic regression trees in geometric semantic genetic programming. In: Proceedings of the Genetic and Evolutionary Computation Conference, GECCO 2018, pp. 1151–1158. ACM, New York (2018)

8. Moraglio, A., Mambrini, A.: Runtime analysis of mutation-based geometric semantic genetic programming for basis functions regression. In: Proceedings of the 15th Annual Conference on Genetic and Evolutionary Computation, GECCO 2013, pp. 989–996. ACM, New York (2013)

9. Vanneschi, L., Silva, S., Castelli, M., Manzoni, L.: Geometric semantic genetic programming for real life applications. In: Riolo, R., Moore, J.H., Kotanchek, M. (eds.) Genetic Programming Theory and Practice XI. GEC, pp. 191–209. Springer, New York (2014). https://doi.org/10.1007/978-1-4939-0375-7_11

10. Kramer, O.: K-nearest neighbors. In: Kramer, O. (ed.) Dimensionality Reduction with Unsupervised Nearest Neighbors. Intelligent Systems Reference Library, vol. 51, pp. 13–23. Springer, Heidelberg (2013). https://doi.org/10.1007/978-3-642-38652-7_2

11. Mucherino, A., Papajorgji, P.J., Pardalos, P.M.: k-nearest neighbor classification. In: Mucherino, A., Papajorgji, P.J., Pardalos, P.M. (eds.) Data Mining in Agriculture. Springer Optimization and Its Applications, vol. 34, pp. 83–106. Springer, New York (2009). https://doi.org/10.1007/978-0-387-88615-2_4

12. Breiman, L.: Random forests. Mach. Learn. **45**(1), 5–32 (2001)

13. Verikas, A., Gelzinis, A., Bacauskiene, M.: Mining data with random forests: a survey and results of new tests. Pattern Recogn. **44**(2), 330–349 (2011)

14. Ziegler, A., König, I.: Mining data with random forests: current options for real-world applications. Wiley Interdisc. Rev. Data Min. Knowl. Discov. **4**, 55–63 (2014)

15. Archetti, F., Lanzeni, S., Messina, E., Vanneschi, L.: Genetic programming for computational pharmacokinetics in drug discovery and development. Genetic Program. Evolvable Mach. **8**(4), 413–432 (2007)

16. Castelli, M., Vanneschi, L., Silva, S.: Prediction of high performance concrete strength using genetic programming with geometric semantic genetic operators. Expert Syst. Appl. **40**(17), 6856–6862 (2013)

17. Castelli, M., Trujillo, L., Vanneschi, L., Popovič, A.: Prediction of energy performance of residential buildings: a genetic programming approach. Energy Buildings **102**, 67–74 (2015)

18. Castelli, M., Vanneschi, L., Silva, S.: Prediction of the unified Parkinson's disease rating scale assessment using a genetic programming system with geometric semantic genetic operators. Expert Syst. Appl. **41**(10), 4608–4616 (2014)

19. Cheng, D., Zhang, S., Deng, Z., Zhu, Y., Zong, M.: kNN algorithm with data-driven k value. In: Luo, X., Yu, J.X., Li, Z. (eds.) ADMA 2014. LNCS (LNAI), vol. 8933, pp. 499–512. Springer, Cham (2014). https://doi.org/10.1007/978-3-319-14717-8_39

20. Galván, E., Schoenauer, M.: Promoting semantic diversity in multi-objective genetic programming. In: Proceedings of the Genetic and Evolutionary Computation Conference, GECCO 2019, pp. 1021–1029. ACM, New York (2019)

21. Chen, G.H., Shah, D.: Explaining the success of nearest neighbor methods in prediction. Found. Trends® in Mach. Learn. **10**(5–6), 337–588 (2018)
22. Cohen, G., Sapiro, G., Giryes, R.: DNN or k-NN: that is the generalize vs. memorize question. ArXiv abs/1805.06822 (2018)
23. Slavinec, M., et al.: Novelty search for global optimization. Appl. Math. Comput. **347**, 865–881 (2019)

Guided Subtree Selection for Genetic Operators in Genetic Programming for Dynamic Flexible Job Shop Scheduling

Fangfang Zhang$^{1(\boxtimes)}$, Yi Mei^1 , Su Nguyen^2 , and Mengjie Zhang^1

^{1} School of Engineering and Computer Science,
Victoria University of Wellington,
PO BOX 600, Wellington 6140, New Zealand
{fangfang.zhang,yi.mei,mengjie.zhang}@ecs.vuw.ac.nz
^{2} Centre for Data Analytics and Cognition,
La Trobe University, Melbourne, VIC 3086, Australia
P.Nguyen4@latrobe.edu.au

Abstract. Dynamic flexible job shop scheduling (DFJSS) has been widely studied in both academia and industry. Both machine assignment and operation sequencing decisions need to be made simultaneously as an operation can be processed by a set of machines in DFJSS. Using scheduling heuristics to solve the DFJSS problems becomes an effective way due to its efficiency and simplicity. Genetic programming (GP) has been successfully applied to evolve scheduling heuristics for job shop scheduling automatically. However, the subtrees of the selected parents are randomly chosen in traditional GP for crossover and mutation, which may not be sufficiently effective, especially in a huge search space. This paper proposes new strategies to guide the subtree selection rather than picking them randomly. To be specific, the occurrences of features are used to measure the importance of each subtree of the selected parents. The probability to select a subtree is based on its importance and the type of genetic operators. This paper examines the proposed algorithm on six DFJSS scenarios. The results show that the proposed GP algorithm with the guided subtree selection for crossover can converge faster and achieve significantly better performance than its counterpart in half of the scenarios while no worse in all other scenarios without increasing the computational time.

Keywords: Guided subtree selection · Scheduling heuristic · Dynamic flexible job shop scheduling · Genetic programming

1 Introduction

Job shop scheduling (JSS) [1] is an important combinatorial optimisation problem that can be applied to almost all areas of our lives such as manufacturing

© Springer Nature Switzerland AG 2020
T. Hu et al. (Eds.): EuroGP 2020, LNCS 12101, pp. 262–278, 2020.
https://doi.org/10.1007/978-3-030-44094-7_17

[2] and cloud computing [3]. The task in JSS is to process a number of jobs by a set of machines. Each job has a sequence of operations. The goal of JSS is to find a good schedule to complete the processing task. An effective scheduling decision-making scheme is the key to enhancing the competitiveness of a modern enterprise. Flexible JSS (FJSS) [4], as a variant of JSS, better reflects the real-world applications than ordinary JSS. In FJSS, one operation can be processed on a set of machines. Except for choosing an operation as the next operation to be processed by an idle machine (*operation sequencing*), we need to assign an operation to a particular machine (*machine assignment*). These two decisions need to be made simultaneously. In addition, many practical scheduling problems are changing over time, for example, due to new job arrivals [5–7]. Dynamic FJSS (DFJSS) is to consider flexible JSS under dynamic environments.

Scheduling heuristics such as dispatching rules [8] are widely used to handle DFJSS. A scheduling heuristic is a heuristic that works like a priority function to evaluate the priorities of operations and machines. To be specific, in DFJSS, a machine that has the highest priority value based on the *routing rule* (i.e. routing scheduling heuristic) will be assigned a job to be processed. An operation with the highest priority value based on the *sequencing rule* (i.e. sequencing scheduling heuristic) will be chosen as the next operation to be processed. There are some rules such as SPT (i.e. shortest processing time) and WIQ (i.e. the workload in the queue of a machine) which have been identified as effective rules for JSS. However, they are manually designed by experts, which is time-consuming. In practice, it is hard to manually design effective rules due to the complexity and diversity of the investigated job shop environments.

Genetic programming (GP) [9], as a hyper-heuristic (GPHH) method, has been successfully applied to automatically evolve scheduling heuristic for JSS [10,11]. GP uses crossover, mutation and reproduction to generate offspring for the next generation. In a typical subtree-based crossover, offspring are created by *swapping the subtrees* of the parents. On the other hand, mutation is generally to maintain diversity within the population and prevent premature convergence. In the common subtree-based mutation, an individual (i.e. parent) is selected, and an offspring is generated by *replacing one of its subtrees* with a new randomly generated subtree.

In traditional GP, subtrees (i.e. function nodes) are randomly chosen to generate individuals. However, the importance of subtrees in each individual can be different. Some subtrees are redundant or less important and removing them might not affect the fitness of an individual too much. On the other hand, some subtrees play important roles for an individual, and losing them will cause considerable loss to the fitness. It may not be an effective way to randomly select subtrees without considering the importance of subtrees. To this end, this paper proposes subtree selection strategies for crossover and mutation to help GP improve the effectiveness of generating new offspring.

The overall goal of this paper is to develop novel guided subtree selection strategies based on the occurrence of features for crossover and mutation to help GP find more effective scheduling heuristics for DFJSS efficiently. The proposed algorithms are expected to speed up the convergence of GP and find effective rules in a shorter time. In particular, this paper has the following research objectives:

- Develop guided subtree selection strategies both for crossover and mutation with the information of the occurrence of features to improve the effectiveness of the evolutionary process.
- Verify the effectiveness and efficiency of the proposed GP algorithm with the guided subtree selection strategy by comparing its performance and convergence curve with the baseline GP counterpart.
- Analyse how the subtree selection strategy affects the evolutionary process of GP.

2   Background

2.1   Dynamic Flexible Job Shop Scheduling

In FJSS problem [12], n jobs $J = \{J_1, J_2, ..., J_n\}$ need to be processed by m machines $M = \{M_1, M_2, ..., M_m\}$. Each job J_j has an arrival time $at(J_i)$ and a sequence of operations $O_j = (O_{j1}, O_{j2}, ..., O_{ji})$. Each operation O_{ji} can only be processed by one of its optional machines $\pi(O_{ji})$ and its processing time $\delta(O_{ji})$ depends on the machine that processes it. It indicates that there are two decisions which are routing decision and sequencing decision in FJSS. In DFJSS, not only the two decisions need to be made simultaneously, but also the dynamic events are necessary to be taken into account when making schedules. This paper focuses on one dynamic event (i.e. continuously arriving new jobs). That is, the information of a job is unknown until its arrival time.

2.2   Genetic Programming Hyper-heuristic for DFJSS

A hyper-heuristic [13] is a heuristic search method that seeks to select or generate heuristics to efficiently solve hard computational search problems. The unique characteristic is that the search space of hyper-heuristic is heuristics instead of solutions. Hyper-heuristic is often incorporated with machine learning techniques to achieve its goal.

GP, as a hyper-heuristic method [14], has been successfully applied to more informative scheduling heuristics for combinatorial optimisation problems such as packing [15,16], timetabling [17], arc routing [18], and JSS [19–22]. Scheduling heuristics, including routing and sequencing rules, are needed in DFJSS in our research. To follow the sequence constraint of operations of a job, we only start to allocate an operation when it becomes a *ready operation*. There are two sources of ready operations. One is the first operation of a job. The second is the operation that its proceeding operation is just finished. Once an operation becomes a ready operation (*routing decision point*), it will be allocated to the machine by the routing rule. When a machine becomes idle, and its queue is not empty (*sequencing decision point*), the sequencing rule will be triggered to choose the next operation to be processed.

Although GP has been successfully applied to DFJSS [19,20], to the best of our knowledge, little research has been conducted on genetic operators to improve the effectiveness of generating offspring. To this end, this paper aims to propose subtree selection strategies for both crossover and mutation to help GP evolve more effective scheduling heuristics for DFJSS.

3   The Proposed GP with Subtree Selection

Figure 1 shows the flowchart of the proposed algorithm. The main process is the same as the traditional GP. There are three different parts. After evaluating all the individuals in the population, the occurrence of each feature is counted based on promising individuals. The occurrence information of features is used to calculate the importance of subtrees of the selected parents. During the evolutionary process, crossover and mutation are conducted based on the proposed corresponding subtree selection strategies. In this way, when generating new offspring by crossover and mutation, the subtrees are selected with guidance.

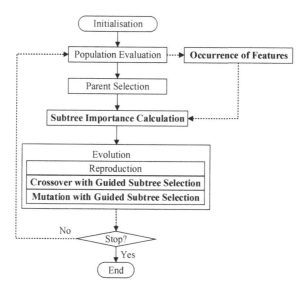

Fig. 1. The flowchart of the proposed algorithm.

According to the proposed algorithm framework, the three research questions in this paper are how to extract feature information to assess the importance of subtrees, how to measure the importance of subtrees, and how to apply the subtree importance information to crossover and mutation. These three questions are studied in the following three sections, separately.

3.1   The Occurrences of Features

An advantage of GP is that it can automatically select important features to build individuals. The features of individuals with good fitness are more likely to be important features. On the other hand, the individuals that contain important features are more likely to be promising individuals. This means that the features involved in promising individuals can be used to measure the importance of subtrees.

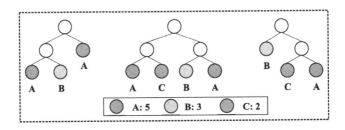

Fig. 2. The occurrence of features in the top three individuals.

In this paper, the occurrence of features in the top ten individuals is further used to assess the importance of subtrees. Our preliminary studies show that top ten individuals tend to have promising fitness which is good for detecting feature characteristics. Another advantage of using the occurrence information of features is that we do not need to put too much extra effort to obtain useful information since the information is already generated during the evolutionary process.

Figure 2 shows an example of how to extract feature occurrence information based on three individuals. These three individuals contain different numbers of features and have different structures. Assuming that they are top three individuals in the population based on the fitness. According to the three individuals, the occurrence of features in all three individuals is counted. The occurrences of feature A, B, and C are 5, 3, and 2, respectively. This information will be used to measure the importance of subtrees in an individual.

3.2   The Importance of Subtrees

An individual (i.e. a tree) can be considered to be composed of multiple subtrees. After a function node is selected, the subtree is determined. The importance of subtrees is measured from bottom to top, and this paper uses the concept *score* to indicate the importance of a subtree. Each feature has its occurrence information at the bottom level of an individual, and the score of their parent node (i.e. the importance of subtree) is set as the average occurrence number of its child nodes. Assuming that importance (i.e. occurrence) of feature A, B and C are ranked as $A > B > C$. If only considering the simplest subtrees (i.e. depth is two) and only take two features, there will be three possible combinations for the subtree which are A and B, A and C, and B and C. The importance of the subtrees should be ranked as $subtree(A, B) > subtree(A, C) > subtree(B, C)$.

Figure 3 shows an example of how to measure the importance of each subtree for an individual. For example, the $subtree_1$ (i.e. in the bottom-left corner) contains two features (i.e. A and B), the score of their parent node is set as 4 (i.e. $(5+3)/2$). The importance of $subtree_3$ is assigned as the average scores of its two subtrees (i.e. $subtree_1$ and $subtree_2$). By analogy, all score of subtrees will be assigned, as shown in Fig. 3.

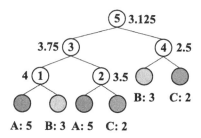

Fig. 3. The importance (i.e. score) of subtrees in an individual.

Taking the subtrees that the depth is two into consideration, there are three subtrees (i.e. indicated by subtree 1, 2 and 4), whose importance are marked as 4, 3.5 and 2.5, respectively. The importance of subtree 1, 2 and 4 are ranked as $subtree_1 > subtree_2 > subtree_4$, which is consistent with the importance measurement design. When looking at all the subtrees, the importance rank of all subtrees in this individual is $subtree_1 > subtree_3 > subtree_2 > subtree_5 > subtree_4$.

3.3 Subtree Selection

Based on the importance of subtrees, the probability of the subtrees that will be selected can be calculated. There are two different techniques to calculate the probability for different purposes (i.e. one for mutation, and the other for both crossover and mutation). The probability is designed proportionally to the scores.

Figure 4 shows the two different techniques to calculate the probability of each subtree in an individual. Figure 4(a) shows the technique that tends to choose the important subtree (i.e. the subtree with a larger score, the higher the probability it will be selected). Let us continue with the previous example in Fig. 3, there are five subtrees with score [3.125, 3.75, 2.5, 4, 3.5]. If we prefer to choose the important subtree, the larger the score of the subtree, the higher the probability it will have. First, we sum up the total score (i.e. $16.875 = 3.125 + 3.75 + 2.5 + 4 + 3.5$). Then, the probability of subtrees is assigned as [0.185, 0.222, 0.148, 0.237, 0.207] (i.e. [3.125/16.875, 3.75/16.875, 2.5/16.875, 4/16.875, 3.5/16.875]). The rank of probability of subtrees is $subtree_1 > subtree_3 > subtree_2 > subtree_5 > subtree_4$.

Figure 4(b) shows the technique that tends to choose the unimportant subtree (i.e. the subtree with a larger score, the lower the probability it will be selected). If we prefer to choose the unimportant subtree, the larger the score of the subtree, the lower the probability it will have. Thus, the score is converted to [1/3.125, 1/3.75, 1/2.5, 1/4, 1/3.5] first. Then, we sum up the total score and get the final probability as we just mentioned. The probabilities of subtrees are shown beside the function nodes. The rank of probability of subtrees is $subtree_4 > subtree_5 > subtree_2 > subtree_3 > subtree_1$.

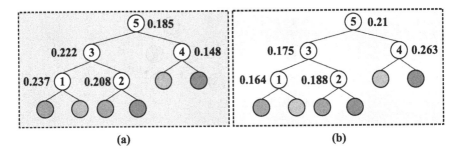

(a)   (b)

Fig. 4. Two different ways to calculate the probability of each subtree for an individual. (a) Tends to choose important subtree while (b) tends to choose unimportant subtree.

Crossover with Guided Subtree Selection. For the crossover, there are two parents (i.e. $parent_1$ and $parent_2$) which are both promising individuals that are selected as parents. Without loss of generality, this paper assumes that $parent_1$ is no worse than $parent_2$. The unimportant subtree from $parent_1$ is expected to be swapped with an important subtree from $parent_2$ to make $parent_1$ an even better individual. Therefore, for $parent_1$, the larger the score of the subtree, the lower the probability it will have. For $parent_2$, the larger the score of the subtree, the higher the probability it will have.

Mutation with Guided Subtree Selection. For mutation, we expect to make the parent produce a better individual by replacing unimportant subtree with a newly generated subtree. We prefer to choose an unimportant subtree, and a larger score of the subtree leads to a lower probability it will be chosen.

3.4   Summary

The purpose of the proposed algorithms is to improve the effectiveness of crossover and mutation by introducing subtree selection strategies instead of choosing subtrees randomly. The occurrence information of features is utilised to measure the importance of subtrees. Then, the subtrees importance information is used to determine the probability that the subtrees will be selected along with the characteristics of crossover and mutation.

4   Experiment Design

To investigate the *effectiveness* of the proposed subtree selection strategies for crossover and mutation, a set of experiments have been conducted. In this section, the experiment design is shown in detail.

4.1   Simulation Model

Assuming that there are 5000 jobs need to be processed by ten machines. The importance of jobs might be different, which are indicated by weights. The weights of 20%, 60%, and 20% of jobs are set as one, two and four, respectively. The number of operations of each job varies by a uniform discrete distribution between one and ten. The processing time of each operation is set by uniform discrete distribution with the range [1, 99]. The number of candidate machines for an operation follows a uniform discrete distribution between one and ten.

In each problem instance, jobs arrive stochastically according to a Poisson process with rate λ. To improve the generalisation ability of the evolved rules for DFJSS problems, the seeds used to stochastically generate the jobs are rotated in the training process at each generation. In addition, in order to make sure the accuracy of the collected data, a warm-up period of 1000 jobs is used.

4.2   Parameter Settings

In our experiment, the terminal and function set are shown in Table 1. The "/" operator is protected division, returning one if divided by zero. The other parameter settings of GP are shown in Table 2.

Table 1. The terminal and function sets.

	Terminals	Description
Machine-related	NIQ	The number of operations in the queue
	WIQ	Current work in the queue
	MWT	Waiting time of a machine
Operation-related	PT	Processing time of an operation
	NPT	Median processing time for next operation
	OWT	The waiting time of an operation
Job-related	WKR	The median amount of work remaining of a job
	NOR	The number of operations remaining of a job
	W	Weight of a job
	TIS	Time in system
Functions	$+, -, *, /, max, min$	As usual meaning

Table 2. The parameter setting of GP.

Parameter	Value
Number of subpopulations	2
Subpopulation size	512
Method for initialising population	Ramped-half-and-half
Initial minimum/maximum depth	2/6
Maximal depth of programs	8
The number of elites	10
Crossover/mutation/reproduction rate	80%/15%/5%
Parent selection	Tournament selection with size 7
Number of generations	51
Terminal/non-terminal selection rate	10%/90%

4.3   Comparison Design

Four algorithms are taken into the comparison in this paper. The cooperative coevolution genetic programming (CCGP) [5] which can be used to evolve routing rule and sequencing rule simultaneously, is selected as the baseline algorithm. Our proposed algorithm, which incorporates subtree selection strategy into the crossover, is named as $CCGP^c$ (i.e. choose subtrees for crossover). The algorithm that incorporates subtree selection into the mutation (i.e. choose subtrees for mutation) is called $CCGP^m$. The proposed algorithm, which incorporates subtree selection by both crossover and mutation, is named as $CCGP^{cm}$. $CCGP^c$, $CCGP^m$ and $CCGP^{cm}$ are compared with CCGP, respectively.

The proposed algorithms are tested on *six different scenarios*. The scenarios consist of three objectives (i.e. max flowtime, mean flowtime, and mean weighted flowtime) and two utilisation levels (i.e. 0.85 and 0.95) [20]. For the sake of convenience, Fmax, Fmean, and WFmean are used to indicate max flowtime, mean flowtime, and mean weighted flowtime, respectively. The evolved best rule at each generation is tested on 50 different test instances, and the mean objective value of them is reported as the objective value of this best rule. This aims to guarantee the accuracy of measuring the performance.

5   Results and Discussions

Thirty independent runs are conducted for the comparison. Wilcoxon rank-sum test with a significance level of 0.05 is used to verify the performance of proposed algorithms. In the following results, "−" and "+" indicate the corresponding result is significantly better or worse than its counterpart. If there is no mark there, that means the performance between them is similar.

5.1   Performance of Evolved Rules

Table 3 shows the mean and standard deviation of the objective value of the four algorithms over 30 independent runs for six DFJSS scenarios. $CCGP^c$ performs significantly better than CCGP for three scenarios (i.e. <Fmean,0.85>, <WFmean,0.85> and <WFmean,0.95>). For the remaining three scenarios, $CCGP^c$ performs as well as the CCGP. In scenario <Fmax,0.85>, although $CCGP^c$ does not achieve significantly better performance than that of CCGP, the mean and standard deviation are smaller than that of CCGP (i.e. still better). However, $CCGP^m$ performs significantly better than that of CCGP only in scenario <Fmean,0.85> and achieves better performance in scenario <Fmax,0.95>. In general, it seems like it is not that effective to apply subtree selection strategy to mutation as it does not get better results in most scenarios. The effectiveness of $CCGP^{cm}$ is similar to $CCGP^c$. Its performance might be mainly due to the role played by applying subtree selection strategy into the crossover.

Table 3. The mean (standard deviation) of the objective value of CCGP, $CCGP^c$, $CCGP^m$, and $CCGP^{cm}$ over 30 independent runs for six DFJSS scenarios.

Scenario	CCGP	$CCGP^c$	$CCGP^m$	$CCGP^{cm}$
<Fmax,0.85>	1211.84(35.27)	1211.68(30.21)	1217.81(28.24)	1215.76(26.41)
<Fmax,0.95>	1942.06(31.70)	1944.84(31.52)	1936.62(23.11)	1955.04(56.65)
<Fmean,0.85>	386.07(3.53)	384.80(1.67)(−)	384.40(2.02)(−)	384.88(1.60)(−)
<Fmean,0.95>	550.99(5.28)	551.94(4.94)	551.20(4.70)	551.12(3.87)
<WFmean,0.85>	832.46(7.25)	829.70(4.83)(−)	832.03(7.33)	830.14(4.26)
<WFmean,0.95>	1110.04(10.82)	1107.59(12.49)(−)	1109.44(12.33)	1107.76(8.08)(−)

Figure 5 shows the convergence curves of the average objective value on the test instances of the four algorithms. To better show the performance of the proposed algorithms, only the curves between generation 20 and 50 are shown in Fig. 5. Except for max-flowtime related scenarios (i.e. <Fmax,0.85> and <Fmax,0.95>) and scenario <Fmean,0.95>, the three proposed algorithms (i.e. $CCGP^c$, $CCGP^m$, and $CCGP^{cm}$) can achieve better performance than that of CCGP. In <Fmean,0.85>, all the proposed three algorithms show their advantages in both convergence speed and final performance, especially $CCGP^m$. In scenario <WFmean,0.85>, $CCGP^c$ has the best convergence speed and performance. In scenario <WFmean,0.95>, $CCGP^m$ convergence faster than $CCGP^c$ before generation 30 roughly, however, it loses to $CCGP^c$ after generation 30. Finally, $CCGP^c$ achieves better performance than that of $CCGP^m$. For minimising max-flowtime, the proposed three algorithms have no obvious advantages. It might be because max-flowtime is more sensitive to the worst case, which is more complex and hard to optimise.

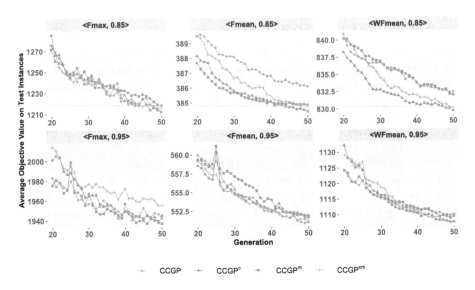

Fig. 5. The convergence curves of CCGP, CCGP^c, CCGP^m, and CCGP^{cm} from generation 20 to generation 50 in six scenarios.

Summary. Based on the results, CCGP^c is the most promising algorithm which shows the effectiveness of improving the crossover operator by subtree selection strategy. CCGP^m is not as promising as CCGP^c. One possible reason is that the mutation rate is low and can not affect the evolutionary process too much. That might also be the reason why the performance of CCGP^{cm} is similar to that of CCGP^c. The other possible reason is that mutation aims to maintain the diversity of the population, and it is better not to guide its direction.

5.2 The Probability Difference

The main idea in this paper is to differentiate the probability of subtrees to be chosen instead of choosing subtrees randomly. The probability difference ($P_s - P_u$) is defined as the difference between the assigned probability (P_s) and the uniform probability (P_u) of the selected subtree. The probability difference can be positive, negative, and zero. If the probability is a positive number, that would mean the current subtree is selected with a higher chance compared with uniform probability. If the probability is a negative number, that means the current subtree is selected with a lower chance compared with uniform probability. If the probability is zero, that means the assigned probability is the same as the uniform one, which will not affect the crossover and mutation operators.

This paper takes CCGP^c in scenario <WFmean,0.85> as an example to show how the proposed subtree selection strategy affects the selection probability on crossover since CCGP^c performs significantly better than other algorithms in this scenario. Figure 6 shows the histogram plot of the probability difference in early generation (i.e. generation 1), middle generation (i.e. generation 25) and late generation (i.e. generation 45) of CCGP^c in scenario <WFmean, 0.85> based on 30 independent runs. The small in the subtitles means the smaller the score of the subtree, the higher probability it will be chosen (i.e. for $parent_1$ in the crossover). The big in the subtitles means the larger the score of the subtree, the higher probability it will be chosen (i.e. for $parent_2$ in the crossover). In general, most of the probability differences are positive numbers and much larger (i.e. more than 0.5) than uniform probability. At the early state (i.e. generation 1), the probability difference is not that higher than that of in the late generation (i.e. generation 25 and 45). This means that the proposed subtree selection strategy for crossover can successfully influence the selection of nodes of individuals.

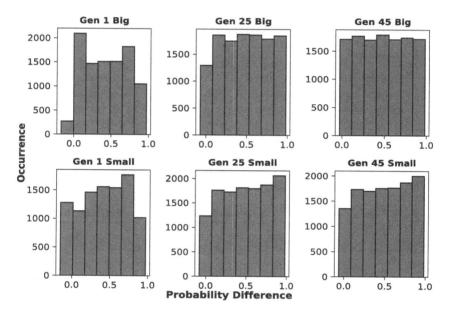

Fig. 6. The histogram plot of probability difference of CCGP^c in generation 1, 25, and 45 in scenario <WFmean, 0.85> based on 30 independent runs.

Figure 7 shows the histogram plot of the probability difference in generation 1, 25, and 45 of CCGP^m in scenario <Fmean, 0.85> based on 30 independent runs. There are only three blocks because CCGP^m only works on the mutation to choose the unimportant subtree (i.e. the smaller the score of the subtree, the higher probability it will be chosen). It is obvious that the number of subtree selections is not that high as that in Fig. 6, because the mutation rate is lower than the crossover rate. The same trend is shown in Fig. 6, the probability difference is becoming larger and larger as the number of generations increases.

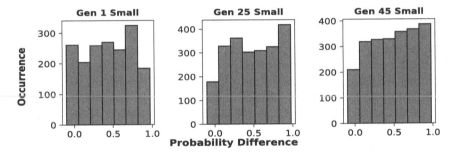

Fig. 7. The histogram plot of probability difference of CCGP^m in generation 1, 25, and 45 in scenario <Fmean, 0.85> based on 30 independent runs.

5.3 The Occurrences of Features

It is interesting to see the trend of the feature occurrence that carries the information. Figure 8 shows the curves of the occurrence of features in routing rules during the evolutionary process of CCGP^c. The MWT (i.e. machine waiting time) is the most important feature for the routing rules in all scenarios. The importance of MWT is much higher than other features. In the scenarios whose utilisation levels are 0.85, WIQ (i.e. the workload in the queue) also plays a second important role. In the scenarios whose have a higher utilisation level (i.e. 0.95), NIQ (i.e. the number of operations in the queue) plays a significant role.

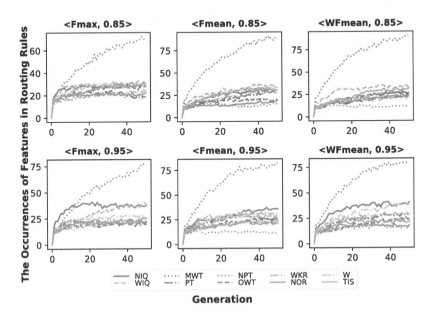

Fig. 8. The curves of the occurrence of features in *routing rules* during the evolutionary process of CCGP^c.

Intuitively, both WIQ and NIQ are important indicators for measuring the workload for machines, they might have the same functions, and one might take over another one. However, we do not know how they work in different scenarios. It is interesting to see that the role of NIQ is significantly higher than that of WIQ in the scenarios that have higher utilisation level. One possible reason is that NIQ is an important factor in busy scenarios, which is an important finding.

Figure 9 shows the curves of the occurrence of terminals in sequencing rules during the evolutionary process of CCGP^c. Different from routing rules, there are three terminals (i.e. WKR, TIS, and PT) play a vital role in minimising max-flowtime. PT and WKR also are two important terminals in minimising mean-flowtime and weighted mean-flowtime. Except for them, W plays a dominant role in weighted mean-flowtime, which is consistent with our intuition. In addition, W plays its role mainly in sequencing rules instead of routing rules.

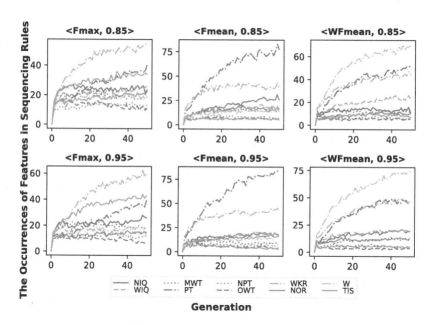

Fig. 9. The curves of the occurrence of features in *sequencing rules* during the evolutionary process of CCGP^c.

5.4 Training Time

Table 4 shows the mean and standard deviation of training time of CCGP, CCGP^c, CCGP^m, and CCGP^{cm} in six different scenarios. There is no significant difference between the four algorithms. It means the proposed subtree selection strategies do not need extra computational cost. This verifies the advantages of utilising the information generated during the evolutionary process of GP.

Table 4. The mean (standard deviation) of **training time** (in minutes) obtained by the involved four algorithms over 30 independent runs for six scenarios.

Scenario	CCGP	CCGP^c	CCGP^m	CCGP^{cm}
<Fmax,0.85>	74(10)	75(11)	83(36)	75(11)
<Fmax,0.95>	86(16)	84(13)	84(12)	83(12)
<Fmean,0.85>	73(10)	73(11)	72(11)	75(13)
<Fmean,0.95>	79(11)	78(14)	77(13)	83(14)
<WFmean,0.85>	73(13)	70(10)	70(10)	73(11)
<WFmean,0.95>	82(13)	81(14)	80(14)	82(13)

6   Conclusions and Future Work

The goal of this paper was to develop subtree selection strategies to improve the effectiveness of crossover and mutation operators to guide GP to improve its convergence speed and evolve more effective scheduling heuristics for DFJSS. The goal was achieved by proposing the guided subtree selection strategy that can utilise the information of the occurrence of features information obtained during the evolutionary process.

The results show that using the proposed guided subtree selection in crossover can speed up the convergence and achieve better performance in half scenarios while no worse in all other scenarios without increasing the computational cost. The proposed subtree selection can successfully guide GP to select important or unimportant subtrees according to the need of genetic operators. The evolved rules have better test performance of given complex job shop scenarios, especially for minimising mean-flowtime and weighted mean-flowtime. An advantage of the proposed algorithms is that incorporating the occurrence of features information needs no extra computational cost. This shows the benefits of making better use of the information during the evolutionary process. In addition, this paper discovered that although both NIQ and WIQ can be used to measure the workload of a machine, NIQ has an important role in busy scenarios while WIQ has a significant role in less busy scenarios.

Some interesting directions can be further investigated in the near future. This work already shows the potential to improve the effectiveness of crossover by choosing subtrees. We would like to find more promising ways to select the subtrees for crossover to further improve its effectiveness.

References

1. Manne, A.S.: On the job-shop scheduling problem. Oper. Res. **8**(2), 219–223 (1960)
2. Tay, J.C., Ho, N.B.: Evolving dispatching rules using genetic programming for solving multi-objective flexible job-shop problems. Comput. Ind. Eng. **54**(3), 453–473 (2008)

3. Nguyen, S.B.S., Zhang, M.: A hybrid discrete particle swarm optimisation method for grid computation scheduling. In: 2014 IEEE Congress on Evolutionary Computation (CEC), pp. 483–490. IEEE (2014)
4. Brucker, P., Schlie, R.: Job-shop scheduling with multi-purpose machines. Computing **45**(4), 369–375 (1990)
5. Yska, D., Mei, Y., Zhang, M.: Genetic programming hyper-heuristic with cooperative coevolution for dynamic flexible job shop scheduling. In: Castelli, M., Sekanina, L., Zhang, M., Cagnoni, S., García-Sánchez, P. (eds.) EuroGP 2018. LNCS, vol. 10781, pp. 306–321. Springer, Cham (2018). https://doi.org/10.1007/978-3-319-77553-1_19
6. Zhang, F., Mei, Y., Zhang, M.: Genetic programming with multi-tree representation for dynamic flexible job shop scheduling. In: Mitrovic, T., Xue, B., Li, X. (eds.) AI 2018. LNCS (LNAI), vol. 11320, pp. 472–484. Springer, Cham (2018). https://doi.org/10.1007/978-3-030-03991-2_43
7. Zhang, F., Mei, Y., Zhang, M.: Evolving dispatching rules for multi-objective dynamic flexible job shop scheduling via genetic programming hyper-heuristics. In: Proceedings of the IEEE Congress on Evolutionary Computation (CEC), pp. 1366–1373. IEEE (2019)
8. Durasevic, M., Jakobovic, D.: A survey of dispatching rules for the dynamic unrelated machines environment. Expert Syst. Appl. **113**, 555–569 (2018)
9. Koza, J.R., Poli, R.: Genetic programming. In: Burke, E.K., Kendall, G. (eds.) Search Methodologies, pp. 127–164. Springer, Boston (2005). https://doi.org/10.1007/0-387-28356-0_5
10. Miyashita, K.: Job-shop scheduling with genetic programming. In: Proceedings of the 2nd Annual Conference on Genetic and Evolutionary Computation, pp. 505–512. Morgan Kaufmann Publishers Inc. (2000)
11. Nguyen, S., Zhang, M., Johnston, M., Tan, K.C.: Genetic programming for evolving due-date assignment models in job shop environments. Evol. Comput. **22**(1), 105–138 (2014)
12. Maccarthy, B.L., Liu, J.: Addressing the gap in scheduling research: a review of optimization and heuristic methods in production scheduling. Int. J. Prod. Res. **31**(1), 59–79 (1993)
13. Branke, J., Nguyen, S., Pickardt, C.W., Zhang, M.: Automated design of production scheduling heuristics: a review. IEEE Trans. Evol. Comput. **20**(1), 110–124 (2016)
14. Burke, E.K., Hyde, M.R., Kendall, G., Ochoa, G., Ozcan, E., Woodward, J.R.: Exploring hyper-heuristic methodologies with genetic programming. In: Mumford, C.L., Jain, L.C. (eds.) Computational Intelligence. ISRL, vol. 1, pp. 177–201. Springer, Berlin (2009). https://doi.org/10.1007/978-3-642-01799-5_6
15. Burke, E.K., Hyde, M.R., Kendall, G., Woodward, J.R.: A genetic programming hyper-heuristic approach for evolving 2-D strip packing heuristics. IEEE Trans. Evol. Comput. **14**(6), 942–958 (2010)
16. Hyde, M.R.: A genetic programming hyper-heuristic approach to automated packing. Ph.D. thesis, University of Nottingham, UK (2010)
17. Bader-El-Den, M.B., Poli, R., Fatima, S.: Evolving timetabling heuristics using a grammar-based genetic programming hyper-heuristic framework. Memet. Comput. **1**(3), 205–219 (2009)
18. Ansari Ardeh, M., Mei, Y., Zhang, M.: A novel genetic programming algorithm with knowledge transfer for uncertain capacitated arc routing problem. In: Nayak, A.C., Sharma, A. (eds.) PRICAI 2019. LNCS (LNAI), vol. 11670, pp. 196–200. Springer, Cham (2019). https://doi.org/10.1007/978-3-030-29908-8_16

19. Zhang, F., Mei, Y., Zhang, M.: A new representation in genetic programming for evolving dispatching rules for dynamic flexible job shop scheduling. In: Liefooghe, A., Paquete, L. (eds.) EvoCOP 2019. LNCS, vol. 11452, pp. 33–49. Springer, Cham (2019). https://doi.org/10.1007/978-3-030-16711-0_3

20. Zhang, F., Mei, Y., Zhang, M.: A two-stage genetic programming hyper-heuristic approach with feature selection for dynamic flexible job shop scheduling. In: Proceedings of the Genetic and Evolutionary Computation Conference (GECCO), pp. 347–355. IEEE (2019)

21. Durasević, M., Jakobović, D.: Evolving dispatching rules for optimising many-objective criteria in the unrelated machines environment. Genet. Program Evolvable Mach. **19**(1), 9–51 (2017). https://doi.org/10.1007/s10710-017-9310-3

22. Hildebrandt, T., Heger, J., Scholz-Reiter, B.: Towards improved dispatching rules for complex shop floor scenarios: a genetic programming approach. In: Proceedings of the 12th Annual Conference on Genetic and Evolutionary Computation, pp. 257–264. ACM (2010)

Classification of Autism Genes Using Network Science and Linear Genetic Programming

Yu Zhang[1], Yuanzhu Chen[1], and Ting Hu[1,2(✉)]

[1] Department of Computer Science, Memorial University,
St. John's, NL A1B 3X5, Canada
{yu.zhang,yzchen,ting.hu}@mun.ca
[2] School of Computing, Queen's University,
Kingston, ON K7L 2N8, Canada

Abstract. Understanding the genetic background of complex diseases and disorders plays an essential role in the promising precision medicine. Deciphering what genes are associated with a specific disease/disorder helps better diagnose and treat it, and may even prevent it if predicted accurately and acted on effectively at early stages. The evaluation of candidate disease-associated genes, however, requires time-consuming and expensive experiments given the large number of possibilities. Due to such challenges, computational methods have seen increasing applications in predicting gene-disease associations. Given the intertwined relationships of molecules in human cells, genes and their products can be considered to form a complex molecular interaction network. Such a network can be used to find candidate genes that share similar network properties with known disease-associated genes. In this research, we investigate autism spectrum disorders and propose a linear genetic programming algorithm for autism gene prediction using a human molecular interaction network and known autism-genes for training. We select an initial set of network properties as features and our LGP algorithm is able to find the most relevant features while evolving accurate predictive models. Our research demonstrates the powerful and flexible learning abilities of GP on tackling a significant biomedical problem, and is expected to inspire further exploration of wide GP applications.

Keywords: Linear genetic programming · Autism spectrum disorders · Human molecular interaction network · Complex networks · Disease-gene association

1 Introduction

Understanding the genetic etiolzgy of complex diseases and disorders is one of the greatest challenges in modern biomedical research [1]. Many common diseases are speculated to have complex genetic architecture, and multiple genes

© Springer Nature Switzerland AG 2020
T. Hu et al. (Eds.): EuroGP 2020, LNCS 12101, pp. 279–294, 2020.
https://doi.org/10.1007/978-3-030-44093-7_18

may contribute collectively to the manifestation of a disease [2,3]. Understanding the association of genes with a specific disease helps better diagnose it, design therapeutic strategies, and even prevent it. The identification of genes associated with a disease, however, requires time-consuming and expensive biological experiments to evaluate a considerable number of possible candidates [4–6].

Computational methods *in silico* can successfully facilitate more targeted downstream biological evaluation experiments [7]. Cooperative endeavors are requested from various research fields, ranging from computer science and statistics to biochemistry. Due to the interdependencies of molecular components, identifying genetic variants contributory to a disease needs not only to systematically study molecular functionality independently but also to look into the interconnectivity of molecular components [8]. In order to identify disease-associated genes, systems biology has seen increasing applications of computational approaches that model the interactions among multiple constitutes in human cellular systems [9–15].

Machine learning and heuristic search algorithms, including artificial neural networks [16], principal component analysis [17], and ensemble algorithms [18,19], have seen increasing and successful applications in biomedicine. Nevertheless, genetic programming, as a powerful learning and modeling algorithm, has not caught up with other comparable algorithms in wide applications.

Genetic programming (GP), as a branch of evolutionary computation, has emerged as a powerful tool to solve machine learning problems [20,21]. This is not only because GP can automatically evolve complex predictive models that map the input instances to the expected outcome [22], but also because of its stochastic and robust nature of the search for diversity and novelty [23–26]. GP has been applied to solve classification and regression problems in physics, economics, engineering, and biology [27–32].

The nature of GP makes it a very promising approach to solving classification problems for autism-associated genes in the molecular interaction network [33–35]. First, it can discover novel non-linear models for high-dimensional data by constructing executable computer programs using arithmetic functions, logical functions, and branching statements. Second, the automatic feature selection of GP is embedded in the process of model evolution. This intrinsic selection of relevant features distinguishes GP from many approaches that manually select features using domain-expertise, or perform feature selection and construct classification models in separate stages. Third, the stochastic population-based search property of evolutionary algorithms allows generating diverse high-quality classification models, which enriches the analysis of model interpretation and feature importance.

Many existing computational methods try to predict new genes with a disease association based on their direct relationships with known disease genes. It is later found that only a relatively small fraction of disease-associated genes/proteins physically interact with each other [36,37]. Genes associated with the same diseases have been found spread on multiple connected components in the molecular interaction network that represents the direct interactions among genes and their protein products.

In this research, we follow the new paradigm that genes involved in the development of a disease may not directly interact with each other but may exhibit similar topological properties in the molecular interaction network. We design a linear GP algorithm in order to learn classification models for predicting autism-associated genes. We first construct a human molecular interaction network (HMIN), which provides a scaffold of the connectivity patterns and structural properties of autism-associated genes. We then evolve classification models represented as linear genetic programs using the network properties of genes in the HMIN as features. The classification performance of our LGP algorithm is evaluated using multiple metrics and the set of predicted novel autism-genes is validated using an independent genetic sequencing dataset.

2   Methods

In this section, we first describe the data collection of positive and negative autism-genes and the construction of the human molecular interaction network. We then present the design and configuration of our LGP algorithm.

2.1   Data Collection

We compile a training set of both positive and negative genes using the databases of SFARI Gene 2.0 [38] and Online Mendelian Inheritance in Man (OMIM) [39]. The SFARI Gene 2.0 database is curated for the autism research community and has a collection of manually annotated autism-associated genes. It assigns each gene a score ranging from 1 (highest association confidence) to 6 (no role in autism) in order to quantify its association with autism. Scores 1 and 2 represent the strongest evidence of autism association, scores 3 and 4 show relaxed criteria of autism association, score 5 marks genes hypothesized but without tested associations, and score 6 genes have no existing evidence supporting their relation to autism. Our second data source, the OMIM, is a comprehensive, authoritative, and updated genetic knowledge base, including thousands of genetic disorders and their associated genes.

For this study, we collect 732 genes of scores 1 to 4 from the SFARI database and 28 genes from OMIM using the entry of autism (all data retrieved in November 2018). Overall, a total number of 760 autism-associated genes are used as positive instances for the supervised training of LGP. Please note that although these 760 autism genes have various association significance levels assessed by the SFARI and OMIM databases, we treat them equally as positive instances for the training of binary classifiers. On the other hand, we collect 1,146 genes that have shown no association as the negative instances curated by brain-disease experts [40]. These positive and negative instances (genes) are used by our LGP algorithm to train classification models.

2.2   Human Molecular Interaction Network

We construct the human molecular interaction network (HMIN) in order to provide a scaffold of gene-gene relationships that helps identify candidate genes according to their structural similarities to known autism genes. We base on a previously well-established human protein-protein interaction network [37], which includes data curated up to the year of 2015, and update it by integrating newly discovered protein-protein interactions using BioGRID version 3.5.167, released on November 25th, 2018 [41].

Our HMIN is an unweighted and undirected network with 23,472 nodes, representing genes, and 405,618 edges, representing their pairwise relationships. The HMIN covers 760 positive autism-associated genes and 1,102 negative genes in our training set (see Sect. 2.1). It includes physical interactions experimentally annotated in human cells, such as transcription factor regulatory interactions, metabolic enzyme-coupled interactions, and protein-protein interactions. The hypothesis is that the manifestation of autism is unlikely the consequence of the dysfunction of a single gene product, but is possibly resulted by various pathological processes that interact, which may be captured in the HMIN [8]. Therefore, we use such an interaction network and aim to discover candidate genes that are structurally similar to known autism-genes.

We use 6 network metrics and graphlet orbit frequencies to describe the local structural properties $\mathbf{x}_v$ of a node (gene) v, which serve as features in order to train our LGP algorithm. These 6 network metrics include *degree, betweenness, closeness, eigenvector centrality, personalized PageRank centrality* [42], and *coreness* [43], which are the most common node importance measurements in the literature of complex networks [44]. A graphlet is a small connected non-isomorphic induced subgraph of a large network [45]. These network properties are defined as follows:

- Degree centrality is the number of edges connected to a node.
- Betweenness centrality measures the extent to which a node lies on paths between other nodes.
- Closeness centrality measures the mean distance from a node to all other nodes in the network.
- Eigenvector centrality is an extension of degree centrality, which awards a node using the centrality scores of its direct neighbors.
- Personalized PageRank is a weighted version of the conventional PageRank. The weights are initialized and customized by users.
- The k-core of graph is a maximal subgraph in which each node has at least a degree of k. The coreness of a node is k if it belongs to the k-core but not to the $(k + 1)$-core.
- Orbits refer to distinct positions of vertices in a graphlet. There are 69 different orbits in 4- and 5-node graphlets [45].

2.3   Linear Genetic Programming Algorithm

Linear genetic programming (LGP) is a GP algorithm that uses a sequence of imperative instructions as its representation [46]. Such a compact representation allows efficient reuses of code and LGP is often considered as having fast fitness evaluations comparing to other GP paradigms [46]. Therefore, LGP holds great potential in applications of analyzing high-dimensional, large-volume data [32,47,48].

In our study, a genetic program is a classification model, whose instructions can be either an assignment or a branching statement. In an assignment statement, an arithmetic operation uses its operands and computes a value that is subsequently stored in a return register. A branching statement breaks the sequential execution of a program. We use IF-GREATER-THEN to skip one subsequent instruction when the condition in the IF statement is evaluated to FALSE.

A *feature register* stores the value of a feature. In our study, each training instance (gene) has 75 network features (6 network measures plus 69 graphlet orbit frequencies). Feature registers are read-only and write-protected, meaning that they can only serve as an operand on the right-hand side of an assignment statement. *Calculation registers* are provided to enhance computational capacity and can be used on both left- and right-hand sides of an assignment statement. The calculation register r[0] is designated as the *output* register, and when a genetic program is executed, the final value stored in r[0] is the outcome of the program. Since we treat the current study as a binary classification problem, Sigmoid function $S(x)$ is used to project the output value into the range of $(0, 1)$. If $S(r[0])$ is greater than 0.5, the instance is classified as autism-associated gene (class one), otherwise, it is predicted not associated with autism (class zero).

For initialization, we randomly generate a population of linear genetic programs with various lengths. The fitness of a program measures the performance of the classifier it represents. We define the fitness function as the *F-measure* of binary classification [49,50], i.e., the harmonic mean of *precision* and *recall*. The definitions are as follows.

$$Precision = \frac{T_P}{T_P + F_P}, \tag{1}$$

$$Recall = \frac{T_P}{T_P + F_N}, \tag{2}$$

$$F\text{-}measure = 2 \cdot \frac{Precision \cdot Recall}{Precision + Recall}, \tag{3}$$

where T_P and F_P denote true and false positive cases, respectively, and F_N is the number of false negative cases.

A set of programs are selected as parents based on their fitness, and we apply two types of variation operators to the parents, including mutation and recombination. We use both macro and micro mutations. A macro mutation inserts a new randomly generated instruction or deletes a randomly selected instruction from a program. A micro mutation alters an element of a randomly selected instruction, such as replacing a operator or a register by randomly generating a new operator or register. Recombination swaps randomly chosen segments of instructions of two parent programs.

Table 1. The parameter configuration of LGP algorithm for classification.

Parameter	Configuration
Fitness function	F-measure
Operator set	$+, -, \times, \div$ (protected), x^y, $|x|$, IF $>$
Program length	$[1, 300]$
Population size	500
Crossover rate	0.9
Mutation rate	0.1
Mutation operators	Macro and micro mutations
Number of calculation registers	200
Number of constant registers	10
Constant bound	$[-2, 2]$
Parent selection	Tournament with size 10
Survival selection	Truncation
Number of generations	1000
Number of runs	200

Survival selection picks fitter programs among the current generation and the offspring to update the population for the next generation. After iterating such an evolutionary process for a predefined number of generations, the program with the best fitness (highest F-measure) serves as the final best model of a run.

2.4   Implementation Settings

We implement our LGP algorithm in C programming language using GCC 8.1. Table 1 shows the parameter configuration for the implementation. The division primitive operator is protected by replacing dividing zero with multiplying one. We adopt a 5-fold cross-validation scheme to detect overfitting. That is, we divide the collected set of positive and negative genes into 5 equally-sized partitions with the same positive/negative ratio, and in each cross-validation iteration, we use the 4 out of 5 partitions to train the LGP algorithm, while the remaining partition serves as a testing set. Therefore, each run of the algorithm produces 5 best classification models on the 5 testing sets.

We carry out 200 independent runs of the LGP algorithm using 200 distinct seed values for random number generator. We perform *intron removal* before executing each linear genetic program in order to accelerate the fitness evaluation [46]. Every algorithm run produces 5 best classification models as a result of the 5-fold cross-validation scheme. Therefore, we obtain a total of 1000 best evolved classification models after 200 runs.

3   Results

3.1   Properties of the HMIN

First, we analyze the global network properties of the HMIN. Table 2 shows some fundamental network properties of the HMIN. Each node has a degree ranging from 1 to 2,393 with an average of 34.562. The network is divided into 4 connected components with sizes {23465, 3, 2, 2}. The network appears sparsely connected and the clustering coefficient is low, which indicates that direct neighbors of the same node may not be direct neighbors themselves. The network shows the small-world effect with an average shortest path length of 3.2 and a diameter of 8.

Table 2. Network properties of the HMIN.

Property	Value
Number of nodes	23,472
Number of edges	405,618
Number of connected components	4
Network diameter	8
Network density	0.001
Clustering coefficient	0.107
Average node degree	34.562
Average shortest path length	3.203

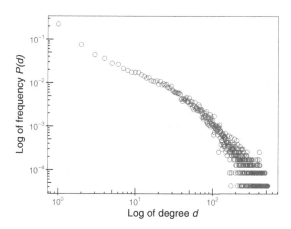

Fig. 1. The node degree distribution of the HMIN. The distribution is approximately power-law, suggested by the straight line correlation in a log-log scale.

The degree distribution of the HMIN is shown in Fig. 1. It approximately follows a power-law distribution, suggesting a scale-free structure of the network.

This indicates that most of the nodes (genes) only interact with a handful of other genes, while some can interact with one or two thousands of others.

3.2 Best Classification Models

Figure 2 shows the fitness (F-measure) distribution of the 1000 best classification models we find. We see that the testing fitness values are more centralized around the mean. The small discrepancy between the training and testing results also suggests a low level of over-fitting.

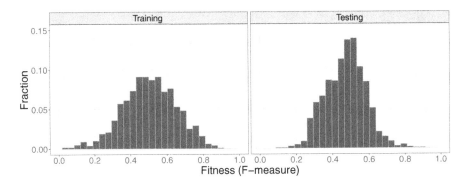

Fig. 2. Fitness distribution of the 1000 best evolved classification models found by the LGP algorithm. The fitness function is defined using the F-measure of classification. A higher F-measure value indicates a better classification performance.

Table 3. The statistics of the classification performance of the 1000 best models.

	MCE	Precision	Recall	AUC
Min	0.301	0.283	0.161	0.217
Median	0.609	0.578	0.598	0.616
Mean	0.613	0.554	0.603	0.624
Max	0.783	1.000	1.000	0.783
Std dev	0.098	0.134	0.112	0.116
5% confidence	0.339	0.325	0.299	0.297
95% confidence	0.577	0.803	0.829	0.696

In addition to fitness, we further look at other statistics of the best classification models. Table 3 summaries the statistics of the testing classification performance of the 1000 best models. The best model achieves a classification error of 0.301, and the area under the curve (AUC) of 0.783.

3.3   Assessment of Feature Importance

Given the stochastic nature of evolutionary algorithms, GP can automatically select a subset of features that are relevant to the classification, as part of the evolution. As a result of such an intrinsic feature selection, the importance of a feature can be assessed based on how often it is selected.

We now investigate how frequently a feature is selected and influential in a best evolved LGP model. Here, an *effective feature* refers to any feature that remains in a linear genetic program after intron removal, and modifies the value stored in the r[0] register when the program is executed. Figure 3(a) illustrates the distribution of the number of effective features in the 1000 best predictive models. Although any subsets of features can be selected by a predictive model, as evolution proceeds the LGP algorithm picks up the most relevant features for

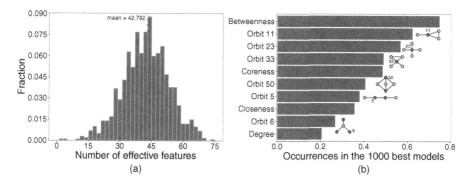

Fig. 3. (a) The distribution of the number of effective features in the 1000 best classification models. An effective feature is defined as any feature that remains in the best models after intron removal. The average number of effective features across the 1000 best models is 42.792. (b) The top 10 most frequent effective features in the 1000 best models. A graphlet visualization is shown next to each orbit feature. The red-colored nodes are the corresponding orbits, and note that there could be multiple nodes in a graphlet locating at the same orbit. (Color figure online)

Table 4. The statistics of the classification performance of the 1000 best classifiers after feature selection.

	MCE	Precision	Recall	AUC
Min	0.228	0.239	0.172	0.187
Median	0.502	0.611	0.607	0.667
Mean	0.476	0.597	0.583	0.667
Max	0.722	1.000	1.000	0.811
Std dev	0.094	0.105	0.122	0.098
5% confidence	0.213	0.302	0.256	0.299
95% confidence	0.667	0.816	0.831	0.773

making a prediction. The majority of the best models select between 30 and 55 effective features. The average number of effective features chosen by the 1000 best classification models is 42.792.

We then only use the top 43 more relevant features and re-run the LGP algorithm for a second round of analysis. Table 4 shows the results of this more focused model search (with feature selection). The best MCE is now 0.228, and the average MCE is reduced by 0.137, comparing to the result of the initial implementation using the full feature set. The average AUC is improved by 0.043 and the best AUC is improved by 0.028. The results suggest that the automatic feature selection of LGP is effective and indeed helps improve the classification performance.

Figure 3(b) shows the top 10 most frequent/important features and their occurrences in the 1000 best predictive models. Four node property measures, including betweenness, corness, closeness, and degree, are among the most important features. In addition, six automorphism orbits from 4-node and 5-node graphlets are found highly relevant to the prediction.

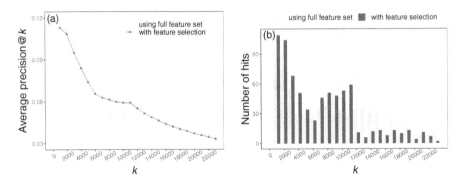

Fig. 4. (a) *Precision@k* and (b) number of hits in each 1000-gene bins averaged across the 1000 best classification models found by the LGP algorithm.

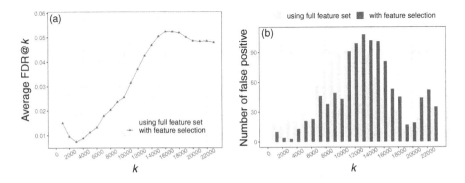

Fig. 5. (a) *FDR@k* and (b) number of false positive cases in each 1000-gene bins averaged across the 1000 best classification models found by the LGP algorithm.

3.4   Evaluation of Autism-Gene Prioritization

We perform further evaluation of the prediction abilities of the LGP algorithm by analyzing other classification performance metrics. Note that a linear genetic program outputs a numerical value projected to the range of $(0, 1)$ for each instance/gene. We consider this output value as the probability of a gene being associated with autism. Thus, we can rank genes based on such an association probability. Please also note that we collect 1000 best evolved models as an ensemble to make the final prediction.

We first calculate $precision@k$ for each best model and then average it across the total 1000 best models to obtain the average $precision@k$. They are defined as follows:

$$precision@k = \frac{|\Delta_{\text{top-}k} \cap \Delta_{\text{positive}}|}{k}, \tag{4}$$

$$average\ precision@k = \frac{precision@k}{1000}. \tag{5}$$

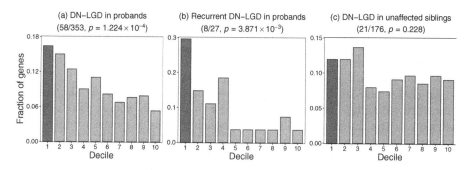

Fig. 6. Distribution of positive (a, b) and negative (c) autism-genes identified in the independent exome-sequencing study in each decile of our LGP prediction rank list. (a) Genes with *de novo* likely gene-disrupting (DN-LGD) mutations in probands (autism affected children). (b) Genes with recurrent DN-LGD in probands. (c) DN-LGD genes identified in unaffected siblings. The first decile is highlighted in blue. (Color figure online)

Here, $\Delta_{\text{top-}k}$ is the set of top k genes from a genetic program's predicted rank list and Δ_{positive} is the set of known autism-genes (positive training instances). The notion $\cap$ is the operation of set intersection, which gives the number of hits at k.

We compute the average $precision@k$ on both rounds of LGP implementation, i.e., without and with feature selection, and compare their results. Moreover, we count the number of hits in each bin of 1000 genes in the rank list. Figure 4 shows the average $precision@k$ and the number of hits in 1000-gene bins. We see that precision drops when k increases, and our LGP algorithm is able to correctly predict positive genes in its top ranks. In addition, using feature selection improves the average $precision@k$ among the high ranks.

We also investigate to what extend our LGP algorithm predicts actual negative genes as being associated with autism. We compute the false discovery rate, $FDR@k$, by replacing $\Delta_{positive}$ with $\Delta_{negative}$ in Eq. (4). We then average the value across 1000 best evolved classification models. Figure 5 shows the average $FDR@k$ using full feature set and selected features, separately. We see that the false discovery rate increases as k increases, and higher ranking bins have less false positive cases than lower bins. In addition, using feature selection considerably reduces the false discoveries.

3.5   Independent Validation of Autism-Gene Prediction

Considering the currently limited understanding of the genetic background of autism, our curated training set of positive genes based on the literature is likely to be incomplete. Therefore, further validation of our prediction results using independent study is necessary. We use a whole exome-sequencing study on autism for this purpose [51]. This study examined 2,508 autism probands (autism affected children), 1,911 unaffected siblings, and their parents in the Simons Simplex Collection (SSC) [52]. The focus of this study is to identify *de novo* likely gene-disrupting (DN-LGD) mutations. It reported 353 target positive genes identified in autism probands, including 27 recurrent genes with a more significant association with autism, and 176 negative DN-LGD genes in unaffected siblings.

We choose the 10, out of the 1000, best LGP models (having the highest testing fitness) with feature selection in order to assess the autism association of each gene in the HMIN. Each LGP best model gives an association probability for a gene, and we average this probability across all 10 best models. This results in a single rank list $\bar{R}$ for all the genes. We look at the genes in each decile of this rank list $\bar{R}$, and compare them with the three gene sets, i.e., DN-LGD in probands, recurrent DN-LGD in probands, and DN-LGD in unaffected siblings, reported in the independent validation study.

For each comparison, we apply a one-tail binomial test in order to assess the significance level. Figure 6 shows the overlap of these independently discovered autism-genes with the genes in our LGP rank list $\bar{R}$. DN-LGD genes are found enriched in our top 10% of the ranking list ($58/353$, $p = 1.244 \times 10^{-4}$). The recurrent DN-LDG genes are further found enriched in the first decile ($8/27$, $p = 3.871 \times 10^{-3}$) too. No significant enrichment of the DN-LGD genes in unaffected siblings (negative genes) is found in the rank list ($21/176$, $p = 0.228$). These results further verify the findings of our approach, i.e., the LGP algorithm is able to find novel candidate genes which are likely associated with autism.

4   Discussion

Many common human diseases and disorders are observed to be inheritable. Understanding what genes and proteins, when mutated or altered in the cell, lead to a specific disease/disorder has the power to illuminate mechanistic explanations of complex phenotypes. Such a knowledge helps better diagnose and treat the disease, and may even prevent it if predicted accurately and acted on effectively at early stages. However, such disease-gene association discovery is a very challenging computational task. It has been found that genes associated with the same disease may not be directly connected in the molecular interaction network. Only a relatively small fraction of disease-associated proteins physically interact with each other. This suggests that the proximity-based gene prediction approaches that search for dense connected communities of interacting genes/proteins in the molecular interaction network, may be ineffective in discovering the collection of candidate disease genes.

Machine learning methods are often employed for modeling the complex nonlinear relationships of combinations of features and the outcome, and has been extensively explored for predicting disease-associated genes. Genetic programming (GP), positioned at the intersection of machine learning and evolutionary computing, has not seen much utilization in such an important application area.

In this study, we designed an algorithm of using network science and linear genetic programming (LGP) to predict autism-associated genes. We constructed the human molecular interaction network (HMIN) and used it as a scaffold for characterizing the structural patterns of autism-associated genes. Then, the LGP algorithm was able to utilize the network features of autism-associated genes in the HMIN in order to predict novel autism-genes, as well as to select the most important network features based on their occurrence frequencies in the best classification models.

A linear genetic program may pick any subsets of features, but only the most influential ones will stay in the final evolved programs. Therefore, the feature selection process is intrinsic and co-evolved with the fitness in the LGP algorithm. We designed a two-stage learning scheme where the full set of network features was used in the first round, and a subset of more important features was used for a focused model search in the second round. Our results showed that the classification performance was improved considerably using the reduced feature set comparing with using all features initially.

Our LGP algorithm achieved good classification performance, quantified using the F-measure, accuracy, precision, recall, area under the curve (AUC), and the false discovery rate (FDR). The predicted genes were successfully validated using an independent sequencing study with newly discovered autism-genes that were not included in our training set of autism-genes.

Our next step is to explore other machine learning techniques that can take network features as input and classify the disease-gene association as the output. These techniques include deep learning, especially graph neural networks, support vector machines, random forests, and gradient boosting machines. It will also be interesting to test other feature selection/engineering methods. We plan to compare their results with that of using our LGP algorithm.

In summary, our research showcased the novel and successful application of a GP algorithm in complex classification model search and automatic feature selection. The advances in biological data collection and computational techniques have equipped us with large volumes of data that describe the properties of biological systems at different levels as well as a comprehensive toolbox of intelligent and powerful learning algorithms. We hope our study can inspire more interdisciplinary research using evolutionary algorithms to better solve complex biomedical problems.

Acknowledgments. This research was supported by the Natural Science and Engineering Research Council (NSERC) of Canada Discovery Grant RGPIN-2016-04699 to TH.

References

1. Loscalzo, J., Kohane, I., Barabási, A.L.: Human disease classification in the postgenomic era: a complex systems approach to human pathobiology. Mol. Syst. Biol. **3**(1), 124 (2007)
2. Griffiths, A.J., Miller, J.H., Suzuki, D.T., Lewontin, R.C., et al.: An Introduction to Genetic Analysis. WH Freeman and Company, New York (2000)
3. Glazier, A.M., Nadeau, J.H., Aitman, T.J.: Finding genes that underlie complex traits. Science **298**(5602), 2345–2349 (2002)
4. Zhu, M., Zhao, S.: Candidate gene identification approach: progress and challenges. Int. J. Biol. Sci. **3**(7), 420–427 (2007)
5. Kwon, J.M., Goate, A.M.: The candidate gene approach. Alcohol Res. Health **24**(3), 164–168 (2000)
6. Tabor, H.K., Risch, N.J., Myers, R.M.: Candidate-gene approaches for studying complex genetic traits: practical considerations. Nat. Rev. Genet. **3**(5), 391–397 (2002)
7. Di Ventura, B., Lemerle, C., Michalodimitrakis, K., Serrano, L.: From in vivo to in silico biology and back. Nature **443**(7111), 527–533 (2006)
8. Barabási, A.L., Gulbahce, N., Loscalzo, J.: Network medicine: a network-based approach to human disease. Nat. Rev. Genet. **12**(1), 56–68 (2011)
9. Almasi, S.M., Hu, T.: Measuring the importance of vertices in the weighted human disease network. PLoS ONE **14**(3), e0205936 (2019)
10. Hu, T., Sinnott-Armstrong, N.A., Kiralis, J.W., Andrew, A.S., Karagas, M.R., Moore, J.H.: Characterizing genetic interactions in human disease association studies using statistical epistasis networks. BMC Bioinf. **12**(1), 364 (2011)
11. Hu, T., et al.: An information-gain approach to detecting three-way epistatic interactions in genetic association studies. J. Am. Med. Inf. Assoc. **20**(4), 630–636 (2013)
12. Hu, T., Tomassini, M., Banzhaf, W.: Complex network analysis of a genetic programming phenotype network. In: Sekanina, L., Hu, T., Lourenço, N., Richter, H., García-Sánchez, P. (eds.) EuroGP 2019. LNCS, vol. 11451, pp. 49–63. Springer, Cham (2019). https://doi.org/10.1007/978-3-030-16670-0_4
13. Goh, K.I., Cusick, M.E., Valle, D., Childs, B., Vidal, M., Barabási, A.L.: The human disease network. Proc. Nat. Acad. Sci. **104**(21), 8685–8690 (2007)
14. Kafaie, S., Chen, Y., Hu, T.: A network approach to prioritizing susceptibility genes for genome-wide association studies. Genet. Epidemiol. **43**(5), 477–491 (2019)

15. Sun, K., Gonçalves, J.P., Larminie, C., Pržulj, N.: Predicting disease associations via biological network analysis. BMC Bioinf. **15**(1), 304 (2014)
16. Ott, J.: Neural networks and disease association studies. Am. J. Med. Genet. **105**(1), 60–61 (2001)
17. Wold, S., Esbensen, K., Geladi, P.: Principal component analysis. Chemometr. Intell. Lab. Syst. **2**(1–3), 37–52 (1987)
18. Yang, P., Li, X., Chua, H.N., Kwoh, C.K., Ng, S.K.: Ensemble positive unlabeled learning for disease gene identification. PLoS ONE **9**(5), e97079 (2014)
19. Dorani, F., Hu, T., Woods, M.O., Zhai, G.: Ensemble learning for detecting gene-gene interactions in colorectal cancer. PeerJ **6**, e5854 (2018)
20. Poli, R., Langdon, W.B., McPhee, N.F.: A Field Guide to Genetic Programming. Published via http://lulu.com (2008)
21. Pappa, G.L., Ochoa, G., Hyde, M.R., Freitas, A.A., Woodward, J., Swan, J.: Contrasting meta-learning and hyper-heuristic research: the role of evolutionary algorithms. Genet. Program. Evol. Mach. **15**(1), 3–35 (2014). https://doi.org/10.1007/s10710-013-9186-9
22. Brameier, M., Banzhaf, W.: A comparison of linear genetic programming and neural networks in medical data mining. IEEE Trans. Evol. Comput. **5**(1), 17–26 (2001)
23. Guven, A.: Linear genetic programming for time-series modelling of daily flow rate. J. Earth Syst. Sci. **118**(2), 137–146 (2009)
24. Agapitos, A., O'Neill, M., Brabazon, A.: Adaptive distance metrics for nearest neighbour classification based on genetic programming. In: Krawiec, K., Moraglio, A., Hu, T., Etaner-Uyar, A.Ş., Hu, B. (eds.) EuroGP 2013. LNCS, vol. 7831, pp. 1–12. Springer, Heidelberg (2013). https://doi.org/10.1007/978-3-642-37207-0_1
25. Nguyen, S., Mei, Y., Zhang, M.: Genetic programming for production scheduling: a survey with a unified framework. Complex Intell. Syst. **3**(1), 41–66 (2017)
26. Parkins, A.D., Nandi, A.K.: Genetic programming techniques for hand written digit recognition. Signal Process. **84**(12), 2345–2365 (2004)
27. Chen, S.H., Yeh, C.H.: Evolving traders and the business school with genetic programming: a new architecture of the agent-based artificial stock market. J. Econ. Dyn. Control **25**(3–4), 363–393 (2001)
28. Liu, K.H., Xu, C.G.: A genetic programming-based approach to the classification of multiclass microarray datasets. Bioinformatics **25**(3), 331–337 (2009). https://doi.org/10.1093/bioinformatics/btn644
29. Link, J., et al.: Application of genetic programming to high energy physics event selection. Nucl. Instrum. Methods Phys. Res., Sect. A **551**(2–3), 504–527 (2005)
30. Hu, T., et al.: An evolutioanry learning and network approach to identifying key metabolites for osteoarthritis. PLoS Comput. Biol. **14**(3), e1005986 (2018)
31. Hu, T., Oksanen, K., Zhang, W., Randell, E., Furey, A., Zhai, G.: Analyzing feature importance for metabolomics using genetic programming. In: Castelli, M., Sekanina, L., Zhang, M., Cagnoni, S., García-Sánchez, P. (eds.) EuroGP 2018. LNCS, vol. 10781, pp. 68–83. Springer, Cham (2018). https://doi.org/10.1007/978-3-319-77553-1_5
32. Zhang, Y., Hu, T., Liang, X., Ali, M.Z., Shabbir, M.N.S.K.: Fault detection and classification for induction motors using genetic programming. In: Sekanina, L., Hu, T., Lourenço, N., Richter, H., García-Sánchez, P. (eds.) EuroGP 2019. LNCS, vol. 11451, pp. 178–193. Springer, Cham (2019). https://doi.org/10.1007/978-3-030-16670-0_12
33. Langdon, W.B., Poli, R.: Foundations of Genetic Programming. Springer, Berlin (2013)

34. Guo, H., Jack, L.B., Nandi, A.K.: Feature generation using genetic programming with application to fault classification. IEEE Trans. Sys. Man Cybern. Part B (Cybern.) **35**(1), 89–99 (2005)
35. Witczak, M., Obuchowicz, A., Korbicz, J.: Genetic programming based approaches to identification and fault diagnosis of non-linear dynamic systems. Int. J. Control **75**(13), 1012–1031 (2002)
36. Ghiassian, S.D., Menche, J., Barabasi, A.L.: A DIseAse MOdule Detection (DIAMOnD) algorithm derived from a systematic analysis of connectivity patterns of disease proteins in the human interactome. PLoS Comput. Biol. **11**(4), e1004120 (2015)
37. Menche, J., et al.: Uncovering disease-disease relationships through the incomplete interactome. Science **347**(6224), 1257601 (2015)
38. Abrahams, B.S., et al.: FARI gene 2.0: a community-driven knowledgebase for the autism spectrum disorders (ASDs). Mol. Autism **4**(1), 36 (2013)
39. Hamosh, A., Scott, A.F., Amberger, J.S., Bocchini, C.A., McKusick, V.A.: Online Mendelian Inheritance in Man (OMIM), a knowledgebase of human genes and genetic disorders. Nucleic Acids Res. **33**(suppl-1), 514–517 (2005)
40. Duda, M., Zhang, H., Li, H.D., Wall, D.P., Burmeister, M., Guan, Y.: Brain-specific functional relationship networks inform autism spectrum disorder gene prediction. Trans. Psychiatry **8**(1), 56 (2018)
41. Oughtred, R., et al.: The biogrid interaction database: 2019 update. Nucleic Acids Res. **47**(D1), D529–D541 (2018)
42. Gleich, D.F.: Pagerank beyond the web. SIAM Rev. **57**(3), 321–363 (2015)
43. Batagelj, V., Zaversnik, M.: An o(m) algorithm for cores decomposition of networks. arXiv preprint cs/0310049 (2003)
44. Newman, M.E.J.: Networks, 2nd edn. Oxford University Press, Oxford (2018)
45. Pržulj, N.: Biological network comparison using graphlet degree distribution. Bioinformatics **23**(2), e177–e183 (2007)
46. Brameier, M.F., Banzhaf, W.: Linear Genetic Programming. Springer, New York (2007)
47. Abraham, A., Ramos, V.: Web usage mining using artificial ant colony clustering and linear genetic programming. In: The 2003 Congress on Evolutionary Computation, CEC 2003, vol. 2, pp. 1384–1391. IEEE (2003)
48. Nag, K., Pal, N.R.: A multiobjective genetic programming-based ensemble for simultaneous feature selection and classification. IEEE Trans. Cybern. **46**(2), 499–510 (2015)
49. Powers, D.M.: Evaluation: from precision, recall and F-measure to ROC, informedness, markedness and correlation. J. Mach. Learn. Technol. **1**, 37–63 (2011)
50. Buckland, M., Gey, F.: The relationship between recall and precision. J. Am. Soc. Inf. Sci. **45**(1), 12–19 (1994)
51. Iossifov, I., et al.: The contribution of de novo coding mutations to autism spectrum disorder. Nature **515**(7526), 216 (2014)
52. Fischbach, G.D., Lord, C.: The simons simplex collection: a resource for identification of autism genetic risk factors. Neuron **68**(2), 192–195 (2010)

Author Index

Printed in the United States
By Bookmasters